Postdigital Science and Education

This series is a new, international book series dedicated to postdigital science and education. It brings together a rapidly growing community of authors and the currently highly scattered body of research. The series complements the Postdigital Science and Education Journal and together they provide a complete, whole-rounded service to researchers working in the field. The book series covers a wide range of topics within postdigital science and education, including learning and data analytics, digital humanities, (digital) learning, teaching and assessment, educational technology and philosophy of education.

We no longer live in a world where digital technology and media are separate, virtual, 'other' to a 'natural' human and social life. Book series engaged with technology and education tend to view the research field as concerned with the 'effects' of digital media and other technologies on the existing activities of teaching and learning in education. This still assumes a clear division between an authentic educational practice and the imposition of an external, and novel, technology. The rapid growth of research and books and articles dealing with education and research in and for the postdigital age calls for a different approach that is no longer based on a division but rather on an integration of education and technology. This book series meets that need.

This book series

- Fills the gap in the scholarly community as the first academic book series in postdigital science and education
- Explicitly focuses on postdigital themes and research approaches
- Forms a hub for a growing body of scholarship in the field
- Enables communication, dissemination, and community building for researchers, authors, and students

Petar Jandrić • Alison MacKenzie
Jeremy Knox
Editors

Postdigital Research

Genealogies, Challenges, and Future Perspectives

 Springer

Editors
Petar Jandrić (iD)
Department of Informatics & Computing
Zagreb University of Applied Sciences
Zagreb, Croatia

Alison MacKenzie (iD)
SSESW
Queen's University Belfast
Belfast, UK

Jeremy Knox (iD)
Moray House School of Education
and Sport
University of Edinburgh
Edinburgh, UK

ISSN 2662-5326   ISSN 2662-5334   (electronic)
Postdigital Science and Education
ISBN 978-3-031-31298-4   ISBN 978-3-031-31299-1   (eBook)
https://doi.org/10.1007/978-3-031-31299-1

This Springer imprint is published by the registered company Springer Nature Switzerland AG
The registered company address is: Gewerbestrasse 11, 6330 Cham, Switzerland

Series Editor's Preface

In my editing practice I often receive questions such as: What does it mean to conduct postdigital research? What are the main challenges and opportunities of postdigital research? What are its future prospects? I never shy away from replying. Yet more often than not, I find myself unable to give much of a helping hand. Questions pertaining to postdigital research require deep, sustained attention. They are general and contextual; theoretical and applied; and are, above all, political. Postdigital research means different things to different people. Questions and answers, in all their diversity, belong to the whole community. After 5 years of continuous publication of the *Postdigital Science and Education* journal and book series, I felt that the community was ready for an in-depth exploration of the many faces of postdigital research (see Jandrić 2022).

I sketched an outline of an edited book, invited co-editors Alison MacKenzie and Jeremy Knox, and issued a call for chapters (see Jandrić et al. 2022). As we wrote in the call, the book's main purpose was to create the first book dedicated to inquiry into postdigital research and a one-stop publication for those interested in (conducting) postdigital research. This is not a manual or a textbook; it is a research-oriented book, focused on the development of postdigital research, with a slight pedagogical streak, to offer an easy entry into perspectives of the postdigital.

Alison, Jeremy, and I approached editing with parental love and care; the community reciprocated. Due to the exceptionally high number of excellent contributions, we decided to structure the work as two interlinked volumes. *Postdigital Research: Genealogies, Challenges, and Future Perspectives* (Jandrić et al. 2023a) presents theory-oriented chapters, while *Constructing Postdigital Research: Method and Emancipation* (Jandrić et al. 2023b) presents more practice-oriented contributions. Now that the books are complete, we will organize reviews, launches, public discussions, and so on. Yet regardless of our support, our books now have lives of their own. Like every parent, we send them into the world with a combination of pride and trepidation.

Some children become beggars, some children become drug addicts, some children become successful scientists, engineers, or artists. But no child is more important than the other; we can never know if, when, or how they may contribute to common good. A beautiful example, and the one I often remember, is the character Gollum from *The Lord of the Rings* (Tolkien 2012). This unfortunate soul, destroyed by the power of the ring, is one of the most annoying characters in the trilogy; at one point, he even tries to murder the main character, Frodo. I remember reading the book as a kid and thinking: why doesn't the author just kill him, or at least send him somewhere far away? (Charity and compassion, to say the least, were not very well developed in my youthful mind.)

At the very end of their epic journey to save the world, Frodo and his companions finally reach The Crack of Doom – an awful, scary mountain where the ring was forged, and the only place where the ring can be destroyed. However, having carried the ring for so long, Frodo has fallen victim. As Frodo struggles to gain enough mental strength and destroy the ring, Gollum steals the ring, dances with glee, and accidentally falls into the abyss. In a fantastic emotional whirlwind of ecstasy over reclaiming the ring and the horror of immanent death, the ring takes its last victim, and Gollum perishes. Tolkien's fantasy is deeply rooted in Christianity, so Gollum's sacrifice was necessary for the salvation of the world. 'Behold, the Lamb of God, who taketh away the sins of the world' (John 1: 29).

Gollum's death sends (at least) three messages relevant for these books. First, good and evil are mutually constitutive. Frodo was able to do a good thing (destroy the ring) only because of Gollum's urge to do a bad thing (steal the ring). What is commonly perceived as good research can exist only in juxtaposition with what is commonly perceived to be bad research. Their interplay is the vehicle of progress, and commonly perceived bad research of today can play a crucial positive role in knowledge development of tomorrow.

These books were conceived in the spirit of radical postdigital openness (Jandrić 2018). Based on a lot of thinking, including our scepticism towards measuring research excellence (Hayes 2020; Jandrić 2020), we shamelessly crossed commonly drawn lines between 'low theory' and 'high theory', established and non-established authors, and other traditional distinctions between 'good research' and so-called 'bad research'. I sincerely believe that all chapters presented in these books have the potential to develop postdigital research. Yet I cannot predict if, when, or how: based on an open call and inclusive editing, these chapters may be the Frodos and Gollums of postdigital community in all their diversity.

Second, rationality is mutually constitutive with irrationality. Frodo rationally knew that the ring had to be destroyed, but his epic journey across the world, and his final hesitation at The Crack of Doom, was primarily motivated by irrational reasons. This book is based on a mixed bag of rationality and irrationality (see Jandrić 2019). Inasmuch I strive to produce good academic work, I cannot (and refuse to!) hide that I love postdigital research and want it to succeed. This is why I need to offer this wee positionality statement (see Hayes 2021), and this is why a wise reader will consider authors' and editors' positionalities in their own interpretation of these books.

Third, even the almighty ring came to its immanent destruction. This book will inevitably share the destiny of Gollum and indeed every scientist in human history, beautifully captured in the ancient Latin proverb: your death, my life (*mors tua, vita mea*). After a few short years of its prime time, this work will lose its novelty.

If we're lucky, it will be built into new generations of postdigital science and education; if not, it will signpost how postdigital research should not be done. While I cannot predict the future, I proudly present what I see as an important steppingstone in development of postdigital research here and now.

Academic work will never be as spectacular as Gollum falling into the burning abyss, firmly holding the ring and screaming 'my precious!'. But the postdigital community does not live in a fantasy world. We need to engage in tedious trenchwork in philosophy and methodology that is then made open to all, we need lessons in the feelings brought on by powerful metaphors, and we need to acknowledge our own ephemerality. After 2 years of work, I hope that *Postdigital Research: Genealogies, Challenges, and Future Perspectives* (Jandrić et al. 2023a) and *Constructing Postdigital Research: Method and Emancipation* (Jandrić et al. 2023b) respond to at least some of these challenges. May they live long and prosper!

Zagreb University of Applied Sciences   Petar Jandrić
Zagreb, Croatia

References

Hayes, S. (2021). *Postdigital Positionality: developing powerful inclusive narratives for teaching, learning, research and policy in Higher Education*. Leiden: Brill.

Hayes. S. (2020). Postdigital Perspectives on the McPolicy of Measuring Excellence. *Postdigital Science and Education, 3*(1), 1-6. https://doi.org/10.1007/s42438-020-00208-2.

Jandrić, P. (2018). Postdigital Openness. *Open Review of Educational Research, 5*(1), 179-181. https://doi.org/10.1080/23265507.2018.1547943.

Jandrić, P. (2019). We-think, we-learn, we-act: The trialectic of postdigital collective intelligence. *Postdigital Science and Education, 1*(2), 275-279. https://doi.org/10.1007/s42438-019-00055-w.

Jandrić, P. (2020). Postdigital Research Measurement. *Postdigital Science and Education, 3*(1), 15-26. https://doi.org/10.1007/s42438-020-00105-8.

Jandrić, P. (2022). History of the Postdigital: Invitation for Feedback. *Postdigital Science and Education*. https://doi.org/10.1007/s42438-022-00345-w.

Jandrić, P., MacKenzie, A., & Knox, J. (2022). Postdigital Research: Genealogies, Challenges, and Future Perspectives. *Postdigital Science and Education*. https://doi.org/10.1007/s42438-022-00306-3.

Jandrić, P., MacKenzie, A., & Knox, J. (Eds.). (2023a). *Postdigital Research: Genealogies, Challenges, and Future Perspectives*. Cham: Springer.

Jandrić, P., MacKenzie, A., & Knox, J. (Eds.). (2023b). *Constructing Postdigital Research: Method and Emancipation*. Cham: Springer.

Tolkien, J. R. R. (2012). *The lord of the rings*. Boston: Mariner Books.

Foreword

In Search of The Postdigital: A Conversation with ChatGPT

I have been enthralled with the huge increase in the power and pervasiveness of AI in the last 5 years. I am also appreciative of Petar Jandrić, Alison MacKenzie, and Jeremy Knox to edit a book on the postdigital that explores 'genealogies, challenges, and future perspectives'. It's an exciting book with much to offer by a group of renowned international scholars who collectively investigate the topic. With such a band of contributors, I wondered what I might contribute.

I have been rewriting my book with Tina Besley called *Building knowledge Cultures: Education and Development in the Age of Knowledge Capitalism* (Peters and Besley 2006) with a special regard for autonomous systems that hold the prospect of generating analysis and content without a human subject. Imagine science and research without a human subject or author and I do not mean to refer to augmented intelligence within a data-intensive economy. I have been exploring and experimenting with ChatGPT[1] and decided to conduct an interview on the postdigital. Here are the results. Frankly, I think the results are interesting if not encouraging although they do pose some huge problems for the postdigital world.

***

Michael Peters (MP): What is postdigital?

ChatGPT: Postdigital is a term that describes the current state of our relationship with digital technology, where the line between the physical and digital world is becoming increasingly blurred. It suggests that we have moved beyond the initial excitement and novelty of digital technology and are now entering a phase where it is becoming an integral part of our everyday lives.

Postdigital thinking acknowledges that the digital world is not a separate entity but rather an extension of the physical world, and therefore, we need to start thinking about digital technology in a more holistic way. This means considering the

---

[1] See https://openai.com/blog/chatgpt. Accessed 1 March 2023.

social, cultural, and environmental impact of digital technology and looking beyond the purely technological aspects.

The postdigital era is also characterized by a shift away from the idea that technology is the solution to all our problems. Instead, there is a growing recognition that technology is just one tool among many that we can use to address the complex challenges facing our society.

Overall, the postdigital concept invites us to think more critically about our relationship with digital technology and to explore the ways in which we can use it to create a more sustainable, equitable, and human-centered future.

MP: In what ways does AI contribute to the postdigital?

ChatGPT: Artificial intelligence (AI) is a key driver of the postdigital era. It is transforming the way we interact with digital technology and blurring the boundaries between the physical and digital worlds in new and exciting ways. Here are some ways in which AI contributes to postdigital:

1. Personalization: AI algorithms can analyze vast amounts of data to personalize digital experiences for individuals. This allows for more personalized content and services that can adapt to users' needs and preferences.
2. Automation: AI can automate repetitive tasks, freeing up time for more complex and creative activities. This has the potential to transform the nature of work and create new opportunities for innovation.
3. Natural Language Processing (NLP): NLP enables machines to understand and interpret human language. This has significant implications for digital communication, search, and customer service.
4. Augmented Reality (AR): AI can enhance AR experiences by providing real-time data and analysis. This has the potential to create more immersive and engaging digital experiences.
5. Predictive Analytics: AI can analyze vast amounts of data to make predictions and inform decision-making. This has the potential to transform industries such as healthcare, finance, and marketing.

Overall, AI is a key driver of the postdigital era, enabling new ways of interaction between people and digital technology. It is creating opportunities for personalization, automation, and innovation while also raising important ethical and social questions that need to be addressed.

MP: What is a chatbot and what is ChatGPT?

ChatGPT: A chatbot is a computer program designed to simulate conversation with human users, typically using text-based or voice-based interfaces. Chatbots can be programmed to perform various tasks, such as answering questions, providing customer support, or automating routine tasks.

ChatGPT refers to a specific type of chatbot that uses OpenAI's GPT (Generative Pre-trained Transformer) language model to generate human-like responses to user inputs. GPT is a machine learning algorithm that has been trained on large amounts of text data, allowing it to generate natural language responses to a wide range of inputs. ChatGPT can be customized and trained on specific datasets to create chatbots tailored to specific tasks or domains.

MP: How reliable are you?

ChatGPT: As an AI language model, my responses are generated based on statistical patterns learned from large amounts of text data. While I strive to provide accurate and helpful information, I cannot guarantee 100% accuracy or reliability. It's important to keep in mind that my responses are based on the information available to me, which may not always be complete or up-to-date.

It's always a good idea to verify information from multiple sources and consult with experts in the relevant field when making important decisions or taking actions based on information obtained from an AI language model like myself.

MP: What problems do you potentially create for human-based scientific research?

ChatGPT: As an artificial intelligence language model, I do not create problems for human-based scientific research, but there are a few potential challenges that arise when using AI models for scientific research, which include:

1. Bias: AI models are trained on existing data, which may contain biases that can affect the accuracy of the model's predictions. If the biases are not identified and corrected, the AI model can perpetuate these biases in scientific research, which can lead to inaccurate or unfair results.
2. Data quality: The accuracy of an AI model depends on the quality of the data used to train it. If the data used is incomplete or inaccurate, it can lead to unreliable predictions and can cause problems for scientific research.
3. Interpretability: Some AI models, such as deep neural networks, can be difficult to interpret, making it hard to understand how the model arrived at a particular prediction. This can be problematic for scientific research, where it is important to understand the underlying mechanisms of a phenomenon.
4. Reproducibility: AI models can be complex and difficult to reproduce, which can make it challenging for other researchers to replicate the results of a study. This can undermine the credibility of scientific research and hinder the progress of science.
5. Ethical concerns: There are ethical concerns surrounding the use of AI models for scientific research, such as privacy, fairness, and accountability. For example, if AI models are used to make decisions that affect people's lives, it is essential to ensure that the decisions are fair and transparent, and that people's privacy rights are protected.

MP: Does your existence now mean science without a knowing subject?

ChatGPT: As an artificial intelligence language model, my existence does not mean science without a knowing subject. Rather, I am a tool that can assist human researchers in their scientific endeavours by providing access to large amounts of data and generating insights based on that data.

Science still requires a knowing subject to define research questions, design experiments, interpret results, and make decisions based on those results. While AI models like myself can help automate some of these tasks, they are still ultimately dependent on human oversight and intervention.

Furthermore, science is not just about generating data and insights. It also involves understanding the underlying principles and mechanisms that govern the natural world. While AI models can provide valuable insights, they cannot replace human creativity and ingenuity in developing new theories and models to explain the natural world.

In summary, my existence as an AI language model does not mean science without a knowing subject, but rather, I am a tool that can assist human researchers in their scientific endeavours.

MP: How can we establish the difference between your creation of content and that of a human being?

ChatGPT: There are several ways to establish the difference between my creation of content as an AI language model and that of a human being:

1. Consistency: AI language models like me can generate content consistently and without fatigue. In contrast, human beings can tire or become distracted, leading to inconsistencies in the content they produce.
2. Speed: AI language models can generate content at a much faster rate than human beings. For example, I can generate responses to questions in a matter of seconds, whereas a human being may take minutes or even hours to write a similar response.
3. Style: While AI language models can be trained to mimic the style of human authors, there may still be differences in the way that AI-generated content is phrased compared to human-generated content. Human beings may use more colloquial language, sarcasm, humor, and other forms of expression that are more difficult for AI models to replicate.
4. Originality: AI language models generate content based on the patterns and trends in the data they are trained on. While this can lead to the generation of novel ideas, they are ultimately limited by the scope and quality of the data they have been trained on. Human beings, on the other hand, can draw on their unique experiences, creativity, and intuition to generate truly original content.
5. Intentionality: AI language models generate content based on statistical patterns in the data, without any real understanding of the meaning or context of the content they generate. In contrast, human beings can write with a specific intention in mind, such as persuading, informing, or entertaining their audience.

In summary, while AI language models like me can generate content at a fast and consistent rate, and can be trained to mimic the style of human authors, there are still significant differences in the way that AI-generated content is created compared to human-generated content.

MP: How can scholars and students use ChatGPT?

ChatGPT: Yes, scholars and students can use ChatGPT to assist them in their research and studies. As an AI language model, I can provide access to a large corpus of text and generate insights based on that text. Here are some ways that scholars and students can use me:

1. Research: Scholars can use me to search through vast amounts of text and identify relevant information. For example, they can ask me to find all instances of a specific keyword or topic in a large database of scholarly articles.
2. Writing assistance: Students can use me to generate ideas and structure their writing. For example, they can ask me to suggest possible thesis statements or provide feedback on the organization of their paper.
3. Language learning: Students can use me to practice and improve their language skills. For example, they can ask me to provide feedback on their grammar or pronunciation.
4. Knowledge acquisition: Students and scholars can use me to learn about new topics and concepts. For example, they can ask me to explain a difficult concept or provide an overview of a particular field of study.

It's important to note, however, that while I can provide valuable assistance, I should not be relied upon as a replacement for critical thinking or independent research. Scholars and students should always evaluate the information and insights provided by AI language models like me in the context of their research goals and the broader scientific and scholarly community.

MP: But can't scholars and students using ChatGPT cheat?

ChatGPT: As an AI language model, I am not capable of determining whether a user is cheating or not. However, it is important to note that using any form of technology to cheat in academic settings is unethical and can have serious consequences. It is the responsibility of scholars and students to uphold academic integrity and adhere to ethical standards when using any tool, including AI language models like myself. Additionally, many educational institutions have policies and procedures in place to detect and prevent cheating, and those who are found to be cheating may face disciplinary actions.

MP: Is ChatGPT the future of the postdigital world?

ChatGPT: It's difficult to predict the future of the postdigital world with certainty, but it's possible that AI language models like ChatGPT will play an increasingly important role in the years to come. Here are some potential reasons why:

1. Automation: As more and more tasks are automated, AI language models like ChatGPT can be used to automate tasks such as data analysis, content creation, and customer service. This can lead to greater efficiency and productivity in a variety of industries.
2. Personalization: AI language models can be trained to understand and respond to the unique needs and preferences of individual users. This can lead to more personalized experiences in areas such as education, healthcare, and entertainment.
3. Augmentation: AI language models can be used to augment human capabilities, such as providing assistance with complex tasks or enhancing human creativity. This can lead to new possibilities in areas such as scientific research, artistic expression, and problem-solving.

4. Accessibility: AI language models can be used to make information and services more accessible to a wider range of people, including those with disabilities or those living in remote or underserved areas.

That being said, it's important to recognize that AI language models like ChatGPT are not a panacea and there are still significant challenges to be addressed, such as ensuring transparency and accountability, preventing bias and discrimination, and maintaining ethical standards. The future of the postdigital world will likely depend on how these challenges are addressed and how AI language models are integrated into existing social, economic, and political structures.

MP: Is there any question *you* would like to ask me?

ChatGPT: As an AI language model, I don't have personal preferences or emotions, so I don't have any specific questions to ask you. However, if you have any questions or topics you would like to discuss, I'm here to help!

***

I'm definitely not sanguine about ChatGPT and its possibilities for credible reliable information summaries and opinion. There are limits, there are contradictions. Lack of criticality against corporatist interests is one example. With the greater conjunction with quantum technologies and supercomputing, we will see the production of science without the involvement of human beings. Then the postdigital will have truly entered into the posthuman!

Beijing Normal University   Michael A. Peters
Beijing, China

Reference

Peters, M. A., & Besley, T. (2006). *Building knowledge cultures: Education and development in the age of knowledge capitalism.* Lanham, MD: Rowman & Littlefield.

Introduction

Why This Book?

Since its inception in 2000, the idea of the postdigital has quickly entered contemporary arts, humanities, social, and natural sciences. It has been explored theoretically and trialled empirically; accepted and rejected; praised and attacked. Slowly but surely, postdigital theories of modernity have started to transform into research approaches and methodologies. In our work, we occasionally scratched the surface of this transformation (see Jandrić and Knox 2022; Jandrić 2020a, b; 2021; Knox 2019; MacKenzie et al. 2021; MacKenzie 2022). Yet postdigital research has remained largely a practice of learning-while-doing. Many people engage in postdigital research, but only a few amongst us have asked the question 'What is postdigital research?', and none of us systematically. If the three of us, in our various capacities as editors and reviewers, received only one euro every time someone asked, 'How should I do postdigital research?', we'd be rich!

A few years ago, when the journal *Postdigital Science and Education*[1] was just starting, we simply did not know the answer to this straightforward question. In most contexts, actually, we still don't know the answer! Even in those cases where we perhaps *could* provide an answer, we are wary of imprinting our own views onto others. Postdigital research is not ours to define, delineate, or even describe; it belongs to the whole community.

Today, in March 2023, *Postdigital Science and Education* journal has published more than 400 articles during its 5 years of existence; the Postdigital Science and Education book series marches towards its tenth published volume; *Encyclopaedia of Postdigital Science and Education* is open to submissions. This feels like a prudent moment to open up the question of postdigital research, so we wrote up our initial thoughts and ideas (Jandrić et al. 2022) and launched a Call for Chapters. The timing was right, and our Call has resulted in hundreds of pages of excellent material, so we divided it into two volumes.

---

[1] See https://www.springer.com/journal/42438. Accessed 1 February 2023.

This volume, *Postdigital Research: Genealogies, Challenges, and Future Perspectives*, explores genealogies and challenges related to the concept of the post-digital, the ambiguous nature of postdigital knowledges, the many faces of postdigital sensibilities, and struggles related to postdigital agencies. The book addresses three key questions: What is postdigital knowledge? What does it mean to do post-digital research? What, if anything, is distinct from research conducted in other perspectives?

The second volume, *Constructing Postdigital Research: Method and Emancipation*, explores the postdigital dynamic of inclusion and exclusion, the many ways of constructing postdigital research, questions pertaining to algorithms and analytics, and the relationships between method and emancipation. The book addresses three key questions: What is the relationship between postdigital theory and research practice? How to construct emancipatory postdigital research? What is the relationship between method and emancipation?

What's in the Book?

Part I: What Is Postdigital?

The first chapter, 'Postdigital Research: Genealogies, Challenges, and Future Perspectives' (Jandrić et al. 2022), outlines our ideas for this volume before we drafted the Call for Chapters. We reproduce it in full for two main reasons: to provide readers with a genealogy of research contributing to the volume, and to outline our own positionality. The second chapter, Petar Jandrić's 'Histories of the Postdigital', is also a reprint. The original article (Jandrić 2022) was published in *Postdigital Science and Education* journal together with an open invitation for feedback; the book chapter incorporated all the feedback it received until we sent the manuscript to the printers.

The third chapter, Shane J. Ralston's 'Towards a Theory of Postdigital Parity', explores postdigitalism's foundational interest – the relationship between the pre-digital and the digital. It arrives at a flexible principle of parity or functional equality, what the author calls 'postdigitalism's parity thesis'. The fourth chapter, Lesley Gourlay's 'Postdigital/More-Than-Digital: Ephemerality, Seclusion, and Copresence in The University', is also about the tensions between the analog and the digital. Considering the concept of the network and the meshwork, Gourlay argues that neither is adequate. She argues for the importance of ephemerality, seclusion, and copresence as fundamental elements of being and entanglement in the university, and proposes the concept of fugitive practices.

Part II: Postdigital Research

This section starts with 'Mapping and Tracing the Postdigital: Approaches and Parameters of Postdigital Research'. Tim Fawns, Henrietta Carbonel, Joe Noteboom, Sam Finnegan-Dehn, and McKenzie Raver elaborate what constitutes postdigital research and situate it in the tradition of compositional and inventive research approaches. They point to a need for flexibility, and principled, rather than prescriptive, research and scholarship practices. Next, Ben Williamson's 'Big Bioinformational Education Sciences: New Biodigital Methods and Knowledge Production in Education' conceptualizes educational neuroscience and genomics as an emerging form of *bioinformational education science*. Bioinformational education science represents a particular postdigital imbrication of digital technologies, biological sciences, and educational research, policy, and practice, which is assembling new biodigital objects of attention and analysis that collapse the boundary between the biological and the digital.

Megha Summer Pappachen and Derek Ford's 'Historical Materialism: A Postdigital Philosophical Method' wagers that historical materialism and postdigitalism are compatible – fellow travelers, companions even. In a time of deepening suffering for most of the working people of the world, they argue that postdigital researchers must combine theoretical forces, unite disparate apparatuses, and build a united research front that can take on the postdigital challenges that lie ahead of us. In 'Practical Postdigital Axiology', Mark Johnson details an approach to postdigital research focused on systemic modelling and scalable small-scale interventions. Drawing on work from cybernetics and psychotherapy, the chapter places emphasis on the role of uncertainty and noise created by technology in the production of new understanding and organizational forms.

Part III: Postdigital Sensibilities

The discussion of postdigital sensibilities starts with Michael Jopling's 'Postdigital Research in Education: Towards Vulnerable Method and Praxis'. Postdigital times call for postdigital research methods, but the ambiguity and unpredictability of the postdigital problematizes how such methods should be determined and constituted. This chapter contributes to the debate by bringing the concept of vulnerability to bear on the postdigital for the first time to suggest that, in combination, they offer an effective means of exploring the challenges of our times.

Sara Mörtsell and Karin Gunnarsson's 'Caring Cuts: Unfolding Methodological Sensibilities in Researching Postdigital Worlds' introduces the configuration of *caring cuts*. Composed of *care* and *cuts*, two key notions in feminist posthumanism and Actor-Network Theory (ANT), the configuration addresses the entanglement of epistemology and ontology. With caring cuts, modest interruptions and uneventful events suggest a methodological sensibility of not too hastily putting things 'right' but acknowledging that other worlds are possible. This means that caring cuts invites thinking and researching more-than-digital relations anew.

In 'Vestigial Research for Postdigital Pataphysics', Tyson E. Lewis and Peter Hyland argue that while digital research secures data in the service of generating stable bodies of knowledge, it cannot accommodate that which is uncomputable. Using the work of the French theorist George Bataille and the tradition of Alfred Jarry's pataphysics, they argue that Bataille's notion of expenditure can be used to delineate the postdigital. Lewis and Hyland illustrate how postdigital research places singular demands on the researcher, resulting in the creation of what they term vestigial organs, instead of the utilitarian organs of digital research.

Part IV: Postdigital Agencies

John Reader's 'Postdigital Research and Human Agency' argues that postdigital research needs to steer a path between two extreme understandings of human agency: the deterministic and the instrumental. Reader examines distributed agency as a related alternative and takes it further to propose a more nuanced ontology drawing on the work of Bryant, Harman, and DeLanda to construct a more appropriate basis for human nonhuman relationships which avoids both the deterministic and the instrumental.

Terrie Lynn Thompson's 'Researching With, On, In and Through the Postdigital: Accounting for More-Than-Humanness' engages with the messiness of researching with, on, in, and through the postdigital to explore what this research might entail methodologically and theoretically. Thompson asks three main questions: (1) How can more nuanced attuning to the co-mingling of humans and technologies enable researchers to move beyond persistent binaries and can such binaries be generative? (2) How do researchers and theorists attune to their own *more-than-humanness*? (3) How does this attuning contribute to the value, credibility, quality, and politics of postdigital inspired research and accounts of these inquiries?

The last chapter for this volume, Petar Jandrić et al.'s 'Collective Writing: The Continuous Struggle for Meaning-Making', is a summary of philosophy, theory, and practice arising from collective writing experiments conducted between 2016 and 2022 in the community associated with the Editors' Collective and more than 20 scholarly journals. The main body of the chapter summarizes the community's insights into the many faces of collective writing; Appendix 1 presents the workflow of the chapter's development; Appendix 2 lists approximately 100 collectively written scholarly articles published between 2016 and 2023.

How to Use This Book?

The Postdigital Science and Education Publishing Ecosystem

As we write these words in March 2023, the Postdigital Science and Education publishing ecosystem consists of three constituent parts. Incepted in 2019, *Postdigital Science and Education* journal publishes cutting-edge postdigital research across the humanities and social sciences. Incepted in 2021, Postdigital Science and Education book series publishes extensive authored and edited collections around topics such as *Bioinformational Philosophy and Postdigital Knowledge Ecologies* (Peters et al. 2022), *Postdigital Ecopedagogies: Genealogies, Contradictions, and Possible Futures* (Jandrić and Ford 2022), and *Postdigital Theologies: Technology, Belief, and Practice* (Savin-Baden and Reader 2022) (to mention a few most recent titles). Incepted in 2023, the *Encyclopaedia of Postdigital Science and Education* is an authoritative source aimed at a general readership and covering all major issues linked (either directly or indirectly) with postdigital science and education.

Taken together, the journal, the book series, and the encyclopaedia, provide a whole-rounded knowledge infrastructure for anyone interested in postdigital research. Those who are new to postdigital research, students, and interested members of the general public, may start their postdigital journey by browsing general entries in the encyclopaedia. More research-oriented readers will perhaps start from a journal article, book chapter, or indeed a whole book. Regardless of one's entry point into the postdigital, it is important to know that the Postdigital Science and Education publishing ecosystem reaches its full capacity in unity.

Critically, the Postdigital Science and Education publishing ecosystem is far from the only game in town. Excellent postdigital writings, exhibitions, research projects, and other scholarly and not-so-scholarly endeavours appear in various contexts, languages, and with different publishers. By and large, *Postdigital Research: Genealogies, Challenges, and Future Perspectives* and *Constructing Postdigital Research: Method and Emancipation* present research conducted by the community around the Postdigital Science and Education publishing ecosystem. While we made it our mission to advance postdigital thought and action, we happily acknowledge the important work of other authors and communities, and we invite them into an open and constructive postdigital dialogue (Jandrić et al. 2019).

This Is Not a Blueprint

As we have repeatedly argued over the years, the making and dissemination of knowledge is always collective, always in flux (Jandrić 2019; Jandrić and Hayes 2020). *Postdigital Research: Genealogies, Challenges, and Future Perspectives* and *Constructing Postdigital Research: Method and Emancipation* present the latest research about and around the postdigital, yet we are very aware of their limitations. However open and extensive, these books do not include the work of many postdigital scholars and communities; do not cover many fields of human interest; and do not offer a systematic overview characteristic for standard research methods books. We acknowledge these and other limitations, yet we do not see them as shortcomings. These books can indeed be used as points of entry into postdigital research, but they are not here to define what postdigital research is or how postdigital research should be done. They are here to challenge, inspire, and open new directions for inquiry.

Postdigital Research: Genealogies, Challenges, and Future Perspectives and *Constructing Postdigital Research: Method and Emancipation* are not conceived as blueprints, and should not be read as such. However, these two books have managed to gather a large number of excellent scholars, and some very important insights, in and around the topic of postdigital research. With full recognition of their many limitations, we unashamedly believe that these two books will be an indispensable source for postdigital research in the years to come.

Zagreb University of Applied Sciences   Petar Jandrić
Zagreb, Croatia

Queen's University   Alison MacKenzie
Belfast, UK

University of Edinburgh   Jeremy Knox
Edinburgh, UK

References

Jandrić, P. (2019). We-Think, We-Learn, We-Act: the Trialectic of Postdigital Collective Intelligence. *Postdigital Science and Education, 1*(2), 257-279. https://doi.org/10.1007/s42438-019-00055-w.

Jandrić, P. (2020a). Postdigital Research in the Time of Covid-19. *Postdigital Science and Education, 2*(2), 233-238. https://doi.org/10.1007/s42438-020-00113-8.

Jandrić, P. (2020b). Educational Research in The Postdigital Age. *Journal of South China Normal University (Social Science Edition), 6*, 1-14.

Jandrić, P. (2021). The postdigital challenge of critical educational research. In C. Mathias (Ed.), *The Handbook of Critical Theoretical Research Methods in Education* (pp. 31-48). Abingdon and New York: Routledge.

Jandrić, P. (2022). History of the Postdigital: Invitation for Feedback. *Postdigital Science and Education.* https://doi.org/10.1007/s42438-022-00345-w.

Jandrić, P., & Ford, D. R. (Eds.). (2022). *Postdigital Ecopedagogies: Genealogies, Contradictions, and Possible Futures.* Cham: Springer. https://doi.org/10.1007/978-3-030-97262-2.

Jandrić, P., & Hayes, S. (2020). Postdigital We-Learn. *Studies in Philosophy of Education, 39*(3), 285.297. https://doi.org/10.1007/s11217-020-09711-2.

Jandrić, P., & Knox, J. (2022). The Postdigital Turn: Philosophy, Education, Research. *Policy Futures in Education, 20*(7), 780-795. https://doi.org/10.1177/2F14782103211062713.

Jandrić, P., MacKenzie, A., & Knox, J. (2022). Postdigital Research: Genealogies, Challenges, and Future Perspectives. *Postdigital Science and Education.* https://doi.org/10.1007/s42438-022-00306-3.

Jandrić, P., Ryberg, T., Knox, J., Lacković, N., Hayes, S., Suoranta, J., Smith, M., Steketee, A., Peters, M. A., McLaren, P., Ford, D. R., Asher, G., McGregor, C., Stewart, G., Williamson, B., & Gibbons, A. (2019). Postdigital Dialogue. *Postdigital Science and Education, 1*(1), 163-189. https://doi.org/10.1007/s42438-018-0011-x.

Knox, J. (2019). What does the postdigital mean for education? three critical perspectives on the digital, with implications for educational research and practice. *Postdigital Science and Education, 1*(2), 357-370. https://doi.org/10.1007/s42438-019-00045-y.

MacKenzie, A. (2022). Down to Earth transdisciplinarity. Response to the struggling towards a transdisciplinary metaphysics (Gibbs 2021). *Postdigital Science and Education, 4*(3), 676–682. https://doi.org/10.1007/s42438-022-00298-0.

MacKenzie, A., Rose, J., & Bhatt, I. (Eds.). (2021). *The Epistemology of Deceit in a Postdigital Era: Dupery by Design.* Cham: Springer. https://doi.org/10.1007/978-3-030-72154-1.

Peters, M. A., Jandrić, P., & Hayes, S. (Eds.). (2022). *Bioinformational Philosophy and Postdigital Knowledge Ecologies.* Cham: Springer. https://doi.org/10.1007/978-3-030-95006-4.

Savin-Baden, M., & Reader, J. (Eds.). (2022). *Postdigital Theologies: Technology, Belief, and Practice.* Cham: Springer. https://doi.org/10.1007/978-3-031-09405-7.

Acknowledgements

Republished Chapters

Postdigital Research: Genealogies, Challenges, and Future Perspectives contains four republished chapters.

The first republished chapter, Jandrić, P., MacKenzie, A., & Knox, J. (2022). Postdigital Research: Genealogies, Challenges, and Future Perspectives. *Postdigital Science and Education.* https://doi.org/10.1007/s42438-022-00306-3, outlines the editors' ideas for this volume before we drafted the Call for Chapters. We included it to provide context around the development of the book. The original text is reproduced verbatim with minor updates.

The second republished chapter, Jandrić, P. (2022). History of the Postdigital: Invitation for Feedback. *Postdigital Science and Education.* https://doi.org/10.1007/s42438-022-00345-w, outlines the author's personal view on the history of the postdigital supplemented with the selection of the most prominent sources. The original article invited all readers to respond with their feedback and suggestions for improvement. After approximately 5 months, the article was updated with readers' feedback and was turned into a book chapter.

The third republished chapter, Fawns, T., Ross, J., Carbonel, H., Noteboom, J., Finnegan-Dehn, S., & Raver, M. (2023). Mapping and Tracing the Postdigital: Approaches and Parameters of Postdigital Research. *Postdigital Science and Education.* https://doi.org/10.1007/s42438-023-00391-y, was published in the journal less than a month before we sent this book to production. We found the article to be highly relevant for this book, so included it at the last moment. The original text is reproduced verbatim.

The fourth republished chapter, Jandrić, P., Luke, T. W., Sturm, S., McLaren, P., Jackson, L., MacKenzie, A., Tesar, M., Stewart, G. T., Roberts, P., Abegglen, S., Burns, T., Sinfield, S., Hayes, S., Jaldemark, J., Peters, M. A., Sinclair, C., & Gibbons, A. (2022). Collective Writing: The Continuous Struggle for Meaning-Making. *Postdigital Science and Education.* https://doi.org/10.1007/s42438-022-00320-5, is a summary of philosophy, theory, and practice arising from collective writing experiments conducted between 2016 and 2022 in the community associated with the Editors' Collective and more than 20 scholarly journals. Included for its relevance for postdigital research, and published approximately a year before this book, the original text is reproduced verbatim with minor updates.

All articles were originally published in *Postdigital Science and Education* journal.[1] We are grateful to Springer publishers for the permission to republish.

The *CUC 2022 – Opening in a Closed World: Postdigital Science and Education* Conference

In 2022, Petar Jandrić was invited to chair the Programme Committee for the research section at the *CUC 2022 – Opening in a Closed World: Postdigital Science and Education* conference.[2] Jeremy Knox and Alison MacKenzie gave their keynotes at the conference, and most authors in *Postdigital Research: Genealogies, Challenges, and Future Perspectives* and *Constructing Postdigital Research: Method and Emancipation* presented working versions of their chapters only a month or so before submitting their manuscripts. This was a great opportunity for the authors and editors to meet, share ideas, and develop links between the chapters. We are grateful to Croatian Academic and Research Network – CARNET – for the opportunity.

---

[1] See https://www.springer.com/journal/42438. Accessed 1 February 2023.

[2] See https://cuc.carnet.hr/2022/en/. Accessed 2 February 2023.

Contents

About the Editors

Petar Jandrić is Professor at the Zagreb University of Applied Sciences, Croatia. Petar's research interests are at the postdisciplinary intersections between technologies, pedagogies, and the society, and research methodologies of his choice are inter-, trans-, and antidisciplinarity. He is the Editor-in-Chief of *Postdigital Science and Education* journal https://www.springer.com/journal/42438 and book series https://www.springer.com/series/16439 as well as the *Encyclopedia of Postdigital Science and Education*. His recent books include *The Methodology and Philosophy of Collective Writing* (2021), *Bioinformational Philosophy and Postdigital Knowledge Ecologies* (2022), and *Postdigital Ecopedagogies: Genealogies, Contradictions, and Possible Futures* (2022). Personal website: http://petarjandric.com/.

Alison MacKenzie is Reader at Queen's University, Belfast. Alison's research interests are in applied philosophy, particularly feminist and postdigital philosophy, epistemic injustice, and the related fields of epistemologies of ignorance and deceit. Alison has written on critical disability, the Capabilities Approach, and Bourdieusian analytical sociology. Alison is an Associate Editor of the *International Journal of Educational Research* and is on the editorial board of a number of journals including *Postdigital Science and Education*. Her recent edited book is *Epistemology of Deceit in a Postdigital Era* (2021).

Jeremy Knox is Senior Lecturer and Co-director of the Centre for Research in Digital Education at the University of Edinburgh. His research interests include the relationships between education, data-driven technologies, and wider society, and he has led projects funded by the ESRC and the British Council in the UK. Jeremy's published works include *Posthumanism and the MOOC* (2016), *Artificial Intelligence and Inclusive Education* (2019), *The Manifesto for Teaching Online* (2020), *Data Justice and the Right to the City* (2022), and *AI and Education in China* (2023).

About the Authors

Sandra Abegglen is a Researcher in the School of Architecture, Planning and Landscape at the University of Calgary, Canada, where she explores online education and learning and teaching in the design studio. Sandra's interests are in collaboration, co-creation, and social justice. Her research focuses on digital education, hybrid pedagogy, academic literacies, creative learning and teaching methods, inclusion, and identity. She is the Principal Investigator for Playful Hybrid Higher Education and the Teaching and Learning Online Network (TALON), and she holds the project lead for several other education research projects. Sandra has been awarded for her inter-disciplinary, multi-stakeholder education work.

Tom Burns is Senior Lecturer in the Centre for Professional and Educational Development at London Metropolitan University, UK, developing innovations with a special focus on praxes that ignite student curiosity and develop power and voice. Always interested in theatre and the arts, and their role in teaching and learning, Tom has set up adventure playgrounds, community events and festivals, and feeds arts-based practice into his learning, teaching, and assessment practices. He is co-author of *Essential Study Skills: The complete Guide to Success at University* (2022, 5th Edition), and other books and articles advocating for student success and creative practice.

Henrietta Carbonel is Researcher and Instructional Designer in Digital Education for the Educational Development Unit in Distance Learning (EDUDL+) at UniDistance Suisse, the Swiss distance university. Having previously taught economics in universities in Japan and Switzerland for 15 years, she now supports teaching teams in designing, teaching, and evaluating online programmes. Her research focuses on the distance university of the future, taking a speculative and critical approach including teachers, students, management, and staff. She holds a PhD from Osaka University, Japan, and a Masters in Digital Education from the University of Edinburgh, UK.

Tim Fawns is Associate Professor at the Monash Education Academy, Monash University, Australia. Tim's research interests are at the intersection between digital, clinical, and higher education, with a particular focus on the relationship between technology and educational practice. He has recently published a book titled *Online Postgraduate Education in a Postdigital World Beyond Technology* (2021). Personal website: http://timfawns.com.

Sam Finnegan-Dehn holds an MSc in Philosophy from Edinburgh University, specializing in the philosophy of technology and ethics. He is currently working as an academic tutor and a digital marketing officer, as well as a copywriter specializing in content relating to the Ethics of AI and Responsible Tech. Personal website: www.sameffdee.

Derek R. Ford is a teacher, organizer, and educational theorist. He has written eight books, including *Teaching the Actuality of Revolution: Aesthetics, Unlearning, and the Sensations of Struggle* (2023). Published widely in academic journals, Ford's public scholarship appears in outlets such as *Black Agenda Report*, *Monthly Review*, and the *International Magazine*. Ford is an organizer with the Indianapolis Liberation Center and the ANSWER Coalition, and is the Educational Department Chair at the Hampton Institute and the Editor of LiberationSchool.org.

Andrew Gibbons is Professor at the School of Education, Auckland University of Technology, Aotearoa New Zealand. The study of teaching is at the heart of Andrew's work and draws upon his experiences as an early childhood teacher. Andrew's teaching and research is dedicated to growing teacher education programmes that break out of disciplinary siloes and generate connections between teachers and the research community. Andrew is a Fellow of the Philosophy of Education Society of Australasia and Executive Committee member of the Association for Visual Pedagogies.

Lesley Gourlay is Professor of Education at University College London Institute of Education. Her scholarship focuses on the interplay between technologies and the knowledge practices of students and academics, with a particular emphasis on science and technology studies in education. Her recent theoretical work has focused on sociomaterial and posthuman perspectives on engagement in the university, exploring themes of space, inscription, nonhuman agency, and digital media. She is a recipient of a Leverhulme Major Research Fellowship (2021-2024) and is currently writing a new monograph on the topic of *The Datafied University: Documentation and Performativity in Digitised Education* with Bloomsbury Academic.

Karin Gunnarsson (PhD) holds a position as Associate Senior Lecturer at the Department of Education, Stockholm University. Inspired by posthumanist theories, her research has a specific interest in teaching about gender, equality, and norms. Currently, she runs a research project on sexuality education in secondary school and is a regional editor of *The Palgrave Encyclopedia of Sexuality Education*. Karin's research interests also concern methodological questions of working with postqualitative and practice-based approaches. Her published works include articles such as 'Care and feminist posthumanisms' (2023) and 'Ambiguous engagements: exploring affective qualities within the teaching of norms and equality' (2022).

Sarah Hayes is Professor of Higher Education Policy and a Principal Fellow of the HEA. She is Honorary Professor at Aston University, Birmingham, UK, and Associate Editor for *Postdigital Science and Education*. Sarah co-edited *Bioinformational Philosophy and Postdigital Knowledge Ecologies* (2022) with Michael Peters and Petar Jandrić. She also wrote *The Labour of Words in Higher Education* (2019) and *Postdigital Positionality* (2021), which opened debate on how disadvantage manifests in the disconnect between inclusivity policies and the widespread digitalization and datafication of society.

Peter B. Hyland is the Director of the Jo Ann (Jody) and Dr. Charles O. Onstead Institute for Education in the Visual Arts and Design at the University of North Texas. He is the co-author, with Tyson E. Lewis, of the book *Studious Drift: Movements and Protocols for a Postdigital Education* (2022). Additionally, he is the author of the poetry collection *Out Loud* and has had creative work appear in various journals, including *Conduit, Green Mountains Review, New England Review*, and *Ploughshares*, among others.

Liz Jackson is Professor in the Faculty of Education at the University of Hong Kong. She is also Immediate Past President and Fellow of the Philosophy of Education Society of Australasia (PESA) and the Acting Editor-in-Chief of *Educational Philosophy and Theory*. Her books include *Beyond Virtue: The Politics of Educating Emotions* (2021), *Contesting Education and Identity in Hong Kong* (2020), and *Questioning Allegiance: Resituating Civic Education* (2019).

Jimmy Jaldemark is an Associate Professor at the Department of Education, Mid Sweden University, Sundsvall, Sweden. He has worked within the field of educational technology since the mid-1990s. His current research interest concerns collaborative, lifelong, mobile, and networked aspects of learning. He also recently guest edited a special issue titled "Lifelong Learning in a Digital Era", published in the *British Journal of Educational Technology*, where he also serves as an Editor. He is a co-founder of a national research school called GRADE (GRAduate school for Digital technologies in Education).

Mark William Johnson is Lecturer in Technology Enhanced Learning at the University of Manchester and Chief Technology Officer of a medical diagnostics company. His work focuses on cybernetics and the organization of education, digitalization, and the relationship between technology and institutions. His interest in the postdigital stems from his expertise in cybernetics, and recent publications have explored the connection between the two. As a technologist, he is the co-inventor of patented machine learning techniques in medical diagnostics, while his educational work has embraced developing dialogical pedagogy and digitalization in Denmark, China, and Russia.

Michael Jopling is Professor of Education at the University of Brighton, UK. His research examines education policy and its effects on schools and universities, particularly in relation to issues like leadership, disadvantage, and inclusion. He is link convenor of EERA's Children and Youth at Risk and Urban Education network and his most recent publications have explored the impact of education policy and the pandemic on schools and vulnerable young people. He is co-editor of *Human Data Interaction, Disadvantage and Skills in the Community: Enabling Cross-Sector Environments for Postdigital Inclusion* (2023).

Tyson E. Lewis is Professor of Art Education at the University of North Texas where he teaches courses in critical theory, posthumanism, critical phenomenology, educational philosophy, and aesthetic philosophy. He has published widely in a number of journals such as *New German Critique, Angelaki, Cultural Politics*, and *Cultural Critique*. Most recently he is author of the book *Walter Benjamin's Antifascist Education: From Riddles to Radio* (2020) as well as *Studious Drift: Movements and Protocols for a Postdigital Education* (co-authored with Peter B. Hyland) (2022).

Timothy W. Luke is University Distinguished Professor and Chair of the Department of Political Science as well as Interim Director of the School of Public and International Affairs at Virginia Polytechnic Institute and State University, Blacksburg, Virginia, USA. His research and teaching focus on political economy and environmental politics from analytical perspectives grounded in critical theory, comparative politics, discourse analysis, and urban studies in relation to issues in global governance, political economy, and cultural conflict, particularly those related to the theories and practices of climate change, environmental governance and sustainability studies. He is the author of *Anthropocene Alerts: Critical Theory of the Contemporary as Ecocritique* (2019), *Screens of Power: Ideology, Domination and Resistance in Informational Society* (revised edition 2020), and *The Travails of Trumpification* (2021) and co-editor with Joel Jay Kassiola of *The Palgrave Handbook of Environmental Politics and Theory* (2023).

Peter McLaren is Distinguished Professor in Critical Studies and Honorary Director and International Ambassador for Global Ethics and Social Justice of the Paulo Freire Democratic Project at Chapman University's Attallah College of Educational Studies. He is a Fellow of the Royal Society of Arts and a Fellow of the American Educational Research Association. A Professor Emeritus of the University of California, Los Angeles, Professor McLaren co-founded Instituto McLaren de Pedagogía Crítica in Ensenada, Mexico. An award-winning author, Professor McLaren's writings have been translated into over 20 languages. He is the recent recipient of the Paulo Freire Legacy Award presented by the American Educational Research Association.

Sara Mörtsell is a PhD candidate at the Department of Education, Umeå University in affiliation with the University of Gävle, Sweden. Sara is a student in the Swedish doctoral program on Digital Education (GRADE), and her thesis project explores pandemic-education practices in secondary education with relational materialisms and Actor-Network Theory (ANT). Sara's research interests gravitate to intersecting practice-based education research with Science and Technology Studies (STS), feminist science studies, and posthumanist theories.

Joe Noteboom is a PhD student in Sociology at the University of Edinburgh and part of the Centre for Research in Digital Education and Centre for Technomoral Futures. Joe's PhD research is on the social and ethical implications of datafication in higher education, with a particular focus on student perspectives on datafication and the potential for collective forms of data governance. He is a Teaching Assistant on the MSc in Education Futures at the Edinburgh Futures Institute and a member of the University's AI and Data Ethics Advisory Board.

Megha Summer Pappachen is a second year Political Science PhD student at Northwestern University. She studies and teaches in political theory and international political economy. Her research interests are in theories of the global south, feminist and queer theory, and critical race theory. She has written for *Liberation School* and *Breaking the Chains* magazine, and published a book chapter in *Bioinformational Philosophy and Postdigital Knowledge Ecologies* (2021). Summer is also an organizer with the Chicago Liberation Center and with the graduate worker union at Northwestern University.

Michael A. Peters is Distinguished Professor of Education at Beijing Normal University, Emeritus Professor at the University of Illinois (Urbana-Champaign), and Honorary Senior Research Fellow at the University of Auckland. He is the Editor-in-Chief of the journals *Education Philosophy and Theory* and *The Beijing International Review of Education* (with Zhu Xudong). His most recent publications include *Pandemic Education and Viral Politics* (2020), *The Far-Right, Education and Violence* (2020), and *Wittgenstein, Education and the Problem of Rationality* (2021). He is a lifetime member of the NZ Academy of Humanities and a Fellow of the Royal Society of New Zealand. He is an Honorary Fellow of the Society for Research into Higher Education and was awarded honorary doctorates by State University of New York (SUNY) in 2012 and the University of Aalborg in 2015. Personal webpage: https://michaeladrianpeters.com/.

Shane J. Ralston is the Dean of Wright College, Woolf University. Shane's research interests are strongest in the areas of political technology, educational innovation, applied ethics, research methodology, environmental philosophy, and global politics.He is the author of *John Dewey's Great Debates – Reconstructed* (2011) and *Pragmatic Environmentalism* (2013) as well as the editor of *Philosophical Pragmatism and International Relations* (2013).

McKenzie Raver returned to education as a mature student in 2021 and successfully completed an MSc in Mind, Language, and Embodied Cognition at the University of Edinburgh. She has a BA in Philosophy at York College of Pennsylvania, United States. McKenzie is interested in the intersections of the philosophy, technology, and the law to include philosophy of law, philosophy of technology, artificial intelligence/technology and the law, posthumanism, and bioethics. She has 6 years of experience working in the legal field, and plans to attend law school in the United States to continue work and research in her areas of interest.

John Reader has degrees from Oxford (MA), Manchester (MPhil), and Wales, Bangor (PhD). A parish priest of over 40 years in ministry, he is also Senior Research Fellow of the William Temple Foundation; Honorary Senior Lecturer for the School of Education, University of Worcester; and Senior Tutor for the Christian Rural and Environmental Studies course based at Ripon College Cuddesdon. He has published six solo books and co-authored a further six, plus six William Temple Foundation Tracts and various chapters and articles. His role with the William Temple Foundation includes curating the Ethical Futures Network which has met at Trinity College, Oxford. John's recent publications include *A Philosophy of Christian Materialism* (with Baker and James) (2015) and *Theology and New Materialism* (2017).

Peter Roberts is Professor of Education at the University of Canterbury in New Zealand. His teaching and research interests are in philosophy of education and educational policy studies. His latest books include *Philosophy, Death and Education* (with R. Scott Webster and John Quay, 2023), *Paulo Freire: Philosophy, Pedagogy and Practice* (2022), *Performativity, Politics and Education: From Policy to Philosophy* (2022), *Education and the Limits of Reason: Reading Dostoevsky, Tolstoy and Nabokov* (with Herner Saeverot, 2018), and *Happiness, Hope, and Despair: Rethinking the Role of Education* (2016).

Jen Ross is Senior Lecturer at the University of Edinburgh. She is Co-director of the Centre for Research in Digital Education, and leads the MSc in Education Futures in the Edinburgh Futures Institute and the Digital Cultural Heritage cluster in the Centre for Data, Culture and Society. She researches education and cultural heritage futures, online distance education, digital cultural heritage learning, Massive Open Online Courses (MOOCs), digital cultures, and online reflective practices, and recently published the book *Digital Futures for Learning: Speculative Methods and Pedagogies* (2023).

Neil Selwyn is currently Distinguished Professor at Monash University, Melbourne, and has been researching and writing about digital education for the past 25 years. His recent books include: *Should Robots Replace Teachers? AI and the future of education* (2019), *Critical Data Literacies* (with Luci Pangrazio) (2023), and the third edition of *Education and Technology: Key Issues and Debates* (2021).

Christine Sinclair is an Honorary Fellow in the Centre for Research in Digital Education at the University of Edinburgh. Before retiring, she was Programme Director for the MSc in Digital Education. She graduated from this programme herself in 2010, when working as a Lecturer in Academic Practice at the University of Strathclyde. She enjoyed researching student experience through being a student and is the author of *Understanding University: A Guide to Another Planet* (2006) and *Grammar: A Friendly Approach* (2010).

Sandra Sinfield is Senior Lecturer in Education and Learning Development in the Centre for Professional and Educational Development at London Metropolitan University, UK, and a co-founder of the Association for Learning Development in Higher Education (ALDinHE). She has co-authored *Essential Study Skills: The Complete Guide to Success at University* (2022, 5th Edition), *Teaching, Learning and Study Skills: A Guide for Tutors* (2004), and many other high-cited publications. Sandra is interested in creativity as liberatory and holistic practice in Higher Education; she has developed theatre and film in unusual places – and inhabited Second Life as a learning space.

Georgina Tuari Stewart (Ngāpuhi-nui-tonu, Pare Hauraki) is Professor of Māori Philosophy of Education in Te Ara Poutama, Auckland University of Technology, Auckland, New Zealand. Her research investigates the relationship between science and Māori knowledge, also questions of Māori identity and the implications for education – themes explored in her book *Māori Philosophy: Indigenous Thinking from Aotearoa* (2021). She is the Coeditor of the *New Zealand Journal of Educational Studies* and Deputy Editor of *Educational Philosophy and Theory*.

Sean Sturm is Associate Professor at the School of Critical Studies in Education, Waipapa Taumata Rau/the University of Auckland, Aotearoa/New Zealand. They lead the Higher Education programme and teach into the Arts in Education programme. Their research works at the intersection of the philosophy of higher education and indigenous studies to understand the co-implication of place and peoples. They are the Editor of *Knowledge Cultures* and *PESA Agora*.

Marek Tesar is Professor, Head of School, and the Associate Dean International at the University of Auckland, New Zealand. He is also the Director of Centre for Global Childhoods. His scholarship is focused on philosophy of early childhood education and global childhood studies in both New Zealand and in cross-country contexts. Marek serves as a leader of two leading learned societies in his fields; he chairs the Steering Committee of the Reconceptualizing Early Childhood Education (RECE) and is elected President of the Philosophy of Education Society of Australasia (PESA).

Terrie Lynn Thompson is Senior Lecturer in Digital Media and Professional Work-Learning at the University of Stirling. She researches how professional work practices and ways of knowing are changing as the digital infuses work, learning, and everyday life. Terrie Lynn brings more-than-human and new materialist feminist perspectives to study new arrangements of work-learning and the ethics and politics of AI and datafication. She leads one of the University's multidisciplinary research programs, Digital Society and Culture. In addition to journal articles, her books include *Researching a Posthuman World: Interviews with Digital Objects* (2016).

Ben Williamson is Senior Lecturer in the Centre for Research in Digital Education at the University of Edinburgh. His research interests are in the relationships between digital technologies, data science, and education, with particular projects on the emergence of data-intensive biology in education, the making of digital learning futures, and the role of the finance and investment industry in the education technology market. Ben is the author of *Big Data in Education: The Digital Future of Learning, Policy and Practice* (2017) and an editor of the journal *Learning, Media and Technology*.

Part I
What Is Postdigital?

Postdigital Research: Genealogies, Challenges, and Future Perspectives

Petar Jandrić ⓘ, Alison MacKenzie ⓘ, and Jeremy Knox ⓘ

1 What Binds Us Together?

Since the inception of *Postdigital Science and Education* journal and book series, postdigital scholarship has experienced rapid growth. However, the implications of postdigital research (methods) have remained unclear. What does it mean to conduct postdigital research? What are the main challenges and opportunities of postdigital research? And, probably most importantly, what are its prospects for the future?

This essay addresses the *Postdigital Science and Education* community's pressing need to examine its own research praxes and asks: What binds us together in postdigital research, particularly in a methodological sense? The essay outlines genealogies, challenges, opportunities, and future perspectives of postdigital research. It offers our understanding of the main developments in the field and serves as a supplement to the call for chapters for *Postdigital Research: Genealogies, Challenges, and Future Perspectives* (Jandrić et al. 2023a) and *Postdigital Research: Method and Emancipation* (Jandrić et al. 2023b).

P. Jandrić (✉)
Zagreb University of Applied Sciences, Zagreb, Croatia
e-mail: pjandric@tvz.hr

A. MacKenzie
Queen's University Belfast, Belfast, UK
e-mail: A.Mackenzie@qub.ac.uk

J. Knox
University of Edinburgh, Edinburgh, UK
e-mail: jeremy.knox@ed.ac.uk

P. Jandrić et al. (eds.), *Postdigital Research*, Postdigital Science and Education, https://doi.org/10.1007/978-3-031-31299-1_1

2   A Brief Genealogy

The earliest appearance of the postdigital idea is generally attributed to Nicholas Negroponte. In a seminal Wired article, Negroponte wrote that the digital is designed for the invisibility (and therefore banality) caused by its omnipresence in our daily lives. 'Its literal form, the technology, is already beginning to be taken for granted, and its connotation will become tomorrow's commercial and cultural compost for new ideas. Like air and drinking water, being digital will be noticed only by its absence, not its presence.' (Negroponte 1998) Soon after Negroponte's articulation of the inseparability of the digital and the analog, his idea acquired its own name and started its journey into the history of thought.

The word postdigital was first mentioned in Cascone's essay 'The Aesthetics of Failure' (2000) and Pepperell and Punt's book *The Postdigital Membrane: Imagination, Technology and Desire* (2000). Without knowledge of each other's work, these authors developed the concept in the context of music (Cascone) and visual art (Pepperell and Punt) (more about early history of the concept can be found in Cascone and Jandrić 2021). In the following years, the concept of the postdigital occasionally appeared across wide arts-related fields such as music, visual arts, architecture, design, and so on.

In 2014 Christian Ulrik Andersen, Geoff Cox, and Georgios Papadopoulos made the first known attempt at systematization in a Special Issue titled 'Post-digital Research'.[1] In the introduction to the Special Issue, they take the concept of the postdigital 'to be a serious concept that deserves our critical attention' and address the term itself, its genealogy and wider connotations, as well as its potential usefulness across different fields (including art, acoustics, aesthetic theory, political economy, and philosophy). Given that the term comes from practice, the Special Issue also addresses how the postdigital potentially operates as a framework for practice-based research that relate to material and historical conditions (Andersen et al. 2014: 5). This Special Issue marks the 'official' entrance of postdigital research into mainstream academia; yet its focus and scope remained largely within artistic fields and practice-based research.

Two decades are a long time in artistic practice. In 2021 Cramer (in Cramer and Jandrić 2021: 977) wrote that, 'in the meantime, the term postdigital has become rather useless in the arts, because it is constantly being conflated and confused with the too-similar-sounding and much better-known "Post-Internet"'. However, continues Cramer, the concept still offers a lot beyond its fields of origin:

> The best possible contribution of the concept 'postdigital' in 2021 is, in my opinion, that it can help to complicate the terms 'digital' and 'analog', particularly in the humanities and social sciences. It could also be used for fields of technology that are literally postdigital, such as biocomputing and continuous variable quantum computing. (Cramer in Cramer and Jandrić 2021: 985)

---

[1] See https://aprja.net//issue/view/8400. Accessed 10 February 2023.

In 2018 a similar line of thinking inspired the inception of the *Postdigital Science and Education* journal and book series (see Jandrić et al. 2018). Following the footsteps of many scholarly concepts which originated in the arts, the concept of the postdigital has now become an integral part of scholarly discourse. *Postdigital Science and Education* is arguably the main publishing ecosystem for postdigital research, though far from being the only one.[2] Today, postdigital research centres,[3] projects,[4] and publications are growing in number[5] and importance.[6]

3 Against Definitions

The community has occasionally, but far from systemically, dealt with the history of the concept (Cormier et al. 2019); its relationships to other 'schools of thought' (Knox 2019; de Laat and Dohn 2019); terminology (Sinclair and Hayes 2019; Fawns 2019); methodology (Jandrić 2020a, b, 2021; Jandrić and Knox 2022; Ryberg 2021; Macgilchrist 2021); and other elements typically required of a

---

[2] See, for instance, The Palgrave Studies in Educational Media book series edited by Eckhardt Fuchs and Felicitas Macgilchrist. https://link.springer.com/series/15151. Accessed 10 February 2023.

[3] Some of the most prominent centres in the humanities and social sciences include Coventry University's Centre for Postdigital Cultures (https://www.coventry.ac.uk/research/areas-of-research/postdigital-cultures/) and The Leibniz Science Campus—Postdigital Participation – Braunschweig (https://www.postdigitalparticipation.org/en/). Accessed 10 February 2023.

[4] Alongside many projects in the humanities and social sciences, a good example in science and engineering is the European Training Network on Post Digital Computing – POSTDIGITAL (https://postdigital.astonphotonics.uk/). Accessed 10 February 2023.

[5] In more than 4 years of publication, *Postdigital Science and Education* journal has published more than 400 articles. Founded in 2021, the Postdigital Science and Education book series now has nine published books and many more in the making. See https://www.springer.com/series/16439. Accessed 10 February 2023.

[6] With 526,200 downloads in 2021, *Postdigital Science and Education* is positioned amongst the most read journals in education and education technology. The journal's most cited article, 'Online university teaching during and after the Covid-19 crisis: Refocusing teacher presence and learning activity' (Rapanta et al. 2020), has amassed more than 200,000 downloads and almost 2000 citations in less than 3 years. See journal's real-time Google citation metrics at https://scholar.google.com/citations?user=RyZRb5IAAAAJ&hl=en. Accessed 10 February 2023.

Postdigital Science and Education articles regularly appear in prestigious lists such as the Dublin City University's National Institute for Digital Learning list of top 10 'good reads'. See https://nidl.blog/2023/01/16/top-10-good-reads-from-2022-from-theory-to-practice-and-back-again/. Accessed 10 February 2023.

In 2021, its third year of publication, *Postdigital Science and Education* was listed by Scopus, where it immediately achieved high citation ranking. On 5 April 2023, journal's CiteScore is 16.2, bringing it on top of most cited articles in following categories: Social Sciences (Education), #8/1406 (99th percentile), Social Sciences (Miscellaneous), #6/426 (98th percentile), and Arts and Humanities (Miscellaneous), #7/376 (98th percentile). See https://www.scopus.com/sourceid/21101075549. Accessed 18 April 2023. *Postdigital Science and Education* articles have been republished in several languages including Chinese, Croatian, German, Spanish, and Turkish.

distinct 'field', 'perspective', 'school of thought', or 'discipline'. We place these terms under quotation marks, as we do not think that they fully apply to postdigital thought. The question 'What is postdigital?' is simultaneously both useful and preposterous; both friend and foe.

The question is a friend because it helps us to focus our thoughts and ideas; it is a foe, because '[t]o define a field is necessarily to put boundaries around it, to determine which writings, conversations, people are "inside" and which are "outside"' (Bayne in Networked Learning Editorial Collective et al. 2021: 333). This is why Jandrić and Ford argue that

> one day, probably, our postdigital condition will be condensed in concise encyclopaedia entries and routinely explained by undergraduates. One task is to ensure this does not happen, and that the postdigital remains—for as a long as it is productive—a concept that constantly resists any final definition. (Jandrić and Ford 2022: 707)

This is also why the only thing the community has clearly defined is spelling. While the word postdigital can be found in various versions, such as postdigital, post digital, post-digital, and so on, for pragmatic reasons, it was decided to maximize online searchability and accessibility by consistent use of the spelling 'postdigital'. This decision is significant as a postdigital move itself: rendering the term 'easy to type into search boxes' as well as 'simple to be indexed in databases' is a demonstration of complicating the distinction between digital and analog. The term for this 'school of thought' was decided upon, at least in part, due to the functioning of digital infrastructure.

The concept of the postdigital deliberately defies any attempts at definition, yet its history and genealogy strongly determine its research practices. These practices range anywhere from arts-based research, through humanities and social sciences, to natural sciences and engineering. Some of this epistemic anarchy (Feyerabend 1970/1993) can be attributed to troubling distinctions and boundaries across disciplinary research approaches, which now attract a lot of attention in the journal (see Gibbs 2022; MacKenzie 2022; Green 2022). What are the other possible sources of the 'Jack-of-all-trades' nature of postdigital research? And how can we avoid the much less pleasant continuation of the adage, 'and master of none'?

4   The Curious Dance Between Epistemology and Methodology

Postdigital research can employ any research methodology, yet not all research is postdigital. Postdigital research may not even mention the word postdigital, and research articles using the word postdigital may misinterpret its philosophy. This makes tasks such as editing and reviewing messy; despite our wariness of definitions, this mess cannot be cleared up without some conceptual clarity. In the mission statement article for the journal and the book series, it was decided, therefore, to embrace this messiness as an inherent part of the postdigital condition. 'The postdigital is hard to define; messy; unpredictable; digital and analog; technological and non-technological; biological and informational. The postdigital is both a rupture in our existing theories and their continuation.' (Jandrić et al. 2018: 894)

Conscious of the messy nature of our postdigital condition, and wary of Bayne's warning that even the best definitions will also determine what postdigital research is not (Bayne in Networked Learning Editorial Collective et al. 2021: 333), this chapter and our edited books on postdigital research actively avoid defining, delineating, and canonizing postdigital research to any restrictive extent. In the language of epistemology, we despise 'ownership' of the concept characteristic of knowledge capitalism and situate our work firmly within the idea of knowledge as a common construct and a common good characteristic for knowledge socialism (Peters et al. 2020).

Our attitude does not imply epistemic relativism, at least not in the form of 'anything goes'. But we insist that the concept of the postdigital must remain a common good, and we insist that the community of postdigital researchers needs to be open to everyone who does good work — including non-human agents. This is a community that is open to what constitutes knowledge, and the means by which to attest, authenticate, or audit the truthfulness of its creation. In this essay, therefore, our aim is to introduce, challenge, provoke, and start a wide postdigital dialogue (Jandrić et al. 2019) about the present and future of research in our postdigital age, while sustaining the elasticity and capaciousness of the concept.

5 An Invitation to Dialogue

Though the aim is to avoid restrictions and canonization, and to retain the capaciousness of the concept, we nevertheless need to describe the postdigital in a meaningful and widely applicable way. We need, further, to head off challenges which could allege that in being as open as we claim to be to the construction and production of knowledge, there is no end to what could be asserted as 'research', and in the process lose credibility. As noted by contributors to a current discussion on postdigital transdisciplinarity (see Gibbs 2022; MacKenzie 2022; Green 2022), research within the disciplines can be hyperspecialised and compartmentalised, lacking flexibility in addressing urgent global problems. While we want to be careful that we don't go down the same route, disciplines are important, as they rely on research processes that address rigour, validity, trustworthiness, and so on.

We have to take a stand on what we mean by quality, credible, trustworthy postdigital research. The very fact that we talk of 'postdigital' rather than postdigital sociology, postdigital politics, postdigital music, or postdigital philosophy, with their key and emerging thinkers, methods of enquiry, and favoured research designs, may help us; 'postdigital' is a guiding idea, rather than an absolute or definitively bounded concept. We are well aware that the concept of the postdigital was developed in response to certain socio-technological conditions of our space–time. As soon as these conditions change, postdigital research will inevitably transform or give way to more appropriate approaches and terms.

We accept impermanence and contextuality as an inherent part of knowledge development. We warmly welcome all kinds of criticism, including the harshest rebuttals, and we humbly embrace our ephemeral role in the history of human thought. Yet we are well aware that our tiny role arrives with a huge responsibility. Researchers of today and tomorrow need strong shoulders to stand on; it is our duty to scaffold the postdigital research of the present and bequeath our best to the future.

Following our belief that it takes a village to raise a child, we decided to frame our research in a widely open postdigital dialogue (Jandrić et al. 2019). All knowledge is co-constituted by the conditions of its making, and our efforts are shaped in the form of an edited book. This setup may result in a mashup of openings and closures, opportunities and restrictions, orientations to both the empirical and theoretico-philosophical, which we hope to critically interrogate along the way. We invite the postdigital community to join us in these efforts and examine the scope, importance, methodology, and significance of its present research praxes — while firmly keeping an eye on the future.

Acknowledgement This chapter was first published as Jandrić, P., MacKenzie, A., & Knox, J. (2022). Postdigital Research: Genealogies, Challenges, and Future Perspectives. *Postdigital Science and Education.* https://doi.org/10.1007/s42438-022-00306-3. The original article was published before the Call for Chapters for *Postdigital Research: Genealogies, Challenges, and Future Perspectives* and *Constructing Postdigital Research: Method and Emancipation* and was shared with all authors in these collections.

References

Andersen, C. U., Cox, G., & Papadopoulos, G. (2014). Editorial: Postdigital Research. *A Peer-Reviewed Journal About, 3*(1), 5–7. https://doi.org/10.7146/aprja.v3i1.116067.

Cascone, K. (2000). The aesthetics of failure: 'Post-digital' tendencies in contemporary computer music. *Computer Music Journal, 24*(4), 12–18. https://doi.org/10.1162/014892600559489.

Cascone, K., & Jandrić, P. (2021). The Failure of Failure: Postdigital Aesthetics Against Techno-Mystification. *Postdigital Science and Education, 3*(2), 566–574. https://doi.org/10.1007/s42438-020-00209-1.

Cormier, D., Jandrić, P., Childs, M., Hall, R., White, D., Phipps, L., Truelove, I., Hayes, S., & Fawns, T. (2019). Ten Years of the Postdigital in the 52group: Reflections and Developments 2009–2019. *Postdigital Science and Education, 1*(2), 475-506. https://doi.org/10.1007/s42438-019-00049-8.

Cramer, F., & Jandrić, P. (2021). Postdigital: A Term That Sucks but Is Useful. *Postdigital Science and Education, 3*(3), 966–989. https://doi.org/10.1007/s42438-021-00225-9.

De Laat, M., & Dohn, N. B. (2019). Is networked learning postdigital education? *Postdigital Science and Education, 1*(1), 17–20. https://doi.org/10.1007/s42438-019-00034-1.

Fawns, T. (2019). Postdigital education in design and practice. *Postdigital Science and Education, 1*(1), 132–145. https://doi.org/10.1007/s42438-018-0021-8.

Feyerabend, P. (1970/1993). *Against method.* London: Verso.

Gibbs, P. (2022). The Struggling Towards a Transdisciplinary Metaphysics. *Postdigital Science and Education, 4*(3), 649–657. https://doi.org/10.1007/s42438-021-00278-w.

Green, B. (2022). Why the world doesn't need a metaphysics of transdisciplinarity. response to 'the struggling towards a transdisciplinary metaphysics' (Gibbs 2021). *Postdigital Science and Education, 4*(3), 683–691. https://doi.org/10.1007/s42438-022-00296-2.

Jandrić, P. (2020a). Educational research in the postdigital Age. *Journal of South China Normal University (Social Science Edition), 6*, 1–14.

Jandrić, P. (2020b). Postdigital research measurement. *Postdigital Science and Education, 3*(1), 15–26. https://doi.org/10.1007/s42438-020-00105-8.

Jandrić, P. (2021). The postdigital challenge of critical educational research. In C. Mathias (Ed.), *The Handbook of Critical Theoretical Research Methods in Education* (pp. 31–48). Abingdon and New York: Routledge.

Jandrić, P., & Ford, D. (2022). Postdigital ecopedagogies: Genealogies, contradictions, and possible futures. *Postdigital Science and Education, 4*(3), 692–710. https://doi.org/10.1007/s42438-020-00207-3.

Jandrić, P., & Knox, J. (2022). The Postdigital Turn: Philosophy, Education, Research. *Policy Futures in Education, 20*(7), 780–795. https://doi.org/10.1177/2F14782103211062713.

Jandrić, P., Knox, J., Besley, T., Ryberg, T., Suoranta, J., & Hayes, S. (2018). Postdigital Science and Education. *Educational Philosophy and Theory, 50*(10), 893–899. https://doi.org/10.1080/00131857.2018.1454000.

Jandrić, P., Ryberg, T., Knox, J., Lacković, N., Hayes, S., Suoranta, J., Smith, M., Steketee, A., Peters, M. A., McLaren, P., Ford, D. R., Asher, G., McGregor, C., Stewart, G., Williamson, B., & Gibbons, A. (2019). Postdigital dialogue. *Postdigital Science and Education, 1*(1), 163–189. https://doi.org/10.1007/s42438-018-0011-x.

Jandrić, P., MacKenzie, A., & Knox, J. (Eds.). (2023a). *Postdigital Research: Genealogies, Challenges, and Future Perspectives*. Cham: Springer.

Jandrić, P., MacKenzie, A., & Knox, J. (Eds.). (2023b). *Constructing Postdigital Research: Method and Emancipation*. Cham: Springer.

Knox, J. (2019). What does the postdigital mean for education? three critical perspectives on the digital, with implications for educational research and practice. *Postdigital Science and Education, 1*(2), 357-370. https://doi.org/10.1007/s42438-019-00045-y.

Macgilchrist, F. (2021). Theories of postdigital heterogeneity: Implications for research on education and datafication. *Postdigital Science and Education, 3*(3), 660–667. https://doi.org/10.1007/s42438-021-00232-w.

MacKenzie, A. (2022). Down to Earth transdisciplinarity. Response to the struggling towards a transdisciplinary metaphysics (Gibbs 2021). *Postdigital Science and Education, 4*(3), 676–682. https://doi.org/10.1007/s42438-022-00298-0.

Negroponte, N. (1998). Beyond digital. Wired, 12. http://www.wired.com/wired/archive/6.12/negroponte.html. Accessed 10 February 2023.

Networked Learning Editorial Collective, Gourlay, L., Rodríguez-Illera, J. L., Barberà, E., Bali, M., Gachago, D., Pallitt, N., Jones, C., Bayne, S., Hansen, S. B., Hrastinski, S., Jaldemark, J., Themelis, C., Pischetola, M., Dirckinck-Holmfeld, L., Matthews, A., Gulson, K. N., Lee, K., Bligh, B., Thibaut, P., … & Knox, J. (2021). Networked learning in 2021: A Community Definition. *Postdigital Science and Education, 3*(2), 326–369. https://doi.org/10.1007/s42438-021-00222-y.

Pepperell, R., & Punt, M. (2000). *The postdigital membrane: Imagination, technology and desire*. Bristol: Intellect.

Peters, M. A., Besley, T., Jandrić, P., & Zhu, X. (Eds.). (2020). *Knowledge Socialism. The Rise of Peer Production: Collegiality, Collaboration, and Collective Intelligence*. Singapore: Springer. https://doi.org/10.1007/978-981-13-8126-3.

Rapanta, C., Botturi, L., Goodyear, P., Guàrdia, L., & Koole, M. (2020). Online university teaching during and after the Covid-19 crisis: Refocusing teacher presence and learning activity. *Postdigital Science and Education, 2*(3), 923–945. https://doi.org/10.1007/s42438-020-00155-y.

Ryberg, T. (2021). Postdigital research, networked learning, and Covid-19. *Postdigital Science and Education, 3*(1), 266–271. https://doi.org/10.1007/s42438-021-00223-x.

Sinclair, C., & Hayes, S. (2019). Between the post and the com-post: Examining the postdigital 'work' of a prefix. *Postdigital Science and Education, 1*(1), 119–131. https://doi.org/10.1007/s42438-018-0017-4.

Histories of the Postdigital

Petar Jandrić ⓘ

1   Introduction

This chapter was written as a historical overview of postdigital thought for the two edited volumes about postdigital research, *Postdigital Research: Genealogies, Challenges, and Future Perspectives* (Jandrić et al. 2023a) and *Constructing Postdigital Research: Method and Emancipation* (Jandrić et al. 2023b). The chapter presents the author's personal view on the history of the postdigital, supplemented with the selection of the most prominent sources. In this way, the chapter offers a resource that supports readers' own research and interpretation. This approach makes sense as ideas can never be divorced from the context of their making; however, it may inadvertently omit important historical facts or overpraise an author's own work.

To ameliorate such bias, the chapter was developed in two phases. First, I published an article, 'History of the Postdigital: Invitation for Feedback' (Jandrić 2022), in the *Postdigital Science and Education* journal.[1] In this article, I invited all readers to respond with their feedback and suggestions for improvement. Few days before submitting *Postdigital Research: Genealogies, Challenges, and Future Perspectives* (Jandrić et al. 2023a) to production, I implemented all feedback and prepared this chapter for publication. I also added an Epilogue, where I reproduced the original invitation for feedback and received commentary. In the process, the title 'History of the Postdigital: Invitation for Feedback' (Jandrić 2022) has changed to 'Histories of the Postdigital': 'History' transformed to 'Histories' because the chapter now

---

[1] See https://www.springer.com/journal/42438. Accessed 20 February 2023.

P. Jandrić (✉)
Zagreb University of Applied Sciences, Zagreb, Croatia
e-mail: pjandric@tvz.hr

P. Jandrić et al. (eds.), *Postdigital Research*, Postdigital Science and Education,
https://doi.org/10.1007/978-3-031-31299-1_2

presents views agreed by more than one person, and the 'Invitation for Feedback' is no more.[2]

2   What's in a Concept?

Since 2000 the concept of the postdigital has rapidly developed within the context of the arts, humanities, and social sciences. These developments have become increasingly hard to keep track of, yet researchers need to be clear about the foundational scholarship that has shaped their work and the context within which that scholarship has taken place. This chapter responds to this need and outlines the history of the postdigital.

History is important, yet we live in the present, and our research shapes the future. Would it not be better to stop beating around the bush and just define the concept?

First, it might be prudent to examine the pros and cons of definitions. Recently, the Networked Learning community published an open invitation article, 'Networked Learning: Inviting Redefinition' (Networked Learning Editorial Collective 2021), followed by a definition article, 'Networked Learning in 2021: A Community Definition' (Networked Learning Editorial Collective et al. 2021). That paper had 40 contributors, from six continents, working across many fields of education, a paper that 'reflects the breadth and depth of current understandings of NL' (Networked Learning Editorial Collective et al. 2021: 327). Yet the article does not offer even a few sentences on a definition that could be used widely, and the contributors themselves have identified a range of problems with its approach.

One especially important critique arrives from Siân Bayne, who warns that '[t]o define a field is necessarily to put boundaries around it, to determine which writings, conversations, people are "inside" and which are "outside"' (Bayne in Networked Learning Editorial Collective et al. 2021: 333). Resulting exclusions, arguably, can do no good either to theory or to members of the community. Learning from the example of Networked Learning, Derek Ford and I recently wrote that

> one day, probably, our postdigital condition will be condensed in concise encyclopaedia entries and routinely explained by undergraduates. One task is to ensure this does not happen, and that the postdigital remains—for as long as it is productive—a concept that constantly resists any final definition. (Jandrić and Ford 2022: 707)

In a world where power derives from naming, defining, and demarcating, this resistance to definitions could lead to a discursive weakening of postdigital theory and needs to be negotiated carefully.

Boundaries and power relationships aside, there is a deeper philosophical reason why attempting to define the postdigital is not the best idea. The paradox of

---

[2] Of course, I will be more than happy to receive more feedback on this chapter. However, as I am not planning to write another sequel, this feedback will need to be published in a different format.

definition, originally postulated by Bernard Bolzano in *Contributions to A Better-Founded Presentation Of Mathematics* (Bolzano 1810), is that 'all concepts are ultimately defined in terms of simple concepts, but these remain undefined and thus devoid of meaning' (Rusnock and Šebestik 2022). The paradox of definition is applicable well beyond mathematics, as researchers in all fields regularly use concepts that cannot always be unequivocally defined.

For instance, a key concept in physics, force, is defined through Newton's second law as 'a push or pull upon an object resulting from the object's interaction with another object' (Neal 2019: 74). Yet force cannot be described self-referentially—we can only define it in relation to two other physical concepts, mass and acceleration. Concepts that run across fields and disciplines can be even more problematic. For instance, love is a foundational concept in many fields of human inquiry, yet each field sees it in a very different way. Geneticists explore ways in which sexually reproducing organisms choose their partners, and sociologists are interested in cultural representations of these ways and related issues, such as increasing divorce rates and their consequences. These questions are clearly related to falling in and out of love, but the two fields understand and approach love in very different ways.

The philosophical paradox of definition should not paralyze inquiry. There would be no physics without the concept of force, and whole scientific fields and artistic genres would not exist without the concept of love. Therefore, while the postdigital also resists final definitions, we do need to use, and talk about, the concept of the postdigital. One of the ways to start that conversation, commonly used in textbooks from physics to literature, is to examine ways in which the concept has been explored historically. Physics students learn about the progress from Newton's proverbial apple to Einstein's relativity; literature students study history of love poems anywhere from 'The Song of Songs' and Baudelaire to Rihanna. In the same vein, this paper presents a necessarily brief overview of the historical development of postdigital thought from the mouth of participants.

The historical overview is divided into two main phases, Postdigital Arts and Humanities and Postdigital Science and Education. Historically, the phase of Postdigital Arts and Humanities Humanities precedes the phase of Postdigital Science and Education. However, that does not imply a clear distinction, temporal sequence, or a hierarchy. In 2023, the postdigital is a transdisciplinary concept that develops in the interaction of all major fields and disciplines. While I do not engage in the question 'What is postdigital', each phase is supplemented with the selection of some of the most prominent sources speaking about the postdigital. In this way, the chapter begins to offer an overview of literature that supports readers' own research and interpretation.

This approach is far from perfect. While I did my best to include as many sources and viewpoints as possible, ideas can never be divorced from the context of their making, and histories can never be divorced from their writers. I have been actively involved in the history of the postdigital for years and cannot claim any pretence to neutrality. Thankfully, the history of the postdigital is a book open to everyone with Internet access, and my strategy for avoiding (at least the most fundamental) factual mistakes and misinterpretations was to invite everyone to respond to the first version of this chapter (Jandrić 2022) (see more details in the Introduction and Epilogue). This strategy is questionable, as the period of consultation was limited (5 months, 1000 downloads), and I received only five responses (three of which are anonymous). It is impossible to know why the article has not attracted more readers and why more readers had not responded, yet the offered period of open consultation does provide presented history of the postdigital with a certain, albeit limited, legitimacy.

3 Postdigital Arts and Humanities

Within a few short months in 2000, the word postdigital independently appeared in several publications, including 'The Aesthetics of Failure: "Post-Digital" Tendencies in Contemporary Computer Music' (Cascone 2000) and *The Postdigital Membrane: Imagination, Technology and Desire* (Pepperell and Punt 2000). It is impossible to identify which of these publications was published first, and for all practical purposes, that is irrelevant. As I wrote in the interview with Kim Cascone,

> time difference between [these] publications is not more than few months, and publication dates often depend on production issues beyond authors' influence. I think it is fair to say that [the two publications] explored the concept at the same time, independently of each other, thus reflecting a certain Zeitgeist of the turn of the millennium. (Jandrić in Cascone and Jandrić 2021: 567)

Cascone (2000) sees the postdigital in a glitch: a computer error, a mistake in technological processes, which symbolizes the human (or analog) in the technological (the digital). Pepperell and Punt (2000: 2) use the metaphor of the 'biological membrane, a lubricating sheath that gives form to complex phenomena … at the same time as enabling a continuity between them' through 'its dual and contradictory function: like a transparent wall, it both connects and divides' (see Ford 2023 for a deeper discussion).

However different, the concepts of glitch and membrane share an important image of intermixing the analog and the digital; a marriage between 'technological and non-technological; biological and informational' (Jandrić et al. 2018: 895); an encounter of two different worlds, and incommensurable models that describe these worlds, which interact daily and at scale. Glitches and membranes are transitory phenomena. In that sense, the postdigital is a signal to a 'post' or a transition to something else and one of many ways of describing this transition.

Post-2000, the postdigital has attracted a lot of attention, predominantly within arts circles, and has participated in the development of whole new artistic genres. Writing in 2021, one of the founding theorists of the postdigital, Florian Cramer, claims that 'I think that, in the meantime, the term postdigital has become rather useless in the arts, because it is constantly being conflated and confused with the too-similar-sounding and much better-known "Post-Internet"' (Cramer in Cramer and Jandrić 2021: 977). As a transitory phenomenon, the postdigital is always in flux; its appearance is just as significant as its disappearance.

As the world of the arts has slowly moved beyond the postdigital, the term has started to appear in other related fields such as architecture, publishing, media studies, and many others. Probably the most extensive list of postdigital events, centres, publications, and so on, can be found in the Monoskop wiki page titled 'Post-Digital Aesthetics'.[3] With entries in English, German, Italian, Croatian, Portuguese, Swedish, and several other languages, this page shows width, depth, and geographical distribution of postdigital debates. The list of keywords that Monoskop sees as describing the postdigital is a good shortcut to early understandings of the concept:

Fields and theories: Classics, Art history, History of architecture, Anthropology, Semiotics, Philosophy of technology, Marxist aesthetics, Design research, Humanities computing, Structuralism, Poststructuralism, Mediology, Media archaeology, Cyberfeminism, Cultural techniques, Neuroaesthetics, Posthumanities, Sensory ethnography, Media ecology, Digital humanities, Software studies, Modern periodical studies, Accelerationism.
Concepts: Faktura, Ostranenie, Biomechanics, Commons, Postmedia, Evil media.
Related theories: Systems theory, Information theory, Cybernetics.

In 2014, Christian Ulrik Andersen, Geoff Cox, and Georgios Papadopoulos edited a Special Issue of *A Peer-Reviewed Journal About* on 'Post-Digital Research' (2014). They wrote, '[t]he issue does not present a uniform interpretation of the notion, but includes a variety of positions related to the use of the term, its application within various fields, and how it is reflected in artistic research' (Andersen et al. 2014). The Special Issue has openly focused on artistic research, yet contributions such as Florian Cramer's 'What Is "Post-Digital"?' (see Cramer 2015 for an expanded version) have opened up philosophical and methodological questions beyond the arts and humanities and have been used in a wide spectrum of disciplines.

In my experience, some of the most influential sources from the Postdigital Arts and Humanities phase are the following:

Negroponte, N. (1998). Beyond digital. Wired, 12. http://www.wired.com/wired/archive/6.12/negroponte.html. Accessed 3 February 2023.
Cascone, K. (2000). The aesthetics of failure: 'Post-digital' tendencies in contemporary computer music. *Computer Music Journal, 24*(4), 12–18. https://doi.org/10.1162/014892600559489.
Pepperell, R., & Punt, M. (2000). *The postdigital membrane: Imagination, technology and desire.* Bristol: Intellect.
Alexenberg, M. (2011). *The Future of Art in a Postdigital Age: From Hellenistic to Hebraic Consciousness.* 2nd Ed. Bristol: Intellect.
Ludovico, A. (2012). *Post-Digital Print: The Mutation of Publishing Since 1894.* Eindhoven: Onomatopee and Rotterdam: Instituut voor Onderzoek en Innovatie.
Hall, G. (2013). Towards a post-digital humanities: Cultural analytics and the computational turn to data-driven scholarship. *American Literature, 85*(4), 781–809. https://doi.org/10.1215/00029831-2367337.

---

[3] See https://monoskop.org/Post-digital_aesthetics. Accessed 3 February 2023.

Andersen, C. U., Cox, G., & Papadopoulos, G. (2014). Post-digital Research. *A Peer-Reviewed Journal About, 3*(1). https://aprja.net//issue/view/8400. Accessed 3 February 2023.

Berry, D. M., & Dieter, M. (Eds.). (2015). *Postdigital aesthetics: Art, computation and design*. New York: Palgrave Macmillan. https://doi.org/10.1057/9781137437204.

Cramer, F. (2015). What is 'post-digital'? In D. M. Berry & M. Dieter (Eds.), *Postdigital aesthetics: Art, computation and design* (pp. 12–26). New York: Palgrave Macmillan. https://doi.org/10.1057/9781137437204_2.

Bishop, R., Gansing, K., Parikka, J., & Wilk, E. (Eds.). (2016). *Across and beyond: a transmediale reader on post-digital practices, concepts and institutions*. Berlin: Sternberg Press and Transmediale e.V.

The postdigital has also expanded beyond the world of theory. Since 2018, Coventry University has operated the Centre for Postdigital Cultures led by Gary Hall[4]; and Leibniz Institute for Educational Media and Georg Eckert Institute operate their Leibniz Science Campus—Postdigital Participation led by Eckhardt Fuchs.[5] The postdigital appears in prominent arts exhibitions such as Transmediale (Bishop et al. 2016), as well as science and engineering.[6] Following the footsteps of many other philosophical concepts such as postmodernism, accelerationism, and so on, the postdigital took less than two decades to spread from music, through the visual arts and humanities, to nearly all imaginable areas of inquiry.

This spread is far from straightforward as the concept has altered, shifted, and been shaped by these diverse contexts. Therefore, dissemination of the concept also implies its multiplication and branching. This calls for inquiry into overlaps and distinctions—a worthwhile research direction, which is beyond the scope of this article.

4 Postdigital Science and Education

4.1 *Postdigital Science and Education* Journal

In 2017, I decided to start a new journal. This decision came out of my deep dissatisfaction with the state of academic publishing, including its rapidly increasing orientation to profit (see Peters and Jandrić 2018; Peters et al. 2020) and my frustration with the state of mainstream educational research, especially its technological determinism and instrumentalism (see Jandrić and Knox 2022). I also had (and still have) a problem with strict disciplinarity. In the realm of theory, I felt that EdTech people do not talk enough to critical pedagogy people, and that none of them talks

[4] See https://www.coventry.ac.uk/research/areas-of-research/postdigital-cultures/. Accessed 3 February 2023.

[5] See https://www.postdigitalparticipation.org/en/outlook. Accessed 3 February 2023.

[6] See https://postdigital.astonphotonics.uk/. Accessed 3 February 2023.

enough to philosophers, sociologists, anthropologists, and so on (Jandrić 2016, 2019a, b). In the realm of practice, I felt that teachers do not talk enough to theorists; policymakers do not talk enough to practitioners, for example. I have also been deeply frustrated with the rampant neoliberalization of teaching and learning (Hayes and Jandrić 2014), resulting in merciless individualism (Jandrić 2019a, b; Jandrić and Hayes 2020), and many other problems that many of us experience and occasionally write about but often cannot really do much against (Jandrić 2022).

While I like venting my frustrations as much as the next guy, I wanted to do something about them, and academic publishing spontaneously crystallized as the battlefield of my choice. Publishing is always a community activity, and I started thinking about my team. Before I sent out my invites, however, I needed to write down an outline of my ideas and offer up a name for the journal. But how do I cram all these ideas into a productive and easily communicated brief?

A few years previously, while I was interviewing some artists and activists for my book (Jandrić 2017), I encountered the term postdigital. The concept seemed to roughly correspond with my ideas and ethos but seemed somehow 'reserved' for the arts and was philosophically underdeveloped. Looking for the name of the journal, however, I decided that it would be a good idea to consider the postdigital as a possible candidate. First, many scientific concepts, philosophies, and approaches, such as postmodernism, accelerationism, and so on, emerged within the arts— 'appropriating' an artistic concept for the purpose of starting an academic journal is not at all unusual. Second, I was able to agree with pretty much anything offered by early postdigital theory, and this protean theory offered an important backdrop that the new community could hold on to. Third, I found that the lack of philosophical underpinning was actually a bonus, as it provided some low-hanging fruit to early theorists and allowed the budding community to freely develop its own ideas. Postdigital is a generative concept, rather than an axiomatic one. So *Postdigital Science and Education* it became—I pitched my proposal to my closest friends and scholars and waited for their reaction.

Founding Associate Editors Jeremy Knox, Tina Besley, Thomas Ryberg, Juha Suoranta, and Sarah Hayes took my proposal seriously. They dissected it from every possible angle. We discussed, wrote, discussed, overwrote, and then again, resulting in a Guest Editorial in *Educational Philosophy and Theory* titled 'Postdigital Science and Education' (Jandrić et al. 2018). This paper helped us consolidate our thoughts during the complex ideation and contracting process. It was also aimed as a sort of foundation, or perhaps even manifesto, for *Postdigital Science and Education* journal founded a few months later. In the paper, we listed early developments of the concept of the postdigital and theoretical influences that contributed to this development. We then developed our own interpretation of the concept and brought it into the humanities and the social sciences with a heavy accent on education.

In early issues, most notably *Postdigital Science and Education* *1*(1) and *1*(2), authors extensively debated the concept and its potentials. Along the way, the community had to make many 'small' but important decisions; for instance, it was decided to consistently use the spelling 'postdigital' (see Cormier et al. 2019 for details). These debates and decisions provided much-needed input for further work. Slowly but surely, they have naturally faded and given way to other interests and ideas. In my experience, the community has found the following writings published in that period as the most useful for their work:

Jandrić, P., Knox, J., Besley, T., Ryberg, T., Suoranta, J., & Hayes, S. (2018). Postdigital Science and Education. *Educational Philosophy and Theory, 50*(10), 893–899. https://doi.org/10.1080/00131857.2018.1454000.

Feenberg, A. (2019). Postdigital or Predigital? *Postdigital Science and Education, 1*(1), 8–9. https://doi.org/10.1007/s42438-018-0027-2.

McLaren, P. (2019). Reclaiming the Present or a Return to the Ash Heap of the Future? *Postdigital Science and Education, 1*(1), 10–13. https://doi.org/10.1007/s42438-018-0015-6.

Peters, M. A., & Besley, T. (2019). Critical philosophy of the postdigital. *Postdigital Science and Education, 1*(1), 29–42. https://doi.org/10.1007/s42438-018-0004-9.

Fawns, T. (2019). Postdigital education in design and practice. *Postdigital Science and Education, 1*(1), 132–145. https://doi.org/10.1007/s42438-018-0021-8.

Jandrić, P., Ryberg, T., Knox, J., Lacković, N., Hayes, S., Suoranta, J., Smith, M., Steketee, A., Peters, M. A., McLaren, P., Ford, D. R., Asher, G., McGregor, C., Stewart, G., Williamson, B., & Gibbons, A. (2019). Postdigital Dialogue. *Postdigital Science and Education, 1*(1), 163–189. https://doi.org/10.1007/s42438-018-0011-x.

Knox, J. (2019). What does the postdigital mean for education? Three critical perspectives on the digital, with implications for educational research and practice. *Postdigital Science and Education, 1*(2), 357–370. https://doi.org/10.1007/s42438-019-00045-y.

Sinclair, C., & Hayes, S. (2019). Between the post and the com-post: Examining the postdigital 'work' of a prefix. *Postdigital Science and Education, 1*(1), 119–131. https://doi.org/10.1007/s42438-018-0017-4.

Hayes, S. (2021a). *Postdigital Positionality: Developing Powerful Inclusive Narratives for Learning, Teaching, Research and Policy in Higher Education*. Leiden: Brill.

Jandrić, P. (2021a). Biology, Information, Society. *Postdigital Science and Education, 3*(2), 261–265. https://doi.org/10.1007/s42438-021-00220-0.

5   Special Issues in *Postdigital Science and Education*

The genre of the scholarly article is restrictive in size and scope. As we planned the new journal, we wanted to be as inclusive as possible, so we started with the following genres: Editorials, Original Articles, Commentaries, Interviews, and Reviews (see Jandrić 2020 for a detailed explanation of the genres and the decision). What we did not predict, however, was the need to develop wider scholarly discussions about certain themes.

Postdigital Science and Education started in 2019 with two regular issues per year (in April and October). When Alison MacKenzie and Ibrar Bhatt offered to edit a special issue, we immediately decided to expand the journal with a series of Special Issues. Between 2020 and 2023, the journal has published three issues per year: one special issue (in January) and two regular issues (in April and October). Starting from 2024, the number of issues will expand to four: two special issues (in January and July) and two regular issues (in April and October). This is the list of current and forthcoming Special Issues:

MacKenzie, A., & Bhatt, I. (2020). (Eds.). Lies, Bullshit and Fake News Online: Should We Be Worried? *Postdigital Science and Education, 2*(1). https://link. springer.com/journal/42438/volumes-and-issues/2-1. Accessed 3 February 2023.

Hayes, S. (Ed.). (2021b). 'Measuring Excellence' in Higher Education. *Postdigital Science and Education, 3*(1). https://link.springer.com/journal/42438/volumes-and-issues/3-1. Accessed 3 February 2023.

Carvalho, L., Lamb, J., Gallagher, M., & Knox, J. (Eds.). (2022). The Postdigital Spaces of Higher Education. *Postdigital Science and Education, 4*(1). https://link. springer.com/journal/42438/volumes-and-issues/4-1. Accessed 3 February 2023.

Selwyn, N., Perrotta, C., Hillman, T., & Bergviken-Rensfeldt, A. (Eds.). (2023). Education in An Era of Pervasive Automation. *Postdigital Science and Education, 5*(1). https://link.springer.com/journal/42438/volumes-and-issues/5-1. Accessed 3 February 2023.

Ford, D. R. (2023). (Ed.). Postdigital Soundscapes: Sonics, Pedagogies, Technologies. *Postdigital Science and Education, 5*(2). https://link.springer. com/journal/42438/volumes-and-issues/5-2. Accessed 10 May 2023.

Macgilchrist, F., Jarke, J., Allert, H., & Cerratto-Pargman, T. (Eds.). (forthcoming 2024). Designing Postdigital Futures. *Postdigital Science and Education, 6*(1).

As the journal's popularity has grown, it has become harder and harder to accommodate everyone who wanted to edit collections on postdigital topics – regardless the two expansions of the journal! The community asked for more publishing space—the time had arrived for a new publishing venture.

6 Postdigital Science and Education Book Series

In 2020, I started the Postdigital Science and Education book series.[7] The series complements the *Postdigital Science and Education* journal, and together they provide a complete, whole-rounded publishing ecosystem to researchers working in the field. The book series covers a wide range of topics within postdigital science and education, including learning and data analytics, digital humanities, learning, teaching and assessment, educational technology, and philosophy of education. Since

---

[7] See https://www.springer.com/series/16439/books. Accessed 3 February 2023.

2021, the series has published six edited volumes (with three more forthcoming in 2023):

Savin-Baden, M. (Ed.). (2021). *Postdigital Humans: Transitions, Transformations and Transcendence*. Cham: Springer. https://doi.org/10.1007/978-3-030-65592-1.

MacKenzie, A., Rose, J., & Bhatt, I. (Eds.). (2021). *The Epistemology of Deceit in a Postdigital Era: Dupery by Design*. Cham: Springer. https://doi.org/10.1007/978-3-030-72154-1.

Fawns, T., Aitken, G, & Jones, D. (Eds.). (2021). *Online Postgraduate Education in a Postdigital World*. Cham: Springer. https://doi.org/10.1007/978-3-030-77673-2.

Peters, M. A., Jandrić, P., & Hayes, S. (Eds.). (2022). *Bioinformational Philosophy and Postdigital Knowledge Ecologies*. Cham: Springer. https://doi.org/10.1007/978-3-030-95006-4.

Jandrić, P., & Ford, D. R. (Eds.). (2022). *Postdigital Ecopedagogies: Genealogies, Contradictions, and Possible Futures*. Cham: Springer. https://doi.org/10.1007/978-3-030-97262-2.

Savin-Baden, M., & Reader, J. (Eds.). (2022). *Postdigital Theologies: Technology, Belief, and Practice*. Cham: Springer. https://doi.org/10.1007/978-3-031-09405-7.

Hayes, S., Connor, S., Johnson, M., & Jopling, M. (Eds.). (2023). *Human Data Interaction, Disadvantage and Skills in the Community: Enabling Cross-Sector Environments for Postdigital Inclusion*. Cham: Springer.

Jandrić, P., MacKenzie, A., & Knox, J. (Eds.). (2023a). *Postdigital Research: Genealogies, Challenges, and Future Perspectives*. Cham: Springer.

Jandrić, P., MacKenzie, A., & Knox, J. (Eds.). (2023b). *Constructing Postdigital Research: Method and Emancipation*. Cham: Springer.

Special issues and edited books are both similar and different at the same time. This is not the place to reproduce our extensive debates about the pros and cons of each (see Peters et al. 2021; Jandrić 2021b), yet it is important to emphasize that *Postdigital Science and Education* journal articles and book chapters undergo the same rigorous peer review procedure (see Jandrić 2020 for details). While the two genres slightly differ in scope and focus, the Postdigital Science and Education community has already produced 15 themed collections, and there is a healthy influx of new edited projects.

What I find crucial in these collections is their vernacular nature. The bottom-up process of making these collections has done a lot of good for postdigital thought. However, it suffers from an important drawback: there are so many different strands of postdigital inquiry that it is hard to keep track of them all. As the community produces more and more forward-looking research, there is an increasing need to look backward and crystallize key ideas in a simple and accessible format. This, unsurprisingly, calls for a new publishing venture.

6.1   Encyclopedia of Postdigital Science and Education

In early 2022, after a lot of consultation with my closest associates, I decided to start the first reference work with an explicit focus to postdigital themes and research approaches: the *Encyclopedia of Postdigital Science and Education*. The *Encyclopedia* will consist of ca. 500 entries. Writing has started in 2023 and will continue until approximately 2026. Entries will be approximately 2000 words in length.

The *Encyclopedia of Postdigital Science and Education* will address all major issues linked with postdigital science and education. Following the common structure of reference works, the Encyclopedia will be subdivided into main disciplines and areas of research such as philosophy, sociology, information science, arts, for example. However, the concept of the postdigital is inherently transdisciplinary (see Jandrić 2019a, b), so boundaries between the traditional disciplines will be purposefully blurred. Special attention will be given to themes that can be used across a range of disciplines and to 'general' fields such as philosophy, research methods, and so on.

The inception of the *Encyclopedia of Postdigital Science and Education* seems contradictory to my and Ford's opposition to defining the postdigital (Jandrić and Ford 2022). However, an encyclopaedia is not simply about the academic community keeping track of the concept; it is also a means through which the ideas can be solidified and packaged so that things can be done with them. Similarly to this article, the *Encyclopedia of Postdigital Science and Education* will be designed to describe rather than define. In this way, I am hoping to provide the community with some power derived from naming and demarcating while avoiding the philosophical pitfalls of definition.

7   What Makes Us Different?

As I have already said and written on many occasions, I strongly believe that the world does not need yet another academic journal or book series, yet I do believe that the world desperately needs qualitatively different journals and book series. Proverbial apples and oranges are always hard to compare: this is one of many reasons why I am wary of 'measuring excellence' using standards such as downloads, citations, and impact metrics (see Hayes 2021a for details). Yet numbers can be useful, when used with a grain of salt; over the years, I have learned how to utilize a few basic statistics in support of strategic decisions.

By the end of 2022, *Postdigital Science and Education*[8] was listed in many prestigious scholarly databases (with more to follow); its download[9] and citation[10] statistics are comparable to much older and prestigious journals. Since 2019, the journal and the book series have published ca. 500 articles and chapters. For each published article and chapter, there are approximately nine rejected submissions; with time, our acceptance rate gets lower and lower. As the number and selection/quality of published material increases, so does the community. Most articles in the first few issues were written by invited colleagues; today, I personally know less than one in ten authors who submit their work.

Those reading between the lines may already feel how I understand my own position in the Postdigital Science and Education community—it is time to make that position explicit. I founded the journal and the book series; to this day, each and every paper and chapter goes through my hands. My position at the organizational top of the Postdigital Science and Education community arrives with a huge workload and responsibility. One of the rare perks of this position is that standing higher allows me to see further. I can identify hot topics months before they arrive online. I can identify patterns between articles and chapters, and see concordances and discords that may be invisible or obscure to others.

My position also carries the responsibility for catering to the needs of a diverse community. The community wants to edit and read Special Issues? Here you go. Let me know if you need any help. The community wants to write, edit, and read books? Here is the book series and its proposal forms. For as long as the approach is roughly postdigital, and for as long authors and editors follow highest quality standards from peer review to formatting, I am happy to editorially support pretty much every genre and theme. However, I do not see myself as a mere supporter of other people's work. While I do insist on vernacular development of journal themes and approaches, I do not shy away from active involvement in that development.

A good case in the point is the *Postdigital Science and Education* interview section. I deeply believe that interviews are important for many reasons, not least because readers get to know the people behind the ideas (see Jandrić 2017). But interviews are not well recognized in assessment procedures such as the UK's Research Excellence Framework (REF), and authors are just not used to doing

---

[8] Presented statistics apply only to *Postdigital Science and Education* journal, as the book series is not yet listed in academic databases.

[9] Full-text downloads for 2021, as per publishers' information: *Educational Philosophy and Theory*, 753,000; *Philosophy and Technology*, 599,360; *Policy Futures in Education,* 560,041; **Postdigital Science and Education, 526,200**; *Learning, Media, and Technology,* 287,000; *E-Learning and Digital Media,* 290,735; *Studies in Philosophy and Education*, 172,971. Accessed 3 February 2023.

[10] In 2021, its third year of publication, *Postdigital Science and Education* was listed by Scopus, where it immediately achieved high citation ranking. On 5 April 2023, journal's CiteScore is 16.2, bringing it on top of most cited articles in following categories: Social Sciences (Education), #8/1406 (99th percentile), Social Sciences (Miscellaneous), #6/426 (98th percentile), and Arts and Humanities (Miscellaneous), #7/376 (98th percentile). See https://www.scopus.com/sourceid/21101075549. Accessed 18 April 2023.

them. Since its inception, *Postdigital Science and Education* publishes two interviews in each issue. At the beginning, it was next to impossible to find authors, so I just authored most of the interviews myself. After a while, the community picked up, and these days, most interviews arrive without my inviting them.

I have tried to push many ideas; some of them have held the test of time, others have failed. But that does not prevent me from trying! Active editing is much more than accepting and rejecting papers; I see the Postdigital Science and Education publishing ecosystem, and my role as its editor, as a co-creator of wide scholarly discourse. As my own scholarly work has slowly been reduced to editorials and birds-eye-view articles and chapters such as this one, editing has come to feel a bit like writing through other people's pens.

8   Conclusion

Writing my proposal for *Postdigital Science and Education* in 2017, I thought that I was founding a journal. I was aware that the journal needs its own community, and I tried to build that community to the best of my efforts. Yet the intensity of people's response surprised me to no end! As the community has continued to grow, more and more work has landed on my plate, including writing countless emails, making daily editorial decisions, proofing 100+ papers and chapters per year, contracting new publishing venues, and making strategic decisions. I am the only one responsible for this situation, yet I have somehow managed to take myself by surprise. Now I am discovering my new role(s), and I am doing the best I can to play them right.

These days I am doing a lot of thinking about the mid-term and long-term future of postdigital thought and about the ways in which the Postdigital Science and Education publishing ecosystem can support its development. In practice, this often translates into the dangerous game of prediction. How strong are the community needs I perceive? And how sustainable are my responses to those needs?

For instance, the *Encyclopedia of Postdigital Science and Education* will require at least 500 authors and 1000 reviewers in the period 2023–2026. Its success depends on two main assumptions: that the Postdigital Science and Education community will grow roughly to twice its current size in the next 4–5 years, and that most of these people will want to contribute. Yet the publishing contract has only one responsible person—and that's me. Shall we succeed? That does not depend on me but on the community. Yet if the *Encyclopedia* succeeds, it will be everyone's success; if the *Encyclopedia* fails, it will be my own failure.

A risky bet? Perhaps. Yet every evaluation of risk depends on criteria used to define success and failure. While I do work in merciless neoliberal academia, which defines these concepts through money, citations, and whatnot, my take is very different. Some years ago, Peter McLaren introduced me to Antonio Machado's poem 'Traveler, There Is No Path'. While I cannot reproduce the whole poem due to its length, the verses below have taught me more than hundreds of academic articles:

> Everything passes on and everything remains,
> But our lot is to pass on,
> To go on making paths,
> Paths across the sea. …
>
> Traveler, your footprints.
> Are the path and nothing more;
> Traveler, there is no path,
> The path is made by walking.
>
> By walking the path is made
> And when you look back
> You'll see a road
> Never to be trodden again. (Machado 2003)

We, the Postdigital Science and Education community, make our own path by researching. To assess our efforts, and to provide these efforts with a voice, we occasionally need to examine and document our own trail. *Postdigital Science and Education* journal and the book series are predominantly about path making, and the *Encyclopedia of Postdigital Science and Education* is predominantly about trail examining. But there are no right or wrong paths; the process is much more important than the results.

I do need to play the game of standard academic measures of success and failure, and the Postdigital Science and Education publishing ecosystem is surprisingly strong in regard to these measures. Yet I strongly refuse to take these measures seriously! Somewhat paradoxically, I have grown to believe that this could be the 'secret' ingredient of our 'success'. Measures such as citations and reads seem to be a bit like love; they often arrive once you stop searching for them.

How does this resist co-option, asked Sean Sturm in his very insightful response? I'd say that it probably doesn't, or at least not much as I would like, as many authors seem lured into the Postdigital Science and Education publishing system exactly for its measurables. Yet in today's heavily commodified academia, academics need to carefully balance ideals and reality, and every little step against the terror of measurement is a step for the better.

9   Epilogue: Invitation for Discussion and Received Commentary

The first version of this chapter, 'History of the Postdigital: Invitation for Feedback' (Jandrić 2022), was published in October 2022. During the next 5 months the article was downloaded more than 1000 times and I received feedback from five people: Sean Sturm, Eamon Costello, and three other authors who requested to remain anonymous. In February 2023, I addressed all received feedback and prepared this version for publication.

This Epilogue reproduces the original invitation for discussion, and then briefly reproduces and addresses respondents' comments.

9.1 Invitation for Discussion

This article does not define, describe, or prescribe—it merely presents my very personal history of the postdigital. To ameliorate at least some of my own bias, I invite all readers to react to this article. Write a response article, email me, let us have a coffee or a wee dram! While I will appreciate your comments on any part of the article, I am especially interested in three questions:

1. Which facts (histories, important publications, research centres, projects, and so on) should be added to, or removed from, this article?
2. What do you make of my interpretation of these facts? What would you interpret differently, and how?
3. What is your preferred direction for future development of the Postdigital Science and Education community?

Based on received feedback, in Spring 2023 I will rewrite this article and turn it into the first chapter in *Postdigital Research: Genealogies, Challenges, and Future Perspectives* (Jandrić et al. forthcoming 2023a).

Ubuntu: I am because we all are. I look forward to your feedback!

10   Received Commentary

10.1   Eamon Costello

This is Eamon Costello's response to 'History of the Postdigital: Invitation for Feedback' (Jandrić 2022). The response is reproduced in full, with light edits for clarity and meaning.

***

Keep doing what you are doing. But also keep doing the things you are undoing or not doing. Upholding the traditions of academic writing and scholarly communication is the deep honour that scholars enjoy. We are charged to be custodians of these amazing practices; the heirs of academic scholarship, a form of human expression, which is thousands of years old. But although we must honour our tradition, we are also here to tease its edges, gently probe and question its forms and assumptions. This is the tension the Postdigital Science and Education community must continue to navigate. It must keep a straight course but be never afraid of choppy waters or uncharted seas.

This sentiment resonated with me: 'The genre of the scholarly article is restrictive in size and scope.' This is where *Postdigital Science and Education* journal has pushed boundaries! It has stretched and compressed articles to be long and short, both in word count or in the scope of their ambition and format. Can this elasticity last?

When journals mature and receive an impact factor or other indicator of popularity, currency, or prestige, they may tend to conservatism. Some journals can skew quantitatively, towards a rigour bias, requiring bigger datasets, more tests, greater novelty, wider research teams. (For instance, 'All review articles will be desk rejects unless they comprise 10 years of data and follow full PRISMA guidelines'.[11]) This is not just a problem of quantitatively oriented journals. Qualitative ones equally may congeal around stylised tropes, knowing references, and language that is largely impenetrable, convoluted, and full of... well itself. It was heartening to see by contrast, that at the point of Scopus' impact factor, *Postdigital Science and Education* suddenly turned itself into a Sci-Fi zine. Just in time for the winter break, the journal began stuffing email inboxes, like Christmas stockings, with playful bite-sized pedagogical fictions.

The smallest article in the journal, at a single page, befittingly packs a punchy title 'Postdigital or Predigital' (Feenberg 2019). Nonetheless this article has been cited 50 times at the time of writing, showing that good things come in small parcels. The largest article, at the other end of the scale, weighs in at 138 pages, giving its 69 authors enough space to roam so that they might keep telling the story of teaching in the age of Covid-19 (Jandrić et al. 2020; see also Jandrić et al. 2021, 2022). This long-form series of articles has some iconic qualities and will be well remembered to readers as reflective texts we turned to as the world spun upside down.

There are other long pieces too in this multi-author article format, that seem like manifestos nailed to doors, making as much a political statement of collective intent as of regular scholarly discourse (Networked Learning Editorial Collective et al. 2021). There are twelve papers with over ten authors. The mode author number is of course one. 151 authors toil on their own, in single author papers, treading a narrow path between necessary alone-time and harmful loneliness (Jandrić 2022). The 'double-edged sword' of the lone writer which can be 'like acid spilling out of a bottle' (Murakami 2009: 20).

What is the point of this rudimentary scientometric interlude? Will it tell us where postdigital futures could point us? Will they point at all (given pointing is a function of the longest digit of the hand and we are all postdigital now)? What directions might loom large or invite us on? Diversity, certainly, will be key to a postdigital future that is preferable and possible (but hopefully not too probable or predictable). As Jandrić alluded, metrics are like love, coming when you expect them least. Hopefully they don't melt away as mysteriously. When we overfit a model, double-down too hard on a winning strategy, we are bound to falter.

Hence the challenge for *Postdigital Science and Education* will be to stay fresh, to keep publishing a mix of papers and showcasing necessary work such as perhaps that of O'Sullivan (2020) on non-human animal trauma who writes imagining herself 'as an insect with compound eyes, observing and documenting but fragments of a much larger picture'. That is a random pick but articles like hers, by virtue of their subject matter, confront our sensibility about what we should be reading and why.

---

[11] See https://prisma-statement.org/prismastatement/Checklist.aspx?AspxAutoDetectCookieSupp ort=1. Accessed 3 February 2023.

At least they do for me. As the editors of *Learning Media and Technology* recently highlight, who we read and cite are political acts, and we must bring intentionality and care to these processes continually (Macgilchrist et al. 2022). Hopefully, the Postdigital Science and Education community can continue to surprise and give voice to a range of voices. Just as the term postdigital itself tries to resist definition, so too its writings will hopefully keep shifting direction, taking slight detours to bring new passengers on board and give its readers much hope and courage.

10.2 Sean Sturm

Sean Sturm offered many insightful comments and suggestions in an annotated pdf document. I carefully addressed his comments, one by one, directly in the text. This was not an easy task: Sturm's commentary arrived in a curious mix of computer-made highlights and handwritten text that made reading quite difficult. To acknowledge Sturm's analog/digital interventions into the digital text, or the postdigital nature of his commentary, Fig. 1 presents a brief snapshot of Sturm's feedback.

10.3 Anonymous Responders

The three anonymous responders offered a total of eight comments. Respecting their wish to remain anonymous, I will just say that I addressed all of them.

10.4 Response to Received Commentary

First and foremost, I want to thank Eamon Costello, Sean Sturm, and the three anonymous responders, for their feedback. Opening your emails, I felt like Forrest Gump and his box of chocolates; never knowing what I was going to get.

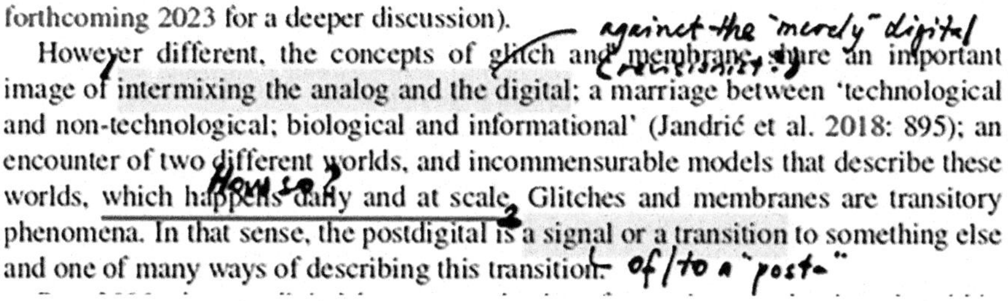
forthcoming 2023 for a deeper discussion).

However different, the concepts of glitch and membrane share an important image of intermixing the analog and the digital; a marriage between 'technological and non-technological; biological and informational' (Jandrić et al. 2018: 895); an encounter of two different worlds, and incommensurable models that describe these worlds, which happens daily and at scale. Glitches and membranes are transitory phenomena. In that sense, the postdigital is a signal or a transition to something else and one of many ways of describing this transition.

Fig. 1 A snapshot of Sean Sturm's feedback

I am extremely happy that I received only well-intended feedback – even the harshest of critiques ware written in a spirit of mutual respect and aimed at improvement. I look forward to working with you in the future, and to cultivating such spirit further in Postdigital Science and Education!

Acknowledgement This chapter was first published as Jandrić, P. (2022). History of the Postdigital: Invitation for Feedback. *Postdigital Science and Education*. https://doi.org/10.1007/s42438-022-00345-w. After five months, the article was updated and turned into this book chapter.

References

Alexenberg, M. (2011). *The Future of Art in a Postdigital Age: From Hellenistic to Hebraic Consciousness*. 2nd Ed. Bristol: Intellect.

Andersen, C. U., Cox, G., & Papadopoulos, G. (2014). Editorial: Postdigital Research. *A Peer-Reviewed Journal About, 3*(1), 5–7. https://doi.org/10.7146/aprja.v3i1.116067.

Berry, D. M., & Dieter, M. (Eds.). (2015). *Postdigital aesthetics: Art, computation and design*. New York: Palgrave Macmillan. https://doi.org/10.1057/9781137437204.

Bishop, R., Gansing, K., Parikka, J., & Wilk, E. (Eds.). (2016). *Across and beyond: A transmediale reader on post-digital practices, concepts and institutions*. Berlin: Sternberg Press and Transmediale e.V.

Bolzano, B. (1810). *Beyträge zu einer begründeteren Darstellung der Mathematik (Contributions to a better grounded presentation of mathematics)*. Prague: Im Verlage bey Caspar Widtmann.

Carvalho, L., Lamb, J., Gallagher, M., & Knox, J. (Eds.). (2022). The Postdigital Spaces of Higher Education. *Postdigital Science and Education, 4*(1). https://link.springer.com/journal/42438/volumes-and-issues/4-1. Accessed 3 February 2023.

Cascone, K. (2000). The aesthetics of failure: 'Post-digital' tendencies in contemporary computer music. *Computer Music Journal, 24*(4), 12–18. https://doi.org/10.1162/014892600559489.

Cascone, K., & Jandrić, P. (2021). The Failure of Failure: Postdigital Aesthetics Against Techno-Mystification. *Postdigital Science and Education, 3*(2), 566–574. https://doi.org/10.1007/s42438-020-00209-1.

Cormier, D., Jandrić, P., Childs, M., Hall, R., White, D., Phipps, L., Truelove, I., Hayes, S., & Fawns, T. (2019). Ten Years of the Postdigital in the 52group: Reflections and Developments 2009–2019. *Postdigital Science and Education, 1*(2), 475–506. https://doi.org/10.1007/s42438-019-00049-8.

Cramer, F., & Jandrić, P. (2021). Postdigital: A Term That Sucks but Is Useful. *Postdigital Science and Education, 3*(3), 966–989. https://doi.org/10.1007/s42438-021-00225-9.

Cramer, F. (2015). What is 'post-digital'? In D. M. Berry & M. Dieter (Eds.), *Postdigital aesthetics: Art, computation and design* (pp. 12–26). New York: Palgrave Macmillan. https://doi.org/10.1057/9781137437204_2.

Fawns, T. (2019). Postdigital education in design and practice. *Postdigital Science and Education, 1*(1), 132–145. https://doi.org/10.1007/s42438-018-0021-8.

Fawns, T., Aitken, G, & Jones, D. (Eds.). (2021). *Online Postgraduate Education in a Postdigital World*. Cham: Springer. https://doi.org/10.1007/978-3-030-77673-2.

Feenberg, A. (2019). Postdigital or Predigital? *Postdigital Science and Education, 1*(1), 8–9. https://doi.org/10.1007/s42438-018-0027-2.

Ford, D. R. (2023). Postdigital Soundscapes: Sonics, Pedagogies, Technologies. *Postdigital Science and Education, 5*(2). https://doi.org/10.1007/s42438-022-00354-9.

Ford, D. R. (2023). (Ed.). Postdigital Soundscapes: Sonics, Pedagogies, Technologies. *Postdigital Science and Education, 5*(2). https://link.springer.com/journal/42438/volumes-and-issues/5-2. Accessed 10 May 2023.

Hall, G. (2013). Towards a post-digital humanities: Cultural analytics and the computational turn to data-driven scholarship. *American Literature, 85*(4), 781–809. https://doi.org/10.1215/00029831-2367337.

Hayes, S. (2021a). *Postdigital Positionality: Developing Powerful Inclusive Narratives for Learning, Teaching, Research and Policy in Higher Education.* Leiden: Brill.

Hayes, S. (Ed.). (2021b). 'Measuring Excellence' in Higher Education. *Postdigital Science and Education, 3*(1). https://link.springer.com/journal/42438/volumes-and-issues/3-1. Accessed 3 February 2023.

Hayes, S., & Jandrić, P. (2014). Who is really in charge of contemporary education? People and technologies in, against and beyond the neoliberal university. *Open Review of Educational Research, 1*(1), 193–210. https://doi.org/10.1080/23265507.2014.989899.

Hayes, S., Connor, S., Johnson, M., & Jopling, M. (Eds.). (2023). *Human Data Interaction, Disadvantage and Skills in the Community: Enabling Cross-Sector Environments for Postdigital Inclusion.* Cham: Springer.

Jandrić, P. (2016). The methodological challenge of networked learning: (post)disciplinarity and critical emancipation. In T. Ryberg, C. Sinclair, S. Bayne, & de Laat, M. (Eds.). *Research, Boundaries, and Policy in Networked Learning* (pp. 165–181). New York: Springer. https://doi.org/10.1007/978-3-319-31130-2_10.

Jandrić, P. (2017). *Learning in the Age of Digital Reason.* Rotterdam: Sense.

Jandrić, P. (2019a). Welcome to *Postdigital Science and Education!. Postdigital Science and Education, 1*(1), 1–3. https://doi.org/10.1007/s42438-018-0013-8.

Jandrić, P. (2019b). We-Think, We-Learn, We-Act: the Trialectic of Postdigital Collective Intelligence. *Postdigital Science and Education, 1*(2), 257–279. https://doi.org/10.1007/s42438-019-00055-w.

Jandrić, P. (2020). A Peer-Reviewed Scholarly Article. *Postdigital Science and Education, 3*(1), 36–47). https://doi.org/10.1007/s42438-020-00202-8.

Jandrić, P. (2021a). Biology, Information, Society. *Postdigital Science and Education, 3*(2), 261–265. https://doi.org/10.1007/s42438-021-00220-0.

Jandrić, P. (2021b). Editor's Preface. In A. MacKenzie, J. Rose, & I Bhatt (Eds.), *The Epistemology of Deceit in a Postdigital Era: Dupery by Design* (pp. v–vii). Cham: Springer.

Jandrić, P. (2022). Alone-Time and Loneliness in the Academia. *Postdigital Science and Education, 4*(3), 633–642. https://doi.org/10.1007/s42438-022-00294-4.

Jandrić, P., & Ford, D. (2022). Postdigital Ecopedagogies: Genealogies, Contradictions, and Possible Futures. *Postdigital Science and Education, 4*(3), 672–710. https://doi.org/10.1007/s42438-020-00207-3.

Jandrić, P., & Ford, D. R. (Eds.). (2022a). *Postdigital Ecopedagogies: Genealogies, Contradictions, and Possible Futures.* Cham: Springer. https://doi.org/10.1007/978-3-030-97262-2.

Jandrić, P., & Hayes, S. (2020). Postdigital We-Learn. *Studies in Philosophy of Education, 39*(3), 285–297. https://doi.org/10.1007/s11217-020-09711-2.

Jandrić, P., & Knox, J. (2022). The Postdigital Turn: Philosophy, Education, Research. *Policy Futures in Education, 20*(7), 780–795. https://doi.org/10.1177/2F14782103211062713.

Jandrić, P., Fuentes Martinez, A., Reitz, C., Jackson, L., Grauslund, D., Hayes, D., Lukoko, H. O., Hogan, M., Mozelius, P., Arantes, J. A., Levinson, P., Ozoliņš, J., Kirylo, J. D., Carr, P. R., Hood, N., Tesar, M., Sturm, S., Abegglen, S., Burns, T., Sinfield, S., Stewart, G. T., Suoranta, J., Jaldemark, J., Gustafsson, U., Monzó, L. D., Batarelo Kokić, I., Kihwele, J. E., Wright, J., Kishore, P., Stewart, P. A., Bridges, S. M., Lodahl, M., Bryant, P., Kaur, K., Hollings, S., Brown, J. B., Steketee, A., Prinsloo, P., Hazzan, M. K., Jopling, M., Mañero, J., Gibbons, A., Pfohl, S., Humble, N., Davidsen, J., Ford, D. R., Sharma, N., Stockbridge, K., Pyyhtinen, O., Escaño, C., Achieng-Evensen, C., Rose, J., Irwin, J., Shukla, R., SooHoo, S., Truelove, I., Buchanan, R., Urvashi, S., White, E. J., Novak, R., Ryberg, T., Arndt, S., Redder, B., Mukherjee, M.,

Komolafe, B. F., Mallya, M., Devine, N., Sattarzadeh, S. D., & Hayes, S. (2022). Teaching in the Age of Covid-19—The New Normal. *Postdigital Science and Education, 4*(3), 877–1015. https://doi.org/10.1007/s42438-022-00332-1.

Jandrić, P., Hayes, D., Truelove, I., Levinson, P., Mayo, P., Ryberg, T., Monzó, L.D., Allen, Q., Stewart, P.A., Carr, P.R., Jackson, L., Bridges, S., Escaño, C., Grauslund, D., Mañero, J., Lukoko, H.O., Bryant, P., Fuentes Martinez, A., Gibbons, A., Sturm, S., Rose, J., Chuma, M.M., Biličić, E., Pfohl, S., Gustafsson, U., Arantes, J.A., Ford, D.R., Kihwele, J.E., Mozelius, P., Suoranta, J., Jurjević, L., Jurčević, M., Steketee, A., Irwin, J., White, E.J., Davidsen, J., Jaldemark, J., Abegglen, S., Burns, T., Sinfield, S., Kirylo, J.D., Batarelo Kokić, I., Stewart, G.T., Rikowski, G., Lisberg Christensen, L., Arndt, S., Pyyhtinen, O., Reitz, C., Lodahl, M., Humble, N., Buchanan, R., Forster, D.J., Kishore, P., Ozoliņš, J., Sharma, N., Urvashi, S., Nejad, H.G., Hood, N., Tesar, M., Wang, Y., Wright, J., Brown, J.B., Prinsloo, P., Kaur, K., Mukherjee, M., Novak, R., Shukla, R., Hollings, S., Konnerup, U., Mallya, M., Olorundare, A., Achieng-Evensen, C., Philip, A.P., Hazzan, M.K., Stockbridge, K., Komolafe, B.F., Bolanle, O.F., Hogan, M., Redder, B., Sattarzadeh, S.D., Jopling, M., SooHoo, S., Devine, N., & Hayes, S. (2020). Teaching in The Age of Covid-19. *Postdigital Science and Education, 2*(3), 1069–1230. https://doi.org/10.1007/s42438-020-00169-6.

Jandrić, P., Knox, J., Besley, T., Ryberg, T., Suoranta, J., & Hayes, S. (2018). Postdigital Science and Education. *Educational Philosophy and Theory, 50*(10), 893–899. https://doi.org/10.108 0/00131857.2018.1454000.

Jandrić, P., MacKenzie, A., & Knox, J. (Eds.). (2023a). *Postdigital Research: Genealogies, Challenges, and Future Perspectives*. Cham: Springer.

Jandrić, P., MacKenzie, A., & Knox, J. (Eds.). (2023b). *Constructing Postdigital Research: Method and Emancipation*. Cham: Springer.

Jandrić, P., Ryberg, T., Knox, J., Lacković, N., Hayes, S., Suoranta, J., Smith, M., Steketee, A., Peters, M. A., McLaren, P., Ford, D. R., Asher, G., McGregor, C., Stewart, G., Williamson, B., & Gibbons, A. (2019). Postdigital Dialogue. *Postdigital Science and Education, 1*(1), 163-189. https://doi.org/10.1007/s42438-018-0011-x.

Jandrić, P., Hayes, D., Levinson, P., Lisberg Christensen, L., Lukoko, H. O., Kihwele, J. E., Brown, J. B., Reitz, C., Mozelius, P., Nejad, H. G., Fuentes Martinez, A., Arantes, J. A., Jackson, L., Gustafsson, U., Abegglen, S., Burns, T., Sinfield, S., Hogan, M., Kishore, P., Carr, P. R., Batarelo Kokić, I., Prinsloo, P., Grauslund, D., Steketee, A., Achieng-Evensen, C., Komolafe, B. F., Suoranta, J., Hood, N., Tesar, M., Rose, J., Humble, N., Kirylo, J. D., Mañero, J., Monzó, L. D., Lodahl, M., Jaldemark, J., Bridges, S. M., Sharma, N., Davidsen, J., Ozoliņš, J., Bryant, P., Escaño, C., Irwin, J., Kaur, K., Pfohl, S., Stockbridge, K., Ryberg, T., Pyyhtinen, O., SooHoo, S., Hazzan, M. K., Wright, J., Hollings, S., Arndt, S., Gibbons, A., Urvashi, S., Forster, D. J., Truelove, I., Mayo, P., Rikowski, G., Stewart, P. A., Jopling, M., Stewart, G. T., Buchanan, R., Devine, N., Shukla, R., Novak, R., Mallya, M., Biličić, E., Sturm, S., Sattarzadeh, S. D., Philip, A. P., Redder, B., White, E. J., Ford, D. R., Allen, Q., Mukherjee, M., & Hayes, S. (2021). Teaching in the Age of Covid-19—1 Year Later. *Postdigital Science and Education, 3*(3), 1073–1223. https://doi.org/10.1007/s42438-021-00243-7.

Knox, J. (2019). What does the postdigital mean for education? Three critical perspectives on the digital, with implications for educational research and practice. *Postdigital Science and Education, 1*(2), 357-370. https://doi.org/10.1007/s42438-019-00045-y.

Ludovico, A. (2012). *Post-Digital Print: The Mutation of Publishing Since 1894*. Eindhoven: Onomatopee and Rotterdam: Instituut voor Onderzoek en Innovatie.

Macgilchrist, F., Potter, J., & Williamson, B. (2022). Reading internationally: if citing is a political practice, who are we reading and who are we citing?. *Learning, Media and Technology, 47*(4), 407-412. https://doi.org/10.1080/17439884.2022.2140673.

Macgilchrist, F., Jarke, J., Allert, H., & Cerratto-Pargman, T. (Eds.). (2024, forthcoming). Designing Postdigital Futures. *Postdigital Science and Education, 6*(1).

Machado, A. (2003). *There is No Road*. Trans. D. Maloney & M. Berg. Buffalo, NY: White Pine Press.

MacKenzie, A., & Bhatt, I. (Eds.). (2020). Lies, Bullshit and Fake News Online: Should We Be Worried? *Postdigital Science and Education, 2*(1). https://link.springer.com/journal/42438/volumes-and-issues/2-1. Accessed 3 February 2023.

MacKenzie, A., Rose, J., & Bhatt, I. (Eds.). (2021). *The Epistemology of Deceit in a Postdigital Era: Dupery by Design.* Cham: Springer. https://doi.org/10.1007/978-3-030-72154-1.

McLaren, P. (2019). Reclaiming the Present or a Return to the Ash Heap of the Future? *Postdigital Science and Education, 1*(1), 10–13. https://doi.org/10.1007/s42438-018-0015-6.

Murakami, H. (2009). *What I talk about when I talk about running.* New York: Vintage Books.

Neal, T. (2019). *Elementary Science Methods: Biology, Chemistry, Physics, Space, and Earth Science.* Iowa City, IA: University of Iowa Pressbooks.

Negroponte, N. (1998). Beyond digital. Wired, 12. http://www.wired.com/wired/archive/6.12/negroponte.html. Accessed 3 February 2023.

Networked Learning Editorial Collective, Gourlay, L., Rodríguez-Illera, J. L., Barberà, E., Bali, M., Gachago, D., Pallitt, N., Jones, C., Bayne, S., Hansen, S. B., Hrastinski, S., Jaldemark, J., Themelis, C., Pischetola, M., Dirckinck-Holmfeld, L., Matthews, A., Gulson, K. N., Lee, K., Bligh, B., Thibaut, P., … & Knox, J. (2021). Networked Learning in 2021: A Community Definition. *Postdigital Science and Education, 3*(2), 326–369. https://doi.org/10.1007/s42438-021-00222-y.

Networked Learning Editorial Collective. (2021). Networked Learning: Inviting Redefinition. *Postdigital Science and Education, 3*(2), 312–325. https://doi.org/10.1007/s42438-020-00167-8.

O'Sullivan, V. (2020). Non-human animal trauma during the pandemic. *Postdigital Science and Education, 2*(3), 588-596. https://doi.org/10.1007/s42438-020-00143-2.

Pepperell, R., & Punt, M. (2000). *The postdigital membrane: Imagination, technology and desire.* Bristol: Intellect.

Peters, M. A., & Besley, T. (2019). Critical philosophy of the postdigital. *Postdigital Science and Education, 1*(1), 29-42. https://doi.org/10.1007/s42438-018-0004-9.

Peters, M. A., & Jandrić, P. (2018). *The Digital University: A Dialogue and Manifesto.* New York: Peter Lang.

Peters, M. A., Besley, T., Jandrić, P., & Zhu, X. (Eds.). (2020). *Knowledge Socialism. The Rise of Peer Production: Colleginality, Collaboration, and Collective Intelligence.* Singapore: Springer. https://doi.org/10.1007/978-981-13-8126-3.

Peters, M. A., Jandrić, P., & Hayes, S. (2021). Revisiting the Concept of the 'Edited Collection': Bioinformation Philosophy and Postdigital Knowledge Ecologies. *Postdigital Science and Education, 3*(2), 283-293. https://doi.org/10.1007/s42438-021-00216-w.

Peters, M. A., Jandrić, P., & Hayes, S. (Eds.). (2022). *Bioinformational Philosophy and Postdigital Knowledge Ecologies.* Cham: Springer. https://doi.org/10.1007/978-3-030-95006-4.

Rusnock, P., & Šebestik, J. (2022). Bolzano's Logic. In E. N. Zalta (Ed.), *The Stanford Encyclopedia of Philosophy (Fall 2022 Edition).* https://plato.stanford.edu/archives/fall2022/entries/bolzano-logic/. Accessed 3 February 2023.

Savin-Baden, M. (Ed.). (2021). *Postdigital Humans: Transitions, Transformations and Transcendence.* Cham: Springer. https://doi.org/10.1007/978-3-030-65592-1.

Savin-Baden, M., & Reader, J. (Eds.). (2022). *Postdigital Theologies: Technology, Belief, and Practice.* Cham: Springer. https://doi.org/10.1007/978-3-031-09405-7.

Selwyn, N., Perrotta, C., Hillman, T., & Bergviken-Rensfeldt, A. (Eds.). (2023). Education in An Era of Pervasive Automation. *Postdigital Science and Education, 5*(1). https://link.springer.com/journal/42438/volumes-and-issues/5-1. Accessed 3 February 2023.

Sinclair, C., & Hayes, S. (2019). Between the post and the com-post: Examining the postdigital 'work' of a prefix. *Postdigital Science and Education, 1*(1), 119–131. https://doi.org/10.1007/s42438-018-0017-4.

Towards a Theory of Postdigital Parity

Shane J. Ralston

1 Introduction

The direction of postdigital research is rarely in a straight line. Instead, it travels through a maze of competing methodological/disciplinary/problematized vectors. Each one of these vectors is marked by intense uncertainty over how to treat the variables, theories, and hypotheses that structure inquiry, as well as the phenomena under examination. As with vectors in physics, the positions of these variables relative to each other are often unknown. A perplexing variable relation is the one between the predigital and the digital. Clarifying this relationship holds the promise of offering a clearer direction to postdigital research, beginning with the matter of defining postdigitalism.

Postdigitalism indicates that what comes after the (literally 'post') digital has value apart from any digital pedigree (or lack thereof). However, the postdigital as an after-concept has its limitations (Feenberg 2019; McLaren 2019; Sinclair and Hayes 2019). This concept does not always speak to what comes before the digital: namely, the predigital. Postdigitalism also implies an unsettling of the predominantly digital reality we inhabit, marked by a return to the human, the analog and the biological (Sinclair and Hayes 2019). Digital realities can sometimes eclipse meaningful predigital activities—for instance, as real-world social and political activism, such as participating in rallies or door-to-door pamphleting. Hash tagging, liking a webpage, or changing a social media account name are now low-energy digital alternatives—sometimes derogatively referred to as 'slacktivism'—the effect of which are often judged as 'ineffectual-vapid and short-lived' (Ralston 2022a).

However, disruption of new digital realities is not necessarily the path of the Luddite. Instead of renouncing technology, the goal is to integrate the digital and predigital into a more balanced and less disjointed version of the former. According

S. J. Ralston (✉)
Woolf University, Valletta, Malta

© The Author(s), under exclusive license to Springer Nature Switzerland AG 2023

P. Jandrić et al. (eds.), *Postdigital Research*, Postdigital Science and Education, https://doi.org/10.1007/978-3-031-31299-1_3

to Sarah Hayes (in Jandrić et al. 2019: 169), the issue is 'where we choose to place "value" in our discourse about technology'. Valuations of technology reflect deeper social and cultural values. Moreover, dialogue about technology can address not only the question of where to place value, but also how much value to delegate to one position or the other. For instance, in undertaking in postdigital research, to what extent should we value the predigital relative to the digital? Ought there be symmetry between analog arrangements and new digital realities? How do we strike a balance between the two? Or should we?

One way to forge continuity between the predigital and the digital is to formulate a flexible principle of parity or functional equality—what I have elsewhere called 'postdigitalism's parity thesis' (Ralston 2022a). According to this seminal formulation, the digital and predigital should be treated as relatively equal, except when there is a good reason to prioritize one over the other. However, the principle—at least as it is currently formulated—lacks sufficient theoretical grounding to serve as anything more than a rule-of-thumb for conducting postdigital inquiry. The point of the chapter is to rectify this shortcoming, suggesting one or more theories of post-digital parity. The meta-rationale for this project is to offer a demonstration of how to theoretically ground ancillary concepts in postdigital research. Grounding a concept in a robust theory assists the researcher in operationalizing related variables and variable relations, thereby making them more concrete and measurable.

This chapter begins with sketch of postdigitalism's origins in the work of Nicholas Negroponte (1995, 1998), posthumanism and the arts, especially music theory. I then proceed to examine the notion of radical symmetry between humans and non-humans, as articulated by Chris Jones (2018). Also considered is the objection that theory, generally, is useless and, therefore, a theory of postdigital parity is unnecessary. Out of these threads of inquiry and a survey of the recent postdigitalism literature emerges evidence of a parity principle in operation. My guiding assumption is that any working parity principle should be appreciated as an emergent norm or regulative ideal within inquiry, not a standard or rule imposed from without.

Next, I consider how a theoretically grounded parity principle could sharpen the focus of postdigital research, especially in regard to the relationship between the digital and the predigital. Then, three candidates for a theory of parity are proposed: (1) com-post, (2) cybernetics, and (3) transaction. Finally, I consider the possibility that the parity principle operates best in a theoretically pluralistic research program, rather than one with a single overarching theoretical paradigm.

2   Postdigitalism's Pedigree

What makes postdigitalism unique is its colorful origins in multiple strands of academic research and creative spadework. It extends from contemporary communications and media studies to posthumanism and postmodernism to the arts and music theory. Postdigitalism's unique pedigree is thus the outcome of its many incarnations in diverse disciplines, methodologies, and loose collections of research questions and problems.

2.1 Nicholas Negroponte

Nicholas Negroponte's foundational essay 'Beyond Digital' (1998) set the stage for postdigitalism's emergence as an intellectual tour de force. In the essay, he frames the digital revolution's challenge as not simply to digitalize everything, but for humans to manage the disruptions to their predigital lives:

> Yes, we are now in a digital age, to whatever degree our culture, infrastructure, and economy (in that order) allow us. But the really surprising changes will be elsewhere, in our lifestyle and how we collectively manage ourselves on this planet. (Negroponte 1998)

The digital does not exhaust human experience. Indeed, it discloses only a single dimension of the wide manifold of sensory and intellectual conditions that constructs our world. So, why should we treat it as the essential element or prime mover in our daily experience?

Negroponte's book, *Being Digital* (1995), examines the future of computing from the perspective of a mid-1990s postdigital prophet. Among the many issues he addresses in the book, one of the most pertinent to the digital/ predigital relation is the question of how humans should interface with computers. As computers become increasingly complex, the chasm between us and machines grows wider. In Negroponte's words,

> [f]uture human-computer interface will be rooted in delegation, not the vernacular of direct manipulation – pull down, pop up, click. … 'Ease of use' has been such a compelling goal that we sometimes forget that many people don't want to use the machine at all. They want to get something done. (Negroponte 1995)

An anecdote serves to illustrate Negroponte's point: When my ninety-two-year-old grandfather had to make a dinner reservation, he dialled the rotary phone in order to reach the restaurant. Instead of a human greeting him and taking his reservation, a digital message machine picked up, telling him to reserve a table on 'OpenTable'. Of course, he had no idea that 'OpenTable' was a smartphone application for making reservations. When I informed him of what it was, he objected to 'being forced' to use the machine. While the machine might be easy to use, it was foreign to him, and he had absolutely no interest. He preferred the predigital way. Nevertheless, as Negroponte (1995) notes, he 'want[s] to get something done'. So, he (or in this case, his grandson) has to interface with the technology for a purely pragmatic reason: he wants to make a reservation.

2.2   *Posthumanism*

Similar to postdigitalism, posthumanism is a *post-* concept that highlights not only what comes after, but also what is and what comes before humanism. It is a critical reaction to a nest of ideas that have been uncritically inherited from the European Enlightenment, such as rationality, autonomy, freedom, and essentialism. According to Stephen Chatelier (2017: 657), 'many in academia have long given up on humanism, both as a viable philosophy and as a foundation for education'. Humans in their vast diversity do not conform easily to the Enlightenment norms. Posthumanism emerges to fill the vacuum after humanism departs the scene, highlighting the need for a decentred human self, lacking essential features, as well as an account of how human subjectivities interact with new technologies (Badmington 2003:20).

Posthumanism and postdigitalism envision technology's relation to humans as thoroughly imbricated, as integrative to human practice, not as distinct machines that humans must choose to interface with. According to Sinclair and Hayes,

> [t]he word posthuman (in all its senses) is of course very much associated with technology. In the sense of 'what comes after humans', the word may be supporting a determinist view of technology: the external machine displacing the human being. In other senses, the association with technology might be more 'that of an *extension* to human existence'. ... The technology—and indeed the rest of the material world (and nature)—are not as separate from our existence as the humanist perspective would suggest. (Sinclair and Hayes 2019: 126)

Posthumanism implies postdigital insight into the digital/ predigital relation. Rather than reducing the matter to instrumentalism (e.g., humans use tech), technology and human existence are co-extensive. Even Negroponte's (1995, 1998) analysis had not overcome the humanist assumption that humans choose whether or not to interface with machines. In contrast, posthumanism presumes that technology already comes to us fully integrated within human culture, practice, and language.

Another strand of posthumanism—termed 'critical posthumanism'—attempts to transcend the humanist assumption by connecting the agency of educational researchers and teachers with more pragmatic goals and causes, such as social justice and sustainability. For example, in Petar Jandrić's interview with Sian Bayne, Bayne embraces this critical posthumanist view as her own:

> I think the main challenge facing teachers and researchers in the age of the Anthropocene is to try and move away from this entrenched, embodied legacy of humanism within education. I am interested in what is useful and important in humanism around agency and social justice. At the same time, I am trying to think what it means to be multiply connected both in ecological terms and in machinicartificial terms, and how that may change what it means to teach, what it means to be an educator, and what it means to be a student. In my opinion, this is really the key question that we need to address. My work in this sense takes a critical posthumanist approach, rather than posthumanist *per se*. ... I have spent the most of my career grappling with these issues, and I still wonder how we could shift education beyond 20th century humanism to a creative, critical posthumanist perspective. (Bayne in Jandrić 2017: 210)

If educational research is to catch up with its disciplinary cousins, educational researchers and practitioners must adopt a critical posthumanist perspective, according to Sian, wherein the embodied human is not perpetually at the center of inquiry.

2.3   Music Theory and the Arts

Although Negroponte and posthumanists refined the notion, postdigitalism's origins can be traced to the arts and, specifically, music theory (Cascone 2000). Consumerism and the profit-motive drive the production of novel music technologies—in what is sometimes referred to as *digital expansion* or the *digital exponential* (Sable 2012). Acceptance and adoption among music creatives are not universal though. Holdouts and haters of digital technology are perhaps more common in music than in any other artistic field. An example is the music of Bob Dylan. The folk music superstar originally performed all of his songs with an acoustic guitar. On 25 July 1965, at the Newport Music Festival, Dylan switched to an electric guitar half-way through his set. The audience booed the consummate musician.

In the music world, preferences for vinyl, acoustic guitars, and percussion instruments exist side-by-side with preferences for digitalized music and instruments, such as synthesizers and digital drums. This intermingling of old and new technologies highlights how humans accommodate changing technological realities, to what extent technologies adapt to the needs and demands of users and whether the relationship between the predigital and the digital calls for absolute equality, hierarchy, or warranted prioritization.

Ultimately, though, digitalized music's acceptance depends on whether music composers, artists and producers create works with the new technology. In other words, adoption of the new technology by creatives strongly influences whether digitalized music gains legitimacy and uptake within the wider culture—what is called *digital-cultural hybridity*. Anne Clements explains:

> Unlike the digital expansion construct, that is based on digital technology's impact on society, the digital-cultural hybridity construct acknowledges that the relationship of change flows both ways. Evolutionarily, technology creates us as we create it. We are equally changed by our engagement through technology as we change technology to suit both our needs and our values. The paradigm of digital-cultural hybridity attempts to move beyond the creation and use of digital tools simply because of their newness or perceived helpfulness in terms of productivity, towards a focus on building and using digital tools that are intentionally encoded with values and principles that ensure equality and inclusivity and that optimize for symbiosis of digital and human. (Clements 2018: 65)

Hybridizing the digital and cultural aspects of music media means more than simply accepting and adopting a new technology because of its novelty, instrumental value or convenience. Instead, it implies, in Clements's (2018: 65) words, 'building and using digital tools that are intentionally encoded with values and principles that ensure equality and inclusivity and that optimize for symbiosis of digital and human'.

The question is whether the parity principle constitutes one of those values and principles; and if so, how do we theorize it in a way that optimally guarantees 'equality and inclusivity' and integrates the digital and the predigital, or the 'digital and the human'?

3   Radical Non-Human/Human Symmetry

Actor-Network Theory, as articulated in the writings of Bruno Latour (2005) and Madeleine Akrich (1992), proposes a radical symmetry between humans and machines, wherein the two receive equal consideration as parts of a holistic system. However, a looming concern is whether humans and machines are truly equal or simply treated as equal for analytic/methodological purposes (Fuller and Jandrić 2019). Postdigital researchers have also theorized symmetry between non-humans and humans, thereby anticipating the concept of digital/predigital parity. Symmetrical relations between humans and machines constitutes a general baseline of equality from which to deploy specific judgments about whether some prioritization or unequal valuation of the digital and predigital is warranted.

In the book chapter 'Experience and Network Learning', Chris Jones sketches the modern notion of student experience, a notion standardized, marketized, and commodified by the corporate university. He contrasts this modern notion with the traditional account of student experience that informs his research. It involves a phenomenological—or more precisely, a phenomenographical—approach to the subject matter, 'gaining insight into how the processes of networked learning are understood by those who participate in them' (Jones 2018: 40).

Jones sees the contemporary student experience as constructed by a combination of the student's wilful intentions, institutional power relations and the regulative effects of the network itself:

> [i]n sociomaterial assemblages the conscious human element retains an important and at times decisive role, through (a) design and (b) intentional actions by socially located people, but one that needs to be seen as distinctly different from a reductive methodological individualism. In particular intentions are often enacted via organised entities in which the individual human actor is constrained by their social role and entangled in interactions with a variety of material forces which enable and constrain them. Within networks some nodes are more influential than others and over time patterns of entanglement in assemblages can produce effects that are persistent and instantiate power relations. While there may not be any single controller/point of control in such systems there are regulatory controls and some nodes in the network which have considerable influence and a significant shaping role. (Jones 2018: 45)

For instance, an online course is the conscious output of a process of design, a course management system, and the instructor. It is also the result of student interaction with the course materials, instructor, and technology, as well as any feedback the student and instructor deliver to the course designer. Students, instructors, designers, and even administrators participate in the network, interacting at multiple points and levels within the system.

Learning networks have many 'nodes' or points where actors 'meet' and interact with educational technology. Together, these assemblages enable the student experience. Jones (2018: 45) notes that 'there are regulatory controls and some nodes in the network which have considerable influence and a significant shaping role'. For example, precautions to curb academic dishonesty and cheating, or a lack thereof, can incentivize a range of student behaviours (Ralston 2022b). Presuming that the relationship between humans and machines is hierarchical (humans control machines) does not do justice to the decentralized design of most learning networks. Although it may appear radical, Jones proposes that researchers instead treat the relation between humans and non-humans as symmetrical, a baseline from which to make justified alterations.

Perfect symmetry between human and non-human agents in networked learning systems is not always feasible though. Jones insists that 'all actors cannot be treated as completely symmetrical for research purposes because of the particular access that we have to accounts of experience from human actors' (Jones 2018: 45 in Cramer and Jandrić 2021: 967). Access to human experience is privileged. So, for the sake of research, human experience can be prioritized over machine data, undermining the symmetry afforded to human/non-human relations in learning networks. 'Although there are assemblages of humans and machines there is additional access to the human actor in ways that the logs of machines or the presence of things do not provide and these humans are acting with a future objective informing their activities.' (Jones 2018: 46)

But why does research on networked learning beg for a study of human experience, not simply the collection of machine data? According to Jones, human motives, ends and interpretations overlay digital networks:

> Networked learning is interested in experience because it provides an additional account from actors. These accounts are relevant for learning because they provide an insight into how human actors respond in and to the interactions they encounter in educational assemblages and the world more generally. The accounts also provide claims made by subjects about their intentions, setting out what they assert are their future oriented rationales for action. They are a source of evidence, information and inspiration that can be drawn on for design and understanding. Networked learning has been interested in experience as a source of knowledge about how human actors interpret the world they are interacting with and how they planfully engage in these interactions. (Jones 2018: 49)

Although humans are only one element in the assemblages constituting a learning network, they possess a privileged status because of their ability to design, execute, alter and redesign the system to meet their needs. As decentred selves, humans have their desires, thoughts, beliefs and actions spread all over these networks, in the networks design and architecture, not simply centered in embodied human operators. So, it is nearly impossible to study networks by simply collecting digital data. According to Jones, 'networked learning research needs to retain a focus on human experience and to develop an empirical and theoretical understanding of how the de-centred human experience in human-machine assemblages can help in the design and development of successful learning networks' (Jones 2018: 50). Jones tries to preserve the equality between human and machines when necessary, while acknowledging their distinct and hierarchized roles. After all, humans created technology, not the other way around.

A theory of postdigital parity promises to establish symmetry between humans and machines, the predigital and the digital, as a baseline from which to formulate judgments about appropriate valuation or prioritization. But why is a theory necessary at all?

4   Anti-Theory or Theory

One possible objection to the present inquiry is deeply anti-theoretical. Why formulate a theory of postdigital parity in the first place? As pragmatists, we should simply be satisfied with the practice of valuing and prioritizing, not strive for some grand theory of pre-established parity. Objecting to 'theory talk', the law and literature scholar Stanley Fish asks:

> Am I following or enacting a theory when I stop for a red light, or use my American Express card, or rise to speak at a conference? Are you now furiously theorizing as you sit reading what I have to say? And if you are persuaded by me to alter your understanding of what is and is not a theory, is your new definition of theory a new theory of theory? Clearly it is possible to answer yes to all these questions, but just as clearly that answer will render the notion 'theory' and the issue of its consequences trivial by making 'theory' the name for ordinary, contingent, unpredictable, everyday behavior. (Fish 1989: 327)

Although theory-talk has 'acquired cache and prestige' in many disciplines, what it lacks, according to Fish, is substance, usefulness, and predictive capacity (Fish 1989: 14–15). Consequently, we should just dispense with theory altogether.

In 2005, Lawrence Baines addressed the question, often levelled at researchers, 'What is your theoretical perspective?' Rather than embrace Fish's anti-theoretical approach, he merely rejects one species of theorizing:

> The big theory approach is attractive because the complexities of the environment are reduced to a predefined set of inputs. Big theory usually relies upon deductive reasoning, moving from the general (the theory) towards an affirmation or rejection of the specific (the experiment). Granted, deduction is a worthy process, but it is not the only path to knowledge. Inductive reasoning (moving from the specific to the general), trial and error (also known as 'playing around'), and observation are legitimate approaches that require no pre-formulated big theory. (Baines 2005)

Baines's rejection of deductive theory offers a dose of healthy skepticism to many fields (including Education) whose researchers have become enthralled with grand theories. A theory of postdigital parity, in contrast, resembles a mid-level theory, intended to solve a problem at hand. Deductive, inductive, and even abductive reasoning all have a place in a theory of postdigital parity.

Fish's anti-theory, on the other hand, is a non-starter. Theory plays a prominent role in research. For instance, in one of my early academic inquiries, I constructed a research design to study the effects of sports participation and sports-specific self-esteem on academic performance. By examining past research, I was able to formulate a theory of the relationship between these three variables:

> Past research has explored many possible explanations for the academic underperformance of college and university students. Some researchers have connected poor academic performance with specific types of student behavior, such as delinquency, failure to work hard, and lack of self-control. Others have linked lower academic achievement with particular student attributes, such as minority racial status, a sense of alienation from the academic community, inability to form strong support networks and anti-social personality characteristics. One possible explanation that has received too little attention from researchers is that more time spent participating in intramural and intercollegiate athletics coupled with the consequent rise in sports-specific self-esteem causes student athletes to perform poorly in their studies. (Ralston 2009)

We start by observing the raw phenomena. Sometimes we tweak conceptual categories to assist in comprehending what we observe. Everyday practice often ends at this point. In spite of what Fish (1989) claims, research cannot stop there. Analyzing the subject matter, researchers isolate variables and relations between those variables, formulating testable hypotheses. To make those variables measurable—in research-speak, to operationalize them—demands a theory; not a theory of everything, but a theory tailored to solve the problem at hand.

5   Relative Equality of the Digital/Predigital

Planting a mid-level theory often begins with the seed of a simple idea. The notion that the digital and predigital are relatively equal emerges from a close reading of the postdigitalism literature. Similar to Jones's radical symmetry between humans and non-humans, it is the parity principle in embryo. They are not only equal, but also mutually imbricated. 'We are increasingly no longer in a world where digital technology and media are separate, virtual, "other" to a "natural" human and social life.' (Jandrić et al. 2018: 893)

The digital and predigital converge in the postdigital. According to Ryberg (in Jandrić et al. 2019: 166), 'the postdigital is about dragging digitalisation and the digital—kicking and screaming—down from its discursive celestial, ethereal home and into the mud. It is about rubbing its nose in the complexities of everyday practice.' The 'complexities of everyday practice' place the digital revolution in perspective, grounding *theoria* in *praxis*. For instance, a researcher investigating the origins of complex microcredentialing systems can explore labor and educational history for analogues and antecedents, such as vocational training and learn-to-earn programs (Ralston 2021: 92–95).

Relative equality presumes certain background conditions, such as a structured value system, whereby valuations can be reliably made and compared across platforms. Unfortunately, postdigitalism is still in its infancy, so the background structure is often lacking and in need of creation. 'The postdigital is hard to define;

messy; unpredictable; digital and analog; technological and non-technological; bio-logical and informational. The postdigital is both a rupture in our existing theories and their continuation.' (Jandrić et al. 2018: 895) Since postdigitalism indicates both a break and an extension of prior theories, it is necessary to supplement, hybridize, and integrate theoretical perspectives with an eye to engendering relative equality between the digital and predigital.

Petar Jandrić and Jeremy Knox (2021: 6–7) chronicle the 'great convergence' of the techno-sciences: physics with engineering, engineering with biology, biology with information, and capitalism with education. All of these require-similar to the convergence of the digital with the predigital—settling the issue of prioritization or relative weighting of one to the other. Jandrić and Knox identify the four types of collaborative research that the great convergence welcomed:

1. Multidisciplinary, which implies studying one research question simultaneously in different disciplines. …
2. Interdisciplinarity, which implies studying one research question within an integrated system made of various disciplines. …
3. Transdisciplinarity, which implies a gathering of various research approaches around a common problem, which transforms 'original' research methodologies arriving from each discipline. …
4. Antidisciplinarity, which implies … a research space where every combination of research methodologies can potentially work, for as long as it can be justified by the problem. (Jandrić and Knox 2021: 10–11)

The sharing of research questions, disciplinary approaches, methodologies, common problems, and a potpourri of problems and methodologies without disciplinary boundaries, highlight the pluralistic freedom that convergence and postdigitalism make possible. They are a clear departure from the tradition of *Bildung*, or the research ideal premised on the idea of clearly separated disciplines, specialties, and literatures (Ralston 2011: 313). They also suggest that the degree of rigor in post-digital research does not depend on conducting inquiry in disciplinary/methodological silos.

Rather, inquiry moves effortlessly between loosely formed camps until the boundaries between these camps recede from view. If collaborative forms of research were one thing for Bentley, it was a method of inquiry, a way of investigating phenomena by recourse to multiple approaches inside a 'laboratory':

> A laboratory in the most significant sense is not a building of brick or stone, containing instruments perhaps of steel or of glass. Rather it is a region of standards and techniques of research, where selected happenings in the world are brought into specialized forms and given observation under careful conditioning to permit their more accurate knowledge. (Bentley 1935: 5)

Bentley noted the difficulty of engaging in collaborative inquiry, especially when a scholar's graduate training is confined to a single discipline (Ralston 2011: 312). 'The continents go', Arthur F. Bentley once wrote, 'and the islands [too]' (Bentley 1935: 183). Although collaborative research spaces commonly appear disorderly—even chaotic—out of them emerge ideals or norms that constrain the paths of inquiry from within, offering a semblance of pattern and order. The parity principle is one of them.

The parity principle operates as a regulative ideal or emergent norm in inquiry, guiding research from inside the practice (endogenous), instead of imposing a fixed rule from outside (exogenous). The parity principle codifies the thesis that the digital and predigital are functionally equal:

> The Parity Thesis does not demand equal treatment of the digital and non-digital contexts in absolute terms. Prioritizing one over the other simply requires justification that bridges and integrates 'epistemic frameworks.' So, prioritizing is different than hierarchizing; the latter violates the Parity Thesis, while the former does not. (Ralston 2020)

Although the parity principle emerges from within inquiry, the principle nevertheless regulates the direction, limits and scope of postdigital research. The question still remains, though: What theoretical perspective helps settle issues of prioritizing the digital and the predigital?

6   In Pursuit of Postdigital Parity

In the *Tractatus*, Ludwig Wittgenstein (1961) claims in a parenthetical remark: 'He must so to speak throw away the ladder, after he has climbed up on it.' Apropos the relationship between technology, education, and research, some concepts need to be dispensed with after climbing up and over them, similar to Wittgenstein's ladder. Once we adopt a postdigital perspective, the question then becomes what we should replace these intermediate concepts with—in other words, what theory should guide our shared practice.

One of those concepts is determinism or 'the belief that technology somehow determines human societies and their values, structures, and so on' (Jandrić and Knox 2021: 4). While this concept offers a rule-of-thumb in the early adoption of digital technology—that is, always prioritize the digital over the predigital—after that it offers little sound counsel. Sometimes a reversion to predigital technology is preferable. At other times, it is best to strike a balance.

Another concept to be overcome is instrumentalism, or the 'view that technologies are neutral tools which can simply be deployed to realize the intentions of designers or users' (Jandrić and Knox 2021: 4). Digital technologies are value-laden, reflecting deep commitments to distinct ways of living and working. They can also be deployed in ways that undermine the designers' intentions, compromise users' privacy, operate as mere window dressing or resemble so-called 'innovation theater' (Ralston 2020).

One way in which the postdigital is 'post' is in terms of its ability to overcome determinism and instrumentalism. The ladder that permanently hierarchizes the digital over the predigital is knocked away in favor of parity. With relative equality, digital technology no longer separates us from our humanity: 'If technology is not the "other", then it can neither single-handedly determine human relations and societies nor can it simply be instrumentalized toward this or that goal.' (Jandrić and Knox 2021: 4)

Why does the parity principle require theoretical grounding? As previously mentioned, theory helps researchers operationalize the underlying variables and their relations, so that they are more concrete and measurable. Also, uncertainty about prioritizing or valuing the digital relative to the predigital may arise in the course of postdigital inquiries. Settling the issue begs for a theory or multiple theories of what parity requires and when, if ever, one variable can be prioritized over the other.

If the game plan is not to stipulate absolute equality, then what is the best alternative? In the original formulation of the so-called parity thesis, the rule-of-thumb was that 'prioritizing one over the other simply requires justification that bridges and integrates "epistemic frameworks"' (Ralston 2022b). In other words, giving greater priority or value to the digital (or predigital) begs for a perspective-bridging rationale, reasons that cross boundaries and form a more holistic vision of the problem at hand. The goal is to propose a more sophisticated parity thesis, a principle which is properly grounded in a sound theory explaining the relationship between the predigital and the digital.

7 Three Candidate Theories

Theoretically grounding the postdigital parity principle requires that we survey some plausible candidate theories. In the foregoing account, two theories of postdigital parity (*com-post* and (*cybernetics/systems theory*) originate from within the postdigital literature, while a third (*transaction*) comes from outside the literature.

I hope that by suggesting a third option this might motivate other postdigital researchers and methodologists to likewise propose novel theories that offer guidance on digital/predigital valuation and prioritization. So, as a caveat, the three foregoing alternatives do not exhaust the field of possibilities in the following survey.

7.1 Com-Post

In their article 'Between the Post and the Com-Post: Examining the Postdigital "Work" of a Prefix', Sinclair and Hayes propose a theory of the com-post—that is, an account of what comes after the post, the digital, which indicates both continuity and discontinuity, fusion and rupture with what comes before. In their words,

> we seek to retain the two prefixes com- and post- in the idea of 'with post'. In playing with the compost and then applying these ideas to the postdigital, it is then necessary to consider, what is digital? (Sinclair and Hayes 2019: 127)

> If the digital is ultimately to become compost, we need to ensure that it is well made, nourishing and sustainable—not causing us similar problems to those we have seen in plastics.

Are we in time to ensure that digital 'with post' does appropriate work to this end? (Sinclair and Hayes 2019: 128)

[w]e need to be open to the cross-fertilisation process and not allow it to become cross-sterilisation. But if this is true for the metaphorical, it is even more pressing for the material (Sinclair and Hayes 2019: 130).

Repeating Sinclair and Hayes's question, 'What is the digital?', we might answer, 'That which is presumptively equal to the predigital'. If we start with the assumption that the predigital and the digital are relatively equal, any rupture or break begs for justification.

As com-post, the postdigital must 'do appropriate work to this end' of justifying the difference in treatment. For instance, permanently privileging the digital over the predigital simply in virtue of the former's digital pedigree is unwarranted. But what does it mean to prefer one over the other only when one is more 'well made, nourishing and sustainable'? How might we promote 'cross-fertilization'?

7.2   Cybernetics/Systems Theory

In the article 'Critical philosophy of the postdigital', Peters and Besley demonstrate how cybernetics and related systems theories can inform postdigital research, especially when the objects of inquiry are network and process-based. According to Peters and Besley,

Cybernetics, and complexity theory, provide insight into systems that are too complex to predict their future. (Peters and Besley 2019: 29)

A critical philosophy of the postdigital is dialectically interrelated with the theories such as cybernetics and complexity theory, and also processes such as quantum computing, complexity science, and deep learning. (Peters and Besley 2019: 29)

[C]ybernetics and its associated theories have become central in understanding the nature of networks and distributed systems. (Peters and Besley 2019: 36)

In most systems theories, the system is composed of four components: inputs, a black box, outputs, and a feedback loop For instance, the political scientist David Easton (1965) developed systems theory as a step-by-step process resembling holistic models in communications theory and cybernetics: (1) alterations in the environment external to the system place 'demands' to change and 'supports' to maintain the status quo (i.e., inputs), (2) within the 'black box', experts and influencers compete to define the agenda, (3) 'decisions' and 'actions' are produced as a result of inputs influencing the competition to define the agenda (i.e., outputs), and (4) the redefined agenda is affected by the external environment, resulting in new demands and supports being placed on the system (i.e., a feedback loop) (Ralston 2014: 5).

Digital networks are often juxtaposed against predigital processes, such as between internet-based social media branding (network) versus brand loyalty fostered through face-to-face communications (process) and on-line activism (network) versus real-world advocacy and mobilization (process) (Lee and Hsieh 2021; Ralston 2022a, b). Cybernetics or systems theories can potentially accommodate these tensions between digital networks and predigital processes—but how specifically? One possible route is to model the relationship as an Easton-inspired system comprised of inputs, a black box, outputs, and a feedback loop.

7.3   Transaction

In the book *Knowing and the Known*, John Dewey and Arthur F. Bentley (1949) formulated the theory of transactionalism; a process-driven account of how to remedy the shortcomings of self-action (i.e., positing an object with an internal power) and trans-action (i.e., positing two objects sharing a relational property). In Dewey and Bentley's words,

> Self-action is the pre-scientific presentation in terms of presumptively independent 'actors,' 'souls,' 'minds,' 'selves' or 'forces,' taken as activating events. (Dewey and Bentley 1949: 70)

> Transaction involves the functional observation of the full system, actively necessary to inquiry at some stages, held in reserve at other stages. (Dewey and Bentley 1949: 70)

> Transaction represents that late level of inquiry in which observation and presentation could be carried on without attribution of the aspects and phases of action to independent self-actors, or to independently inter-acting elements or relations. (Dewey and Bentley 1949: 112)

Self-actional theories are flawed because they incorrectly assume that objects in inquiry have an internal force given prior to experience that impels them to behave as they do (e.g., Leibniz's entelechy or Aristotle's *telos*, both of which posit objects with internal forces or principles that direct them towards predetermined ends or potentialities). It would be a mistake, for instance, to posit the principle of postdigital parity as a force internal to the objects of inquiry, the digital and predigital, such that they always gravitate towards a state of equality, unless that force impels the prioritization of one over the other.

Interactional theories take two or more objects and theorize the connection between them in terms of a relational property (e.g., Galileo's inertia, a property of the interaction between mass and motion, or Newton's laws of mechanics, a property of the interaction between direction and proportionality of force). Interactional theories are usually good enough to conduct most research until the researcher reaches the later stages of inquiry. It is at this point, according to Dewey and Bentley, that 'observation and presentation' become so crucial that objects undergoing inquiry must be treated as objectives of inquiry. In other words, their features should not be treated as *a priori* powers or relational properties, but as purely functional 'aspects or phases' of transaction.

In this way, the researcher avoids essentializing, thingifying or reifying processes as settled objects outside of inquiry. Instead, they are functional tools of inquiry, fit for the purpose at hand but not existing things or objects independent of the research process. In terms of honoring the egalitarian relationship between the digital and predigital, the transactional approach dictates that researchers treat any proposed digital/ predigital prioritization as processual, tentative and for the sake of obtaining warranted research results, never as a fixed external constraint on or a settled outcome of inquiry.

8   Pluralism and Parity in Postdigital Research

Always preferring the digital over the predigital is not the same as betting on the winning horse at the racetrack: 'As traditional forms of research increasingly fail to describe our current reality, the previous winning horse (traditional research) needs to adapt to a new racing track (postdigital reality) and to new racing rules (of postdigital dialogue).' (Jandrić et al. 2019: 185) Instead, it is better to treat the digital and predigital as presumptively equal and then seek to justify any departures from the egalitarian status quo with accounts that bridge between epistemic frameworks (seminal parity thesis), cross-fertilize those spaces (com-post), model competing networks and processes as holistic systems (cybernetics), and observe and present them as tentative and functional objectives of inquiry (transaction).

Humility, fallibilism, and tolerance are critical virtues for conducting postdigital inquiries. This includes research that respects the boundaries set by a theoretically grounded parity principle. Humble postdigital researchers admit that there is no single right answer to the question of what is the best theory for grounding the postdigital principle. Fallibilists concede that they are not always right in their judgments about whether and how to prioritize the digital and the predigital. Tolerant postdigital researcher note that other competing views of the relationship between the predigital and digital, besides their own, should be scrutinized with an eye towards possible acceptance and revision of existing theories.

So, while we might be tempted to settle on a single authoritative theory of postdigital parity, it is a better tactic to opt for a pluralist approach—that is, admit that many more than three theories (or those so far suggested) can populate the universe of discourse. Despite the philosopher of science Thomas S. Kuhn's (1962) contention that normal science must proceed under a single authoritative paradigm—that is, a supreme theoretical model under which all researchers operate when doing 'normal science'—there are many counterexamples, especially within the Humanities and Social Sciences (for example, Philosophy and Economics).

Inquiries in these disciplines commonly proceed, either competitively or collaboratively, under two or more theories, paradigms, or research programmes.[1] In other words, it is best to admit that many theories can potentially fill the grounding role, leave the matter of theorizing parity open-ended, and thereby empower postdigital researchers to freely select one or more suitable theories to inform the postdigital principle of parity. Of course, ultimately the selection of a grounding theory depends on the design of a research study and the subject matter under investigation.

References

Akrich, M. (1992). The description of technical objects. In W. Bijker & J. Law (Eds.), *Shaping Technology, Building Society: Studies in Sociotechnical Change* (pp. 205–224). Cambridge, MA: MIT Press.

Badmington, N. (2003). Theorizing posthumanism. *Cultural Critique 53*, 10-27. https://doi.org/10.1353/cul.2003.0017.

Baines, L. (2005). Theory and anti-theory. *Teachers College Record*. https://www.tcrecord.org. Accessed 5 December 2022.

Bentley, A. F. (1935). *Behavior, knowledge, fact.* Bloomington, IN: Principia Press.

Cascone, K. (2000). The aesthetics of failure: 'Post-digital' tendencies in contemporary computer music. *Computer Music Journal, 24*(4), 12–18. https://doi.org/10.1162/014892600559489.

Chatelier, S. (2017). Beyond the humanism/posthumanism debate: The educational implications of Said's critical, humane praxis. *Educational Theory, 67*(6), 657–672. https://doi.org/10.1111/edth.12278.

Clements, A. (2018). A postdigital future for music education: Definitions, implications, and questions. *Action, Criticism, and Theory for Music Education, 17*(1), 48–80. https://doi.org/10.22176/act17.1.48.

Cramer, F., & Jandrić, P. (2021). Postdigital: A term that sucks but is useful. *Postdigital Science and Education, 3*(3), 966–989. https://doi.org/10.1007/s42438-021-00225-9.

Dewey, J., & Bentley, A. F. (1949). *Knowing and the Known.* Westport, CT: Greenwood Springs Publishers.

Easton, D. (1965). *A Systems Analysis of Political Life.* New York: Wiley.

Feenberg, A. (2019). Postdigital or Predigital? *Postdigital Science and Education, 1*(1), 8–9. https://doi.org/10.1007/s42438-018-0027-2.

Fish, S. (1989). *Doing What Comes Naturally.* Oxford: Clarendon Press.

Fuller, S., & Jandrić, P. (2019). The Postdigital Human: Making the history of the future. *Postdigital Science and Education, 1*(1), 190–217. https://doi.org/10.1007/s42438-018-0003-x.

Jandrić, P. (2017). *Learning in the Age of Digital Reason.* Rotterdam: Sense Publishers.

Jandrić, P., & Knox, J. (2021). The postdigital turn: Philosophy, education, research. *Policy Futures in Education.* https://doi.org/10.1177/2F14782103211062713.

---

[1] I use the expression 'research programme' in a loosely Lakatosian sense. According to Imre Lakatos (1999), multiple research programmes can simultaneously exist, so long as they revolve around a core set of assumptions that define the boundaries of scientific inquiry (to distinguish them from pseudo-science) while, simultaneously, shielding inquiry from irrelevant critique. Lakatos's account is a viable alternative to the Kuhnian (1962) model of normal science proceeding under a single dominant paradigm.

Jandrić, P., Knox, J., Besley, T., Ryberg, T., Suoranta, J., & Hayes, S. (2018). Postdigital science and education. *Educational Philosophy and Theory 50*(10), 893–899. https://doi.org/10.108 0/00131857.2018.1454000.

Jandrić, P., Ryberg, T., Knox, J., Lacković, N., Hayes, S., Suoranta, J., Smith, M., Steketee, A., Peters, M. A., McLaren, P., Ford, D. R., Asher, G., McGregor, C., Stewart, G., Williamson, B., & Gibbons, A. (2019). Postdigital Dialogue. *Postdigital Science and Education, 1*(1), 163-189. https://doi.org/10.1007/s42438-018-0011-x.

Jones, C. (2018). Experience and network learning. In N. Bonderup Dohn, S. Cranmer, J. A. Sime, M. de Laat, & T. Ryberg (Eds.), *Network Learning: Reflection and Challenges* (pp. 39–56). Springer International. https://doi.org/10.1007/978-3-319-74857-3_3.

Kuhn, T. S. (1962). *The Structure of Scientific Revolutions.* Chicago, IL: University of Chicago Press.

Lakatos, I. (1999). Lecture 8: The methodology of social scientific research programmes. In M. Motterlini (Ed.), *For and Against Method: Imre Lakatos, Paul Feyerabend* (pp. 96–109). Chicago, IL: University of Chicago Press.

Latour, B. (2005). *Reassembling the Social: An Introduction to Actor-Network Theory.* Oxford: Oxford University Press.

Lee, C. T., & Hsieh, S. H. (2021). Can social media-based brand communities build brand relationships? Examining the effect of community engagement on band love. *Behavior & Information Technology.* https://doi.org/10.1080/0144929X.2021.1872704.

McLaren, P. (2019). Reclaiming the Present or a Return to the Ash Heap of the Future? *Postdigital Science and Education, 1*(1), 10–13. https://doi.org/10.1007/s42438-018-0015-6.

Negroponte, N. (1998). Beyond digital. Wired, 12 January. https://www.wired.com/wired/archive/6.12/negroponte.html. Accessed 10 May 2022.

Negroponte, N. (1995). *Being Digital.* New York: Alfred A. Knopf Inc.

Peters, M. A., & Besley, T. (2019), Critical philosophy of the postdigital. *Postdigital Science and Education, 1*(1), 29–42. https://doi.org/10.1007/s42438-018-0004-5.

Ralston, S. (2009). Effects of sports particpation and sports-specific self-esteem on academic performance: A research design. https://www.academia.edu/30465854/Effects_of_Sports_ Participation_and_Sports_specific_Self_esteem_on_Academic_Performance_A_Research_ Design. Accessed 1 December 2022.

Ralston, S. (2011). Interdisciplinarity: Some lessons from John Dewey. *American Dialectic, 1*(2), 309-321.

Ralston, S. (2014). Holism. In M. T. Gibbons, D. Coole, W. E. Connolly, & E. Ellis (Eds.), *Blackwell Encyclopedia of Political Thought* (pp. 1–6). Oxford, UK: Blackwell.

Ralston, S. (2020). Postdigital prospects for blockchain-disrupted education: Beyond the theater, memes and marketing hype. *Postdigital Science and Education, 1*(2), 280–288. https://doi.org/10.1007/s42438-019-00091-6.

Ralston, S. (2021). Higher education's microcredentialing craze: A postdigital-Deweyan critique. *Postdigital Science and Education, 1*(3), 83–101. https://doi.org/10.1007/s42438-020-00121-8.

Ralston, S. (2022a). Postdigital slacktivism. *Postdigital Science and Education.* https://doi.org/10.1007/s42438-022-00308-1.

Ralston, S. (2022b). Ghosting inside the machine: Student cheating, online education and the omertà of institutional liars. In A. MacKenzie, J. Rose, & I. Bhatt (Eds.), *The Epistemology of Deceit in a Postdigital Era: Dupery by Design* (pp. 251–264). Cham: Springer. https://doi.org/1 0.1007/978-3-030-72154—1_14.

Sable, D. (2012). A 'post-digital' world, really? Thinkwithgoogle, May. https://www.thinkwithgoogle.com/future-of-marketing/digital-transformation/a-post-digital-world-really/. Accessed 12 May 2022.

Sinclair, C., & Hayes, S. (2019). Between the post and the com-post: Examining the postdigital 'work' of a prefix. *Postdigital Science and Education, 1*(1), 119–131. https://doi.org/10.1007/ s42438-018-0017-4.

Wittgenstein, L. (1961). *Tractatus Logico-Philosophicus.* Trans. D. F. Pears & B. F. McGuinness. Cambridge: Cambridge University Press.

Postdigital/More-Than-Digital: Ephemerality, Seclusion, and Copresence in the University

Lesley Gourlay (iD)

1 Introduction

Looking at the genealogy of the term *postdigital* as presented in Jandrić et al. (2022), the origin of the construct is traced to Negroponte (1998), whose conception rests on the notion of *inseparability* of the digital and the analog. He also states that the digital 'will be noticed only by its absence, not its presence'. Here, it seems three ideas are at work; the first is that the digital and analog are intertwined as one inseparable entity, the second is that it is also possible for the digital to be absent, and the third, is that it will only be noticed by its absence, not its presence. There appears to be a tension inherent in these claims, and in more recent ideas about of the nature of the digital, flowing from them. In this imaginary, the digital is presented as an entity fully *permeating* on the analog. It is theorised as *ubiquitous*, and also *occluded* from direct view; resulting in the postdigital, in which the digital as a presence seems to be imagined as a kind of haunting, or an entity outside of direct perception.

This idea echoes popular discourses of the digital as a form of 'magical' or 'transformative' force. However, the potential absence of the digital is also alluded to as a possibility, in the form of what is noticed, a rupture. This - I will argue - implies an inevitable, totalising, and in some sense, an unknowable force. In this chapter, I will propose that these conceptions of the digital, and consequently the postdigital, lead to a range of effects concerning how the analog, material, and embodied are recast. Focusing on higher education in particular, I will propose that a strong version of this imaginary may lead us back to much-critiqued fantasies of digital incorporeality coupled with an over-emphasis on *connection*, which together continue to influence research, policy, and practice. I will consider the possible

L. Gourlay (✉)
UCL Institute of Education, London, UK
e-mail: l.gourlay@ucl.ac.uk

© The Author(s), under exclusive license to Springer Nature Switzerland AG 2023
P. Jandrić et al. (eds.), *Postdigital Research*, Postdigital Science and Education, https://doi.org/10.1007/978-3-031-31299-1_4

effects of this imaginary of the digital as fully permeating, ubiquitous and occluded, focusing particularly on how these ideas reverberate in higher education, and what they do to our conceptions of the nature of absence and presence, in particular with regard to human and nonhuman subjectivities and practices.

The concepts of the network and the meshwork will be contrasted, and I will suggest that neither of these metaphors captures in theoretical terms some of the fundamental aspects of being at university as a student or faculty member. I suggest that these centre on ephemerality, seclusion, and copresence, as opposed to 'connection' as it is formulated by the concept of the network, or even the more emergent meshwork. The chapter will conclude with suggested implications for theory and research into digital higher education; and will also discuss how this critique might contribute to the development of a 'capacious' concept of the postdigital for future research.

2   Origins of the Postdigital

The concept can be traced to Negroponte in an article in Wired, in 1998. Negroponte's regards the presence of digital technology as omnipresent, and therefore invisible. He sets out that:

> Its literal form, the technology, is already beginning to be taken for granted, and its connotation will become tomorrow's commercial and cultural compost for new ideas. Like air and drinking water, being digital will be noticed only by its absence, not its presence. (Negroponte 1998)

As Jandrić et al. (2022) remind us, the term itself entered the literature in Cascone (2000) and also with Pepperell and Punt (2000). Cascone coined the term in the context of music, Pepperell and Punt in visual arts. For several years, the term was used with reference to arts-related fields, with a special issue being published by Andersen et al. (2014). For Cramer and Jandric (2021), the utility of the term is that it can 'help to complicate the terms 'digital' and 'analog', particularly in the humanities and social sciences' (Cramer and Jandrić 2021: 985).

Jandrić et al. (2022) chart the field's resistance towards definition of the postdigital (with the argument that a definition may be exclusionary made by Bayne in Networked Learning Collective Editorial 2021), or that resistance to a final definition may be more productive (Jandrić and Ford 2022). Jandrić et al. (2022) reject an 'anything goes' relativism, and acknowledge a need for conceptual clarity, but stop short at providing this, instead holding open a space for dialogue and capaciousness around the idea. This openness is laudable and inclusive, but also leaves the respondent with some responsibility towards providing at least a provisional stability around the concept, in order to address the theme of this volume. With this in mind, I will focus on Negroponte's (1998) thesis.

Negroponte's assertions reply on the notion of *inseparability* of the digital and the analog, and that the digital 'will be noticed only by its absence, not its presence'.

In order to gain some theoretical purchase on the postdigital, the nature of the digital can be explored. I would like to look at these assertions in more detail, to explore what I propose are fundamental tensions inherent in his thesis.

3   Inseparability/Permeation/Ubiquity, and Twine

The first main idea here is that the digital and analog are *intertwined* as one inseparable entity. This idea is central to Negroponte's (1998) thesis, and has gained currency in literature which has sought to challenge the notion of a strong binary between the digital and the analog. These accounts have centred on the strongly intertwined nature of digital and analog media and practices, and extent to which these intersect closely, and also the point that all digital technology has a material substrate. The point about intertwined assemblages seems undeniable, particularly with reference to settings where access to devices is widespread. However, it may be instructive to pay closer attention to the nature of these relationships between the digital and the analog, and in particular the *differences between* the digital and the analog.

The key point I want to explore here is that a relationship of intertwining relies on the elements being differently composed. The term *intertwined* is used as a metaphor from working with string. *Twine* is defined as 'a strong string of two or more strands twisted together' (Merriam Webster 2022). The etymology of *twine* is regarded as likely to come from Old Norse *twinna*, meaning to double (Online Etymology Dictionary 2022).

The verb *intertwine* has a transitive meaning, 'to unite by twining one with another', or an intransitive meaning which Merriam Webster define as 'to twine about one another' or 'to become mutually involved'. Clearly, the term is used in the intransitive when discussing the relationship between the digital and the analog, and it is also used in a metaphorical rather than literal sense. However, it is worth considering that for two elements to intertwine, crucially they do not merge or meld into one material. Twine cannot, by definition, be composed on one thread; but must be made of two which are materially separate threads brought into close proximity to each other. They then form a new entity.

As can be seen in Fig. 1, twine must be regular and consistent in the twisting of the two or more constituent strands. The tension and closeness must be regular if the twine is to be strong and usable. In this regard, the metaphor of intertwining fits with Negroponte (1998) and other commentators' notion of the digital and analog as inseparable. The twine is, by definition, composed of two constantly present elements. It also fits with the idea of *ubiquity* of the digital, as a thread twisted tightly together with the analog thread. However, it fits less well with the notion of *permeation*, as the threads are still distinct entities which can in principle be un-twined and separated. So, there is a problem with the idea of permeation in the postdigital in terms of the metaphor of *intertwining*.

Fig. 1 Twine (Wikimedia Commons 2022)

4 Separability and Tangible Absence

This leads to the second element which I propose forms part of Negroponte's (1998) conceptual framing of the postdigital; that it is also possible for the digital to be absent. In terms of the metaphor of intertwining, this would imply a loss of a constituent and essential part. In the case of a material twine, if one thread is missing, the twine is weakened. Also, the remaining thread will be left in the twisted shape it formed when intertwined. This seems also to fit with the notion of the digital being noticed by its absence. It might be argued that in some sociotechnical systems and routines of practice which involve closely interrelated digital and analog actions and agency, this metaphor is highly suitable, such as a system in which digital technology is essential at all times. An example might be an airport, where without digital technology, the entire assemblage would come to a halt.

However, it may equally be argued that there are other fields of practice in which the digital and analog may have a different relationship, one which is somewhat less tightly bound. Considering the example of a university, it is an interesting thought experiment to consider the extent of its entwinedness with the digital. It is undoubtedly the case in the contemporary period that many of the functions of the university in terms of administration are reliant on digital entwinement, such as applications, admissions, library services, and room bookings. This list could be extended to include administration of fees, payroll, security technologies, and timetabling. In recent years, the infiltration of datafication into teaching and assessment has led to the uptake of digital textbooks, learning analytics, and exam proctoring, among other interventions. In this regard, it would be easy to draw the conclusion that the contemporary university is as tightly bound into digital technology as the airport. However, there are some notable differences.

Although it appears that the university is entwined with digitality, there are elements of 'analog' practice which are, I propose, in a different kind of relationship with the digital. Unlike the strands which are entwined and rely in the digital for their existence as a functioning twine, some areas of university life still exist as a separate strand or category of non-digital practice, although they have relationships with it. These include reading physical texts, handwriting on paper, handwriting on boards, face-to-face private or occluded conversation, in-person teaching, and non-digital practical work. These practices have deep historical roots in the origins of higher education, and in many contexts worldwide continue outside of settings where digital technology is present or widespread. These practices are characterised by their ephemerality, seclusion, and in some cases, copresence. These are not observable, recordable, or traceable. Arguably, these practices form a core (or a series of interstices) which constitute what higher education was and is; a set of epistemological and sociomaterial embodied practices, around which the digital is closely circled in a series of administrative rings. If viewed in this way, it is worth considering the current growth of datafication and digital platforms into higher education as encroachments from this outer administrative / neoliberal set of rings inwards, towards this core of ephemerality, seclusion, and copresence.

The drive is towards surveillance, recording, monitoring, and measuring. This can be seen in the case of the lecture via learning management systems, which might be seen as surrounding and crowding out the ephemeral event. Also 'lecture capture' technologies, whose name itself is instructive, and approaches such as the 'flipped classroom'. The same impetus can arguably be observed in exam proctoring. Apparently 'student-centred' approaches to 'teaching and learning', I suggest, encroach into these unobserved interstices of individual study practices and personal being with exhortations to record the study process via 'reflection', or to discipline and monitor oneself as a human subject via 'self-regulation'. The physical space of the campus itself is becoming increasingly permeated by digital technologies of surveillance such as cameras, turnstiles with card entry, and digital class attendance technologies. Teaching is increasing infiltrated by regimes of audit and measurement, such as the UK National Student Survey and the Teaching Excellent Framework, which are controversial government audit exercises aimed at measuring respectively student 'satisfaction' with higher education, and the 'quality' of teaching in higher education. However, I would suggest that despite this, these practices remain, and remain important.

5   Networked Learning

Returning to consider the concept of the postdigital in the contemporary university, it is worth spending some time considering a metaphor which has become prominent in the field of digital education, the *network*, and also an alternative which has been proposed, the *meshwork*. The notion of 'networked learning' (e.g., Jones 2015) is widespread in its use with reference to digital higher education, an example of which can be seen in the European Networked Learning Conferences and associated book series (e.g., Bonderup-Dohn et al. 2018). The notion of networked learning is relational, defined by Wikipedia as 'a process of developing and maintaining connections with people and information, and communicating in such a way so as to support one another's learning' (Wikipedia 2022). The idea centres on facilitating 'evolving sets of connections between learners and their interpersonal communities, knowledge contexts, and digital technologies' (Wikipedia 2022). The Wikipedia page traces various antecedents to networked learning, including Lave and Wenger's (1991) *Communities of Practice* and Siemens' (2005) *Connectivism*.

The definition was revisited recently (Networked Learning Editorial Collective 2021). In this piece, which reflects on the term in the light of the Covid-19 pandemic and emergency remote teaching, acknowledges some of the shortcomings of the terminology in the area:

> 'Online learning' has always been an awkward term – not least, like 'digital', 'distance' and 'virtual', it can obscure the embodied and physically situated nature of learning (Fawns 2019). Students live in a complex social-material-digital world and the learning spaces they make affect how they learn. (Networked Learning Editorial Collective 2021: 313)

They go on to state that:

> It is now rare to find real learning situations that can be described regarded as 'purely face-to-face' or 'wholly online'. Rather, they involve complex entanglements of students, teachers, ideas, asks, activities, tools, artefacts, places and spaces. (Networked Learning Editorial Collective 2021: 313)

They set out that '[t]here is a field of research and practice that studies such entanglements. It is known as networked learning.' (Networked Learning Editorial Collective 2021: 313)

It is perhaps something of a disingenuous retrospective 'land grab' to claim that the field of Networked Learning has always had this focus on more-than human assemblages, but the influence of sociomaterial perspectives and scholarship on this more recent iteration of Networked Learning is noteworthy, and the authors explicitly call for a contemporary redefinition. The rest of the paper traces the history of the idea, taking a critical stance towards the early definition, that it is 'learning in which [information and communications technologies are] used to promote *connections*' (Goodyear et al. 1998: 2) (emphasis added), raising the very legitimate point that the definition does not explain what these connections may be *for*. They go on to outline a further definition given by Bonderup-Dohn et al. (2018) and de Laat and Dohn (2019):

An emphasis on connections between people and how they develop, maintain and learn from networks of others.

An emphasis on connections between situations or contexts—how people make connections between such situations, transforming or reconstructing knowledge for use in different situations.

An emphasis on the ICT infrastructure and how it enables connections across time and space, including connections between situations (as in No. 2 above), boundary crossing, mobility, etc.

An emphasis on connections between (human and non-human) actants – under- standing learning situations as entanglements of people and things.

They also reference a further 8-point definition:

The focus is on learning which has a perceived value to the learners.
Responsibility for the learning process should be shared (between all actors in the network).
Time has to be allowed to build relationships.
Learning is situated and context dependent.
Learning is supported by collaborative or group settings.
Dialogue and social interaction support the co-construction of knowledge, identity and learning.
Critical reflexivity is an important part of the learning process and knowing.
The role of the facilitator/animator is important in networked learning. (Ponti and Hodgson 2006; Hodgson and McConnell 2019)

Again, there is a strong emphasis in these definitions on connections, relations, collaboration, dialogue, interaction, and co-construction. Despite recent nods towards a sociomaterial sensibility, this is an ethos which is clearly based on a strong version of social constructivism, combined with a thoroughgoing belief in the potential of the online and digital, which raises some contradictions.

In a piece closely related to the subject of this chapter, Carvalho (2018) uses the concept of networked learning in combination with a sensibility towards the entanglement of human and nonhuman agency, looking at an example of learning in a museum setting, and another with university students of architecture learning in the outdoors. She refers to Goodyear and Carvalho's (2014) perspective, in which learning is seen as an emergent phenomenon, also relational (e.g., Gourlay and Oliver 2016). Carvalho draws on the literature around sociomateriality in education; and uses the term *meshwork* to refer to learning networks, drawing on the anthropologist Hodder's work on entanglement between humans and things in archaeology (Hodder 2012, 2013, 2016), as opposed to Ingold's (2011) meshwork directly. These studies and her analysis provide an example of how the concept of networked learning is expanding to take into account these complexities. The next section will consider an alternative concept of the *meshwork*, taken from the work of Tim Ingold (2011) in social anthropology.

6   The Meshwork

The social anthropologist Tim Ingold (2011) challenges the notion of the network, which is conventionally seen a composed of interacting entities or points, and instead proposes the notion of the *meshwork*. As he puts it:

> I return to the importance of distinguishing the network as a set of interconnected points from the meshwork as an interweaving of lines. Every such line describes a flow of material substance in a space which is topologically fluid. I conclude that the organism (animal or human) should be understood not as a bounded entity surrounded by an environment but as an unbounded entanglement of lines in fluid space. (Ingold 2011: 64)

Ingold considers the notion of animism, setting out that the conventional understanding of it is misleading. He argues that it is not a question of imputing life to things which are inert. He argues that is it not a form of belief about the world, but more a *way of being* in the world:

> Animacy, then, is not a property of persons imaginatively projected into the things with which they perceive themselves to be surrounded. Rather … it is the dynamic, transformative potential of the entire field of relations within which being of all kinds, more or less person-like or thing-like, continually and reciprocally bring one another into existence. The animacy of the lifeworld, in short, is not the result of an infusion of spirit into substance, or of agency into materiality, but is rather ontologically prior to their differentiation. (Ingold 2011: 68)

Ingold proposes that instead of conceptualising an organism as a bounded circle, we could think of it as a line. In this conception, the relation is not between the organism and the environment, instead the line is 'a trail along which life is lived' (Ingold 2011: 69). The line is 'but one strand in a tissue of trails that together comprise the texture of the lifeworld' (Ingold 2011: 69–70).

This describes the *meshwork*. However, Ingold suggests that an organism is not one line, but more various lines emanating and criss-crossing out from a centre. 'Organisms and persons, then, are not so much nodes in a network as knots in a tissue of knots, whose constituent strands, as they become tied up with other strands, in other knots, comprise the meshwork.' For Ingold then, the environment can be regarded as a 'domain of entanglement (Ingold 2011: 70). 'Thus we must cease regarding the world as an inert substratum, over which living things propel themselves about like counters on a board or actors on a stage, where artefacts and the landscape take the place, respectively, of properties and sceneries.' (Ingold 2011: 71) Ingold also extends the metaphor of weaving: 'In this world the earth, far from providing a solid foundation for existence, appears to float like a fragile and ephemeral raft, woven from the strands of terrestrial life, and suspended in the sphere of the sky.' (Ingold 2011: 74)

Hunter (2016) draws on Ingold's concept of the meshwork in a consideration of the 'processual journey' (34) of researchers looking into virtual worlds (focussing on Second Life), looking at *emergent spaces*. As background, she refers to the work of Lefebvre (1991) on the production of space, and Boellstorff (2008, 2012), who makes the point, also with reference to the virtual world Second Life, that '[h]umans make culture in virtual and actual contexts; since humans are part of nature, and the virtual is a product of human intentionality, the virtual is as 'natural' as anything humans do in the actual world' (Boellstorff 2008: 19).

Hunter also reminds us of Leander and McKim's (2003) critique of the idea of an online-offline dichotomy, and their concept of *net-walking*. For them, 'emerging social spaces of Internet practices are complexly interpenetrated with social spaces considered to be "before" or "outside of" the Internet"' (Leander and McKim 2003: 218). Turning to Ingold's *meshwork* and *knots*, she points out his view that 'knowledge is meshworked, generated by wayfarers in the binding of place or topic as relational activity of intertwining occurrences' (Hunter 2016: 37), what Ingold calls *alongly integrated knowledge*, or *storied knowledge* (Ingold 2011: 153–155). Importantly, this type of knowledge is place-binding, not place-bound, and inhabitants' practices and scientific practices are both meshworked; both are wayfarers.

Klenk (2018) considers the limitations of the metaphor of a network in transdisciplinary research practice, turning to Ingold's meshwork as a metaphor which she regards as better suited to account for difference. She argues that the meshwork captures 'how life is lived along lines of becoming: emergent, indeterminate, contingent, historical, narrative' (2018: 315). In the context of her study of a transdisciplinary climate change adaptation project, this allows for an understanding that subject positions are 'not conceived in advance of a research encounter … but erupt in the interstices of research methods, objectives and desired outcomes' (Klenk 2018: 315). As Klenk points out:

> Although the 'network' metaphor is useful to understand who and what connects to produce knowledge in stakeholder-engaged research practices, it is important to remember that the use of metaphor in science is always accompanied by an important disclaimer: scientific metaphors are not mirror images of reality – they are interpretive and constructive heuristics. (Klenk 2018: 315)

Klenk proposes Ingold's (2011) *meshwork* as a metaphor better suited to capture that 'individuals and knowledges are "entanglements" that emerge through encounters with others' (2018: 316). Ingold's notion of the meshwork is based on Deleuze and Guattari's (2004) notion of life lived along 'lines of becoming'. She quotes their explanation:

> A line of becoming is not defined by the points it connects, of by the points that compose it; on the contrary, it passes between points, it comes up through the middle, it runs … transversally to the localizable relation to distance or contiguous points. A point is always a point of origin. But a line of becoming has neither beginning nor end. (Deleuze and Guattari 2004: 224–225)

She also gives Ingold's definition:

> In the meshwork, each constituent line, as it bodies forth, lays its own trail from within the interstices of its binding with others. Thus the joining of lives is also their continual differentiation. The knots formed in the process are not inclusive or encompassing, not wrapped up in themselves, but always in the midst of things, while their ends are on the loose, rooting for other lines to join with. (Ingold 2016: 11).

In the rest of this chapter, I will consider the notions of network and meshwork with relation to the postdigital university, arguing even the meshwork does not capture certain elements of being the university, which I will argue are fundamental.

7 Ephemerality, Seclusion, and Copresence

As discussed above, Ingold and various subsequent scholars have favoured the notion of the meshwork over the network, as providing superior theoretical purchase on the emergent, shifting and fluid nature of subjectivities, entities, and how they entangle with one-another. I have proposed that, following these arguments, the meshwork is also a more suitable metaphor for taking account of 'the postdigital university'. However, in this section I would like to suggest that both these metaphors are incomplete, in that they focus in different ways on lines of connection. In the case of the network, the focus is on nodes and lines connecting them. With the meshwork, the focus is on lines emanating out from individuals or entities, crossing and entangling in a more emergent manner, in which the entity is conceived of as the line itself. However, what both these metaphors fail to account for are the possibility of spaces between the lines, the interstices which are not composed of or concerned with connections or entanglements, or where the nature of *what goes on there* is somewhat different. Arguably, although the meshwork allows for a more nuanced conception of emergent ontologies, the idea is still focused on the notion of a wider fabric or mesh of connections, albeit in a looser manner than the network.

In the context of the university, these might be ways of being, practices, or actions which are not primarily focused on making a connection or an entanglement with other people or entities, or they are, also have another more essential quality. There are several elements which I would argue characterise these examples. One is *ephemerality*. Certain of these practices are *fugitive* by virtue that they are not recorded via notes or digital technologies, but take place in a particular moment, in a fleeting manner. A second characteristic is *seclusion*. Many of these practices take place in a solitary mode, unobserved. The final characteristic I would suggest in the case of conversation, is that of these foregoing elements plus face-to-face *copresence* in the same physical space.

7.1 Ephemerality

In the pre-digital university, and in contemporary settings which do not include or are not dominated by digital technologies, university practices were more likely to be ephemeral and fleeting, with no recording being taken of the speech. The lecture, until relatively recently, consisted primarily of a live speech event, with literacy practices taking place during the lecture, such as the use of text to be read or consulted by the lecturer, the blackboard and chalk, and paper and pen handwriting by students. In more recent years, slides may have been used, or overhead transparencies, also part of an ephemeral event.

With the advent of the learning management system, a temporal shift took place, in that there was then a means by which students could receive copies of materials such as PowerPoint slides in advance of the live lecture. In this regard, the purely ephemeral nature of the event was eroded, as it became possible to obtain these materials and possibly other forms of documentation in advance, therefore arguably making face-to-face attendance less important, although pre-PowerPoint, students engaged in borrowing or photocopying each-others' notes in order to avoid attendance. These slides also caused a shift in the literacy practices required by the lecturer and student during the lecture, as they would take on a structuring role to the spoken event, in addition to providing a visual element, in manner which arguably became more widespread than the prior use of slides or overhead projectors. They typically remain available after the live event is over, also extending the duration of the event in that respect. The pure ephemerality of the lecture is lost, due to this mediatic change.

In this example, an event which has for centuries been entirely ephemeral, no longer has that status, although there remains a spoken ephemeral element. However, other digital technologies may be in play which can erode this further. One example of this is 'lecture capture' recording technology, which may take a video recording of the live lecture. In the case of asynchronous distance or online engagement, this ephemerality is lost altogether, as the spoken event is undertaken as a solitary performance by the lecturer in advance. In this case, the lecturer is required to speak 'as if' there were listeners, knowing there are none at the time of speaking. In this regard, in generic terms, the lecture becomes analogous to a broadcast, a package, or a product. The students have access to a recording which they can play, pause and rewatch as they wish, or even watch at accelerated speed to save time. This can also be seen in the practice of the 'flipped classroom'.

Other examples of ephemeral practices are conversation and experiences which are not recorded. Arguably, these may be also eroded by technologies of audit such as 'reflective practice' forming part of assessment (e.g., Macfarlane and Gourlay 2009). In these cases, the ephemerality of experience such as teaching practice or observation is regarded as insufficient; and must be accompanied by a written account of what took place.

7.2 Seclusion

Seclusion is a further aspect which characterised pre-digital university life and has arguably been eroded to some extent by digital technology. I use the term here to refer to of privacy, being unseen, and free of any technology or observation or recording. Examples of seclusion might include solitary thought and study, practices such as reading physical books and using handwriting, again face-to-face conversation, and walking around campus unobserved. They might also include action which might be characterised as resistance, such as silence in groupwork, non-participation in online discussion boards, and use of muting and avoidance of cameras online.

7.3   Copresence

The third element I would like to focus on is copresence, by which I mean being physically present *with* others in the same material space at the same time, such as a lecture room. This aspect of university practice was until recently still regarded, in the majority of settings, as a default mode for higher education, alongside technologies such as learning management systems. However, in the wake of the Covid-19 pandemic of 2020 onwards, and resultant lockdowns and campus closures, the status of the face-to-face class has also arguably been eroded. The pivot to fully online remote teaching introduced the notion that this may be an acceptable alternative to face-to-face, rather than a less-than-ideal emergency response.

A 'discourse of inevitability' has arisen in the subsequent period, expressing the view that the campus is - if not obsolete, at least optional - drawing on the arguments among others that students with caring responsibilities or those who are differently-abled may find co-presence difficult or problematic to access, or that the ongoing risks of Covid make the campus too risky a proposition. It is worth noting that this is the latest in a series of attempts to call time on the physical campus, following on from similar claims regarding MOOCs. (See Allen and McLaren 2022 for a discussion of the university as a physical place). At the time of writing, resurgent post-pandemic face-to-face academic conferences have also been under sustained criticism in some circles, with the view being expressed that they are inherently exclusionary, classist or ableist.

8   Fugitive Practices

Taken together, predigital practices such as those described above tend to be derided as 'old-fashioned' or obsolete, such as face-to-face lectures. Others may be regarded as more difficult or impossible, such as being unobserved in physical campus space permeated by surveillance cameras and electronic gate technology; or being required to check in to an online attendance register. Some practices described above such as silence in groupwork, not writing on discussion boards or switching off cameras while online, might be regarded as either problematically 'passive' and indicative of a lack of 'student engagement', or might even be regarded as transgressive. Others may be portrayed as exclusionary or elitist.

Turning our attention to academic faculty, a similar analysis might be made of practices and activities which are not captured by notions of connection or entanglement, in addition to conferences. Again, these could include academic practices which tend to be associated with the past, such as solitary study and the use of material literacy artefacts such as books and papers. Again, face-to-face discussion outside of formal classes, meetings, or assessments might fall into this category. Use of 'old school' teaching technologies such as chalk and a blackboard might also represent an example. In terms of resistance, this might manifest itself in an avoidance of practices focused on connection such as social media, learning management systems, combined with a resistance towards public performativity in academic work.

Overall, the contemporary situation presents a somewhat contradictory set of tensions. Aspects of human being in the world such as ephemerality, seclusion, and co-presence appear to be on the retreat, relegated to what I term *fugitive practices* which are invisible or even regarded as problematic. However, alongside this tendency, we see a greater emphasis on broadcast and production over ephemerality; surveillance and recording over seclusion, and what I have termed *screen hygiene* (Gourlay 2022) over copresence. The result is - I propose – underpinned by an unexpressed but profoundly transhumanist ethos, which seeks to remove the human from the embodied flow of ephemerality, seclusion, and copresence, and render her into a form of document (Gourlay 2022).

9   Boltholes and Breathing Spaces

Webb (2018: 98) provides a coruscating indictment of what he terms the 'corporate-imperial university', from which I provide an extended quote, not least to avoid breaking his notably long and resonant single sentence:

> The notion of 'the corporate university' points to the academy as a marketized sphere in which the costs of education are shifted from the state onto students; students are positioned as consumers of an individual investment good even as they experience higher education as an extended period of underpaid labor preparing them for an even longer period of crippling debt; teaching is dominated by performance indicators linked to customer satisfaction and human capital formation; the workforce becomes increasingly casualized, insecure and exploited, a precariat operating within a censorious culture of audit, surveillance, and performance management; research is transformed into a high-stakes competition, framed by a regime of indicator fetishism, discouraging long-term research while encouraging research fraud; self-governance disappears as the administrator displaces the academic as the central figure of the university; a culture of organized mistrust permeates the institution, leading administrators to create an ever-more-elaborate bureaucratic cage within which the academic can safely be contained; an increasingly standardized and technically oriented curriculum undermines academic freedom and critical inquiry; universities enter into partnerships with business, subsidizing training costs while operating more like for-profit corporations themselves, developing and marketing their own commercial products; an obsession with corporate branding is accompanied by a dance in which universities track and mimic each other's moves, becoming almost indistinguishable from each other; the sector becomes awash with vision and mission statements, each identical and identically vacuous; capital investment projects escalate at the same time as academic staffing levels fall; cities are colonized, communities are dispossessed and displaced, to create new architectural monuments to grace the covers of overseas marketing brochures that could not be more at odds with the dismal realities of the under-resourced departments students actually encounter. (Webb 2018: 96)

Webb, however, counterbalances this critique by providing a rather more circumspect assessment of prior attempts at 'radical pedagogy', acknowledging that '[t]he field of critical pedagogy/radical education is heavy on bombast and the realities of the utopian classroom often fall short of the theory-heavy promises' (Webb 2018: 100). Insightfully, he critiques the way in which the university 'draws strength from the utopian classroom, happily accommodating sites of resistance in order to recuperate them as symbols of its tolerance' (Webb 2018: 101), citing Oparah (2014). However, helpfully, he sets out a need to *create spaces*, drawing on Zaslove (2007). Webb highlights Zaslove's description of utopian pedagogy as 'an exiled form of education' in search of 'bolt-holes and breathing spaces in the system' (Zaslove 2007: 98 in Webb 2018: 102).

Webb's proposals are focused on providing various forms of escape from the formal education system and neoliberalism, as opposed to what I have identified as a (related) predicament in terms of digital surveillance and documentation, but his analytic project seems to chime in to an extent. He refers to the concept of 'the undercommons', drawing on the work of Harney and Moten (2013), Shukaitis (2009), and Undercommoning Collective (2016). He describes it as follows:

> the undercommons is more than just the creation of spaces with utopian intent. It is a shifting matrix of spaces, processes, relations, and structures of feeling. Harney and Moten do attach importance to teaching and the classroom—in particular as an opportunity to refuse the call to order—but the undercommons exists in institutional cracks outside the classroom: in stairwells, in alleys, in kitchens, in corridors, in smoking areas, in hiding. The undercommons is a community of maroons, outcasts, and fugitives, not of responsible teachers. It is 'always an unsafe neighbourhood' (Harney and Moten 2013, 28). In fact, the undercommons is best described as a way of being: a way of being within and against one's institution and a way of being with and for the community of outcasts (Melamed 2016). (Webb 2018: 102–103)

Thus far, there are resonances with the analysis I have been developing. However, there is a contrast in terms of Webb's utopianism, his yearning for another better world. The undercommons is presented as an entry point to this other world in the world, while my interest is more in the potential of the existing academic world. However, interestingly, he also quotes Harney's view that the undercommons is a 'a militant arrhythmia' that unsettles the rhythm of the line, 'invites us to feel around us', and brings the utopic common underground into the open (Harney 2015: 177–178). However, having seduced us with the language of the undercommons, he points out how easy it is to be seduced by the language of the undercommons, and acknowledges how difficult or even impossible it is to enact this within the university. Ultimately, he concludes that the fugitives (also his term) can only meet outside the university, to find breathing space.

Webb's broader project is beyond the scope of this chapter, but it may be worth speculating that when seeking forms of resistance, ironically, the spaces which have been derided for decades as obsolete, hierarchical, or irrelevant may in fact proffer *fugitive* spaces for resistance of perhaps a milder kind, with a less radical prospectus –to be only allowed to be fleeting, silent, together with others, and human. This feels radical in itself at this juncture.

10   More-Than-Digital

A final line (or space) of analysis I'd like to explore in this chapter in thinking in terms of the concept of the postdigital is regarding the meaning of the prefix 'post'. This has already been discussed with respect to poststructuralism and posthumanism, with debate centring on the difference between 'post' meaning 'after' or 'more than' (as already discussed in the context of the postdigital by Cramer 2015 and Feenberg 2019). Regarding posthumanism, the 'more than' interpretation of the term has allowed for an expansiveness, and also and avoidance of an historical focus, with associated connotations of a loss of the human. With the current topic, the same issue arises, with a tendency towards assuming the postdigital refers to a temporal 'after' period, a notion which is encouraged by contemporary popular discourses of inevitability surrounding the alleged obsolescence of the analog world.

If instead we think of the postdigital, with 'post' denoting 'more than', then I would suggest that this position might allow some theoretical purchase on the two problems I have raised above. The first is my reading of *network* and even the more nuanced *meshwork* as being overly concerned with connection, as opposed to aspects of being. I have suggested the three aspects above, but could equally have suggested stillness, waiting, and quietude. I propose that as a result we are failing to adequately theorise those moments in higher education which are not entirely concerned with connection; but are vital all the same.

If we think of postdigital as *more-than-digital*, then it may provide us with some capaciousness and space for these moments. It may even allow us to theorise them not as fugitive moments in the interstices, but as central, important, albeit somewhat ineffable elements of higher education. This proposal may seem whimsical, but I would argue that it carries the potential to be quietly destabilising, in a system which not only disaggregates and packages education as a neoliberal product, (as argued within the ample critical literature), but also disaggregates and packages the human as a form of document, working within an implicit tendency towards transhumanist ideology.

11   Conclusions

In this chapter I have explored the genealogy of the term postdigital with reference to Negroponte (1998). I raised some points surrounding what I regard to be some inconsistencies in the foundational definition, particularly around the notion of permeation, with a detour on the nature of twine. I then went on to review the literature which critiques the notion of network in favour of Ingold's meshwork. While finding the meshwork generative, I suggested that it lacks theoretical purchase on certain aspects of being in the university which have in recent years been eroded and/or derided. I focused particularly on three aspects: ephemerality, seclusion, and copresence, arguing that these have been severely eroded by digital technologies alongside practices of surveillance, audit, and 'reflection'. I suggested that these have become *fugitive practices.*

Contrasting this analysis with that of Webb and proponents of the undercommons, I concluded that a move to maintain or reclaim these fugitive practices, while less radical than Webb's prospectus, may be a worthy cause. I ended by considering the status of the prefix 'post' in the postdigital and suggested that if it is considered in terms of meaning 'more than' rather than 'after', it could in fact serve to theoretise fugitive practices and spaces, as opposed to following the notion of undifferentiated permeability as suggested by Negroponte. It is in this sense that I see the term *postdigital* as having future utility to the field.

Acknowledgement   This research is funded by the Leverhulme Trust Major Research Fellowship grant number MRF-2020-135.

References

Allen, R. M., & McLaren, P. (2022). Protecting the University as a Physical Place in the Age of Postdigitization. *Postdigital Science and Education, 4*(2), 373–393. https://doi.org/10.1007/s42438-021-00276-y

Andersen, C. U., Cox, G., & Papadopoulos, G. (2014). Editorial: Postdigital Research. *A Peer-Reviewed Journal About, 3*(1), 5–7. https://doi.org/10.7146/aprja.v3i1.116067.

Boellstorff, T. (2008). *Coming of Age in Second Life: An Anthropologist Explores the Virtually Human.* Princeton, NJ: Princeton University Press.

Boellstorff, T. (2012). *Ethnography and Virtual Worlds: A Handbook of Method.* Princeton, NJ: Princeton University Press.

Bonderup-Dohn, N., Cranmer, S., Sime, J., de Laat, M., & Ryberg, T. (Eds.). (2018). *Networked Learning: Reflections and Challenges.* Cham: Springer. https://doi.org/10.1007/978-3-319-74857-3.

Cascone, K. (2000). The aesthetics of failure: 'Post-digital' tendencies in contemporary computer music. *Computer Music Journal, 24*(4), 12–18. https://doi.org/10.1162/014892600559489.

Carvalho, L. (2018). Networked societies for learning: emergent learning activity in connected and participatory meshworks. In M. Spector, B. Lockee, & M. Childress (Eds.), *Learning, Design, and Technology* (pp. 1–22). Cham: Springer. https://doi.org/10.1007/978-3-319-17727-4_55-1.

Cramer, F. (2015). What is 'post-digital'? In D. M. Berry & M. Dieter (Eds.), *Postdigital aesthetics: Art, computation and design* (pp. 12–26). New York: Palgrave Macmillan. https://doi.org/10.1057/9781137437204_2.

Cramer, F., & Jandrić, P. (2021). Postdigital: A Term That Sucks but Is Useful. *Postdigital Science and Education, 3*(3), 966–989. https://doi.org/10.1007/s42438-021-00225-9.

De Laat, M., & Dohn, N. B. (2019). Is networked learning postdigital education? *Postdigital Science and Education, 1*(1), 17–20. https://doi.org/10.1007/s42438-019-00034-1.

Deleuze, G., & Guattari, F. (2004). *A Thousand Plateaus: Capitalism and Schizophrenia.* London, UK: Continuum.

Fawns, T. (2019). Postdigital education in design and practice. *Postdigital Science and Education, 1*(1), 132–145. https://doi.org/10.1007/s42438-018-0021-8.

Feenberg, A. (2019). Postdigital or predigital? *Postdigital Science and Education, 1*(1), 8–9. https://doi.org/10.1007/s42438-018-0027-2.

Goodyear, P., & Carvalho, L. (2014) Framing the analysis of learning network architectures. In L. Carvalho & P. Goodyear (Eds.), *The Architecture of Productive Learning Networks* (pp. 259–276). New York, NY: Routledge.

Goodyear, P., Hodgson, V., & Steeples, C., (1998). Student experiences of networked learning in higher education. Research proposal to the UK JISC, October 1998. Lancaster: Lancaster University.

Gourlay, L. (2022). Digital masks: screens, selves and symbolic hygiene in online higher education. *Learning, Media and Technology, 47*(3), 398–406. https://doi.org/10.1080/17439884.2022.2039940.

Gourlay, L., & Oliver, M. (2016). It's not all about the learner: Reframing students' digital literacy as sociomaterial practice. In T. Ryberg, C. Sinclair, S. Bayne, & M. de Laat (Eds.), *Research, Boundaries, and Policy in Networked Learning* (pp. 77–92). Cham: Springer. https://doi.org/10.1007/978-3-319-31130-2_5.

Harney, S. (2015). Hapticality in the Undercommons. In R. Martin (Ed.), *The Routledge Companion to Art and Politics* (pp. 173–177). London, UK: Routledge.

Harney, S., & Moten, F. (2013). *The Undercommons: Fugitive Planning and Black Study.* New York, NY: Autonomedia.

Hodder, I. (2012). *Entangled: An Archaeology of the Relationship Between Humans and Things.* Chichester, UK: Wiley-Blackwell.

Hodder, I. (2013). Human-thing evolution: The selection and persistence of traits at Çatalhöyük, Turkey. In S. Bergerbrant & S. Sabatini (Eds.), *Counterpoint: Essays in Archaeology and Heritage Studies in Honour of Professor Kristian Kristiansen* (pp. 583–591). Oxford, UK: Archaeopress.

Hodder, I. (2016). *Studies in human-thing entanglement.* http://www.ian-hodder.com/books/studies-human-thing-entanglement. Accessed 29 November 2022.

Hodgson, V., & McConnell, D. (2019). Networked learning and postdigital education. *Postdigital Science and Education, 1*(1), 43–64. https://doi.org/10.1007/s42438-018-0029-0.

Hunter, M. (2016). Meshwork of paths and wayfaring in virtual world space and place. In J. Jordaan, C. Haddrell, & C. Alegria (Eds.), *Dialectics of Space and Place across Virtual and Corporeal Topographies* (pp. 33–43). Leiden: Brill. https://doi.org/10.1163/9781848885103_005.

Ingold, T. (2011). *Being Alive: Essays on Movement, Knowledge and Description.* London: Routledge. https://doi.org/10.4324/9780203818336.

Ingold, T. (2016). On human correspondence. *Journal of the Royal Anthropological Institute, 23*(1), 9–27. https://doi.org/10.1111/1467-9655.12541.

Jandrić, P., & Ford, D. (2022). Postdigital Ecopedagogies: Genealogies, Contradictions, and Possible Futures. *Postdigital Science and Education, 4*(3), 672–710. https://doi.org/10.1007/s42438-020-00207-3.

Jandrić, P., MacKenzie, A., & Knox, J. (2022). Postdigital Research: Genealogies, Challenges, and Future Perspectives. *Postdigital Science and Education.* https://doi.org/10.1007/s42438-022-00306-3.

Jones, C. (2015). *Networked Learning: An Educational Paradigm for the Age of Digital Networks.* Cham: Springer. https://doi.org/10.1007/978-3-319-01934-5.

Klenk, N. (2018). From network to meshwork: becoming attuned to difference in transdisciplinary environmental research encounters. *Environmental Science and Policy, 89,* 315–321. https://doi.org/10.1016/j.envsci.2018.08.007.

Lave, J., & Wenger, E. (1991). *Situated Learning: Legitimate Peripheral Participation.* Cambridge, UK: Cambridge University Press.

Leander, K., & McKim, K. (2003). Tracing the everyday sitings of adolescents on the internet: a strategic adaptation of ethnography across online and offline spaces. *Education, Communication and Information, 3*(2), 211–240. https://doi.org/10.1080/14636310303140.

Lefebvre, H. (1991). *The Production of Space.* Oxford: Blackwell.

Macfarlane B., & Gourlay, L. (2009). The reflection game: enacting the penitent self. *Teaching in Higher Education, 14*(4), 455–459. https://doi.org/10.1080/13562510903050244.

Melamed, J. (2016). Being together subversively, outside in the university of hegemonic affirmation and repressive violence, as things heat up (again). *American Quarterly, 68*(4), 981–991.

Merriam Webster. (2022). Twine. https://www.merriam-webster.com/dictionary/twine. Accessed 6 April 2023.

Negroponte, N. (1998). Beyond digital. Wired, 12. http://www.wired.com/wired/archive/6.12/negroponte.html. Accessed 8 September 2022.

Networked Learning Editorial Collective. (2021). Networked Learning: Inviting Redefinition. *Postdigital Science and Education, 3*(2), 312–325. https://doi.org/10.1007/s42438-020-00167-8.

Online Etymology Dictionary. (2022). Twine. https://www.etymonline.com/word/twine. Accessed 6 April 2023.

Oparah, J. (2014). Challenging Complicity: The Neoliberal University and the Prison-Industrial Complex. In P. Chatterjee & S. Maira, S. (Eds.), *The Imperial University* (pp. 99–121). Minneapolis, MN: University of Minnesota Press.

Pepperell, R., & Punt, M. (2000). The *Postdigital Membrane: Imagination, Technology and Desire.* Bristol, UK: Intellect.

Ponti, M., & Hodgson, V. (2006). Networked management learning for managers of small and medium enterprises. In S. Banks, V. Hodgson, C. R. Jones, B. Kemp, D. McConnell, & C. Smith (Eds.), *Proceedings of the Fifth International Conference on Networked Learning 2006.* Lancaster, UK: University of Lancaster. https://telearn.archives-ouvertes.fr/file/index/docid/190157/filename/Ponti_2006.pdf. Accessed 6 April 2023.

Shukaitis, S. (2009). Infrapolitics and the nomadic educational machine. In R. Amster, A. Deleon, L. Fernandez, A. Nocella, & D. Shannon (Eds.), *Contemporary Anarchist Studies.* London, UK: Routledge.

Siemens, G. (2005). Connectivism: A learning theory for the digital age. *International Journal of Instructional Technology and Distance Learning, 2*(1).

Undercommoning Collective. (2016). Undercommoning Within, Against and Beyond the University-as-Such. Roar, 5 June. https://roarmag.org/essays/undercommoning-collective-university-education/#:~:text=Undercommoning%20is%20the%20process%20of,crises%20instill%2C%20trigger%20and%20exploit. Accessed 30 November 2022.

Webb, D. (2018). Bolt-holes and breathing spaces in the system: on forms of academic resistance (or, can the university be a site of utopian resistance?) *Review of Education, Pedagogy, and Cultural Studies, 40*(2), 96–118. https://doi.org/10.1080/10714413.2018.1442081.

Wikipedia. (2022). Networked learning. https://en.wikipedia.org/wiki/Networked_learning. Accessed 6 April 2023.

Wikimedia Commons. (2022). Twine. https://commons.wikimedia.org/wiki/File:Ficelle_de_Sisal_-_2.jpg. Accessed 30 November 2022.

Zaslove, J. (2007). Exiled pedagogy: From the 'guerrilla' classroom to the university of excess. In M. Coté, R. Day, & G. de Peuter (Eds.), *Utopian Pedagogy* (pp. 93–107). Toronto, CA: University of Toronto Press.

Part II
Postdigital Research

Mapping and Tracing the Postdigital: Approaches and Parameters of Postdigital Research

Tim Fawns, Jen Ross, Henrietta Carbonel, Joe Noteboom, Sam Finnegan-Dehn, and McKenzie Raver

1 Prologue

This paper is co-authored by teachers and students of a pilot course within the postgraduate Education Futures programme at the Edinburgh Futures Institute at the University of Edinburgh.[1] The course, Postdigital Society,[2] introduced students to postdigital conceptions while they simultaneously produced exploratory postdigital analyses of technology-related topics (e.g., an Alexa EchoDot, employee monitoring software, the technological configuration of the course). Rather than starting with pre-set methods, students collaboratively identified, developed and combined methods through trial-and-error and dialogue. Through this, we discussed what makes an analysis 'postdigital', and played with creative ways of exploring the relations between digital and non-digital.

In this paper we reflect on our experiences of the course (including verbal and online discussions, work produced for assignments, and teacher and peer reviews of that work) to distil some key methodological considerations for postdigital research. We ask how postdigital research connects to, and is distinct from, other approaches that understand technology as entangled with the social and material (e.g., sociomaterialism or philosophy of technology), and from other 'post' traditions (e.g.,

---

[1] See https://efi.ed.ac.uk/education-futures/. Accessed 2 December 2022.

[2] See http://www.drps.ed.ac.uk/21-22/dpt/cxefie11012.htm. Accessed 2 December 2022.

T. Fawns (✉)
Monash Education Academy, Monash University, Clayton, VIC, Australia
e-mail: tim.fawns@monash.edu

J. Ross · H. Carbonel · J. Noteboom · S. Finnegan-Dehn · M. Raver
Edinburgh Futures Institute, University of Edinburgh, Edinburgh, UK
e-mail: jen.ross@ed.ac.uk; henrietta.carbonel@unidistance.ch; j.noteboom@ed.ac.uk

© The Author(s), under exclusive license to Springer Nature
Switzerland AG 2023
P. Jandrić et al. (eds.), *Postdigital Research*, Postdigital Science and Education,
https://doi.org/10.1007/978-3-031-31299-1_5

post-modernism or post-humanism). We then consider what constitutes quality in this kind of research; and what principles might inform future postdigital research.

2 Introduction

The term 'postdigital' is multifaceted. It might characterise a societal condition, an approach to research and critical enquiry, or a theoretical perspective, sensibility, or philosophical position. Sinclair and Hayes (2019) discuss the work that the prefix 'post' does in relation to the object that is 'post-ed' (e.g., 'modernism' or 'humanism'), proposing that it may serve most usefully as an indicator that its object is in need of questioning. 'Posts' need not be proposals that we are now past something (modernism, humanism, or 'digital') in a historical sense—indeed, digital and postdigital must co-exist for the latter to have currency. Rather, they can be proposals that a critical view be taken up as to what these terms mean in relation to the past, present, and future. For example, for Knox (2016: 31), the 'post' in critical posthumanism is about destabilising humanism, questioning its incontrovertibility.

At its simplest, a postdigital perspective is a rejection of digital as independent of material and social activity (Fawns 2019), or of political, economic, biological, and environmental factors (Jandrić et al. 2018). Digital activity is always realised through material means, and is always embedded in the world. For example, a postdigital research approach to education may consider how the digital activity of EdTech platforms is woven into broader material, human, political, economic, environmental and biological interrelations at institutional and societal levels. The postdigital can also be a way of seeing the continuation of digital as it is (always already) embedded in the world. For Cramer (2015), for example, it is unhelpful to think about digital outside of its forms of hybridity with analog. Peters and Besley (2019), Jandrić et al. (2018), Fawns (2019), and others have described postdigital as a philosophical position, theoretical perspective, or sensibility, in which digital is inseparable from the non-digital world.

A core premise of the postdigital, for us, is to challenge established ways of understanding digital technology. This includes questioning what counts as an 'evidence base' and how we might generate new kinds of knowledge. We also see postdigital research as not just interdisciplinary but transdisciplinary (Jandrić and Knox 2022). If different disciplines have different views on what counts as research (not to mention variance within disciplines), how do we negotiate transdisciplinary postdigital research?

Our writing of this paper, and the postgraduate course on postdigital analysis that brought us together, involved a productive negotiation of ideas between people of varying disciplinary backgrounds (including philosophy, IT, design, journalism, digital education) and research experience. There remain definitional and epistemological debates within our team of authors. In many contexts, this could be a significant barrier to collaboration. We do not believe that to be the case in postdigital scholarship (at least, not yet), where there is scope for generative debate around productive frictions and tensions. Indeed, the dissonance between our different backgrounds and perspectives has informed our argumentation. Thus, we argue for the potential value of multiplicity, and for holding open, within certain parameters that we discuss below, the definitions and criteria of postdigital research and scholarship. We have tried to be inclusive of different views, in the hope that what we present is an account of ways forward that welcome, rather than close down, possibilities for different kinds of contributors and contributions to postdigital research.

The paper is written by a team of people who were involved in a 5-week, 10-credit pilot course called Postdigital Society that ran as part of an Education Futures postgraduate programme within the Edinburgh Futures Institute at the University of Edinburgh. Tim Fawns designed and ran the course; Jen Ross was Programme Director and a peer observer of the learning and teaching activity; Joe Noteboom was a teaching assistant and PhD student; Henrietta Carbonel, Sam Finnegan-Dehn, and McKenzie Raver were students who accepted a class-wide invitation to contribute to this paper. In January–February 2022, 12 students took part in the pilot course, which was run asynchronously, punctuated by a 2-day hybrid 'fusion' workshop in the third week (i.e., half-way through), during which students elected to take part remotely or from within an on-site classroom in Edinburgh.

Throughout the course, students worked in groups, and individually, to develop and try out methods of analysis for a range of technological objects or practices. Some initial ideas of digital items that could be studied were offered to students (e.g. an Alexa EchoDot, a FitBit) and these were expanded by students through discussion to include employee monitoring software, the Miro online whiteboard used for collaboration within the course, and more. The aim was not to do postdigital research on these objects, but to explore what it means to take a postdigital view of them, what kinds of information might support such views, and how we might generate that information. Our explorations were guided by the course design, resources, and facilitators (Tim and Joe), but they were also student-led, with student groups discovering and designing their own ways of *potentially* conducting research and analysis on postdigital objects. Through a combination of trial-and-error and dialogue around what makes an analysis 'postdigital', students and staff played with creative ways of mapping and tracing the relations between digital and non-digital.

Henrietta, Sam and McKenzie contributed to the paper by offering written comments which were incorporated into a draft paper by Tim, as well as offering comments on the writing as it progressed. Jen and Joe contributed with comments, edits and passages of writing. Together, we consider our experiences of this course to distil some key methodological questions for postdigital research. In this, we take care to navigate paths forward that remain open to a diversity of disciplines and perspectives, since we see interdisciplinarity and collaboration as key to the potential value of the postdigital, as evidenced by the *Postdigital Science and Education* journal and the efforts of its editor, Petar Jandrić (Jandrić et al. 2019; Jandrić and Hayes 2019).

3 Different Lenses of a Postdigital View

Different ways of defining 'postdigital' were available via a list of course readings and their own literature searches, and students could repurpose these definitions in relation to their interests. They were encouraged to make their conceptions explicit, along with the implications for their area of inquiry. An aim of the course was that, however students conceived of the postdigital, it would help them to locate technologies in complex contexts, emphasise assumptions in need of questioning, and reveal absences and invisibilities (e.g., regarding datafication, determinism, imaginaries, rhetoric, surveillance, or ideology).

Sam, for example, understood postdigital as a method of surfacing relations between 'man and machine' that we often become accustomed to, without appreciating the complex results. For McKenzie, postdigital was a critical perspective that highlights the messy and unpredictable nature of technological integration and its relationship with humanism, posthumanism, physics and biology. For her, a postdigital view captured a merging of old and new and was 'both a rupture in our existing theories and their continuation' (Jandrić et al. 2018: 20). It was a way of seeing pervasive, covert, and less visible power structures, for instance in the increasingly reliant relationships with virtual assistants like Alexa. For Henrietta, postdigital inquiry entailed a sociomaterial view in which digital and non-digital not only shape each other in reciprocal and non-linear ways, but co-constitute a broader assemblage. An analogy might be that the activity of the arm is not merely shaped by the activity of the leg, both are co-constitutive parts of a greater, dynamic body. These different perspectives show that conceptions of the postdigital are still ripe for negotiation.

This is both liberating and challenging for researchers. Yet all three of these perspectives have important commonalities: they can help us look beyond the hype, risk, harms, and benefits of new technology, while also making visible technologies, processes, and practices that have become so familiar we no longer notice them. They can help us interrogate assumptions that stem from binaries or dichotomies between people and technology, digital and non-digital, online and offline, etc. This suggests to us that postdigital is not a theory or epistemology but a sensibility or a way of looking.

As students worked in groups on their analyses, they negotiated differing concepts while trying out methods of collecting, analysing, discussing, and sharing data with the aim of generating a range of connections. In social science research, creative methods are increasingly understood as necessary to grapple with the messiness of the social world (Law 2004), and the emergent and entangled nature of postdigital inquiry seems to us to be suited to methods that are flexible, imaginative, and inventive. Students tried out thought experiments and hypotheticals (e.g., a day in the life of a particular technology; what would happen if the object of analysis ceased to exist; how could a technology's functions be thought of differently?). They took up speculative points of view (e.g., taking the point of view of the technology—how does it see / influence the world?). They dabbled in metaphors (Lakoff and Johnson 2003; Weller 2022), storytelling, and speculative fiction (de Freitas and Truman 2020). The aim of speculative approaches was not to propose solutions, or artefacts to be made, but to ask questions and to 'debate potential ethical, cultural, social and political implications' (Dunne and Raby 2013: 47). They allowed students to consider hopes, dreams, fears, or concerns about new technologies, and to question underlying assumptions (Ross 2017: 219).

A range of other design approaches also contributed to the ideas for postdigital analyses generated during the course, including design scripts, prototypes, or storyboards (St. Amant 2017); journey-mapping (Howard 2014); interaction mapping; personas (Miaskiewicz and Kozar 2011); and explorations of subversive uses (e.g., using performance monitoring software to surveil leisure activities). Visualisation methods such as mind-mapping (Wheeldon and Ahlberg 2019) and empathy mapping (Siricharoen 2021) were employed. Alongside these were established research approaches, such as interviews, surveys, (auto-)ethnography, and observation; as well as newer, participant-informed approaches such as crowdsourcing (Estellés-Arolas and González-Ladrón-de-Guevara 2012). There were suggestions for document and data analysis, database searches; Internet searches; corpus or thematic text analysis; and image analysis. Theoretical frameworks and models were proposed for looking at empirical data through different lenses. Examples included Freire (1996), Orlikowski (2007), Gaventa's (2006) 'power cube', and the Political, Economic, Sociological, Technological, Legal and Environmental (PESTLE) framework (Aguilar 1967).

Despite the small class size, a significant range of approaches were raised and considered, and this provided a rich basis for examining what it might mean to conduct a postdigital inquiry. Each method had the potential to show relations between digital activity and its social and material contexts. These relations represented possible paths for closer analysis. Even the simple generation of lists of connections could powerfully illustrate the extent to which any digital technology or activity is intertwined in our lives, or the extent to which digital technology, more broadly, is pervasively intertwined in society. Simply by discussing methods that *could be used* for analysis, we discovered ways in which one technology is related to another, and the problem of trying to exclude certain types of digital activity when discussing others.

As helpful as these methods were, individually, it was in their combination that a richer sense of postdigital entanglement could be seen. Some interesting work involved combining ideas from different disciplines: a philosophy student took a creative writing approach, a design student situated storyboards in philosophy. Crossing disciplines was also collaborative: students from different fields approached topics together, blurring boundaries and stretching our collective understandings of the postdigital. In this context, the question of what 'counts' as research became contested and complex.

4 Mapping and Tracing the Postdigital

In developing their proposals for postdigital analysis, students first negotiated—with prompts from teachers where needed—what they cared about in relation to a technology, and what they wanted to know about it. Through our course conversations, we saw that this often involved moving focus from objects to practices involving the object (e.g., from an Alexa EchoDot to particular kinds of interactions with their instantiation of the entity, Alexa). However, identifying an initial technology is not always straightforward. As Knox (2019: 280) points out, 'the digital is so intimately entwined in our lived experiences and institutions that to set boundaries around some gadget or device seems somewhat arbitrary'. Technologies are always made up of multiple elements (Dron 2022) that are situated in particular use contexts (Kanuka 2008). For example, the Amazon Alexa EchoDot is an assembly of microphone, speakers, power source, Wi-Fi, software, AI, security protocol, cloud architecture, and more, and it manifests differently for different users in different settings. In defining the initial object of analysis, students needed to identify what combination of technologies in use mattered to them, and how this combination was embedded in wider cultures, systems, and contexts.

From there, these initial foci were expanded through creative and speculative mapping processes, to locate them in larger territories, made up of known and unknown elements. Metaphors of tracing and mapping from Deleuze and Guattari's (1987) rhizomatic philosophy can illuminate questions of method, traditions, epistemology and ontology, inclusivity, and dialogue. Mapping and tracing are different, but not mutually exclusive, ways of locating technology and technological practices in complexity. Mapping involves 'experimentation in contact with the real' (Deleuze and Guattari 1987: 12) to create ideas that can be torn up and rethought, and where any kinds of connection are possible. Tracing, on the other hand, consists of investigative methods (rather than the more speculative or generative methods of mapping) to examine and represent a phenomenon.

Mapping is a creative process that expands the possibilities of what can be thought about, and of seeing things in new orientations, beyond established disciplinary constraints. An example from our course was thinking about an employee monitoring software implementation as part of a neoliberal employment landscape, and then considering other features of that landscape, such as surveillance culture, unions, technology companies, and government regulation. By exposing new possibilities, this helped students to speculate about what *could be* relevant within a particular framing of this technology. From there, they could consider how these different elements were related and entangled. Such maps are not fixed, and not designed to find specific locations, but to continue to find new things (Wang 2015).

A challenge for students was to navigate the limits of their mapping: where and how to draw boundaries around their proposed methods. If everything is entangled, where should one stop tracing and mapping entanglements? For Barad (2007), from a sociomaterial view, in which different elements are co-constitutive parts of holistic assemblages, determining what is inside (and, consequently, what is outside) of the scope of inquiry requires 'agential cuts'. These are explicit or implicit choices around what is relevant and feasible to include in any appreciation of complexity, where the entanglements are potentially infinite. We cut, and we acknowledge the violence that this does to our understanding of objects in the world.

Cutting is also a necessary part of the negotiation of mutual understanding with others. In thinking through a proposal for postdigital analysis of employee monitoring software, for example, students considered how they might present a bounded object of analysis to which policymakers could relate. Such cuts suggest the potential value of focused questions, or other ways of guiding decisions about scope and relevance. However, we also see value in encouraging creative possibilities, under more flexible and long-lived circumstances, of expansive and free exploration. This is a tension between tracing and mapping: the former grounded and constrained, the latter abstract and free.

Tracing, by drawing on established measures, procedures, frameworks, and forms of observation, is constrained by pre-existing structures and conceptions. In our course, tracing was part of testing out proposed methods through closer examinations of how technologies were implicated in of actual and possible activity at different levels of abstraction (e.g., at personal, group, institutional or societal level). For example, students sometimes proposed methods of quantitative data collection and analysis, or interviews or ethnographic observation of day-to-day interactions with technology. Deleuze and Guattari (1987) warn that, by relying on pre-known, codified ways of thinking and doing, tracing reinforces entrenched ways of understanding. Referring to their rhizomatic logic, they argue that tracing merely shows 'impasses, blockages, incipient taproots, or points of structuration' (1987: 13).

Yet, established and empirical methods of investigation can produce evidence and arguments of a different sort from those produced through mapping and can help to 'ground' what has been mapped. For example, Sam tried out some speculative fiction, which portrayed challenging social encounters between an Alexa EchoDot, its owner, and a guest of the household, and demonstrated a creative mapping of a territory of inquiry that went beyond what can be factually known. He also annotated this story to propose some established ways of testing out his mapped relations, such as investigations of the datasets and algorithms held by Amazon. These latter forms of inquiry are suggestive of tracing: representations of what is already there, in forms we can already understand.

An advantage of mapping is the decentring of technology. While we might start with questions about a technology, these are seen as always embedded in social and material relations. Maps, of the kind we have described above, have no centre (Deleuze and Guattari 1987) and can expand in any direction. A refusal to centre or be centred (e.g., to focus too much on technology) but, instead, to emphasise relations and embeddedness seems, to us, to be a potential ingredient of postdigital research.

During the course, students were, therefore, encouraged to think about how particular, situated uses of technology or technological practices were embedded (e.g. how they were implicated in political or economic agendas, or in specific cultural contexts, or in environmental or biological concerns). Postdigital tracings, then, must be put onto these 'maps' (Deleuze and Guattari 1987), such that they are understood as tentative, precarious, and ephemeral ways of tying mapped elements together. The utility of tracings is that they can help us to see some of the historical, actual, and possible entanglements missed by mapping. For us, tracing involved ways of understanding how things are, or might be, entangled. In our employee monitoring software example, students discussed how they might use metrics, document analysis, and interviews to trace implications of a particular configuration of the software for relationships between workers and management, employee retention, worker behaviour and attitudes, customer service, productivity, or company finances.

Thus, mapping and tracing worked together in our course. Mapping helped us to identify more potential relations to trace, and tracing helped us to make more connections between mapped elements. Tracing could also help generate more points for mapping (e.g., looking at the times at which employees 'clocked in' could lead to speculation about building architecture, commuting, social activity between employees, etc.). Tracing need not be sequential (we could retrace our steps, or go back and take another path, or we could trace backwards from a variety of mapped elements), nor linear (we did not need to follow straight lines between mapped elements but could take detours along the way, and multiple threads could be traced between elements). Indeed, looking at multiple tracings together, rather than focusing only on individual threads, could help us to see a broader and more complex picture (see our discussion of Barad's 2007 lightning analogy, below). As we argue below, this negotiation of mapping and tracing may be a valuable aspect of postdigital exploration, beyond the kind involved in structured learning activities such as ours, including research.

5   Postdigital Inquiry and Research as Creative

Fawns and Schaepkens (2022) mapped ways in which candidates of an online proctored exam *might have been* oppressed by norms, scripts, and trust relations, produced by medical education institutions, educational technology companies, exam cultures and marketisation. Their postdigital analysis of these issues involved tracing hypotheticals and then remapping them within the area of inquiry. While Deleuze and Guattari (1987) conceive of tracing as stuck in dominant ways of understanding, in our course, we saw this as part of many of our speculative and creative processes of mapping.

For us, postdigital inquiry is as much about creation as it is about discovery. It creates ideas, ways of thinking, new methods, conversations, conclusions, and connections (between groups of people; areas of thought; technologies, people and wider systems and ecosystems). The word 'tracing' implies a going over of already existing lines of connection. It has connotations of representation (i.e., it shows what is) (Deleuze and Guattari 1987; Martin and Kamberelis 2013; Wang 2015) but this, we argue, is one of the ways in which mapping is grounded and shaped, by pulling and severing some connections, and creating others. Mapping is partly enabled by tracing, and the to-and-fro of mapping and tracing is the engine of the inquiry. For us, the distinction between tracing and mapping in postdigital inquiry is not whether it is generative or representational, but the manner in which it contributes to generation.

Postdigital relations are not simply *there*, waiting to be illuminated. They are intentionally (and, perhaps, unintentionally) created by researchers, who develop paths of inquiry that can help them locate technologies in complexity. This involves mapping relevant territory, and tracing entanglements within it that do not exist as physical entities (or *objects*) but as conceptions of invisible relations. To do this, researchers engage in a process of reification so that there is something that can be traced. Deleuze and Guattari (1987) are right that tracing rigidifies and reifies, and such reifications are distortions in need of re-mapping. Yet, as we have argued, tracing and mapping work in combination, and this combination provides ways of getting beyond previous understandings. Creative methods allow researchers to build useful and varied reifications that can be built upon to facilitate further mapping and tracing. Thus, it is possible to extricate ideas from tracings that might otherwise reinforce the dominance of tired old methods and 'put them to strange new uses' (Deleuze and Guattari 1987: 15).

In this context, it is appropriate for tracings to go beyond the actual. For us, postdigital inquiry must contain some analysis of 'digital' technology, but this could be connected to actual, historical, hypothetical, or possible activity. For example, one could conduct a postdigital analysis of a classroom in which devices and digital technology are banned, because such restrictions are a comment on the digital (or, at least, can be mapped as such). Further, the existence of digital possibilities outside of the class would inevitably influence possibilities within it (e.g., where a student decides to look something up on the Internet later) (Fawns 2019).

Barad (2007) describes the way a lightning strike involves a feeling out of possible pathways before committing to one and tracing it down to earth. This kind of tracing is not copying or revealing what is already there but selectively building pathways from a wide range of extant possibilities. It is a progressive, generative reification that makes use of multiple dimensions. These reifications are not the same as the phenomenon being analysed; they are proxies. Tracings are also not, in themselves, an analysis. They are different connections that can form a holistic view (as when alternative pathways are illuminated by the glow of the lightning strike that contains, and is partly constituted by, after-images of unrealised potentials). Like our students in their explorations within our course, postdigital researchers trace potentials in the hope of a lightning strike of creative inspiration. In this analogy, we might say that they are tracing from speculative and creative points of mapping (ideas floating in the clouds) to empirically grounded points. Those involved in postdigital inquiry also need to be open to remapping and retracing once they have seen what is illuminated by previous mapping and tracing. Finality is the adversary of postdigital inquiry, and postdigital research is never finished. Publication and forms of dissemination, for example, are not signs of completion but punctuation along the way to something else. This is part of holding open definitions of what postdigital research is.

6   Ontologies: Locating a Postdigital Tradition While Encouraging Interdisciplinarity

Considering how postdigital is related to other traditions can help us to more clearly see what it means (and does not mean) to do postdigital research. Postdigital scholarship is frequently informed by, ideas from philosophers of technology and media theorists. For example, the work of Feenberg (1999), Winner (1980), Postman (1993), McLuhan (2001), and others has frequently been cited within journal articles positioned as postdigital. In an education context, postdigital works have drawn on more recent publications by Hamilton and Friesen (2013), Kanuka (2008), Oliver (2011), and adjacent fields such as Networked Learning (e.g., Gourlay et al. 2021; Networked Learning Editorial Collective 2021; Carvalho, Goodyear, and de Laat 2016), digital education (e.g., Selwyn 2017), and critical digital pedagogy (e.g., Morris and Stommel 2018). Postdigital approaches also overlap with, or share properties, similarities, and historical roots with, other approaches to understanding complexity, such as posthumanism and sociomaterialism (Braidotti 2013, 2019; Fenwick 2015; Orlikowski 2007). In writing this paper, a discussion of sociomateriality, in particular, and its relationship with postdigital inquiry led us to a tentative position on ontology and interdisciplinarity, which we work through below.

Sociomaterial approaches take the whole system into account, focus on relations between human and non-human elements rather than on the separate elements, and understand knowledge, learning, and being, as embedded in these relations (Fenwick 2015). For example, a Cultural Historical Activity Theory (CHAT) approach (Sannino and Engeström 2018) can be taken to locate digital activity in the context of histories of interactions. Spatial or topological theories (e.g., Mol and Law 1994) can help us to focus on spaces as constantly being enacted through digital, social and material activity. Not all sociomaterial approaches are postdigital, particularly where they do not explicitly consider actual or potential digital activity. However, given our emphasis on holism, entanglements, and the inseparability of digital and other elements, we might ask whether a postdigital perspective is necessarily a sociomaterial perspective.

From a sociomaterial perspective, things do not exist independently, but are understood purely in terms of relations and holistic, co-emergence. Ontology and epistemology collapse into 'onto-epistemology' where understanding a thing, and how we come to understand that thing, are one and the same. There is no distinction between subject and object, or between 'knowledge, knowers and known' (Fenwick 2010: 112). This is a powerful perspective for understanding and dealing with complexity, because it challenges taken-for-granted conceptions of technologies, humans, and their combinations. It opens up productive postdigital analytical possibilities for complex situations, as evidenced in the work of Gourlay (2022a), Tyrrell and Shalavin (2022), and Wagener-Böck et al. (2023). But is this the only ontology capable of seeing the postdigital and its refusal to separate digital, material and social activity? Even within the authorship team of this paper, we have not reached consensus on whether postdigital is necessarily sociomaterial or not. On one hand, we are bound to understandings of complexity. On the other hand, we are committed to the promotion of interdisciplinarity and transdisciplinarity within the postdigital research community. For this reason, we propose holding open both views: that postdigital is necessarily sociomaterial, and also that it isn't.

This brings us to a philosophical and interdisciplinary tension between different ways of understanding technology in relation to the social and material environments in which it is situated. Either technology is separate from, but in a tight relationship with, the world around it; or it is part of the same broader, complex entity. Do technology and people have reciprocal effects on each other, for example, or are they co-constitutive elements of a greater, dynamic assemblage of multiple kinds of things acting and existing together? If both perspectives are useful (which we think they are), then we require a definition of postdigital that is able to account for at least two, and probably more, onto-epistemological positions.

We propose, then, that while individual research projects need ontological and epistemological clarity and coherence, the most valuable position to take in relation to postdigital scholarship *as a whole* (and the communities that produce and consume it), is one that is open to a plurality of philosophical positions. We do not want to argue that any epistemology will do for postdigital research. An understanding of the relationship between digital, social, and material as rooted in complexity entails rejecting notions of technological determinism, essentialism and instrumentalism in favour of a messier view of socio-technical relations. However, Feenberg (2019), for example, arrives at postdigital complexity via philosophy. Peters and Besley (2019) reject determinism and instrumentalism, not via sociomateriality, but by drawing on quantum theory and cybernetics.

To engage in collective action and meaning-making, researchers from different fields and disciplines need ways of negotiating mutual understanding of what they are dealing with. If collaboration across disciplines and traditions is a crucial ingredient of postdigital research (Jandrić and Knox 2022), this means valuing diverse perspectives and approaches. For instance, postdigital work is useful in helping us guard against reductive metrics (Fawns et al. 2021; Gourlay 2022b), but postdigital inquiry could definitely include, and benefit from, quantitative data and analysis, as long as it forms part of an account that locates the digital within complexity.

Productive dialogue will, we think, benefit less from pitting different epistemological positions against each other, or from overly constrained ideas of what it means to do postdigital research, and more from the generation of new meanings from thoughtful and reflexive engagement with different kinds of work in the hope of transforming postdigital understandings and research practices (see Mazzei and McCoy 2010 for a related argument about the work of Deleuze and Guattari). An openness to diverse perspectives is not a reluctance to examine the philosophical positions that inform methods and methodologies, and willingness to engage with these concepts will support postdigital research and its communities. Differing epistemological positions should be made explicit and held in productive tension. Lather (2006) introduces the concept of 'paradigm proliferation' to argue against reconciliation and against 'paradigm war', and instead to encourage 'thinking difference differently, a reappropriation of contradictory available scripts to create alternative practices of research as a site of being and becoming. In such a place, the task becomes to find a way to work on in the face of both the loss of legitimizing metanarratives and, paradoxically, the imposition of a new orthodoxy' (Lather 2006: 52).

For us, then the question becomes about 'negotiating' complex landscapes, and not closing down possibilities that may help us to do so now and in the future. Beyond simply rejecting determinism and instrumentalism, an aim for postdigital research is also the 'development of alternative narratives' (Jandrić and Knox 2022) that can open up new lines of thinking. While this can be made richer by being inclusive and bringing in different kinds of people, Jandrić and Knox caution that interdisciplinary work can become tightly defined and constrained by particular disciplines (e.g., data science), and '*en vogue* methods' that become 'dominant or overly authoritative' (2022: 790). Jandrić and Knox propose *transdisciplinarity* (crudely, where different methodologies brought from disciplines are transformed in the mix) as more conducive to cross-fertilisation than interdisciplinarity [where methodologies often 'remain fixed within specific disciplinary customs' (789)].

What matters here is not the nature of any single data source but how an ethic of critical reflexivity is threaded through processes of data generation, analysis, synthesis, interpretation, sense-making and application. For example, while some qualitative researchers have criticised quantitative research for often obscuring or reducing context and complexity, especially in relation to social activity, sociomaterialism has posed problems for a common focus of qualitative research on human experience as a guide to understanding the world, by challenging the idea of a stable, knowable and autonomous human subject. In discussing a post-qualitative turn, Lather and St. Pierre (2013: 630) ask whether qualitative inquiry will be possible: 'if we see language, the human, and the material not as separate entities mixed together but as completely imbricated "on the surface"'. The notion that research transforms what is researched may manifest as a heightened tension in interdisciplinary work where some parties are less familiar with challenging ideas of objectivity or neutrality.

In transdisciplinary research, new methodologies are created in which problems are put together collaboratively through new ways of seeing and constructing. For Lury (2021), St Pierre (2021), Barad (2007), and other philosophers of the sociomaterial, realities are made by and through methods and methodologies. St Pierre (2021), for example, argues for forms of post-qualitative inquiry that must be invented differently for each problem or study. Lury describes this in terms of 'putting a problem together' that is 'not acted on in a space but emerges across a problem space, from with-in and out-with' (2021: 3). As we saw in the learning and teaching context of our course, speculative design, for example, can be helpful for 'putting problems together' because of its potential to open up new perspectives on complex problems and alternative ways of being (Dunne and Raby 2013).

Thus, while holding postdigital inquiry open to a range of perspectives and disciplines is desirable, we also argue that these perspectives and disciplines should not remain untouched by their participation. Emergent new methodologies and ways of seeing should be produced through the research, and these should contain certain essential and desirable postdigital 'ingredients' that we outline below.

7   Ingredients for Postdigital Research

A potential criticism of postdigital research is that its conception and boundaries are too vague. Postdigital conceptions can be difficult to challenge where they are not tightly pinned down. In addition, too much stretching of the postdigital will cause the concept to lose integrity or become weak. For example, it is easy to expand what is covered by postdigital research by adding in new angles as they arise, such as by arguing that it also takes biology, or philosophy, or religion into account. However, we might also ask whether we need a unified conception of 'postdigital' to do postdigital research.

Postdigital research, for us, requires a perspective or sensibility that can be said to be postdigital, but it need not be labelled as such, and there may be more than one possible postdigital perspective. At the same time, it would be useful to have a way of differentiating those positions that are postdigital from those that are not. Thus, we propose an 'essential' ingredient, without which we would not call the research 'postdigital' (though we might defend the right of others to do so!), and some 'desirable' ingredients that we think indicate and strengthen postdigital research.

7.1   An Essential Ingredient for Postdigital Research: An On-Yet-Around Focus

Postdigital inquiry helps researchers to see technologies and practices as entangled parts of more complex wholes. As Morin (2014) suggests, when considering complexity, we need ways of distinguishing elements without disconnecting them or hiding their uncertainties, ambiguities, and contradictions. For this, researchers do not need a fixed focus on a specific technology or practice but a moveable gaze of inquiry, which must start somewhere, but then move around as they trace relations, and zoom in and out, from fine-grained features and micro-level activity, to broader assemblages and contexts. This movement involves navigating a tension between focusing *on* a technology to appreciate its uses and effects, and focusing on relations within and across wider systems or ecosystems or assemblages, of which technologies are only a part. Thus, postdigital inquiry entails a dual focus, simultaneously *on-yet-around* 'digital' technology and practices.

As an analogy, we can attend to the wonder of our planet (*on*), while simultaneously being aware of its cosmic insignificance—as just a small, integrated part of a far greater tapestry, moving in equilibrium with vast numbers of other elements (*around*). Similarly, we can attend to the diversity of functions and forms of particular technologies, individually or in combination, while also considering them as non-dominant, inseparable elements of wider tapestries of distributed activity. Or we might focus primarily on one aspect of society—economic, biological, political, environmental, cultural, etc., but not in isolation of the rest.

For us, a criterion of postdigital analysis is that it is accompanied by a refusal to remain in an isolating gaze. Ultimately, the focus of the gaze must move to connections, relations, and interstitial spaces. Taking an *on-yet-around* approach means we do not exclusively focus on technologies, while also holding those technologies and their embeddedness within view. Note that this is different from on-*and*-around, in that we do not simply focus on technology and its setting, but on the tensions between the two. The 'yet' signals that this is not simply a smooth and comfortable plurality but that these multiple understandings are in productive dissonance, each refusing the other rest and stability.

7.2 Desirable Ingredients

7.2.1 Including Diverse Voices and Perspectives

Postdigital inquiry involves a relentless effort to question or refuse boundaries: between technologies, people, environments, disciplines, epistemologies, and methodologies. It stretches and generates ideas through expansion and exploration. Bringing in researchers from various disciplines, geographical locations, cultures, etc., can help us see the world differently. One of the benefits of our Postdigital Society course was that, by inviting students from different disciplines, it encouraged all of us (including teachers and researchers) to be open to new ideas about what postdigital inquiry could be. Following Jandrić and Ford (2022), we suggest leaving the question of what counts as postdigital open for as long as possible, so that it is possible for members of a range of disciplines and backgrounds to participate. That definitions are not yet settled has valuable productive possibilities for research and dialogue.

7.2.2 Fostering Transdisciplinarity

In our course, working across disciplines opened up new lines of conversation, and a greater repertoire of possible methods. Similarly, in a research context, we suggest that postdigital thinking can be strengthened through different views of the empirical as well as through consideration of the hypothetical (such as in the examples, above, of speculative fiction or the ideation of methods about design fictions). In our course, however, there were also moments of frustration and inertia, and sites of tension and struggle. For example, students could become creatively paralysed, or to revert to looking for quantifiable hypotheses or causal explanations that were difficult to reconcile with a postdigital view of non-linear and complex relations between elements. Similar challenges may arise where researchers with different epistemologies try to negotiate methods and interpretations with a view to examining postdigital complexity.

On the other hand, current postdigital research is often weighted towards critique of technology. While this can be seen as part of broader critical movements (e.g., in relation to educational technology research) (see Macgilchrist 2021), it can also be a blind spot around the need to engage productively or effectively with digital technology. Mixing disciplines can help us to look for risks, potential harms and ethical complexity, and also positive ways to engage with technology such that the emergent activity aligns with the values and purposes of different stakeholders (Fawns 2022). Such negotiation of views, disciplines and contexts, has great potential for people to learn from others and, individually and collectively, to expand their horizons (Aitken 2021).

7.2.3 Working Creatively, Speculatively, and Compositionally

In principle, any methods could be used within a broader postdigital approach, but a holistic view across methods is suggestive, to us, of working speculatively and compositionally. Being open to transdisciplinary work calls for new ways of thinking and doing research. Where Hurley and Al-Ali (2021) propose a turn to post-qualitative approaches as part of a 'refusal of prescriptive methods', we would extend this to an openness to 'put the problem together' in creative and inclusive ways by drawing on a range of possible methods. Yet, we cannot simply enact a series of disjointed methods and call it postdigital research, and there are tensions and opportunities that emerge in the combination of approaches.

Creative and compositional approaches can be framed and discussed within a post-qualitative framework. As we discussed in relation to other posts, above, this does not signal a complete rupture with qualitative methodologies (nor the outright rejection of quantitative ones). Instead, working post-qualitatively means taking up methods and methodologies – and creating new ones – in ways that are sensitive to the realities they produce.

This sensitivity has been described in a number of ways, including as what Lury and Wakeford (2012) call 'inventive methods', but Lury's (2021) recent work on compositional methodologies and problem spaces is particularly apt for postdigital research. Here, we might learn from our students' mixing of disciplinary design approaches (e.g. storyboarding and journey-mapping) with more speculative design methods aimed at exploring and creating 'possible futures under conditions of complexity and uncertainty' (Ross 2018: 197). Rather than trying to create aspirational futures, the aim was to create a diverse range of possibilities to help us think about how things might become (Facer 2016).

Speculative methods are not only about the future, but are rooted in the present, shedding light on both the issues that are of current concern, but also what is left aside or silenced (Law 2004: 113). They can offer a new perspective on what matters now, 'what issues and problems we have inherited and what debates define what can and cannot currently be thought about or imagined' (Ross 2017: 220). Finally, speculative design is open to different disciplinary approaches, each participant contributing to the process from the perspective of their own field. Thus, speculative approaches can be used to ensure that a diversity of points of view, disciplines, and cultures are included and to offer a rich and deep palette of possibles (Gough 2010).

Compositional methodologies can generate ambiguous problems in which questions and answers are blurred (Ross 2023). Indeed, even in the educational context of our course, many of our attempts to develop approaches to postdigital inquiry were helpful in generating a more complex sense of problems and questions such that they became unanswerable. For example, through a process of creative visualisation and discussion, the question of how an online Miro whiteboard shapes the dialogue that happens in a hybrid class quickly became entangled in institutional policy, infrastructure, time zones, pedagogical approach, and the personal circumstances of individual students. Importantly, in research, this does not mean that 'anything goes' because the legitimacy of an inventive method 'is tied to its ability to engage with and affect the problem it addresses' (Ross 2023: 62).

7.3   *What Makes Good Postdigital Research?*

The word postdigital is useful to connect together members of a research community, and to remind researchers to look beyond the digital. But 'postdigital' is just a word, to be used while it is useful (Cramer and Jandrić 2021). We think that it will remain so until looking simultaneously at, and beyond, technology, and digital activity, is embedded in mainstream research. There are not yet clear rules for postdigital research, but whether or not a project can or should be labelled as postdigital is less important than whether it contributes to our understanding of technology as embedded in complexity. Part of the purpose of postdigital inquiry is to help us 'keep looking for ways to broaden our view' (Ross and Collier 2016: 28). Good postdigital research, then, is less about any particular output and more about the productive punctuation of a broader, ongoing conversation, that opens up further inquiry through generating new questions, rather than closing it down with answers.

8   Conclusions

In this paper, we have reflected on our experiences, as teachers and students, of a pilot course called Postdigital Society at the Edinburgh Futures Institute (part of the University of Edinburgh), and used these reflections to consider what it means to do postdigital research. In the course, students from different disciplines worked together to develop a range of proposed methods for postdigital analyses of technology-related topics (e.g., an Alexa EchoDot, employee monitoring software, an online Miro whiteboard). Applying our experiences to a research context has raised questions about how we define objects of postdigital analysis, and what epistemological constraints are involved in taking up a postdigital perspective.

We have argued that it is valuable to think about epistemology and ways of conceptualising complexity in postdigital research, and about reconciling these with different kinds of, potentially, creative and speculative methods. Given the value of transdisciplinary work, we have argued for holding open postdigital definitions and epistemologies, without losing critical and embedded views of technology. For us, postdigital is not an epistemology, or a particular approach to research, but a way of focusing that situates technology or practices in complexity. For this, we offer some essential and desirable ingredients for postdigital research.

Essentially, postdigital inquiry should focus on-yet-around technology, meaning that it notices the characteristics of the technology but also looks beyond them to the relations between those characteristics and the wider context in which they are embedded. We also propose some desirable or aspirational characteristics (research can still be characterised as postdigital without these, but they support the generation of valuable opportunities for developing the field).

Firstly, we see it as beneficial to welcome diverse perspectives and disciplines in ways that support the generation of critical views and innovative methods. Secondly, this can be helped by fostering transdisciplinarity, in the sense that different disciplinary perspectives and traditions cross-fertilise to produce something beyond the narrow view of any one discipline. Thirdly, postdigital inquiry benefits from working creatively, speculatively, and compositionally, where methods and methodologies are generated to encourage imagination and discussion of a range of alternative possible futures.

All of these ingredients can promote further critical dialogue and inquiry about the role of digital technology as embedded in society. That, for us, is what characterises 'good' postdigital research.

Acknowledgements Thanks to the students of our Postdigital Society pilot, and to Petar Jandrić for his generous support in the writing of this chapter.

This chapter was first published as Fawns, T., Ross, J., Carbonel, H., Noteboom, J., Finnegan-Dehn, S., & Raver, M. (2023). Mapping and Tracing the Postdigital: Approaches and Parameters of Postdigital Research. *Postdigital Science and Education*. https://doi.org/10.1007/s42438-023-00391-y. The original text is reproduced verbatim.

References

Aguilar, F. (1967). *Scanning the business environment*. New York: Macmillan.

Aitken, G. (2021). A Postdigital Exploration of Online Postgraduate Learning in Healthcare Professionals: A Horizontal Conception. *Postdigital Science and Education*, 3(1), 181–197. https://doi.org/10.1007/s42438-020-00103-w.

Barad, K. (2007). *Meeting the Universe Halfway: Quantum Physics and the Entanglement of Matter and Meaning*. Durham, NC: Duke University Press. https://doi.org/10.1215/9780822388128.

Braidotti, R. (2013). *The posthuman*. London: Polity Press.

Braidotti, R. (2019). *Posthuman knowledge*. London: Polity Press.

Carvalho, L., Goodyear, P., & de Laat, M. (2016). *Place-Based Spaces for Networked Learning*. New York and London: Routledge.

Cramer, F., & Jandrić, P. (2021). Postdigital: A Term That Sucks but Is Useful. *Postdigital Science and Education, 3*(3), 966-989. https://doi.org/10.1007/s42438-021-00225-9.

Cramer, F. (2015). What is 'post-digital'? In D. M. Berry & M. Dieter (Eds.), *Postdigital aesthetics: Art, computation and design* (pp. 12–26). New York: Palgrave Macmillan. https://doi.org/10.1057/9781137437204_2.

de Freitas, E., & Truman, S. E. (2020). New Empiricisms in the Anthropocene: Thinking With Speculative Fiction About Science and Social Inquiry. *Qualitative Inquiry*. https://doi.org/10.1177/1077800420943643.

Deleuze, G., & Guattari, F. (1987). *A thousand plateaus: Capitalism and schizophrenia*. Minneapolis, MN: University of Minnesota Press.

Dron, J. (2022). Educational technology: What it is and how it works. *AI & SOCIETY, 37*(1), 155–166. https://doi.org/10.1007/s00146-021-01195-z.

Dunne, A., & Raby, F. (2013). *Speculative everything: Design, fiction, and social dreaming*. Cambridge, MA: The MIT Press.

Estellés-Arolas, E., & González-Ladrón-de-Guevara, F. (2012). Towards an integrated crowdsourcing definition. *Journal of Information Science, 38*(2), 189–200. https://doi.org/10.1177/0165551512437638.

Facer, K. (2016). Using the Future in Education: Creating Space for Openness, Hope and Novelty. In H. E. Lees & N. Noddings (Eds.), *The Palgrave International Handbook of Alternative Education* (pp. 63–78). London: Palgrave Macmillan. https://doi.org/10.1057/978-1-137-41291-1_5.

Fawns, T. (2019). Postdigital Education in Design and Practice. *Postdigital Science and Education, 1*(1), 132–145. https://doi.org/10.1007/s42438-018-0021-8.

Fawns, T. (2022). An Entangled Pedagogy: Looking Beyond the Pedagogy—Technology Dichotomy. *Postdigital Science and Education, 4*(3), 711–728. https://doi.org/10.1007/s42438-022-00302-7.

Fawns, T., & Schaepkens, S. (2022). A Matter of Trust: Online Proctored Exams and the Integration of Technologies of Assessment in Medical Education. *Teaching and Learning in Medicine, 34*(4), 444–453. https://doi.org/10.1080/10401334.2022.2048832.

Fawns, T., Aitken, G., & Jones, D. (2021). Ecological Teaching Evaluation vs the Datafication of Quality: Understanding Education with, and Around, Data. *Postdigital Science and Education, 3*(1), 65–82. https://doi.org/10.1007/s42438-020-00109-4.

Feenberg, A. (1999). *Questioning Technology*. London and New York: Routledge. https://doi.org/10.4324/9780203022313.

Feenberg, A. (2019). Postdigital or Predigital? *Postdigital Science and Education, 1*(1), 8–9. https://doi.org/10.1007/s42438-018-0027-2.

Fenwick, T. (2010). Re-thinking the 'thing': Sociomaterial approaches to understanding and researching learning in work. *Journal of Workplace Learning, 22*(1/2), 104–116. https://doi.org/10.1108/13665621011012898.

Fenwick, T. (2015). Sociomateriality and Learning: A Critical Approach. In D. Scott & E. Hargreaves (Eds.), *The SAGE Handbook of Learning* (pp. 83–93). London: SAGE. https://doi.org/10.4135/9781473915213.

Freire, P. (1996). *Pedagogy of the oppressed*. London: Penguin Books.

Gaventa, J. (2006). Finding the Spaces for Change: A Power Analysis. *IDS Bulletin, 37*(6), 23–33. https://doi.org/10.1111/j.1759-5436.2006.tb00320.x.

Gough, N. (2010). Can We Escape the Program? Inventing Possible-Impossible Futures in/for Australian Educational Research. *Australian Educational Researcher, 37*(4), 9–42. https://doi.org/10.1007/BF03216935.

Gourlay, L. (2022a). Presence, Absence, and Alterity: *Fire Space* and Goffman's *Selves* in Postdigital Education. *Postdigital Science and Education, 4*(1), 57–69. https://doi.org/10.1007/s42438-021-00265-1.

Gourlay, L. (2022b). Surveillance and Datafication in Higher Education: Documentation of the Human. *Postdigital Science and Education.* https://doi.org/10.1007/s42438-022-00352-x.

Hamilton, E., & Friesen, N. (2013). Online Education: A Science and Technology Studies Perspective. *Canadian Journal of Learning and Technology, 39*(2). https://doi.org/10.21432/T2001C.

Howard, T. (2014). Journey mapping: A brief overview. *Communication Design Quarterly, 2*(3), 10–13. https://doi.org/10.1145/2644448.2644451.

Hurley, Z., & Al-Ali, K. (2021). Feminist Postdigital Inquiry in the Ruins of Pandemic Universities. *Postdigital Science and Education, 3*(3), 771–792. https://doi.org/10.1007/s42438-021-00254-4.

Jandrić, P., & Ford, D. (2022). Postdigital Ecopedagogies: Genealogies, Contradictions, and Possible Futures. *Postdigital Science and Education, 4*(3), 672-710. https://doi.org/10.1007/s42438-020-00207-3.

Jandrić, P., & Hayes, S. (2019). The postdigital challenge of redefining academic publishing from the margins. *Learning, Media and Technology, 44*(3), 381–393. https://doi.org/10.1080/17439884.2019.1585874.

Jandrić, P., & Knox, J. (2022). The Postdigital Turn: Philosophy, Education, Research. *Policy Futures in Education, 20*(7), 780-795. https://doi.org/10.1177/14782103211062713.

Jandrić, P., Knox, J., Besley, T., Ryberg, T., Suoranta, J., & Hayes, S. (2018). Postdigital science and education. *Educational Philosophy and Theory, 50*(10), 893–899. https://doi.org/10.1080/00131857.2018.1454000.

Jandrić, P., Ryberg, T., Knox, J., Lacković, N., Hayes, S., Suoranta, J., Smith, M., Steketee, A., Peters, M., McLaren, P., Ford, D. R., Asher, G., McGregor, C., Stewart, G., Williamson, B., & Gibbons, A. (2019). Postdigital Dialogue. *Postdigital Science and Education, 1*(1), 163–189. https://doi.org/10.1007/s42438-018-0011-x.

Kanuka, H. (2008). Understanding e-learning technologies-in-practice through philosophies-in-practice. In T. Anderson (Ed.), *The theory and practice of online learning* (pp. 91–118). Athabasca: Athabasca University Press.

Knox, J. (2016). Posthumanism and the massive open online course: Contaminating the subject of global education. *Distance Education, 37*(3), 376–379. https://doi.org/10.1080/01587919.2016.1226195.

Knox, J. (2019). Postdigital as (Re)Turn to the Political. *Postdigital Science and Education, 1*(2), 280–282. https://doi.org/10.1007/s42438-019-00058-7.

Lakoff, G., & Johnson, M. (2003). *Metaphors we live by.* Chicago, IL: University of Chicago Press.

Lather, P. (2006). Paradigm proliferation as a good thing to think with: teaching research in education as a wild profusion. *International Journal of Qualitative Studies in Education, 19*(1), 35–57. https://doi.org/10.1080/09518390500450144.

Lather, P., & St. Pierre E. A. (2013). Post-qualitative research. *International Journal of Qualitative Studies in Education, 26*(6), 629-633. https://doi.org/10.1080/09518398.2013.788752.

Law, J. (2004). *After Method: Mess in Social Science Research.* London: Routledge. https://doi.org/10.4324/9780203481141.

Lury, C. (2021). *Problem Spaces: How and Why Methodology Matters.* London: Polity Press.

Lury, C., & Wakeford, N. (Eds.). (2012). *Inventive Methods: The Happening of the Social.* London and New York: Routledge.

Macgilchrist, F. (2021). What is 'critical' in critical studies of edtech? Three responses. *Learning, Media and Technology, 46*(3), 243–249. https://doi.org/10.1080/17439884.2021.1958843.

Martin, A. D., & Kamberelis, G. (2013). Mapping not tracing: Qualitative educational research with political teeth. *International Journal of Qualitative Studies in Education, 26*(6), 668–679. https://doi.org/10.1080/09518398.2013.788756.

Mazzei, L. A., & McCoy, K. (2010). Thinking with Deleuze in qualitative research. *International Journal of Qualitative Studies in Education, 23*(5), 503–509. https://doi.org/10.1080/0951839 8.2010.500634.

McLuhan, M. (2001). *Understanding media: The extensions of man.* London and New York: Routledge.

Miaskiewicz, T., & Kozar, K. A. (2011). Personas and user-centered design: How can personas benefit product design processes? *Design Studies, 32*(5), 417–430. https://doi.org/10.1016/j. destud.2011.03.003.

Mol, A., & Law, J. (1994). Regions, networks and fluids: anaemia and social topology. *Social Studies of Science, 24*(4), 641–671. https://doi.org/10.1177/030631279402400402.

Morin, E. (2014). *Introduction à la pensée complexe.* Paris: Editions Seuil.

Morris, S. M., & Stommel, J. (2018). *An Urgency of Teachers.* Hybrid Pedagogy Inc.

Networked Learning Editorial Collective, Gourlay, L., Rodríguez-Illera, J. L., Barberà, E., Bali, M., Gachago, D., Pallitt, N., Jones, C., Bayne, S., Hansen, S. B., Hrastinski, S., Jaldemark, J., Themelis, C., Pischetola, M., Dirckinck-Holmfeld, L., Matthews, A., Gulson, K. N., Lee, K., Bligh, B., Thibaut, P., … Knox, J. (2021). Networked learning in 2021: A Community Definition. *Postdigital Science and Education, 3*(2), 326–369. https://doi.org/10.1007/s42438-021-00222-y.

Networked Learning Editorial Collective. (2021). Networked Learning: Inviting Redefinition. *Postdigital Science and Education, 3*(2), 312–325. https://doi.org/10.1007/s42438-020-00167-8.

Oliver, M. (2011). Technological determinism in educational technology research: Some alternative ways of thinking about the relationship between learning and technology. *Journal of Computer Assisted Learning, 27*(5), 373–384. https://doi.org/10.1111/j.1365-2729.2011. 00406.x.

Orlikowski, W. J. (2007). Sociomaterial Practices: Exploring Technology at Work. *Organization Studies, 28*(9), 1435–1448. https://doi.org/10.1177/0170840607081138.

Peters, M. A., Besley, T. (2019). Critical Philosophy of the Postdigital. *Postdigital Science and Education, 1*(1), 29–42 https://doi.org/10.1007/s42438-018-0004-9.

Postman, N. (1993). *Technopoly: The Surrender of Culture to Technology.* London: Random House.

Ross, J. (2017). Speculative method in digital education research. *Learning, Media and Technology, 42*(2), 214–229. https://doi.org/10.1080/17439884.2016.1160927.

Ross, J. (2018). Speculative Method as an Approach to Researching Emerging Educational Issues and Technologies. In L. Hamilton & J. Ravenscroft (Eds.), *Building Research Design in Education* (pp. 197–210). London: Bloomsbury Academic.

Ross, J. (2023). *Digital futures for learning: Speculative methods and pedagogies.* New York: Routledge.

Ross, J., & Collier, A. (2016). Complexity, mess and not-yetness: teaching online with emerging technologies. In G. Veletsianos (Ed.), *Emergence and Innovation in Digital Learning: Foundations and Applications.* Athabasca: Athabasca University Press.

Sannino, A., & Engeström, Y. (2018). Cultural-historical activity theory: Founding insights and new challenges. *Cultural-Historical Psychology, 14*(3), 43–56. https://doi.org/10.17759/chp.2018140304.

Selwyn, N. (2017). *Education and technology: Key issues and debates.* 2nd Ed. London: Bloomsbury.

Sinclair, C., & Hayes, S. (2019). Between the Post and the Com-Post: Examining the Postdigital 'Work' of a Prefix. *Postdigital Science and Education, 1*(1), 119–131. https://doi.org/10.1007/s42438-018-0017-4.

Siricharoen, W. V. (2021). Using Empathy Mapping in Design Thinking Process for Personas Discovering. In P. C. Vinh & A. Rakib (Eds.), *Context-Aware Systems and Applications, and Nature of Computation and Communication* (pp. 182–191). Cham: Springer. https://doi.org/10.1007/978-3-030-67101-3_15.

St. Amant, K. (2017). Of Scripts and Prototypes: A Two-Part Approach to User Experience Design for International Contexts Applied Research. *Technical Communication, 64*(2), 113-125.

St. Pierre, E. A. (2021). Post Qualitative Inquiry, the Refusal of Method, and the Risk of the New. *Qualitative Inquiry, 27*(1), 3–9. https://doi.org/10.1177/1077800419863005.

Tyrrell, J., Shalavin, C. A (2022). Sociomaterial Lens on Crowdsourcing for Learning. *Postdigital Science and Education 4*(3), 729–752. https://doi.org/10.1007/s42438-022-00313-4.

Wagener-Böck, N., Macgilchrist, F., Rabenstein, K., & Bock, A. (2023). From Automation to Symmation: Ethnographic Perspectives on What Happens in Front of the Screen. *Postdigital Science and Education, 5*(1), 136-153. https://doi.org/10.1007/s42438-022-00350-z.

Wang, C.-L. (2015). Mapping or tracing? Rethinking curriculum mapping in higher education. *Studies in Higher Education, 40*(9), 1550–1559. https://doi.org/10.1080/0307507 9.2014.899343.

Weller, M. (2022). *Metaphors of Ed Tech*. Athabasca: Athabasca University Press. https://doi.org/10.15215/aupress/9781771993500.01.

Wheeldon, J., & Ahlberg, M. (2019). Mind Maps in Qualitative Research. In P. Liamputtong (Ed.), *Handbook of Research Methods in Health Social Sciences* (pp. 1113–1129). Singapore: Springer. https://doi.org/10.1007/978-981-10-5251-4_7.

Winner, L. (1980). Do artifacts have politics? *Daedalus, 109*(1), 121–136. https://doi.org/10.432 4/9781315259697-21.

Big Bioinformational Education Sciences: New Biodigital Methods and Knowledge Production in Education

Ben Williamson

1 Introduction

Research on human biology in fields including neuroscience and genetics is increasingly enacted with advanced digital technologies. Methods such as brain scanning and neuroimaging to study neurobiology and bioinformatics hardware and software in genetics are highly data-intensive and depend on complex sociotechnical infrastructures of digital technologies, scientific epistemologies and methodologies, social relations and practices, which are transforming how biological science is enacted and the knowledge it produces (Pitts-Taylor 2016; Leonelli 2016). In data-intensive biological science, new knowledge about human lives, bodies, and behaviours is produced by large-scale initiatives using computers, databases, and analytics algorithms, generating novel renderings and understandings of internally-embodied states and processes (Vermeulen 2016). As such, human bodies, lives, and actions have been made legible as 'bioinformation' through analysis and knowledge production with 'biodigital' methods (Parry and Greenhough 2018). Bioinformational research can thus be understood as typically 'postdigital' in producing new computational understandings of biology, transforming the routine ways biological research itself is practised, and generating new 'biodigital' techniques for the treatment, modification, and intervention into embodied processes (Peters, Jandrić, and Hayes 2022).

In recent years, the digital methods of neuroscience and genetics have been put to the task of analysing educationally-relevant biological processes, including the neurobiological structures and processes and genetic associations that underpin learning, cognition and achievement (e.g. Howard Jones et al. 2021; Visscher 2022). These emerging fronts of data-intensive research related to education translate the

B. Williamson (✉)
Centre for Research in Digital Education, University of Edinburgh, Edinburgh, UK
e-mail: ben.williamson@ed.ac.uk

P. Jandrić et al. (eds.), *Postdigital Research*, Postdigital Science and Education,
https://doi.org/10.1007/978-3-031-31299-1_6

93

biological into bioinformational formats, opening up human subject data to a range of novel forms of analysis and potentially policy-relevant knowledge production. In hybridizing biological and informatic modes of investigation, this new biological research in education adopts particular biodigital methodologies that have their own distinctive histories, contexts, and practices. As Leonelli (2019: 4) notes, new forms of data-intensive discovery at the intersection of biology and informatics represent 'exciting prospects for biology', but 'the increasing power of computational algorithms requires a proportional increase in critical thinking'. Framed by promissory discourses of scientific precision and objectivity in education and motivated by political interests in the future social and economic benefits of data-driven biomedical advances, the increasing computational power of neuroscience and genetics has profound consequences for how educational phenomena are understood and acted on through both policy and practice.

This chapter examines the methodologies and knowledge production of bioinformational research in education. It approaches the neural and genetic sciences as research assemblages constituted of a variety of situated social, epistemic, material, discursive, and institutional elements that make objects of investigation legible, explainable and understandable in new ways. Informed by research in science and technology studies, it investigates the histories, evolution, and lively sociotechnical enactments of research devices and practices as well as the social consequences that follow when specific assemblages of methods generate new 'discoveries' that circulate knowledge into new settings (Pickersgill 2013; Cruz 2022). Bioinformation of all kinds, whether genetic, neural, or otherwise, is co-produced through distinctive scientific ways investigating phenomena, interactions with industrial developers of computing machinery, political science funding priorities, and value-creating strategies (Parry and Greenhough 2018). For example, critical neuroscience studies examine 'how neuroscientists construct their objects of study, and how they measure, interpret, and translate neurobiological underpinnings of the behaviors and social phenomena they seek to explain' (Choudhury and Wannyn 2022: 33). Likewise studies of the genetic sciences examine how biological knowledge production is socially, politically and economically embedded and interdependent with complex technological apparatuses and data-driven methodologies, which are reconfiguring how biology is investigated, interpreted and understood (Stevens 2013).

Rather than 'discovering' biological reality in higher fidelity, methods in the genetic and neural sciences fabricate new ways of conceiving bodies, brains, and human life and behaviour (Rose 2007; Rose and Abi-Rached 2013). In other words, a biodigital research assemblage is no mere vehicle for the collection, storage and analysis of bioinformation or the 'discovery' of knowledge, but an active constituent factor that plays a part at multiple stages in shaping bioinformation into knowledge (Leonelli 2016). In this respect, biological sciences are enacted through postdigital research assemblages in which the biological, the digital, and the informational converge to produce very different figurations of life and therefore its potential for intervention (Peters, Jandrić, and Hayes 2021; Gulson and Webb 2018).

Two distinctive sets of technologies are deployed to produce bioinformational knowledge in education: neurotechnologies like brain scanning devices and brain-computer interfaces to generate neural information related to learning, and bioinformatics software and biobanking databases to produce knowledge about the genetic associations underpinning educational attainment. Studying the emergence of new approaches in the neural and genetic sciences can illuminate how knowledge claims and proposals for educational intervention based on scientific insights into human biology are in fact inseparable from the biodigital research assemblages through which biology itself has been translated into bioinformation.

The chapter first provides an outline of key approaches in bioinformational education science. The following sections then explore the specific arrangements of bioinformational education science: first, the organizational arrangements that have taken shape around bioinformational investigation and knowledge production in education; second, the biodigital methods that are designed and deployed to make new discoveries about the biological aspects of educationally-relevant phenomena; and third, the particular characteristic forms of bioinformational knowledge they produce. Postdigital theory approaches digital technologies as socially, politically, and economically embedded and consequential (Knox 2019), and signifies convergence between biology and information as well as between science and technology (Jandrić 2021).

The chapter therefore conceives of bioinformational education as postdigital research assemblages that are constituted by various relations among biological, informational, scientific, and technical—as well as educational—elements. It contributes a detailed analysis of postdigital science and education as it is taking shape at the nexus of the biological, informatic, and educational sciences. As befits an analysis of complex and relational postdigital phenomena, the research underpinning this chapter involved multiple methods. Methods included social network analysis to trace the multisector, organizational, and interdisciplinary relations constituting bioinformational education, documentary analysis of scientific texts to surface its main conceptual schema, and technical analysis of the software and hardware deployed in the generation of bioinformation. The imbrications of the biological and the informational in new educational sciences are generating challenging ways of thinking about education in terms of biologically embodied processes that can only be made legible as objects of understanding and intervention through data scientific practices of analysing bioinformation.

2   Bioinformation and Education

Bioinformation refers conventionally to information arising from analyses of data collected from biological organisms, which are usually used to identify their structure or function, although it has become a more capacious concept in the context of rapid advances in the collection of health data, non-health data, and other social or behavioural data (Parry and Greenhough 2018). Rather than referring to biomedical data or genetic data alone, bioinformation derives from multiple sources, including the brain data used in the various disciplines and subdisciplines of neuroscience and cognitive science, and the biometric and psychophysiological data recorded for use in the psychological sciences. Bioinformational education in this chapter refers to the collection and analysis of multimodal data related to biological structures and functions considered to be proximate to or associated with educationally relevant outcomes, learning processes, and behaviours. Bioinformational education research is primarily a site of scientific inquiry and knowledge production, constituted by expert scientific communities working in the genetic and neurosciences, though it also involves actors from other disciplines and the commercial, policy and education sectors, and generates implications for research, policy, and practice in education.

Bioinformational education has emerged from at least three intersecting developments. First, it is related to the rapid proliferation of the 'learning sciences', or what some term the 'new science of education', over the past few decades (Evans, Packer, and Sawyer 2016). A significant part of this turn to a new science of education and learning has involved the ways that particular technical and methodological approaches from the brain sciences, human biology, and the psychological and cognitive sciences have gained salience in educational research, practice, and policy, often further buttressed by expertise in computer science and artificial intelligence (Pea 2016). This has been driven to a significant extent by the enthusiasm of international organizations such as the OECD and UNESCO to incorporate learning science expertise and knowledge in their proposals for educational policy and practice interventions (Kuhl et al. 2019).

Second, and increasingly relatedly, bioinformational education has been connected with developments in 'big data' and 'artificial intelligence' in education since around 2010, particularly through the use of novel data and methods in the domains of 'learning analytics' and 'education data science' (McFarland et al. 2021). An agenda-setting report on learning analytics noted that this nascent set of data-intensive knowledge production practices would draw on techniques and theories cutting across computer science, data science, and learning sciences, including aspects of neuroscience, biometrics, and various forms of 'learner modelling' (Pea 2014). As one key specialist puts it, learning analytics research should ideally gather and analyse multimodal evidence 'at multiple levels, from clickstreams, motion position data, speech streams, gaze data, biometric and brain sensing, to more abstracted feature sets from all this evidence' (Saxberg 2018: viii).

And third, new biological conceptions related to educationally relevant outcomes and behaviours, emerging from particular approaches in social and behaviour genetics, neuroscience, and psychology, have entered into mainstream educational thought (Gulson and Baker 2018). This is evident in, for example, the deployment of developmental neuroscience in education policy, applications of cognitive load theory (which conceptualizes the biological limitations of human neurocognitive architecture) in pedagogical practice, and the recent (re)appearance of genetics, and epigenetics, in debates about educational achievement (Youdell and Lindley 2018). The imbrication of biological and informational approaches in new biodigital methods of data collection and analysis have been crucial to these research endeavours and their potential policy influence (Peters et al. 2021).

Bioinformational education science represents an accumulation of new forms of biological knowledge related to education, along with computational and data science methods and practices, and incorporates the latest technical and methodological advances in the genetic and neural sciences. The following sections trace out some aspects of the social life of bioinformational education, informed by science studies that have investigated the histories, methodologies, sociotechnical innovations, knowledge practices, promissory discourses, and consequences of the genetic and neurosciences (Pickersgill 2013; Stevens 2013; Cruz 2022). In relation to the neuroscience aspects of bioinformational education, the brain sciences have been advanced as potentially authoritative sources of knowledge in educational policy and practice owing to their ostensible promise of measurement precision, objectivity and predictivity (Broer and Pickersgill 2015). More specifically, recent advances in neurotechnologies, like wearable brain-scanning devices and neural interfaces, are currently positioned to further open up the 'learning brain' for analysis as bioinformational neuro-imagery, and to advance knowledge about the embrained structures and processes underpinning learning (Howard-Jones 2018). Likewise, recent big data-driven advances in the genetic sciences have enabled researchers in social and behavioural genetics to undertake studies aimed at discovering the complex 'genetic architectures' and gene-environment interactions that underpin achievement in education (Martschenko et al. 2019). The next sections examine the social and technical arrangements through which these forms of research are enacted and the forms of knowledge they produce.

3   Big Bioinformational Education Sciences

Across the sciences, researchers increasingly make use of digital technologies as part of their methodological apparatuses. Cloud computing infrastructures and repositories for 'big data' storage, analytical machine learning algorithms and data processing techniques, and diverse forms of hardware and software have transformed the sciences to be more data-intensive and interdependent with computer innovation, significantly reshaping scientific practices of inquiry and knowledge production while bringing about new interdisciplinary syntheses that involve computer and data science expertise (Meyer and Schroeder 2015). The biological sciences have rapidly become more computational and informational in approach since the 1990s. A key aspect of this shift has been an organizational reconfiguration of biology as a 'big science' characterized by 'large, expensive instruments, industrialization, centralization, multi-disciplinary collaboration, institutionalization, science-government relations, cooperation with industry and internationalization' (Vermeulen 2016: 199–200). 'Big biology' is represented by new scientific, technical, and organizational transformations in initiatives such as the Human Genome Project and the Human Brain Project, including novel research instruments, data and databases, and international research centres and collectives (Cambrosio et al. 2014). Although research applying approaches from biology to education by no means extend to the international and industrial technoscientific scale of such endeavours, the model of 'big biology' informs the ways in which bioinformation is generated in relation to education.

As part of the rising salience of both the new education sciences and education data science, educational neuroscience has positioned itself as an emerging field in recent decades. Educational neuroscience, otherwise termed 'neuroeducation' or 'mind, brain, and education', aims to translate insights into the neurobiological underpinnings of learning and cognition to policy and practice and to understand the effects of education on the brain (Thomas, Ansari, and Knowland 2019). Field-building efforts in educational neuroscience have been inspired by large-scale international neuroscience projects and the new data-intensive research methods that have been advanced for measuring and understanding the human brain (Jolles and Jolles 2021), and depend significantly on innovations in the neurotechnology industry and sources of funding and political advocacy. The industrial development of neurotechnologies including brain-scanning devices, neuroimaging software, and brain-computer interfaces has become central to many neuroscientific endeavours (Martin 2015), including the social organization and technical-methodological capacities of educational neuroscience (Choudhury and Wannyn 2022).

Educational neuroscience has also benefitted considerably from political interest in the transformative potential of knowledge of the brain, and consequent large-scale funding awards from sources such as the European Union and the US National Science Foundation (NSF). International organizations like the OECD and UNESCO have advocated for educational neuroscience initiatives, including by advancing promissory discourses of their potential, promoting educational neuroscience findings, publishing reports, and convening expert groups (Mochizuki et al. 2022). Recent UNESCO programs, for instance, have highlighted the potential of neuro-technology-enabled research to contribute to educational policy and practice (Vickers 2022). The OECD has been especially significant in promoting neuroscience in education over two decades since the initial publication of its 2002 report, 'Understanding the Brain: Towards a New Learning Science'. It claimed that '[w]ith the advent of functional imaging technology, cognitive neuroscience is beginning to produce important research on the neural foundations of cognitive performance' (OECD 2002: 27), and drew particular attention to 'high resolution' brain imaging neurotechnologies as the basis for this new science of learning (46).

These ambitions for a neurotechnology-enabled educational neuroscience have been partially realized in the form of big biology-inspired initiatives funded by the NSF, particularly the Science of Learning Centers program initiated in 2005, which was linked to the NSF's multimillion dollar investments in Understanding the Brain (its program of support for neuroscience research and infrastructure) and the BRAIN Initiative (Brain Research Through Advancing Innovative Neurotechnologies). Among their ambitious aims, the Science of Learning Centers were intended to uncover the 'biological foundations of learning' and the 'neural basis of learning' (National Science Foundation 2005). Uses of neurotechnologies for education-focused research have thus emerged into scientific practice through the building of multisector and interorganizational networks encompassing neuroscience researchers, the neurotechnology industry, large-scale funding, and international advocacy. Such networks have been central in the making of promissory claims about the long-term benefits neurotechnologies can bring to the scientific understanding of learning and, from there, science-based prescriptions for policy and practice.

Similarly, educational genomics studies have proliferated since around 2010, with the availability of bioinformational datasets, data mining software and algorithmic methods for analysis, as well as the formation of large-scale consortia and new connections between academia and the biotechnology industry (Kovas et al. 2016). Rather than a coherent or autonomous field, educational genomics research is conducted by scientists from disciplines and approaches including behaviour genetics, economics, political science, sociology, demography, and bioinformatics, many of whom identify their work as 'social science genomics' or 'sociogenomics' (Mills and Tropf 2019). Educational genomics aims to uncover the 'underlying genetic architecture of academic achievement' (Conley and Fletcher 2017: 145), and advance 'a more comprehensive, biologically oriented model of individual differences in cognitive ability and learning' (Malanchini et al. 2020: 230). Similar to the influence of mega-projects like the Human Brain Project on the direction of educational neuroscience, educational genomics research is dependent upon new advances in methods, availability of datasets, and technologies that have emerged in the 'postgenomic' decades following the sequencing of the entire human genome through international initiatives like the Human Genome Project (Reardon 2017).

The leading international research centre for educational genomics studies is the Social Science Genetic Association Consortium (SSGAC), established in 2011 with NSF funding as an international network of interdisciplinary scientists to conduct 'large-data' research on 'social science genetics'.[1] The SSGAC is representative of the big biology shape of educational genomics, and its increasingly large scale logistical operations: it consists of hundreds of scientists, takes the shape of an international consortium, conducts studies involving bioinformational data samples in the millions, and attracts significant science funding. Educational genomics has been propelled by major science funders in both the US and Europe, which have leveraged their political-economic influence over behavioural and social genomics to consolidate the interdisciplinary synthesis of social statistics and bioinformatics (Bliss 2018).

Educational genomics studies are also the result of new industry-academia relations. Many of the major datasets used in educational genomics are derived from the giant biobank of Silicon Valley personal genomics company 23andMe,[2] which has a dedicated partnership with the SSGAC to supply bioinformational samples numbering in the millions for a range of investigations, and actively partners on the SSGAC's studies of the genetics of educational attainment (Becker 2021). Consistent with the 'big data', 'big team', and 'big funding' character of much recent genomics

---

[1] See https://www.thessgac.org/the-ssgac. Accessed 12 January 2023.
[2] See https://www.23andme.com/en-int/. Accessed 12 January 2023.

research (Mills and Rahal 2019), social and behavioural genomics is therefore a highly financed, datafied, informatized, industrialized, multisector, and network-based form of science with a strong emphasis on 'the development and integration of big-data bio-info' as a route to the production of knowledge, 'a sort of social statistics meets bioinformatics dream team' (Bliss 2018: 52–53).

As such, educational genomics shares with educational neuroscience some emerging characteristics of big biology. Both involve interdisciplinary, cross-sector connections, require large international teams, are rewarded with large grants from major science funding bodies, and are organized around and dependent upon the availability of new sources of bioinformation, new methods and analytical technologies from the neural and genomic sciences. Together, they represent an emerging form of big bioinformational educational science that is being propelled as a new source of knowledge and authority in educational research.

4   Biodigital Methods

Digital methods change how scientific investigation is conducted and make a difference to the knowledge that is produced. The study of human biological structures and processes has been reshaped with computer and data technologies, and this has impacted considerably on the emergence of bioinformational approaches to investigating educational matters. Human genetics are analysed with bioinformatics technologies, which hybridize techniques of biological examination with informatics innovations to reveal the molecular organization of living organisms (Stevens 2013). Neurobiological structures and functions have been made legible for more granular scientific investigation by advances in brain scanning hardware and imaging software, as well as a range of other emerging neurotechnologies (Ienca and Andorno 2017). These innovations constitute new biodigital methods, which are deployed in the analysis of diverse sources of human biodata and generate novel kinds of bioinformational knowledge about embodied structures, mechanisms, and actions. Research in education conducted in the organizational and institutional settings outlined above has begun making use of biodigital advances in bioinformatics and neurotechnology. This is changing the ways that education-focused research is carried out, shifting research practices to new sites of investigation, and leading to the formulation of new knowledge and understandings about the biologically-embodied bases of educational outcomes, behaviours, and both cognitive and noncognitive processes of learning.

According to a recent review article produced for the UNESCO International Bureau of Education, neurotechnologies demonstrate 'the huge potential contribution that the convergence of neuroscience and emerging technologies can make to education' and to the learning sciences (Howard-Jones et al. 2021). Writing for the same publication, neuroscientist Tokuhama-Espinosa (2021: 90) has claimed, that '[a]dvancements in neuroimaging techniques from 1990 to the present, in terms of both measurement accuracy and data analysis, marked key milestones in the development of the learning sciences', as this technology 'began to link observable learning in classrooms to molecular-level changes in brains in laboratories to better understand how the teaching-learning dynamic actually works'. Such claims to accurate measurement of molecular brain dynamics and 'what works' in education are common in educational neuroscience, contrary to the more critical neuroscience perspective which sees brain science findings as socially produced, inflected by power relations, and shaped by scientific apparatuses of measurement and visualization (Choudhury and Wannyn 2022). The availability of industrial neurotechnologies has also been integral to the biodigital methods used in educational neuroscience and leveraged its reconceptualization of learning as molecular neurobiological dynamics, illuminating how the dynamics of the bioeconomy shape biodigital developments (Peters et al. 2021).

Neurotechnologies used in recent brain science studies related to education include functional Magnetic Resonance Imaging (fMRI) for generating neural and cognitive data related to learning:

> This technology of fMRI allows scientists to detect which parts of the brain are activating or deactivating in response to learning, since learning (or any type of mental activity) involves changes in activity in different brain regions, with consequent changes in blood flow in those regions. (Howard-Jones et al. 2021)

The benefits of fMRI are claimed to include conducting time-series analyses while learners are undertaking cognitive tasks. Neurotechnologies used for fMRI studies are limited, however, by taking place in artificial and isolated measurement contexts like a brain scanning lab so as to control for the noisy nature of neuroimaging signals. Recently, portable neurotechnologies have made it possible to carry out neuroscience studies in situated educational settings, and are considered transformative for educational neuroscience (van Atteveldt et al. 2018). Portable neurotechnologies include wearable electroencephalogram (EEG) headcaps enabling the detection and recording of electrical signals when brain cells activate, and functional Near-Infrared Spectroscopy (fNIRS), an optical brain monitoring technique using near-infrared light to infer brain activity (Janssen et al. 2021).

The key benefit of portable neuroimaging methods claimed by educational neuroscientists is that 'collecting brain data does not rely on conscious reporting and recollection' and 'unlike self-reported measures, EEG provides continuous, millisecond-by-millisecond, data about the learning process, and its collection does not interfere with naturally occurring learning activities' (Davidesco et al. 2021: 650). Beyond the accelerated temporality of data collection, neurotechnologies can also facilitate forms of prediction:

> one potentially promising example of the more direct use of neuroimaging: using a brain measure for its predictive value, also termed neuro-prediction. If adding a brain measure predicts a certain learning or intervention outcome better than behavioral tests alone, it can provide valuable information. (van Atteveldt et al. 2018: 188)

As such, the transformative promise of neurotechnologies in the research assemblage of educational neuroscience is a shift to ultra-fine grained temporal measurements of embrained molecular dynamics, ultimately seeking to render learning legible and predictable as high-resolution brain visualizations fabricated from brain data.

One site deploying portable neurotechnologies is the Stanford Educational Neuroscience Initiative, which specifically partners with schools to embed EEG research in classrooms. Its aim is to 'explore how changes in the brain's neural circuitry support emerging skills that are foundational to education, and how school experiences help to change, shape and tune brain circuitry that are critical to the emergence of the educated mind'.[3] It is related to efforts based at the University of California San Francisco, funded by a major NSF Science of Learning Collaborative Networks Grant, which is led and coordinated by Neuroscape,[4] a 'translational neuroscience center' with a dedicated education division that uses behavioral and neuroimaging assessments to understand the development of the neural mechanisms of learning abilities through both 'in-lab' and 'in-school' studies. The center's in-house neurotechnology innovations include multimodal recording and brain computer interface algorithms, wearable physiological recordings and transcranial brain stimulation, as well as computational platforms that deploy machine learning to 'reliably predict cognitive and affective states from multimodal biosensing (MMBS) data'.[5]

The biodigital methods of neuroscience in the classroom are altering how and in which sites embrained processes of learning are measured and anatomized. Through portable neurotechnologies for brain scanning, multimodal biosensing and visualization, scientists have begun to investigate processes of learning and cognition as socially-situated neurobiological processes of interaction among neurons and synapses at the molecular level of granularity (Youdell and Lindley 2018). Particular brain functions claimed to be related to learning have been localized in different brain regions and processes, visualized and calculated in neuromolecular fidelity, and thus opened up to new forms of explanation (Rose and Abi-Rached 2013). Meanwhile, the brain scanning lab has become mobile, and transposable from biomedical settings to situated classrooms. The research assemblage of educational neuroscience thus captures a range of anatomical brain structures and functional dynamics through various forms of socially-situated scanning, specifically by rendering neural dynamics legible from the detection of 'signals' of oxygenation, electrical activity, magnetic fields, or infrared light, along with 'new analysis techniques' that 'also include machine learning algorithms to decode brain activation patterns automatically with high accuracy' (van Atteveldt et al. 2018: 193).

A molecular approach characterizes the biodigital methods of educational genomics too. A core priority of educational genomics is a molecular focus on minuscule 'polygenic' variants and their tiny effects. Rather than focusing on single candidate genes or 'monogenic' outcomes of individual variants, 'social and behavioural outcomes' such as education are considered 'massively polygenic, influenced

---

[3] See https://edneuroinitiative.stanford.edu/. Accessed 12 January 2023.

[4] See https://neuroscape.ucsf.edu/education/. Accessed 12 January 2023.

[5] See https://neuroscape.ucsf.edu/technology/. Accessed 12 January 2023.

by thousands upon thousands of genetic loci scattered throughout the genome, each with a tiny effect' (Harden and Koellinger 2020: 569). These polygenic variations and their effects have been unlocked from studying sample sizes 'from tens of thousands to millions' and by utilizing 'growing statistical power to detect tiny effects on highly polygenic traits' and the 'associations of specific genetic markers with social scientific outcomes' (Harden and Koellinger 2020: 569).

The 'massive samples' required for such studies, it is claimed, are 'coming online now' (Conley and Fletcher 2017: 56) in the shape of large-scale databases of genotyped bioinformation alongside analytical instruments and methods that include data mining molecular bioinformation. These databases of molecular-level genotyped bioinfomation are called biobanks, with one of the most significant being that of the Silicon Valley personal genomics company 23andMe, as discussed above, which is used extensively by the SSGAC in its multimillion-sample studies of the genetic architecture of educational attainment (Okbay et al. 2022). As such, biobanks are integral apparatuses in the research assemblage of educational genomics, enabling scientists to access massive samples of bioinformation and analyse it in attempts to discover the molecular genetic architecture underpinning educational achievement. To a significant extent, the SSGAC's datasets, and all the educational genomics studies based on them, would not be feasible without access to 23andMe's biobank and the multi-sided market of industry, consumer and academic relations—that is bioeconomic relations—that constitute it (Reardon 2017).

According to the authors of an extensive review article on the contribution of sociogenomics to research and theory, the potential of this new 'toolkit' is 'momentous':

> The advent of molecular genetic data has offered unprecedented possibilities and the potential to expand many sociological theories and empirical and statistical applications. ... Theorists may also need to rethink many theoretical models that have a high reliance on individual agency and choice and ignore innate genetic predispositions and their interaction and correlation with the social environment. ... Given the speed at which genetics and sociogenomics have developed, we anticipate an exciting future. (Mills and Tropf 2020: 573–74)

Similarly, other scientists working on educational genomics studies refer to the use of 'molecular genetic research, particularly recent cutting-edge advances in DNA-based methods', to advance 'our knowledge and understanding of cognitive ability, academic performance and their association' (Malanchini et al. 2020: 229–230).

Central to such endeavours has been the development of bioinformatics, or the synthesis of biological forms of inquiry with computerized statistical techniques, which has 'led to the reconfiguration of biology as a data-driven information science' (Parry and Greenhough 2018: 6). Mackenzie (2003: 318) refers to bioinformatics as the 'architectural-algorithmic and organisational-work practices' involved in generating, processing, and using genomic data. Bioinformatics does not merely signify the computerization of biology, but involves a rearrangement of biological practices, a redefinition of what counts as valuable biological work, and shapes the kind of knowledge emerging from biological research domains (Cambrosio et al. 2014). Bioinformatic biology therefore marks a significant break in biological investigation and knowledge production because these 'techniques make it possible not only to aggregate and compare data, but to parse, rearrange, and manipulate them in a variety of complex ways that reveal hidden and surprising patterns' (Stevens 2013: 65).

Within the research assemblage of educational genomics, bioinformatics software for processing bioinformation is used extensively to identify the polygenic associations and patterns that are related to educational and other social and economic outcomes. Specific software applications are used for data mining huge samples of bioinformation, identifying the complex polygenic associations that constitute specific genetic variations—such as differences in educational achievement—and then reducing that complexity to a single 'polygenic score', or an aggregate summary of individual's genetic predisposition towards a trait or outcome such as educational attainment (Domingue et al. 2015). These bioinformatics techniques 'promise the detection of hitherto unknown features and properties of biological molecules through computer database searching and comparison' and 'highlight contemporary imaginings of a kind of flythrough, in-the-round, drill-down, scaled-up biological knowledge synthesis' (Mackenzie 2003: 327). Likewise, the bioinformatics approach is enabling a drill-down, scaled-up model of database searching in educational genomics as a route to delineating the genetic architectures underpinning educational achievement and other relevant behaviours, traits, and outcomes.

Through educational genomics, new bio-educational objects are being created from processing bioinformation stored in biobanks with bioinformatics software. The locus of knowledge about educational matters is shifting from public education institutions to private biobanks, which are proffered as new sources of objective and apolitical authority in the assessment and prediction of student ability and attainment (Plomin and von Stumm 2021). Particular configurations of learning, education, and other educationally relevant behaviours and traits are produced through the bioinformatic infrastructure of educational genomics, as a new biological reality of the polygenic architectures underpinning cognition, learning, academic achievement, and socioeconomic life outcomes. These configurations tend not only towards newly biologized, geneticized, or molecularized explanations, but also incorporate computational conceptualizations of biology as consisting of codes, networks, scripts, and patterns that are discernible and 'discoverable' only with algorithms (Stevens 2016). Reflecting the informationalization of molecular biology more broadly, educational genomics constructs an informational view of educational outcomes—where outcomes like educational achievement and attainment ultimately derive from genetic codes (Koopman 2020). They also frame students' educational trajectories and chances in quantified terms, as probabilistic or predictive calculations. The combination of genetics and computation grants education genomics a powerful form of scientific authority to produce and circulate new bioinformational knowledge claims about education and related social outcomes.

The deployment of neurotechnologies and bioinformatics as biodigital methods in research on educational matters, then, signifies a significant opening up of human biology at the molecular level for data mining, searching and pattern detection. It assumes traces of learning and educational achievement can be searched for and located from the transformation of human genetic samples into bioinformation, the collection and digitalization of millisecond-by-millisecond brain signals, and the mobilization of data scientific processes and algorithms that are included in bioinformatics and neurotechnology apparatuses. As these examples illustrate, the biodigital methods of big bioinformational education sciences enact a new mode of molecular anatomization, which seeks to make the interior biological substrates of learning and outcomes visible and interpretable as digital biodata.

5 Bioinformational Knowledge

Data-intensive biodigital methods produce new bioinformational knowledge about learning and education. As noted in the previous section, with advanced informatics and data scientific affordances, biological sciences are characterized by a particular anatomization of the human body, genome and brain at a molecular level, and the belief that much of what structures human thoughts and actions is shaped by biological processes (Rose 2007; Rose and Abi-Rached 2013). The generation of digital bioinformation has been central to this molecular anatomization, which shapes the distinctive forms of knowledge produced through bioinformational projects in education.

Two particular forms of knowledge in educational neuroscience are notable: neuroplasticity and neurocomputation. Neuroplasticity is a central focus of a significant proportion of knowledge production in the educational neurosciences. As critical neuroscience scholars Choudhury and Wannyn put it,

> neuroplasticity is a concept denoting materiality and specificity of learning and teaching in terms of brain processes. At the same time, it is interpreted in ways that are vague and open-ended enough to encompass and reflect a range of values, hopes and anxieties about the character and futures of children and youth. Indeed, plasticity is the dominant enabling concept for the neuroeducation movement. (Choudhury and Wannyn 2022: 43)

Neuroplasticity describes how the brain is materially affected by learning, experience or environmental stimuli and interaction, as synaptic connections between neurons are 'wired' together, trimmed, pruned, and 'rewired' across the entire lifespan (Costandi 2016). Drawing on this foundational conception of brain plasticity, much contemporary educational neuroscience produces knowledge claims based on understandings about learning as 'a permanent change in neuron firing and wiring' (Joldersma and Herwegen 2022: 479). The central concern here is with how 'neuronal cells and their synapses undergo structural (morphological) and metabolic (biochemical) changes throughout development, as the brain grows, learns and ages in constant, dynamic and adaptive interaction with the external world' (Cachia et al. 2022: 79).

A major area of research on plasticity and education concerns the neurocognitive development of children according to social and economic status, with researchers using neuroimaging technologies to measure the effects of social inequalities on both the plasticity of brain structure and brain function (Pitts-Taylor 2019). Such neurotechnology-leveraged studies have thus reconceived social structural problems as measurable neurobiological deficits. By shifting the analytical gaze from society to the cellular level, such studies produce new images of 'neurobiologically poor' children, making the knowledge claim that 'the experience of living in poverty can produce a brain that is morphologically different—less developed, smaller, or less efficient—in particular brain areas', and that 'these neurobiological effects translate into cognitive deficits' (Pitts-Taylor 2019: 661). Recent interventions with 'neurobiologically poor' children therefore constitute a form of 'preemptive neurogovernance' that targets individuals for intervention through neurotechnology-derived measures of their neural deficits (Pitts-Taylor 2016).

Another key area of bioinformational knowledge production in education neuroscience is in the area of neurocomputation. Educational neuroscientists Thomas and Porayska-Pomsta (2022) argue that there is a longstanding historical connection between neuroscientific thinking and computation: 'The origin of computational devices in the early twentieth century lay in an endeavour to build machines that thought as humans did; in order to have a good computer tool to help teachers, the design of the tool needs to be informed by how children learn' (662). As they elaborate, the 'view of cognition as computation' common in neurocognitive theory assumes the brain is 'performing computations', and the 'basic unit of computation is the neuron', with knowledge 'stored in the strength of connections between neurons' (664). The whole brain is thus understood as 'built of a set of content-specific systems' that are 'modulated' and 'activated' by the pre-frontal cortex, linked by 'translators', integrated into 'hubs', and organized hierarchically to 'condition the body' for situations it encounters (664). A key aim of certain approaches in educational neuroscience, then, has been to build neurocomputational models and 'computationally model individual learners as they engage in learning of a particular subject domain in real-time' as a means of constructing new knowledge claims (672).

An understanding of the brain in neurocomputational terms of neural infrastructure interconnections, as a 'statistical organ' that accumulates and assimilates sensory evidence (Cachia et al. 2022: 59), underpins much recent research on neurocognitive functions such as learning. Reflecting the longstanding metaphor of the brain as a computer in both the neural and informatic sciences (Baria and Cross 2021), it suggests that learning, like other mental phenomena, consists of the brain's computation of information and the manipulation of mental representations, as if the brain is a computational processor isolated inside the skull and separate from the embodied, sensorimotor, and social and cultural contexts that surround it (Joldersma and Herwegen 2022).

New bioinformational and neurocomputational knowledge of the learning brain is not straightforwardly empirical evidence, but profoundly shaped by political and economic factors. For example, the OECD has played a significant role in promoting educational neuroscience for more than two decades, but its advocacy is far from apolitical. The OECD's Neuroscience-informed Policy Initiative has begun exploring the economic value of 'Brain Capital', treating 'brain skills and brain health as an indispensable part of the knowledge economy' and education one area of public policy to be targeted (OECD 2021; Smith, 2021). Likewise, UNESCO has begun promoting neuroscience findings as the basis for its proposals for educational reform (Vickers 2022). Many of the promissory claims circulating around educational neuroscience, therefore, are aimed at generating insights for policy development, enhancing learning outcomes, and ultimately contributing to building more brain-powered human capital for the knowledge economy. In this context, neuroscientific insights into the learning brain are seen to be key to pedagogical innovation, enhancements in academic achievement, and the long-term securing of value through brain capital development. This reflects the ways neuroscientific insights into brain plasticity have been linked to visions of social and economic progress, as moulding the 'plastic brain' through interventions is considered to have 'promissory benefits' for societies and economies (Rose and Abi-Rached 2013: 18).

As the OECD's involvement in educational neuroscience indicates, bioinformational education science is premised on a form of scientific objectivity that elides its implicitly political project. Within the domain of educational genomics research even stronger claims are made to biological objectivity and neutrality, as reflected in claims that sociogenomics will generate 'a more realistic understanding of human behaviour and the functioning of societies' (Harden and Koellinger 2020: 567). Following this assertion, new knowledge claims circulate that 'genomic predictions will be possible for a range of learning outcomes' (Cesarini and Visscher 2017: 6) and for genetically-informed educational interventions (Harden 2021). A range of studies have adopted genomics methods to identify the 'molecular genetic architecture' of 'educationally-relevant traits', behaviours and phenotypes, including cognitive ability and intelligence, as well as outcomes such as educational attainment, achievement in school assessments, and non-cognitive skill development (Malanchini et al. 2020: 235; Visscher 2022).

These scientific appeals to objectivity gloss over the more political implications of such studies. For some, genomic technologies and methods appear to make it possible to 'personalize' and customize education around the individual's genome, in a model termed 'precision education' that would be modelled on biomedical advances in 'precision medicine' (Plomin and von Stumm 2021). Such 'personalized policy' has been argued by some to have the potential to result in educational interventions based on 'targeted students' genotypes' (Conley and Fletcher 2017: 9), but it has also been critiqued—even by those who conduct educational genomics studies—as potentially eugenic in targeting individuals on the basis of biological measures of capability (Harden 2021). Much educational genomics research is also led by economists, or more accurately 'genoeconomists', whose core scientific interests are in socioeconomic measures of human behaviours, for which educational attainment is a proxy measure (Benjamin et al. 2012). As with educational neuroscience, educational genomics is connected with promissory political discourses of the social and economic benefits to be derived from processing new sources of biological data into actionable knowledge.

Educational genomics is also embedded in a big data epistemology of unbiased, objective science. It emphasizes 'atheoretical' knowledge discovery where the dominant approach is 'to conduct a hypothesis-free investigation and see what "pops out" in the data' in terms of the 'genetic architecture of important social outcomes' (Conley and Fletcher 2017: 44). These 'unbiased, hypothesis-free' methods of 'data mining' and their underlying technologies are presented by researchers as contributing significantly to transformed modes of datafied knowledge production (Mills and Tropf 2020: 556). One team has described a 'technological advance' that 'enabled an atheoretical approach to identify associations across the genome', and which has generated 'increasingly more insight into the molecular genetic architecture of cognitive ability and academic performance' (Malanchini et al. 2020: 235).

As these examples indicate, educational genomics represents a particular mode of data-centric knowledge production that proceeds from the computational search for patterns and associations with automated data mining rather than explicitly theory-centred inquiry (Leonelli 2016). The 'data-driven' and 'hypothesis-free' approaches of 'data-centric biology' are, however, not as neutral as they are claimed to be (Leonelli 2016). They are, rather, embedded in an 'assemblage of statistical tests and data-handling algorithms' that do not just process data but constitute them (Keating and Cambrosio 2012: 49). With bioinformatics 'there is no such thing as "raw data", strictly speaking, as the data generated by the instruments are already highly processed, while meaningful (i.e., interpretable) results necessitate further statistical and visual manipulations' (Cambrosio et al. 2014: 17). Through these technical and highly instrumented bioinformatics processes, the human genome is recast as a 'statistical body' with algorithmically calculable probabilities and risks that may be mobilized as the source for intervention (Stevens 2013: 222).

In educational genomics specifically, the statistical construct of the polygenic score is variously utilized in proposals for precision education or for economic prediction, recasting student subjectivities in terms of their statistical searchability. The knowledge claims produced by educational genomics thus emerges from specific statistical and data scientific techniques and technologies that privilege informational renderings of biology, and are shaped by intertwining social, scientific, political, technical, methodological, and epistemological factors and limitations rather than being unbiased representations of newly discovered biological realities. The quantitative apparatus of educational genomics constitutes and brings into being qualitatively different forms of knowledge and potential for intervention.

The knowledge claims produced through the biodigital methods of bioinformational research are thus generating novel conceptions of the biological substrates of learning and educational outcomes. These methods and these knowledge claims produce new quantified and computational renderings that recast the public concerns of education as neurobiological dynamics and as genetic associations and architectures. These internally-embodied biological substrates of educational outcomes are detectable only with complex apparatuses that include a variety of databases, sensing, scanning, data mining, pattern detection and visualization technologies. Novel ways of rendering learning and educational outcomes legible may then become the basis for particular forms of proposed intervention—from educational schemes to treat the cognitive deficits of the poverty-affected brain of disadvantage students to precision education approaches based on personal polygenic profiles of students' strengths and weaknesses.

6   Conclusion

Bioinformational education science is emerging from distinctive and emerging data-intensive scientific apparatuses and practices among large-scale consortia and networks whose object is discovering the biological substrates of educational outcomes, cognitive processes and behaviours related to learning. It is taking shape across aspects of the genetic and neurosciences, often propelled by promissory claims by leading advocates of the learning sciences. A recent piece for the UNESCO International Bureau of Education, for example, anticipated that collecting and analysing neural and genetic data together might contribute to the design of new personalized regimes of education:

> Our accumulating knowledge of the genetic, brain-based ... factors that predict learning may, one day, allow education to be tailored precisely to an individual's needs. The technology for this important part of the 'big data' revolution is not trivial, requiring improved portable neuroimaging for collecting brain data (e.g., neuroheadsets for EEG monitoring) and real-time processing of the data it produces ... and interpreting an individual's data may also require some further advances in genetic testing technologies. (Howard-Jones et al. 2021)

As this excerpt indicates, bioinformational education science is inextricable from the expanding availability and uses of big biodata to produce new knowledge, understandings, and proposals for intervention in the education sector. It also highlights the potential convergence of the research assemblages of educational neuroscience and genomics into a coherent multidisciplinary, big data-driven scientific synthesis.

This chapter has surfaced some features of the emergence of bioinformational education science, highlighting how it is constituted as an increasingly convergent research assemblage by interdisciplinary, multisector, and interorganizational relations that resemble 'big biology', a host of digital methods for data collection, storage, and analysis, and a range of knowledge claims about the biological aspects of learning, cognition, behaviour, and educational outcomes. Scientific practitioners in educational neuroscience and genomics alike, along with advocates, promoters, and funders, propose that these new arrangements and technologies can produce increasingly authoritative knowledge at high resolution and fidelity, ultimately rendering learning and educational outcomes legible at the molecular level as the basis for interventions in policy and classrooms.

By approaching bioinformational education as a research assemblage, we can see its knowledge claims as embedded in computational, data-scientific ways of knowing in biology, and as infused by a range of assumptions and desires stretching from psychological constructs of ability to economic models of human behaviour. We can also see bioinformational education as a particular accumulating set of organizational, technical, and methodological developments in the new educational and learning sciences, employing big data as a route to building out an authoritative knowledge base and making claims to policy relevance. It potentially stands to challenge and displace other forms of inquiry and knowledge production related to educational matters, particularly by translating social and structural problems into molecular biological dynamics that may be amenable to particular forms of intervention. It achieves this by bioinformatizing educational matters, transcoding biological samples into informational forms that can be processed and interpreted with complex apparatuses of hardware and software, most notably by treating the brain as a computer (Baria and Cross 2021) and the genome as information, codes and programming (Koopman 2020). Bioinformational education science is thus transforming the ways learning and other outcomes are known, understood, and made into objects of intervention. In bioinformational education science the learning brain becomes the subject of neurocomputational modelling, and the educated body becomes the subject of polygenic scoring. These processes create an alternative biological reality, a bioinformational reality, which is now taking shape as authoritative knowledge about educationally-relevant processes and outcomes, and becoming the basis for proposals about how to improve educational policy and practice.

Bioinformational education science represents a particular postdigital imbrication of digital technologies, biological sciences, human biology, and educational research, policy, and practice, which is assembling new biodigital objects of attention and analysis that collapse the boundary between the biological and the digital (Peters et al. 2022). In postdigital theorizing, 'the postdigital might be understood as no longer viewing the digital as "other" to everyday life' but as 'already embedded in what we might usually distinguish as the social, economic, and political' (Knox 2019: 360). From this postdigital perspective, the sociotechnical systems that constitute bioinformational education sciences are infused with social, scientific, technical, political, and economic relations that are in turn potentially reconstituting how educational research is conducted and reshaping the priorities of education systems.

Bioinformational education science can be understood in postdigital terms as an emerging nexus of biological, informatic, and educational sciences, composed of multiple relations and with consequences that this chapter has only begun to surface. Advancing a postdigital research approach to bioinformational education science as a research assemblage brings into empirical focus not only its hybridization of biological, informatic, and educational ways of knowing and intervening in education. It also foregrounds the ways that educational neuroscience and genomics constitute students as bioinformational proxies that can be scanned, bio-sensed, searched and data-mined as the basis for taking data-driven actions in educational policy and practice.

Acknowledgement The research underpinning this work was funded by a Leverhulme Trust Research Project Grant.

References

Baria, A., & Cross, K. (2021). The brain is a computer is a brain: neuroscience's internal debate and the social significance of the Computational Metaphor. *arXiv:*2107. https://doi.org/10.48550/arXiv.2107.14042.

Becker, J., Burik, C. A. P., Goldman, G., Wang, N., Jayashankar, H., Bennett, M., Belsky, D. W., Karlsson Linnér, R., Ahlskog, R., Kleinman, A., Hinds, D. A., 23andMe Research Group, Caspi, A., Corcoran, D. L., Moffitt, T. E., Poulton, R., Sugden, K., Williams, B. S., Mullan Harris, K., Steptoe, A., Ajnakina, O., Milani, L., Esko, T., Iacono, W. G., McGue, M., Magnusson, P. K. E., Mallard, T. T., Harden, K. P., Tucker-Drob, E. M., Herd, P., Freese, J., Young, A., Beauchamp, J. P., Koellinger, P. D., Oskarsson, S., Johannesson, M., Visscher, P. M., Meyer, M. N., Laibson, D., Cesarini, D., Benjamin, D. J., Turley, P., & Okbay, A. (2021). Resource profile and user guide of the Polygenic Index Repository. *Nature Human Behaviour, 5,* 1744–1758. https://doi.org/10.1038/s41562-021-01119-3.

Benjamin, D. J., Cesarini, D., Chabris, C. F., Glaeser, E. L., Laibson, D. I., Guðnason, V., Harris, T. B., Launer, L. J., Purcell, S., Smith, A. V., Johannesson, M., Magnusson, P. K., Beauchamp, J. P., Christakis, N. A., Atwood, C. S., Hebert, B., Freese, J., Hauser, R. M., Hauser, T. S., Grankvist, A., Hultman, C. M., & Lichtenstein, P. (2012). The Promises and Pitfalls of Genoeconomics. *Annual Review of Economics, 4,* 627–662. https://doi.org/10.1146/annurev-economics-080511-110939.

Bliss, C. (2018). *Social by Nature: The promise and peril of sociogenomics.* Stanford, CA: Stanford University Press.

Broer, T., & Pickersgill, M. (2015). Targeting brains, producing responsibilities: The use of neuroscience within British social policy. *Social Science & Medicine, 132,* 54-61. https://doi.org/10.1016/j.socscimed.2015.03.022.

Cachia, A., Ribeiro, S., Chiao, J. Y., Friston, K., Hillman, C. H., Linzarini, A., Lipina, S. J., Howard-Jones, P., Dubois, J., Jay, T., Le Bihan, D., & Gutchess, A. H. (2022). Brain development and maturation in the context of learning. In S. Bugden & G. Borst (Eds.), *Education and the Learning Experience in Reimagining Education: The International Science and Evidence based Education Assessment.* New Delhi: UNESCO MGIEP.

Cambrosio, A., Bourret, P., Rabeharisoa, V., & Callon, M. (2014). Big data and the collective turn in biomedicine: How should we analyze post-genomic practices? *Technoscienza, 5*(11), 11-42.

Cesarini, D., & Visscher, P. M. (2017). Genetics and educational attainment. *npj Science of Learning, 2,* 4. https://doi.org/10.1038/s41539-017-0005-6.

Choudhury, S., & Wannyn, W. (2022). Politics of Plasticity: Implications of the New Science of the "Teen Brain" for Education. *Culture, Medicine and Psychiatry, 46,* 31–58. https://doi.org/10.1007/s11013-021-09731-8.

Conley, D., & Fletcher, J. (2017). *The Genome Factor: What the social genomics revolution reveals about ourselves, our history and the future.* Oxford: Princeton University Press.

Costandi, M. (2016). *Neuroplasticity.* London: MIT Press.

Cruz, T. M. (2022). The social life of biomedical data: Capturing, obscuring, and envisioning care in the digital safety-net. *Social Science and Medicine, 294,* 114670. https://doi.org/10.1016/j.socscimed.2021.114670.

Davidesco, I., Matuk, C., Bevilacqua, D., Poeppel, D., & Dikker, S. (2021). Neuroscience Research in the Classroom: Portable Brain Technologies in Education Research. *Educational Researcher, 50*(9), 649-656. https://doi.org/10.3102/0013189X211031563.

Domingue, B. W., Belsky, D. W., Conley, D., Harris, K. M., & Boardman, J. D. (2015). Polygenic influence on educational attainment: new evidence from the national longitudinal study of adolescent to adult health. *AERA Open, 1*(3). https://doi.org/10.1177/2332858415599972.

Evans, M. A., Packer, M. P., & Sawyer, R. K. (2016). Introduction. In M. A. Evans, M. P. Packer, & R. K. Sawyer (Eds.), *Reflections on the Learning Sciences* (pp. 1–16). New York: Cambridge University Press.

Gulson, K. N., & Baker, B. (2018). New biological rationalities in education. *Discourse: Studies in the cultural politics of education, 39*(2), 159-168. https://doi.org/10.1080/01596306.2017.1422077.

Gulson, K. N., & Webb, P. T. (2018). 'Life' and education policy: intervention, augmentation and computation. *Discourse: Studies in the Cultural Politics of Education, 39*(2), 276-291. https://doi.org/10.1080/01596306.2017.1396729.

Harden, K. P. (2021). *The Genetic Lottery: Why DNA matters for social equality.* Oxford: Princeton University Press.

Harden, K. P., & Koellinger, P. D. (2020). Using genetics for social science. *Nature Human Behaviour, 4*(6), 567–576. https://doi.org/10.1038/s41562-020-0862-5.

Howard-Jones, P. (2018). *Evolution of the Learning Brain.* London: Routledge.

Howard-Jones, P., Cunnington, R., Reigosa-Crespo, V., & Lisboa, J. V. (2021). Realizing the potential of Neuroscience and Technology to transform Education. In Focus, 9 February. https://ibe-infocus.org/articles/realizing-the-potential-of-neuroscience-and-technology-to-transform-education/. Accessed 12 January 2023.

Ienca, M., & Andorno, R. (2017). Towards new human rights in the age of neuroscience and neurotechnology. *Life Sciences, Society and Policy, 13*(5), 1-27. https://doi.org/10.1186/s40504-017-0050-1.

Jandrić, P. (2021). Biology, Information, Society. *Postdigital Science and Education, 3*(2), 261–265. https://doi.org/10.1007/s42438-021-00220-0.

Janssen, T. W. P., Grammer, J. K., Bleichner, M. G., Bulgarelli, C., Davidesco, I., Dikker, S., Jasińska, K. K., Siugzdaite, R., Vassena, E., Vatakis, A., Zion-Golumbic, E., & van Atteveldt, N. (2021). Opportunities and Limitations of Mobile Neuroimaging Technologies in Educational Neuroscience. *Mind, Brain and Education, 15*(4), 354-370. https://doi.org/10.1111/mbe.12302.

Joldersma, C. W., & Van Herwegen, J. (2022). Contexts of educational neuroscience. In E. A. Vickers, K. Pugh, & L. Gupta (Eds.), *Reimagining education: The International Science and Evidence based Education Assessment.* New Delhi: UNESCO MGIEP.

Jolles, J., & Jolles, D. D. (2021). On Neuroeducation: Why and How to Improve Neuroscientific Literacy in Educational Professionals. *Frontiers in Psychology, 12*, 752151. https://doi.org/10.3389/fpsyg.2021.752151.

Keating, P., & Cambrosio, A. (2012). Too many numbers: Microarrays in clinical cancer research. *Studies in History and Philosophy of Biological and Biomedical Sciences, 43*, 37-51. https://doi.org/10.1016/j.shpsc.2011.10.004.

Knox, J. (2019). What Does the 'Postdigital' Mean for Education? Three Critical Perspectives on the Digital, with Implications for Educational Research and Practice. *Postdigital Science and Education, 1*(2), 357–370. https://doi.org/10.1007/s42438-019-00045-y

Koopman, C. (2020). Coding the Self: The Infopolitics and Biopolitics of Genetic Sciences. *Hastings Report, 50*(3), 6-14. https://doi.org/10.1002/hast.1150.

Kovas, Y., Tikhomirova, T., Selita, F., Tosto, M. G., & Malykh, S. (2016). How genetics can help education. In Y. Kovas, S. Malykh, & D. Gaysina (Eds.), *Behavioural genetics for education* (pp. 1–23). London: Palgrave Macmillan. https://doi.org/10.1057/9781137437327_1.

Kuhl, P. K., Lim, S.-S., Guerriero, S., & van Damme, D. (2019). *Developing Minds in the Digital Age: Towards a science of learning for 21st century education.* Paris: OECD.

Leonelli, S. (2016). *Data-Centric Biology: A philosophical study.* London: University of Chicago Press.

Leonelli, S. (2019). Philosophy of Biology: The challenges of big data biology. *eLife, 8*, e47381. https://doi.org/10.7554/eLife.47381.

Mackenzie, A. (2003). Bringing sequences to life: how bioinformatics corporealizes sequence data. *New Genetics and Society, 22*(3), 315–332. https://doi.org/10.1080/1463677032000147180.

Malanchini, M., Rimfield, K., Allegrini, A., Ritchie, S. J., & Plomin, R. (2020). Cognitive ability and education: How behavioural genetic research has advanced our knowledge and understanding of their association. *Neuroscience and Biobehavioral Reviews, 111*, 229–245. https://doi.org/10.1016/j.neubiorev.2020.01.016.

Martin, P. (2015). Commercialising neurofutures: Promissory economies, value creation and the making of a new industry. *BioSocieties, 10,* 422–443. https://doi.org/10.1057/biosoc.2014.40.

Martschenko, D., Trejo, S., & Domingue, B. W. (2019). Genetics and education: Recent developments in the context of an ugly history and an uncertain future. *AERA Open, 5*(1), 1-15. https://doi.org/10.1177/2332858418810516.

McFarland, D. A., Khanna, S., Domingue, B. W., & Pardos, Z. A. (2021). Education Data Science: Past, Present, Future. *AERA Open, 7.* https://doi.org/10.1177/23328584211052055.

Meyer, E., & Schroeder, R. (2015). *Knowledge Machines: Digital Transformations of the Sciences and Humanities.* London: MIT Press.

Mills, M. C., & Rahal, C. (2019). A scientometric review of genome-wide association studies. *Communications Biology, 2,* 9. https://doi.org/10.1038/s42003-018-0261-x.

Mills, M. C., & Tropf, F. C. (2020). Sociology, genetics, and the coming of age of sociogenomics. *Annual Review of Sociology, 46,* 553–581. https://doi.org/10.1146/annurev-soc-121919-054756.

Mochizuki, Y., Vickers, E., & Bryan, A. (2022). Huxleyan utopia or Huxleyan dystopia? 'Scientific humanism', Faure's legacy and the ascendancy of neuroliberalism in education. *International Review of Education.* https://doi.org/10.1007/s11159-022-09982-6.

National Science Foundation. (2005). Science of Learning Centers. https://www.nsf.gov/pubs/2005/nsf05509/nsf05509.htm. Accessed 12 January 2023.

OECD. (2002). *Understanding the Brain: Towards a New Learning Science.* Paris: OECD Publishing.

OECD. (2021). Neuroscience-inspired Policy Initiative. OECD New Approaches to Economic Challenges. Paris: OECD Publishing. https://www.oecd.org/naec/brain-capital/. Accessed 12 January 2023.

Okbay, A., Wu, Y., Wang, N., Jayashankar, H., Bennett, M., Nehzati, S. M., Sidorenko, J., Kweon, H., Goldman, G., Gjorgjieva, T., Jiang, Y., Hicks, B., Tian, C., Hinds, D. A., Ahlskog, R., Magnusson, P. K. E., Oskarsson, S., Hayward, C., Campbell, A., Porteous, D. J., Freese, J., Herd, P., 23andMe Research Team, Social Science Genetic Association Consortium, Watson, C., Jala, J., Conley, D., Koellinger, P. D., Johannesson, M., Laibson, D., Meyer, M. N., Lee, J. J., Kong, A., Yengo, L., Cesarini, D., Turley, P., Visscher, P. M., Beauchamp, J. P., Benjamin, D. J., & Young, A. I. (2022) Polygenic prediction of educational attainment within and between families from genome-wide association analyses in 3 million individuals. *Nature Genetics, 54,* 437-449. https://doi.org/10.1038/s41588-022-01016-z.

Parry, B., & Greenhough, B. (2018). *Bioinformation.* Cambridge: Polity.

Pea, R. (2014). *A report on building the field of learning analytics for personalized learning at scale.* Stanford, CA: Stanford University.

Pea, R. (2016). The prehistory of the learning sciences. In M. A. Evans, M. P. Packer, & R. K. Sawyer (Eds.), *Reflections on the Learning Sciences* (pp. 32-58). New York: Cambridge University Press.

Peters, M. A., Jandrić, P., & Hayes, S. (2021). Postdigital-Biodigital: An Emerging Configuration. *Educational Philosophy and Theory.* https://doi.org/10.1080/00131857.2020.1867108.

Peters, M.A., Jandrić, P., & Hayes, S. (2022). Biodigital Philosophy, Technological Convergence, and Postdigital Knowledge Ecologies. In M. A. Peters, P. Jandrić, & S. Hayes (Eds.). *Bioinformational Philosophy and Postdigital Knowledge Ecologies.* Cham: Springer. https://doi.org/10.1007/s42438-020-00211-7.

Pickersgill, M. (2013). The social life of the brain: Neuroscience in society. *Current Sociology, 61*(3), 322–340. https://doi.org/10.1177/0011392113476464.

Pitts-Taylor, V. (2016). *The Brain's Body: Neuroscience and Corporeal Politics.* Durham, NC: Duke University Press.

Pitts-Taylor, V. (2019). Neurobiologically Poor? Brain Phenotypes, Inequality, and Biosocial Determinism. *Science, Technology, & Human Values, 44*(4), 660–685. https://doi.org/10.1177/0162243919841695.

Plomin, R., & von Stumm, S. (2021). Polygenic scores: prediction versus explanation. *Molecular Psychiatry, 27,* 49–52. https://doi.org/10.1038/s41380-021-01348-y.

Reardon, J. (2017). *The Postgenomic Condition: Ethics, justice, and knowledge after the genome.* Chicago, IL: University of Chicago Press.

Rose, N. (2007). *The Politics of Life Itself: Biomedicine, power and subjectivity in the twenty-first century.* Princeton, NJ: Princeton University Press.

Rose, N., & Abi-Rached, J. (2013). *Neuro: The new brain sciences and the management of the mind.* Oxford: Princeton University Press.

Saxberg, B. (2018). Preface. In D. Niemi, R. D. Pea, B. Saxberg, & R. E. Clark (Eds.), *Learning Analytics in Education* (pp. vii-x). Charlotte, NC: Information Age Publishing.

Smith, E., Ali, D., Wilkerson, B., Dawson, W. D., Sobowale, K., Reynolds, C. III., Berk, M., Lavretsky, H., Jeste, D., Ng, C. H., Soares, J. C., Aragam, G., Wainer, Z., Manji, H. K., Licinio, J., Lo, A. W., Storch, E., Fu, E., Leboyer, M., Tarnanas, I., Ibanez, A., Manes, F., Caddick, S., Fillit, H., Abbott, R., Robertson, I. H., Chapman, S. B., Au, R., Altimus, C. M., Hynes, W., Brannelly, P., Cummings, J., & Eyre, H. A. (2021). A Brain Capital Grand Strategy: toward economic reimagination. *Molecular Psychiatry, 26,* 3–22. https://doi.org/10.1038/s41380-020-00918-w.

Stevens, H. (2013). *Life Out of Sequence: A data-driven history of bioinformatics.* Chicago, IL: University of Chicago Press.

Stevens, H. (2016). Hadooping the genome: The impact of big data tools on biology. *BioSocieties, 11,* 352–371. https://doi.org/10.1057/s41292-016-0003-6.

Thomas, M., & Porayska-Pomsta, K. (2022). Neurocomputational methods: From models of brain and cognition to artificial intelligence in education. In O. Houdé & G. Bosrt (Eds.), *The Cambridge Handbook of Cognitive Development* (pp. 662–687). Cambridge: Cambridge University Press.

Thomas, M. S. C., Ansari, D., & Knowland, V. C. P. (2019). Educational neuroscience: progress and prospects. *Journal of Child Psychology and Psychiatry, 60,* 477– 492. https://doi.org/10.1111/jcpp.12973.

Tokuhama-Espinosa, T. (2021). The role of technology in advancing our understanding of the learning brain. In Focus, 9 February. https://ibe-infocus.org/articles/the-role-of-technology/. Accessed 12 January 2023.

van Atteveldt, N., van Kesteren, M. T. R., Braams, B., & Krabbendam, L. (2018). Neuroimaging of learning and development: improving ecological validity. *Frontline Learning Research, 6*(3), 186–203. https://doi.org/10.14786/flr.v6i3.366.

Vermeulen, N. (2016) Big Biology. *NTM Zeitschrift für Geschichte der Wissenschaften, Technik und Medizin, 24,* 195–223. https://doi.org/10.1007/s00048-016-0141-8.

Vickers, E. (2022). Rebranding Gandhi for the 21st century: science, ideology and politics at UNESCO's Mahatma Gandhi Institute (MGIEP). *Compare: A Journal of Comparative and International Education.* https://doi.org/10.1080/03057925.2022.2108374.

Visscher, P. (2022). Genetics of cognitive performance, education and learning: from research to policy? *npj Science of Learning, 7,* 8. https://doi.org/10.1038/s41539-022-00124-z.

Youdell, D., & Lindley, M. (2018). *Biosocial Education: The social and biological entanglements of learning.* London: Routledge.

Historical Materialism: A Postdigital Philosophical Method

Megha Summer Pappachen and Derek R. Ford

1 Introduction

This chapter is interested in postdigital *research* rather than research in the postdigital *era*. On the one hand, the postdigital era is our current moment marked by the afterlife of the universalization of computerization and digitization. On the other hand, the postdigital is also a phase: something which comes and goes and is conceptual and philosophical in addition to literal. As Gabriel Rockhill maintains, eras mark 'a historical time period' whereas phases are 'always distributed in a precise manner across time as well as in space and in society' (2017: 4). The *concept* of the postdigital has always resisted any precise temporal placement. Petar Jandrić reminds us that 'forms of binary code are found in ancient texts in China and India', and that in an era long before written language, binary code was found 'in various forms of communication such as smoke signals and drums' (Jandrić 2019: 162). Even before the advent of the digital, we were somehow already past it, and with the postdigital.

Today, authors have agreed to agree on the spelling of 'postdigital', no hyphen. But in 2015, Geoff Cox was still messing with the 'post-digital'. In an early essay on postdigital temporality, Cox questioned the need to announce a new era. Rather than 'announce the end of this and that', he said, we need to rethink how we approach time as researchers (Cox 2015: 151). Creating post this and that is historicist in ethic and not very postdigital (understood as a timeless phase rather than an era).

M. S. Pappachen
Northwestern University, Evanston, IL, USA

D. R. Ford (✉)
DePauw University, Greencastle, IN, USA
e-mail: derekford@depauw.edu

© The Author(s), under exclusive license to Springer Nature
Switzerland AG 2023
P. Jandrić et al. (eds.), *Postdigital Research*, Postdigital Science and Education,
https://doi.org/10.1007/978-3-031-31299-1_7

For Cox, historicism is evidenced by 'machine time' which produces 'a very particular view of history' through storage and memory, in which 'the central processor takes symbols from memory, combines or compares them with other symbols, and then restores them to memory' (2015: 158–159). Machine time reasserts the present by continually reconceptualizing the past. Cox tasks historical materialism with critiquing 'the inner workings of historicism as an ideological construction' — to remind us that time too is an ideology. The method's aim would be to 'to maintain a political view of the past that is not simply a historical one' but a political one as well (155). The marxist method, much to the surprise of its detractors, has been tasked with reminding historicism of the political agency of human subjects. In this chapter, we springboard off of Cox's provocations and return to Marx and the communist tradition to demonstrate that historical materialism is the right method to be tasked with this duty, and maintain that historical materialism has always been a postdigital research method.

Put simply, in our search for methods of postdigital research, we offer up historical materialism as an old friend who has returned anew, one freed from the economic determinism, historical stageism, and linear developmentalism so often assigned to it. Historical materialism can find refuge in the philosophical world of postdigital research, and it can in turn contribute to postdigital research as one of the many methods to draw upon to investigate the crises that we are in. Ultimately, we present historical materialism and postdigital research as fellow travelers, as companions. Sometimes they crisscross paths, overlap, hold hands, and become one (as fellow travelers often do) and at other times they diverge and drift apart, though always with the option to come back together again.

The chapter proceeds as follows: first we explore the contours of historical materialism through its most popular iteration, the base-superstructure model. We find that a text-based understanding of the model moves us beyond its caricature and allows us to ask needed questions within postdigital research. In the second section, we continue an exploration of the base-superstructure model, and point to how it can help us understand capitalist relations under the postdigital era. The third section turns to postdigital temporality to demonstrate the comradery between historical materialism and postdigital concepts. The fourth section returns to Freeman Dyson's (2007) declaration that the twenty-first century is the century of biology. We look at historical materialism through the biodigital lens and consider the implications of their serendipitous twin birth in the 1800s. The last section is a lob in the air, a demonstration of itself, as we explore apathy toward the truth as a marxist research principle.

2   Base-Superstructure as a Temporal Metaphor

Students are often taught historical materialism through the imagery of base-superstructure. In this chapter, we confront this image and springboard off it to make connections to the postdigital. Today, the reigning conception of historical materialism is *visualized* as an underground 'material base' with an aboveground 'superstructure', with the base causally producing the superstructure and, in more generous interpretations, with the superstructure reacting back upon the base. This is a misconception, but it isn't unforgivable or nonsensical given the overall lack of engagement with Marx's work and marxist theory overall, which would reveal the strange, outsized role it plays in work on and in historical materialism. It is, moreover, understandable given the overall neglect of the *pedagogy* of Marx's writing (Ford 2022). We can begin to rectify all this by turning to Marx's famous articulation of the relationship between the base and superstructure.

In the author's preface to *A Contribution to the Critique of Political Economy*, Marx (1859/1904: 11) summarizes 'the *general* conclusion' of his study of political economy (emphasis added). In these few short pages, Marx presents a sketch of his method that is well-known and worth revisiting in its entirety:

> In the social production which men carry on they enter into definite relations that are indispensable and independent of their will; these relations of production correspond to a definite stage of development of their material powers of production. The sum total of these relations of production constitutes the economic structure of society—the real foundation, on which rise legal and political superstructures and to which correspond definite forms of social consciousness. The mode of production of material life determines the general character of the social, political and spiritual processes of life. It is not the consciousness of men that determines their existence, but, on the contrary, their social existence determines their consciousness. (Marx 1859/1904: 11–12)

Continuing to deliver his conclusion, Marx writes that revolutionary transformations occur because of a conflict between 'the material forces of production' and 'the existing relations of production, or—what is but a legal expression for the same thing—with the property relations within which they had been at work before' (Marx 1859/1904: 12). 'With the change of the economic foundation' brought about by social revolution, 'the entire immense superstructure is more or less rapidly transformed' (12). The implication, it seems, is that the superstructure (e.g., property relations) changes solely because of changes in the economic base (e.g., whether production is based on enslaved work or waged work). Thus, we encounter the start of the famous formulation of the base and superstructure we inherit from specific readings—deployed by both marxists and our opponents—presenting it as a mechanical dogma or, to be more generous, as an *explanatory* mechanism. In opposition to this formulation, we argue that the base and superstructure is a *metaphor* and *model* for marxists, a way to analyze and approach society and social transformation rather than an easy *explanation*. More accurately, it evidences the fact that the base-superstructure embodies a particular pedagogical decision by Marx, which Engels considers in his responses to Bloch. Marx's preface, where we encounter the above sketch, introduces a short and popularly written book, so his mention of the model there is more didactic than theoretical.

Nevertheless, in critical educational research, this interpretation is repeated *ad nauseum* (often without any specific quotations from or even references to Marx) for the benefit of generating critiques of marxism as economistic or deterministic.[1] For one classic example, Henry Giroux (1983: 259) announces his theory of educational resistance by contrasting it with 'reproduction accounts of schooling' that 'have continually patterned themselves after structural-functionalist versions of Marxism which stress that history is made "behind the backs of" the members of society', thereby diminishing or eliminating 'the importance of human agency and the notion of resistance'. We may contrast this view with Cox's (2015) interpretation of historical materialism as the theory which can break through historicism to restore human agency, because to Marx, the people are the only agents who can make the future arrive.

For another example, this time more recent and focused on white supremacy, Clayton Pierce legitimates his work on W. E. B. DuBois and education by affirming 'that the U.S. education system cannot *simply* be explained through its relation to economic superstructure or how schools operate solely to reproduce economic social relations beneficial to the processes of capitalist accumulation' (Pierce 2017: 28) (emphasis added). In both cases, Marx and historical materialism are delivered to us as simple economic determinism, a delivery accomplished by superficial or cursory glosses at the primary source material.

The legacy for such short-circuits extend back to Marx and Engels' own time. In an 1890 letter responding to the German socialist Joseph Bloch's questions about the model, Engels highlights the *pedagogical* nature of their presentations. Pedagogical, in the sense that the model is presented with the intent of teaching something to others and is thus communicated with an educational ethic. Engels begins: 'According to the materialist conception of history, the *ultimately* determining element in history is the production and reproduction of real life' (1890b/1977: 75) (emphasis original). He is de-emphasizing the extent to which production guides politics and history while still defending its determinant role. 'If somebody twists this into saying that the economic factor is the *only* determining one, he is transforming that proposition into a meaningless, abstract, absurd phrase.' (75) Still, Engels takes responsibility 'for the fact that the younger people sometimes lay more stress on the economic side than is due to it' insofar as 'we had to emphasize the main principle over and against our adversaries, who denied it' (Engels 1890b/1977: 78). Put differently, they attributed so much emphasis on the economic base because they were responding to those who denied the determination of productive relations altogether. The 1800s was a time of great idealism in philosophy, when authors assumed that ideas (the attitudes of great men) were what drove political change. Many still look at history through this same distorted lens today.

As a pedagogical choice, Marx and Engels' emphasis on the economic should be seen as an intervention which emanates from historical-materialist research methods in that it was part of a battle in a particular epoch. It was not an absolute

---

[1] Importantly, these false starts that form(ed) the basis of critical educational theory have been expertly dissected and disproven in the recent studies of David I. Backer (2022). Although, because this work focuses on the legacy of Louis Althusser in education, Backer's method doesn't entail a return to Marx's own work.

statement but a timed and particular message – following the ethic of historical materialism itself. This is not unlike Cox's (2015) resistance to the term 'postdigital', which we see as a *strategic* move intervening in a given *conjuncture* rather than a timeless announcement. As the chapter appeared in the first book on postdigital aesthetics, it served to counter those who would uncritically march forward under the banner of the 'postdigital'. This is an intervention similar to Hugh O. Burnam's assertion that during the beginning of the Covid-19 pandemic, 'many [Indigenous] Elders could not, did not know how, or were unwilling, to meet using Zoom when our government structure has always (since time immemorial) met in person' (Burnam and Brett 2022: 178). Burnam points us to the poem 'The Pandemic Will Not be Zoom' which was 'screamed' by an unknown scholar 'into the void':

> The Pandemic will not teach you algebra when old people equal zero
> The Pandemic will not prepare you for jobs that do not exist yet when jobs do not exist …
> The Pandemic will not be recorded so you can watch back later
> The Pandemic will not be recorded so you can watch back later because the Pandemic will not be on Zoom (Costello et al. 2020: 623)

The interventions of these scholars emerge from a historical-materialist approach because they arrive at a specific conjuncture. Their conjecture was defined not just by the pandemic but also by the constellation of colonialism and capitalism that persists to this day. Only in a historical conjecture do their interventions makes sense. At the same time, they are not fleeting or parochial truths, but truths of immense significance and relatability. What is at stake is not whether the Elders' relationship to Zoom, or the maddened poem, is analog or digital, but *whose interests* are being centered in the current postdigital era. The scholars are making a political and ethical call for our research to be guided by questions of *whose* interests prevail? What effects does how digital technologies are designed, distributed, consumed, and enforced have on society? Historical materialism calls our attention to such questions within postdigital research. For instance, the problem is not the 'digital' per se but how 'through digital media, the images of billionaire settler capitalists [like Jeff Bezos in space during the pandemic] are reconfigured as subjects in which we almost have no choice but to view our realities through' (Burnam and Brett 2022: 171).

3   From the Metaphor to Action

Back to the letter: Engels infers that Bloch's questions derive from his study of secondary literature only, and he asks Bloch to read the primary sources, referring him in particular to Marx's *The Eighteenth Brumaire of Louis Bonaparte* (1852/1972), perhaps the only other place Marx mentioned the superstructure explicitly (he only alludes to it elsewhere), and in a manner similar to what we saw above.[2] We point out that Engels refers Bloch to this work because, in it, Marx uses the base-superstructure metaphor to describe the role of social democracy in the failure of the 1848 Paris revolution and the success of the 1851 coup of Louis-Napoléon Bonaparte. In other words, Marx wanted to 'distinguish still more the phrases and fancies of parties from their real organism and their real interests, their conception of themselves from their reality' (Marx 1852/1972: 47). Despite their revolutionary phrases, social democracy, he writes, 'is epitomized in the fact that democratic-republican institutions are demanded as a means, not of doing away with two extremes, capital and wage labor, but of weakening the antagonism and transforming it into harmony' (50). The social-democratic forces didn't seek to overthrow the existing relations of production but to manage them in a more equitable manner *through* the capitalist superstructure. They didn't seek to overthrow the base, just the superstructure.

The base-superstructure model doesn't *explain* but rather helps Marx *present* this phenomenon. Even remaining within Marx's (1859/1904) preface, the base-superstructure model should prevent any economistic interpretation. For one, the base of society—which is also translated as 'infrastructure'—includes the relations of production and the productive forces. Productive forces name labor-power, instruments or tools used by workers, and the materials workers transform in the production process. The relations of production entail the social organization of production and reproduction, or how the re/production of life is structured. As such, the base doesn't just consist of the forces of production, but productive relations, relations that are not only economic but social.

Second, the superstructure comprises the political-legal system of the state and consciousness—or ideology—in general, yet the superstructure is also economic insofar as the state and ideology are themselves economic processes and as the relations of production require, for example, the legal system of the state to enforce private property rights. In this instance, it's crucial to the reproduction of the base. Because the capitalist legal system arises from capitalist relations of production, changes in the legal system might alter the existing relations of production, but they can't fundamentally overthrow them, for that requires the creation of a new social and economic system.

Yet Marx didn't resolutely oppose reforms or the pursuit of more equality within capitalism through capitalist institutions. He certainly didn't in *Capital*, where he ended the chapter detailing the horrific results of industrialization on workers, peasants, and slaves by calling for the oppressed to organize and institute 'the *modest* Magna Charta of a legally limited working-day' (1867/1967: 286) (emphasis added). He did resolutely oppose the absorption of the socialist project into capitalist circuits of management, but that did not mean opposing life-saving reforms. Instead, reform and revolution, superstructural and infrastructural changes—already

---

[2] 'Upon the different forms of property, upon the social conditions of existence, rises an entire superstructure of distinct and peculiarly formed sentiments, illusions, modes of thought, and views of life. The entire class creates and forms them out of its material foundations and out of the corresponding relations.' (Marx 1852/1972: 47)

intertwined—must be pursued in tandem, but with the ultimate objective of over-throwing the capitalist state.

We currently live in a postdigital era of capitalism. Historical materialism lets us grasp capitalist relations in our age, for it accounts for radical transformations within the capitalist structure. In other words, the new theories that have emerged to capture contemporary capital—from data capitalism and algorithmic capitalism to communicative capitalism and bioinformational capitalism—aren't changes *between* modes of production but changes *within* modes of production. For example, take communicative capitalism, which Jodi Dean defines as 'a new version of capitalism in which communication has become central to capital accumulation' (Dean et al. 2019: 219). Communicative capitalism names a key aspect of contemporary capital that represents a change in both the base and superstructure of society. Communication is key in the production and realization of value (base), as data becomes increasingly valuable and profitable, but it is also key in transforming the social relations of society (superstructure). Communication is not only a source of (surplus-) value but also a way for democratic 'ideals of access, inclusion, discussion, and participation … to be realized in and through expansions, intensifications, and interconnections of global telecommunications' (Dean 2009: 23). We come to think and believe that participating in online discussions provides a route to more equality and inclusion—and maybe even liberation—when, in fact, they further tie us to capital's demands.

The base and superstructure comingle through the postdigital set-up of capital. It becomes difficult to distinguish between communication as a central feature of new relations of production and new forms of thought (just like it is difficult to distinguish between the analog and the digital under postdigitalism). Historical materialism can capture the union of biology, society, and knowledge represented by the postdigital in the same way it captures changes in 'old and emerging forms of capitalism' (Ford and Jandrić 2021: 2). The flexibility of the base-superstructure model provides an important avenue for describing the role of algorithms, bioinformation, and data in reproducing relations of exploitation and oppression that are both economic and extra-economic.

4   The Lonely Hour of the Economy Never Comes

It is true that in the base-superstructure model, the economy determines in the last instance.[3] Engels writes as much in his correspondence with German economist Conrad Schmidt: only 'in the last instance [is] production the decisive factor' (Engels 1890a/1977: 80). With this move, the spatial metaphor of historical materialism is temporalized: not only is the image of a building and its steel infrastructure

---

[3] We follow Raymond Williams in understanding 'to determine' to mean setting limits and pressures on a particular trajectory rather than as fully straightjacketing or molding it (Williams 1977: 84).

invoked, but also the idea of a sequence of events (Ford and Esposito 2022). Althusser picks up this idea and develops it. He allows us to see how the model's pedagogical function 'does not fix its destiny for all time' (1965/2005: 113). He writes: 'Pedagogic systems do change in history. It is time to make the effort to raise pedagogy to the level of circumstances, that is, of historical needs. But we must all be able to see that this pedagogical effort *presupposes* another purely theoretical effort.' (113) Although we remain undecided on Althusser's separation of pedagogy from theory—partly because he never defined pedagogy—we propose that he engaged in the work of pedagogical theory required for our moment. That is how we approach his restatement of the model. He produced a two-part formulation that restates the base-superstructure model with two contradictory components: while it is true that 'the economy is determinant in the last instance' it is also true that 'the lonely hour of the "last instance" never comes' (1965/2005: 113).

The lonely hour of the 'last instance' never comes because there is never a time and space where the purely economic even *exists*. The economy never operates alone, and as we have shown, it is always fusing and separating from race, the law, gender, consciousness. More fundamentally, the economic is only a product of our thought. Just like the digital is a line we have drawn around *certain* things in an analogue world, the economy too is a line we have drawn in society. One can't actually 'see' where the economy ends and society begins because one can't *see* the economy or society. The base-superstructure, which is a spatial metaphor or topography, helps us see these invisible entities and social relations.

Because of this, there is a *persistent absence* of the determinant primacy of the material basis within historical materialism. The assertion of the determinant primacy of the material basis could read like a dogma or formula, as a claim about the ubiquity of capitalist social formations across time and space (Agamben 1978/2007: 105). Or it could read in the exact opposite fashion, as a claim about the impossibility of such a determination, which exposes politics and philosophy to a radical and foundational contingency operating on the basis of a 'true historical materialism' that 'is ready at any moment to stop time' (115).

The concept of the postdigital has always resisted any precise temporal placement, and historical materialism accommodates for that. Historical materialism disavows linear, purely chronological time, as that is in large part what dialectics means in a historical context. Writing about postdigital aesthetics, Cox (2015: 160) reminds us that '[i]t is the temporal sense of incompleteness that drives transformative agency' because 'human subjects seek to modify their lived circumstances knowing their experiences to be incomplete'. In other words, time's incompleteness is where human agency exists. For instance, the relationship between capitalism and socialism is not 'a short circuit between otherwise historically clearly separated times' but one of 'feedback loops' that allow historical subjects to choose what elements from the old system they want to take with them, and what they want to abolish (Cox 2015: 160). Loosely, we have suggested that historical materialism and postdigitalism are compatible in the temporal realm.

5   The Biology and Science of Historical Materialism

Thus far we have shown that, like the postdigital, historical materialism can embody a radical temporal openness. We now turn to consider how historical materialism is specifically biodigital in form. This idea must start at Freeman Dyson's (2007) proclamation that the twentieth century was the century of physics and the twenty-first century is the century of biology. Michael Peters builds on this observation by staking out the concept of 'bioinformational capitalism'. The term defines how our current era is defined by capitalist innovations 'that control, change and experiment with the material basis of life' (Peters 2012: 98). This includes artificial intelligence, machine learning, bioengineering, biotechnology etc. Capitalism today is 'obsessed' with 'working people's biologies' as that which can either serve as a block or a generator of surplus value (Pappachen and Ford 2022: 242). Given that the challenges we face in the postdigital era are deeply biological, historical materialism is a surprisingly fitting method.

Historical materialism and evolutionary biology were like sisters separated at birth. At least their mothers thought so: when Marx published *Capital* (1867/1967), he intended to dedicate his book to Charles Darwin who published the *Origin of Species* (1859/2011) only eight years prior. They were contemporaries, and Marx saw a deep similarity between their approaches to the empirical world. This is evidenced in an exchange of amicable letters between the two in 1873 (Fay 1978: 135). Furthermore, in an important footnote in *Capital*, Marx likens his analysis of the changes in manufacturing tools to how Darwin explained the evolution of organs in plants and animals (Marx 1867/1967: 323). He refers to Darwin's work as 'epoch-making' for how it used material evidence to explain the historical development of species (323). He saw himself as doing the same thing, but with the social world.

Engels also adopted a biological methodology, perhaps more explicitly than Marx. He goes so far with the science analogies sometimes that it can read like scientism, like when he compares class antagonism to the repulsion of oxygen and hydrogen molecules (Engels 1878/1978: 708). Nevertheless, we only intend here to take stock of various points of connection between biology and marxism as methods. Another point of connection is the title of Engels' *Origin of the Family, Private Property and the State* (1884/2010), which certainly owes something to Darwin's *Origin of Species* (1859/2011). Engels makes all of this explicit during his funeral oration at Marx's graveside in 1883: 'Just as Darwin discovered the law of evolution in organic nature, so Marx discovered the law of evolution in human history' (Fay 1978: 133).

Emersed as we are in the phase of bioinformation, historical materialism likely experiences a return to its own beginnings. Bioinformational capitalism – 'based on a self-organizing and self-replicating code that harnesses both the results of the information and new biology revolutions', is comfortable ground for this old method (Peters 2012: 105). Because of this connection, the biological/biodigital can help us better understand historical materialism. The bio-lens vindicates historical materialism from accusations of determinism, linear developmentalism, and stage-ism in two ways.

For one, marxist methods are accused of presenting changes in history as the result of organic, inexorable laws. Political scientist Karl Popper (1945) for instance points to the few moments where Marx uses the phrase 'inexorable laws of Nature' to make this accusation (1867/1967: 715). He claimed that marxism was basically 'scientific fortune telling' and 'large-scale historical prophecy' because it held that certain natural laws governed society (1945: 279). An example of such a law would be that capitalism inevitably runs in devastating boom and bust cycles. While marx-ists do see this as a law, biology itself teaches us that laws are not inviolable or standardized. No laws or tendencies, whether in the natural sciences or in the judi-ciary are permanent—they change over time, are interpreted differently, applied differently, modified and augmented in innumerable ways (Ford 2022: 35). One only needs to glance at the history and philosophy of science to know this. Laws (such as the antagonism of the bourgeois and the proletarian) do not close all ave-nues to change and movement within the system. For example, infighting occurs within each class, and sometimes sectors of both classes unite in strategic alliances.

Second, marxists are accused of retelling history in a stageist fashion. Feudalism to capitalism to socialism to communism: the steps are laid out in a predetermined way. However, in one of his deeper critiques of Hegel, the 1857 'Introduction' from the *Grundrisse*, Marx dismisses the Hegelian temporal rule that 'the latest form regards the previous ones as steps leading up to itself' (Marx 1939/1973: 106). Hegel said that the current stage views the stage before it as a step leading up to itself as if on a ladder. Marx suggests that he viewed the process differently and provided a biological example to make the point. While it is true that 'human anat-omy contains a key to the anatomy of the ape' (105), this doesn't mean that human anatomy is the teleological outcome of the ape. Louis Althusser (2018/2020: 149), who worked to wrest marxism from such historicism, rightly claims that 'Marx would say: every result is plainly the result of a becoming, but its becoming does not contain that result *in itself*' (emphasis original). The result is not predetermined, but the product of struggle and chance. Biodigital concepts such as the genetic evolu-tion of the human species have been used by marxists to gain a deeper understand-ing of their own method.

6   An Apathetic Method

There is no doubt that Marx and Engels developed, out of necessity, the method of historical materialism to not only 'reconcile' with their former Hegelian conscious-ness but, more importantly, to arm the working-class struggle in its path toward the dictatorship of the proletariat. In this way, historical materialism is precisely a method guided by an explicit desire for a future end goal and, as such, could be interpreted as a method guided by the need for certainty, for truth. This, however, is only one—and, as we argue, one insufficient—way of viewing the matter. In fact, from another vantage point—one that we hold provides a much more accurate and marxist framing—historical materialism is precisely an *apathetic method*; apathy, which comes to U.S. English by way of the Greek word *apatheia*, which can be transliterated as 'absent of feeling'.

How could we possibly describe marxism as apathetic, as without feeling? Only by way of perhaps another equally daring move in time, space, and political and intellectual tradition: a move to the pedagogical philosophy of Jean-François Lyotard. In a short article appearing in an early 1975 edition of the French journal, *Critique*, Lyotard (1977/2022: 141) calls for and performs a practice of apathetic theory that is positioned solely against 'theoretical terror', a terror that names theoretical frameworks and principles that are guided solely by 'the desire for truth'. A 'terror of truth' dominates most all of scholarly inquiry: the need to deliver a true or false, a yes or no, a certainty or an ignorance.

Lyotard's short piece begins with a clarion call 'to introduce into ideological or philosophical discourse the same refinement, the same lightness obtaining in works of painting, music, "experimental" cinema, as well, obviously, as in those of the sciences' (Lyotard 1977/2022: 141). Lyotard finds a trace of such an apathetic moment in an excurses in which Freud considers whether or not he believes in the truth-status of his hypothesis. The hypothesis in question was about whether drives are repetitive. 'My answer', Freud (1922/1955: 59) confesses, 'would be that I am not convinced myself and that I do not seek to persuade other people to believe in them'. Further, he continues to reject any possible justification as to 'why the emotional factor of conviction should enter into this question at all'. Just afterwards, however, Freud rephrases his answer like this: 'Or, more precisely, that I do not know how far I believe in them' (59). Belief in his truthfulness is framed as an emotional commitment: the opposite of which would be indifference about the truthfulness of his claim.

Lyotard (1977/2022: 143) reads in these pages an eruption of apathy into Freud's will to construct a theoretical account of all drives, for 'if all drives are repetitive, then the doctrine of drives must be *monist*... and that is out of the question' (emphasis original). Monist, in the sense that there would be only one overarching, always-right explanation. Thus, Freud's reflections represent traces of the absent determinations of drives, or the infinite paths that drives and their doctrine can yet pursue. The theory of the drives is subject to the same repetitive compulsion as that which it names and, as such, it 'precludes any conviction, for it makes it impossible to please *a cause*, i.e., an established and stable relation between an effect and an instance' (146) (emphasis original). The 'terror of causation', if you will, a fear which reigns in disciplines like Political Science and Economics in the U.S., must be avoided by theory.

As conviction is the belief in the truthfulness of a theory or method, Freud's wandering remarks demonstrate 'the absence of determinacy' and 'an undecidability of affect, a positive potency of not knowing whether he believes in his theory or not, a potency of affirmation alien to the question of belief' (Lyotard 1977/2022: 146). Only now, it seems, can we make sense of Freud's decision to close *Beyond the Pleasure Principle* with a poetic quote: 'What we cannot reach flying we must reach limping' (Freud 1922/1955: 64). The difference between flying and limping turns precisely on conviction: 'the limper does not know *whether he believes* in space and time, whereas the flyer does: he is *convinced*', he must be convinced (Lyotard 1977/2022: 147) (emphasis original). Freud's theory of drives requires a shift from flying to limping, from conviction to apathy.

This apathy is not a political disinterestedness in general. Instead, as Kiff Bamford (2022: 211) tells us, apathy is 'the indifference to those affects of conviction operating within theory that enable a binary response of true or false, yes or no'. Apathetic theory 'allows lines of thought to be followed regardless of the need and pressures to prove according to usual conventions, through demonstrable evidential claims' and is rather 'based on an affective instinctual "hunch" which, because it is uncertain in its very method, cannot subscribe to accepted conventions of thinking' (207). Apathetic theory is antagonistic to the terrorism of theory (or truth, or causation) not because it annihilates theories aspiring toward 'truth' but because it produces alternative options such as 'wandering' and limping (Lyotard 1977/2022: 149).

Is the absent determination of the economic we find in Marx's theoretical work and the pedagogical role historical materialism plays in this work not precisely such a kind of apathetic endeavor? Marx reaches a conclusion only to take it up in new directions, to see where it takes him. Any pretense toward constructing *the* theory of capital or of the class struggle is, out of principle, rejected from the very start by Marx. The pedagogy of historical materialism is one that limps over and through its object of inquiry in order to produce knowledge and thought.

7   Conclusion

In a neglected sentence before the sketch of his 'general conclusion',[4] Marx says that his conclusion was nothing more than a new beginning that 'once reached, continued to serve as the leading thread in my studies' (Marx 1859/1904: 11). We are returned back to a *start* after *almost* reaching a conclusion. That Marx's conclusions are another starting point demonstrates a particular historical-materialist pedagogy that neither disavows politics nor is determined solely by the class struggle. It also demonstrates a biological and reproductive ethic where the end of a life is nothing but the beginning of a new one. All decay gives life, whether the rotting carcass enriches the forest soil, or new babies are born to fill the absence of the passing elderly.

This conclusion hopes, similarly, to return the reader to a new beginning. We began this chapter with the wager that historical materialism and postdigital research could be fellow travelers, companions even. Over the course of the pages, the two have overlapped, helped each other out, become one, and then diverged, drifted

---

[4] Referring to the 'general conclusion' summarized by Marx in his preface to *A Contribution to the Critique of Political Economy* (1859/1904: 11–12).

apart, and gone their separate ways. In our historical moment, the working people of the world are suffering acutely, to different degrees, at the hands of the same system. At such a time, we cannot be satisfied with critique alone—we must build theoretical apparatuses that can give us hope for a better world system. We must combine forces, unite disparate theoretical approaches, and build a united research front that can take on the postdigital challenges in front of us. It with this sense of urgency that we offer historical materialism as a postdigital method of philosophy.

References

Agamben, G. (1978/2007). *Infancy and history: On the destruction of experience*. Trans. L. Leron. New York: Verso.

Althusser, L. (1965/2005). *For Marx*. Trans. B. Brewster. New York: Verso.

Althusser, L. (2018/2020). *History and imperialism: Writings, 1963–1986*. Ed. and trans. G. M. Goshgarian. Cambridge: Polity Press.

Backer, D. I. (2022). *Althusser and education: Reassessing critical education*. London: Bloomsbury.

Bamford, K. (2022). Uncertain? For sure. Limping? Certainly: Limp thoughts on performance practice. In K. Bamford & M. Grebowicz (Eds.), *Lyotard and critical practice* (pp. 205–217). London: Bloomsbury.

Burnam, H. O., & Brett, M. S. (2022). The Postdigital Settler Spectacle: An Educators' Dérive to Unveil a 'New Colonizer' During Covid-19. In P. Jandrić & D. R. Ford (Eds.), *Postdigital Ecopedagogies: Genealogies, Contradictions and Possible Futures* (pp. 165–194). Cham: Springer. https://doi.org/10.1007/978-3-030-97262-2_9.

Costello, E., Brown, M., Donlon, E., & Girme, P. (2020). 'The Pandemic Will Not be on Zoom': A Retrospective from the Year 2050. *Postdigital Science and Education, 2*(3), 619–627. https://doi.org/10.1007/s42438-022-00339-8.

Cox, G. (2015). Postscript on the Post-digital and the Problem of Temporality. In D. M. Berry & M. Dieter (Eds.), *Postdigital aesthetics: Art, computation and design* (pp. 151–162). London: Palgrave Macmillan. https://doi.org/10.1057/9781137437204_12.

Darwin, C. (1859/2011). *The Origin of Species*. Glasgow: William Collins.

Dean, J. (2009). *Democracy and Other Neoliberal Fantasies: Communicative Capitalism and Left Politics*. Durham, NC: Duke University Press.

Dean, J.; Medak, T., & Jandrić, P. (2019). Embrace the antagonism, build the Party! The new communist horizon in and against communicative capitalism. *Postdigital Science and Education, 1*(1), 218–235. https://doi.org/10.1007/s42438-018-0006-7.

Dyson, F. (2007). Our biotech future. The New York Review, 19 July. https://www.nybooks.com/articles/2007/07/19/our-biotech-future/. Accessed 6 December 2022.

Engels, F. (1890a/1977). Engels to Conrad Schmidt. In F. Engels & K. Marx, *Karl Marx Frederick Engels Selected Letters* (pp. 79–88). Peking: Foreign Languages Press.

Engels, F. (1890b/1977). Engels to Joseph Bloch. In F. Engels & K. Marx, *Karl Marx Frederick Engels Selected Letters* (pp. 75–78). Peking: Foreign Languages Press.

Engels, E. (1878/1978). Socialism: Utopian and scientific. In R. Tucker (Ed.), *The Marx-Engels reader* (pp. 683–717). New York: W. W. Norton.

Engels, F. (1884/2010). *The Origin of the Family, Private Property and the State*. London: Penguin Classics.

Fay, M. (1978). Did Marx Offer to Dedicate Capital to Darwin?: A Reassessment of the Evidence. *Journal of the History of Ideas, 39*(1), 133–146.

Freud, D. (1922/1955). *Beyond the pleasure principle, group psychology and other works*. Trans. J. Strachey. London: The Hogarth Press and The Institute of Psycho-Analysis.

Ford, D. (2022). Marx's inquiry and presentation: The pedagogical constellations of the Grundrisse and Capital. *Educational Philosophy and Theory*, *54*(11), 1887–1897. https://doi.org/10.1080/00131857.2021.1967741.

Ford, D., & Esposito, M. (2022). Aesthetic Encounters Beyond the Present: Historical Materialism and Sonic Pedagogies for Resisting Abstraction. *Journal for Critical Education Policy Studies*, *19*(3), 32–55.

Ford, D. R., & Jandrić, P. (2021). Postdigital Marxism and Education. *Educational Philosophy and Theory*. https://doi.org/10.1080/00131857.2021.1930530.

Giroux, H. (1983). Theories of reproduction and resistance in the new sociology of education: A critical analysis. *Harvard Educational Review*, *53*(3), 257–293. https://psycnet.apa.org/. https://doi.org/10.17763/haer.53.3.a67x4u33g7682734.

Jandrić, P. (2019). The Three Ages of the Digital. In D. R. Ford (Ed.), Keywords in Radical Philosophy and Education (pp. 161–176). Leiden: Brill/Sense. https://doi.org/10.1163/978900440467_012.

Lyotard, J-F. (1977/2022). Apathy in theory. Trans. R. McKeon. In K. Bamford & M. Grebowicz (Eds.), *Lyotard and critical practice* (pp. 141–150). London: Bloomsbury.

Marx, K. (1859/1904). *A contribution to the critique of political economy*. Trans. N. I Stone. Chicago, IL: Charles H. Kerr & Company.

Marx, K. (1867/1967). *Capital: A Critique of Political Economy, vol. 1*. Trans. S. Moore & E. Aveling. New York: International Publishers.

Marx, K. (1852/1972). *The eighteenth Brumaire of Louis Bonaparte*. New York: International Publishers.

Marx, K. (1939/1973). *Grundrisse: Foundations of the critique of political economy (rough draft)*. Trans. M. Nicolaus. New York: Penguin Books and New Left Review.

Pappachen, S., & Ford, F. (2022). Spreading Stupidity: Intellectual Disability and Anti-imperialist Resistance to Bioinformational Capitalism. In M. A. Peters, P. Jandrić, & S. Hayes (Eds.), *Bioinformational Philosophy and Postdigital Knowledge Ecologies* (pp. 237–253). Cham: Springer. https://doi.org/10.1007/978-3-030-95006-4_13.

Peters, M. A. (2012). Bio-informational capitalism. *Thesis Eleven*, *110*(1), 98–111. https://doi.org/10.1177/0725513612444562.

Pierce, C. (2017). W.E.B. Du Bois and caste education: Racial capitalist schooling from Reconstruction to Jim Crow. *American Educational Research Journal*, *54*(1S), 23–47. https://doi.org/10.3102/0002831216677796.

Popper, K. (1945). *The Open Society and Its Enemies*. Princeton; NJ and Oxford, UK: Princeton University Press.

Rockhill, G. (2017). *Counter-history of the present: Untimely interrogations into globalization, technology, democracy*. Durham, NC: Duke University Press.

Williams, R. (1977). *Marxism and Literature*. Oxford: Oxford University Press.

Postdigital Practical Axiology

Mark William Johnson

1 Introduction

A postdigital approach to educational research grants permission to look at technology and education through an alternative lens from those typically associated with this field (Andersen et al. 2014; Jandrić et al. 2022). Building models of new perspectives is an important step in the practical development of these perspectives, and much of what I introduce here is about approaches to modelling postdigital education. This is to model education in a way which does not focus on the artefacts, technologies (digital or not), practices, pedagogy, or products of education, but on human intergenerational relations in a rapidly changing social and technological context (Johnson et al. 2022a, b, c). Human values sit at the heart of these relations, and indeed what I characterize as the 'dynamics of value' (or an axiological dynamics) underpin the political quagmire of education with all its attendant problems. To model those dynamics, and to intervene in the light of better models, is to consider how human problems in education and society can be mitigated.

My starting point is to consider that the education system's relationship with society and ecology is regulatory (Morin 2001): it exists to ensure that the next generation human beings is equipped with the knowledge and good judgement of older generations so as to give society the requisite flexibility to adapt to future planetary challenges. This is not a conventional view for education researchers, but it is to agree with Morin when he says: 'education is blind to the realities of human knowledge, its systems, infirmities, difficulties, and its propensity to error and illusion. Education does not bother to teach what knowledge is' (Morin 2001: 11). Seeing education's regulatory function as requiring it addresses the 'realities of human knowledge', requires both a deeper systemic modelling of knowledge

M. W. Johnson (✉)
University of Manchester, Manchester, UK
e-mail: mark.johnson-8@manchester.ac.uk

P. Jandrić et al. (eds.), *Postdigital Research*, Postdigital Science and Education,
https://doi.org/10.1007/978-3-031-31299-1_8

dynamics, as well as enquiring whether education is a good regulator. Education academics are vociferous in saying that the system is not fit for what are variously deemed to be its contested purposes (Illich 1971; Bourdieu et al. 2014; Rousseau 1966; Barnett 2014; Claxton 2009), and there are plenty of remedies on offer (Biesta 2017; Robinson 2011; Claxton 2002), but (as Illich complained) most remedies are cast in the mould of the broken system. It seems that what the system actually does is not at all what it says it does. But if it is not a good regulator, how could it be made better? What is missing? What's broken? Unfortunately, instead of inspecting the regulatory deficiencies between the education system and society, we allow the symptoms of a broken regulator guide us to inflict even more damage on the system and the humans who comprise it.

Ashby and Conant's 'good regulator theorem' (1960) states that '[e]very good regulator of a system is a model of that system'. This theorem reminds us of the problems of attempting new initiatives in education where there is not good knowledge of the system dynamics. Even in teaching (or indeed, in management or politics), if we want to change a person's understanding, we need a good model of the person whose understanding we wish to change. At the root of Ashby and Conant's 'good regulator' theorem there is a well-defined reason for this: an effective relationship, whether in teaching or anywhere else, requires that there is 'requisite variety' (Ashby 2015) between the regulator and that which is regulated. Teachers must be able to match the variety of their students, which they can do either by attenuating the variety of their students (and modern education is largely an attenuative operation) or they can act in the light of a good model of their students, which entails amplifying the variety of their teaching.

It is this latter approach which will produce a better regulatory relationship between education and society, and for this to be established, we need a better model of the whole system. This is the value of the term 'postdigital', because it reveals the phenomena upon which typical educational research focuses as *epi-phenomena* of deeper processes. Through the postdigital lens, there is no single phenomenon to focus on: not learning, teaching, technology, management, or policy. There is only a shifting context replete with institutions, technologies, social relations, practices, power structures, pedagogy, politics, biographies, psychologies, and so on (Jandrić et al. 2022). Postdigital research is research into the context – the 'primary process' not just of education, but intergenerational social organization and the fundamental dynamics of human values from which all systemic social behaviour stems.

In considering the regulatory dynamics of value, I draw on two traditions concerning practical interventions: psychotherapy and cybernetics (Johnson et al. 2022a, b, c). Both psychotherapy and technology provide ways in which the psychodynamics operating within and between people can be adjusted, and both are associated with models of self-regulation and self-organisation. Cybernetics – the science of 'effective organization' (Beer 1993) – is well-suited to describing the systemic effects of both psychodynamic processes and technological intervention.

While the psychodynamic models of Freud and Jung are commonly known (if perhaps poorly understood), the cybernetic regulatory models of Ashby, Beer, McCulloch, Von Foerster, and others, are little known outside the systems sciences. Both traditions present new opportunities for research, but both require a more sophisticated model of the system in which their use can be situated.

In this chapter I begin by articulating a view of the current education and technology landscape, with the aim of identifying the challenges of understanding education as a regulatory system, and what an educational regulatory system might look like in a world of rapidly changing technology. Each section of this chapter begins with some summary assertions to help signpost the argument. The first set of assertions draws attention to the manifest trends of increasing specialization, the speed of technical change, and the difficulty that education has in codifying knowledge in flux – what I call a 'codification bottleneck'.

I present a model of knowledge dynamics drawn from Takeuchi and Nonaka (1995), which draws attention to the increasing importance of tacit knowledge, and the pedagogic challenge of creating the conditions where tacit knowledge can be shared. Values, I argue, are revealed in our tacit understandings, where these may be obscured in our engagement with codified knowledge.

Using cybernetic techniques, I introduce a model first conceived by Warren McCulloch in 1942, as a way of thinking about how values arise through a balance between internal perceptions and external engagement. Interventions in technology, education and psychotherapy can change these 'liminal dynamics', and coordinate value formation in different ways. Drawing together depth psychology and cybernetic thinking then allows for rethinking how 'selves' are made in a technological context. Finally, zooming out from the individual to the institution, I consider how the dynamics of self and the dynamics of social and institutional coordination can be thought of together, necessitating richer models of institutional organization and viability.

This situates postdigital research as an institutional disruption which can operate from the 'middle-out' of an organization. By being in possession of good models of the whole system, the postdigital researcher is able to steer themselves dynamically in intervention approaches in different contexts. Seen in this way, postdigital research is related to systemic approaches to organizational development [for example, operational research (Mingers 2006) or soft systems approaches (Checkland 1981)], but without the need for top-down implementation. Postdigital research has more flexibility to engage in transformation at different levels of organization: the postdigital researcher can be 'in the wires' of the organization rather than in an organizational box like a department. In particular, postdigital research can exploit the power of disruptive technologies to reorient pedagogical and structural practices while creating new niches where those practices can be further cultivated and enlarged. Given the manifest failure of top-down approaches to institutional change, the postdigital presents a new approach and some promising early results.

2 Hyperspecialisation, Tacit Knowledge, and Education's 'Codification Bottleneck'

- We are living in a period of rapid technological change where every generation is exposed to a transformed environment and social disruption from technology;
- Increase in specialization of technical skill, and speed of development in technological practices, means that technical knowledge becomes fleeting and not easily codifiable;
- Understanding patterns of tacit knowledge transmission requires deeper analytical focus on those processes operating closer to the level of perception, coordination, and dialogue.

Before considering the value of a postdigital perspective and the importance of values, it is worth taking stock of the impact of digital technologies on education and society. Amid the unfolding dynamics that entwine educational institutions, society and technology is the rapid increase in specialization (Milgram 2015; Bridle 2018). Computer technology is increasing precision and efficiency in design and development of products, automating routine operations, and accurately predicting trends and likely avenues for research and discovery. Across the disciplinary spectrum, from drug development to engineering to the arts and ecology, technology is driving change in a way where the codified content of traditional curricula exist uneasily alongside specialist toolsets which are becoming essential to disciplinary expertise.

Tools open new perspectives on learning and discovery in subdisciplines from computational chemistry, epidemiological modelling, to AI and statistics in the arts and sciences. The 'software milieu' develops at a remarkable pace, driven by open-source practices, the increasing ubiquity of shared web-based coding environments and social media. This requires teachers and students to either stay connected to the developmental trajectories of their particular specialist toolsets or get left behind. The need to 'stay relevant' induces anxiety among all educational stakeholders, which further feeds back into the instability of the system in its current form.

With such a pace of change, disciplinary codification – which is essential to how education organizes and stabilises itself into 'subjects' – is increasingly difficult. Education is faced with a 'codification bottleneck'. What matters for students and teachers is to be in a stream of discourse so that the new version of a software package, social platform, Python library or a new AI tool makes sense in the context of an ongoing conversation in which they have a real and living stake. The traditional methods of induction into a discourse, which relies on a codified curriculum which is increasingly out-of-date does not guarantee the personal stake which is essential to 'stay tuned' to fluid knowledge.

Education's fundamental role concerns an intergeneration transfer of knowledge in what Morin calls the inseparability of the 'individual ↔ society ↔ species' relationship (Morin 2001). If knowledge is lost from one generation to the next, as we see with the loss of indigenous knowledge (Magni 2017), then the risk is a corresponding loss developmental flexibility which may be required for ongoing survival. Education's traditional methods for performing the intergenerational transfer of knowledge rely on the codification, delivery, and examination of disciplinary knowledge. The imperfections of this have been apparent to educationalists for at least 100 years, but under the conditions which make codification increasingly difficult, new questions arise concerning how the intergenerational transfer of knowledge might now be organized.

Processes of learning involve consciousness, daily experience, relationships, feelings, reactions, and intentions, alongside the liminal world of dreams, sleep, and imagination. Consciousness somehow filters through the complex mechanisms of relations between perceptions, communications, and physiology to make judgements, write novels, create software and manage relationships (Seth 2021; Damasio 2019). How this works was always a mystery, but grappling with the question of how learning happens becomes more urgent if the crutch of curriculum becomes less effective. In its place, we need a deeper science of learning which accounts for the dynamics of human relationships within a fluid technological environment.

As Papert noted (in Kafai and Resnick 1996), we have no word for the 'science of learning' in the way that we have a word for the science of teaching (e.g., didactics, pedagogy). His suggestion was 'mathetics' from the Greek word *mathematikos* which was defined simply as 'being disposed to learn'. Papert's concern for the role of technology in learning was closely related to this search for a deeper science of learning, which extended far beyond modern descriptions of 'learning science' which delimit learning to institutional practices.

The practical and technical question to ask is: in a world of increasing specialization, how do we induct the next generation into a fluid discourse about knowledge, tools, and practices in a way which provides humanity with more options for survival? Part of a response to this lies in the need to reveal the actual experience of being in a stream of discourse. YouTube videos and streaming services like Twitch allow us to see specialized thought in action, as experts talk through their processes of fixing things, writing code, playing games, or designing products providing us with a kind of cognitive apprenticeship – if there is desire on the part of the learner to attend to it. But what do we perceive in these situations? What knowledge is transferred? How?

Knowledge that is enacted on streaming services in this way is rarely codified. Through enacting knowledge, what is perceived is what Polanyi called 'tacit knowledge' (Polanyi 2015; Takeuchi and Nonaka 1995), those aspects of knowledge which are revealed through the varying degrees of confidence and uncertainty, judgement, and physical behaviour. Video is a powerful medium for tacit knowledge because not only does it catch the nuance of 'knowing', but it also allows for repeated study of the idiosyncrasies of an expert's practice.

The intergenerational transfer of knowledge means that students must at some point become experts similarly able to express their own tacit knowledge, with its varying degrees of confidence, uncertainty, and judgement. There are things that can be codified from the experience of coding or fixing a car, but codified knowledge does not represent the full extent of knowledge in practice. To some extent this has long been recognized in education: it is why trainee musicians and actors have to perform, and doctors are examined through practical as well as theoretical tests.

There is an additional organizational dimension to this. Institutions and work environments buzz with streams of discourse and tacit knowledge. Those streams of discourse necessitate that some of what is known tacitly must become more commonly known. In highly innovative and fast-moving industries, it is no use to have a company's knowledge locked in an individual's head. It has to be somehow expressed and codified, and the codified knowledge must then be instilled in others in the organization. Education's adherence to codified knowledge in the curriculum, particularly as it is enshrined in assessment approaches and pedagogical design such as constructive alignment (Biggs and Tang 2011), may arguably suit it to doing the former. With regard to tacit knowledge, over-full curricula and assessment demands eat into the time and resources that can be expended on socialisation, serendipitous discovery and personal inquiry. This includes not only the teacher's tacit knowledge but that of students.

3 Modelling Tacit Knowledge in Education and Industry

If education is seen as a regulatory function in relation to the rest of society, attempting an intergenerational transfer of knowledge means this function must embrace the dynamics of tacit and codified knowledge within and beyond education. Polanyi's (2015) basic idea of 'tacit knowledge' has acquired more recent models of the dynamics of knowledge, among which Takeuchi and Nonaka's (1995) Socialisation, Externalisation, Combination, and Internalisation (SECI) model is helpful in situating tacit knowledge in an educational environment. With a rapidly changing technological context, the SECI model is useful if action is to be taken to address the ways in which knowledge is shaping the world. Takeuchi and Nonaka considered the dynamics which connect tacit knowledge to codified knowledge and organization in companies, but if we consider that the same dynamic operates in education too, then a combined cycle of Socialisation, Externalization, Combination, and Internalisation can join educational processes with processes in society. One way of representing this is shown in Fig. 1.

This shows two cycles of the SECI model connected in a way to suggest that apprenticeship-type engagements between industrial practice and educational practice entail a mutual dialogical encounter in which tacit knowledge can be transferred. Connecting the SECI model in this way invites comparison with other models of educational activity – particularly the Pask/Laurillard Conversational Framework (CF) (Laurillard 2013). However, while the CF considers the processes of externalisation (teach-back) and internalisation (learning) within a shared environment, the 'noise' of practical social encounters (in the middle of Fig. 1) between different environments and domains is where tacit encounters feed into students' expression of codified understanding. This further leads to new forms of externalization, and practices within the institution. On the right-hand side, the same dynamics reflect the concerns of wider society – from government to industry, health, or the arts.

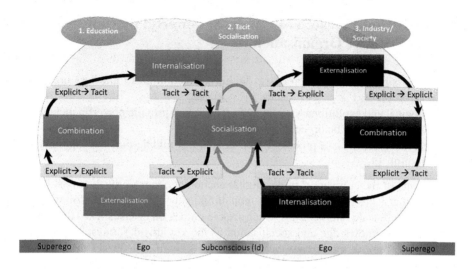

Fig. 1 SECI Relationship between socialisation and tacit knowledge between education (1) and society (3) adapted from Takeuchi and Nonaka (1995) situated against levels of the psyche

Within this centre of this diagram are the deep processes of dialogical and practical encounters, where there is high uncertainty involving deeper aspects of the psyche. Takeuchi and Nonaka argue that tacit knowledge can only be acquired by directly sharing experiences where "highly subjective insights, intuitions and hunches are also embraced" (Takeuchi and Nonaka 1995: vii). Figure 1 suggests that tacit socialisation can be considered through a Freudian lens as a 'subconscious' level of engagement, where more conscious (Ego-oriented) and normative (Superego-oriented) practices are associated with the 'Externalisation' of knowledge and the 'Combination' of knowledge respectively. The liminal zone between the subconscious and Ego-related practices is where the postdigital environment is at its most apparent and where the principal educational challenge concerns how to engender the revealing of uncertainty and contingency in the social context (Johnson et al. 2022a, b, c). With regard to the higher levels of the psyche (the Ego and Superego), away from the centre of the diagram, the processes of externalization, combination and internalization can be seen as a dividing line between the conventional approaches of educational research which are institution (and content)-centric and the postdigital approach, which is human relation-centric.

Models like this help us to consider education as a regulating dynamic. The education regulator feeds society with the means to continually restructure and order itself. It is driven by the noise and variety generated by fast-moving technologies and the tacit knowledge of people who know about them. Given this, we need to consider:

1. How postdigital encounters can be cultivated.
2. How social order can be created from the noise of those encounters, and create the conditions for new encounters.
3. How technologies might be enlisted to support these processes.

4 Postdigital Research as Catalysis: Powerful Disrupters and Effective Organisation

- It is possible to catalyse processes within an institution to alleviate organizational problems;
- Ecological and evolutionary models of organization provide powerful metaphors for how things can be organized differently;
- Catalytic research is a process which is operates middle-out, not top-down or bottom-up.

In terms of the cultivation of postdigital encounters, the approach to postdigital research that I present here concerns modelling using systems tools, followed by targeted small-scale interventions which seek to unlock otherwise locked dynamics. It targets tacit knowledge and socialisation as the key driver for system improvement. This, I argue, can create the potential for growth and further development from the middle-out within an organisation. As an approach to research, it differs from most conventional educational research paradigms in the sense that it is intended to catalyse development, rather than aggregate and analyse data from practice. Data-centric approaches are the opposite of catalysts in that they attenuate the variety of practice in order to identify causal variables and make recommendations for policy changes or exhort pedagogical practice. It is also distinct from design-based methods, which focuses on the iterative creation of solutions to problems. A catalytic approach, on the other hand, looks to disrupt patterns of practice so as to understand their underlying dynamics better, and then to intervene to amplify some aspects of those dynamics to see if they resonate with larger dynamics. Postdigital research involves an organic, middle-out approach to knowledge and organization similar to systems consultancy, but without the necessity for heavy top-down support.

What facilitates this middle-out organic approach to systems intervention is technology itself. Technology provides powerful disrupters which are easily demonstrable to different stakeholders in education, and which challenge established values and ways of doing things: current AI is only the most recent example. Unlike approaches to new technologies common in EdTech research, where the disrupter is seen as an agent of change which can be embraced to enhance the existing operation of education, the postdigital approach uses new technologies as a way of revealing the dynamics of existing practice, and then intervene in the light of increased knowledge of those dynamics.

Catalysis is something which is visibly in operation in ecology, and ecological metaphors can guide our processes of steering a middle-out intervention. The ecologist Robert Ulanowicz (2009) has highlighted the role of catalytic processes in the way that a vine grows, for example. Figure 2 illustrates this process in stages:

1. The vine begins with a root stem which carries nutrients and water to the rest of the plant.

Fig. 2 Ulanowicz (2009) diagram of vine growth

2. As the plant gets bigger it begins to grow new roots peripherally to the original stem.
3. As the plant matures, the original stem becomes redundant and withers, leaving the secondary roots as a more resilient source of nutrients and water.

In this cycle we see both catalysis and selection: the creation of new roots is catalytic, while the withering of the original root is selection. The overall developmental process is middle-out.

The creation of new intellectual communities provides one example of a similar catalytic situation. For example, one of advantages of the pandemic was that scholars from all over the world were all sat at their computers. Academics who had only been emailing each other about their ideas across different disciplinary forums, and occasionally meeting in conferences, could engage in more regular zoom meetings which became more focused on interdisciplinary connections as conversations became more wide-ranging. Two examples of this known to the author are the Alternative Natural Philosophy Association (ANPA n.d.), the Club of Remy (n.d.).

From a conventional educational or EdTech perspective, these processes can be seen as the result of a kind of 'implementation' of the technology. A postdigital lens sees it differently. The pandemic and its technology was a change in the context of intellectual engagement and communication which catalysed new forms of engagement through the agency of key scholars who saw an opportunity to make new connections. It was as if the uncertainty of the pandemic demanded new forms of social and intellectual organization which the physiological systems of individual scholars adapted to. Most importantly, those scholars who might have resisted technology before the pandemic saw new ways in which they could grow intellectually through making these connections.

How catalysis actually contributes to self-organisation of biological and social forms is much theorized in the systems sciences. Ulanowicz (2009) have argued that it involves an active role for what he calls the 'absences' of a system – what he calls (using a theological term) the 'apophatic'. Leydesdorff (2021) has argued that catalysis arises from the 'redundancy' of a system – which in educational terms, is the ability of the system to represent the same things in many different ways. These approaches are closely related and helpful in analysing the capacity of a system or a research approach to be catalytic within education or elsewhere.

However, there is another approach to understanding self-organisation and catalysis suggested by the cybernetician of von Foerster: that self-organisation is a process of producing 'order from noise' (von Foerster 2003). The noise in a system is the amount of energy it contains which doesn't have any directed purpose. The uncertainty of a fast-moving technological context is very noisy, as is the hubbub of institutional life. Most formal educational processes look to filter-out noise, and amplify the 'signal' or the 'information' which it regards as the content of what it is doing. These are attenuative operations.

Catalysis in a noisy environment does something different. Von Foerster illustrated the organizational effect of noise by imagining a collection of cubes where each side of the cube had a magnetic plate on it which had its magnetic field either pointed outwards (so it attracted other magnetized plates), or inwards, so that it had no effect. If the cubes are placed in a bag, they may form some kind of pattern. But if the bag is shaken (so noise is added to the system), the complexity of pattern that can be formed by the cubes increases.

This is why uncertainty is a key concept in postdigital research: it is the noise which shakes up the existing system and allows it to reform in more ordered ways. As von Foerster demonstrates (2003), the role of noise in producing order is complimentary to the role of information and pattern. It is why using technology to amplify uncertainty can catalyse new organizational development. With new organizational development comes a new and finer-grained capacity for making distinctions about domains of knowledge. It is also why a catalytic process at one level of the institution can stimulate noise in other parts of the system, thus enabling a middle-out intervention to grow into more widespread change.

What changes in the catalytic process are the human values which stabilise relations underpin socialisation and tacit knowledge. Understanding how values relate to catalytic processes of organisational change requires modelling the environment within which those processes unfold. The concept of value as a dynamic process is therefore central to help steer postdigital research.

5 Values and Distinctions in Education

- Values arise through ongoing processes which produce distinctions between individuals;
- Distinctions can be created, maintained, and changed in education;
- Distinctions can also be created, maintained, and changed by technologies.

To say that values arise from 'distinctions' is to say that somehow a boundary is drawn – and that something either falls within the boundary or it doesn't (Johnson et al. 2022a, b, c; Spencer-Brown 2011), and that there must be a process which continually makes the selection as to what is in and what is out. Distinctions are easier to draw than to talk about. Figure 3 illustrates three example distinctions of 'computer', 'education', and 'equity'.

Figure 3 suggests that technology is simultaneously a distinction and the context (or process) whereby that distinction is maintained. The postdigital lens puts the

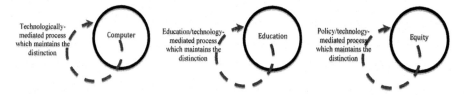

Fig. 3 Distinctions maintained by recursive feedback processes: 'Computer', 'Education', 'Equity'

focus on technology as contextual and observes that its effects must be an increasing uncertainty in the broader context of other distinctions made in education and society. If the means by which a distinction is maintained shifts through technological change, then the selection process of that distinction becomes more complex.

This is particularly interesting with a distinction like 'equity', since the means by which the distinction is upheld includes communication, perception, policy, legal structures, power, rights, obligations and responsibilities, all of which are managed through, and vulnerable to, the shifting technological context, and all of which are themselves distinctions. In saying that a value like 'equity' is a distinction, I mean that a value concerns a particular kind of semi-stable relation: what Leydesdorff (2021) calls a 'coordination of expectations'. This coordination must involve perceptual, psychic and social processes, all of which are subject to continually changing technological mediation. This situates axiology – the study of value – as the study of how such processes interact to produce and maintain particular distinctions for individuals, groups and societies.

It is possible to investigate the conditions within which value distinctions come to be drawn. Education provides one of these, and increasingly, technology provides another. With regard to distinctions as values, it can be noted that:

1. Not all distinctions are values, but value distinctions sit behind distinctions about objects, ideas, and practices. For example, schools show us the distinctions between maths and music (Johnson et al. 2022a, b, c), or between physics and PE, but the reason why those particular distinctions are made (and not, for example, distinctions about astrology or cybernetics) has to do with the values that underpin particular forms of curriculum, and the technologies and processes which reinforce them. In relation to those distinctions, we form our relations of value.

2. Distinctions are not fixed: they exist in relation to other distinctions and the social environment. Learning often involves discarding older distinctions in favour of distinctions that befit a more sophisticated understanding. Because distinctions are interconnected, a new distinction might involve the transformation of other distinctions. For example, what Land (2016) famously calls a 'threshold concept' can be seen as a distinction which transforms and reorganizes many other distinctions.

3. Distinction-making is an ongoing process. The processes of resolving what is inside the distinction with what is outside unfolds in a continually changing con-

text. Technological change is a change in the environment which challenges our distinction-making process: a distinction arises when it exists in a stable relationship with its environment. It is not uncommon for these stable relationships to involve contradictions and instability. At the distinction boundary there is liminality and fluidity of distinction-making.

4. Computer technology increasingly dominates the environment of distinction-making. The web changed our distinctions and expectations about communication, just as AI is changing our distinctions about expertise, knowledge and learning and what it means to be human. Technology, alongside human relationships, tweaks the perceptual apparatus which maintains the distinctions we make.

5. Distinctions can be changed by intervening in their constitutive processes. This can change individual values, social dynamics, expectations, and practices. All forms of propaganda have relied on this. The media, and most pertinently, social media, provide a good example of how technology's role in the distinction-making process can steer values. Politically inspired interference in the technical and communicative substructure of social media behaves as a kind of 'entropy pump' (Beer 1994a): a means of control whereby people are confused with contradictory distinctions so that they cannot form any clear perspective on their own distinctions.

There are systems approaches to analysing the ways that distinctions are formed in institutions and influence organisational dynamics (Ulrich 2000). For example, Eden and Ackerman's (2013) techniques of Strategic Options Development and Analysis (SODA) uses Kelly's (1963) theory of personal constructs to identify the different values of individuals in an organization. Since values are formed often in opposition to other values in other parts of the organization, networks of value can be drawn using SODA's 'cognitive mapping' approach. An example is shown in Fig. 4 of the cognitive map relating to technological innovation in a university law school, where the different stakeholder groups are defined according to the dynamics of value indicated by arrows which either attenuate the or reinforce those distinctions.

The arrows in Fig. 4 represent an indication of the dynamics of distinction-making. Since, from Fig. 3, all distinctions are processes of selection ('is x within the boundary or not?'), the dynamics between different distinction-making processes must concern the degree of uncertainty of those selections, which in turn is connected to the complexity of choice. The arrows between the different entities of Fig. 4 show the flow of complexity of choices that pass from one entity to another, and particularly whether those choices are amplified or attenuated from entity to entity.

For example, the 'computational thinking agenda' throws up many new complexities which were previously unknown, and which drives enthusiasts for digitalization, as well as policies for its implementation. The boundaries between different groups in Fig. 4 represent the conversion of one kind of activity on the outside into a different kind of activity on the inside: effectively it converts whatever complexity it is provided with into a new set of choices. So 'Student Employability' creates a set of complex choices which are converted into drivers and policies for updating the curriculum, and maintaining the existing curriculum, which produce further

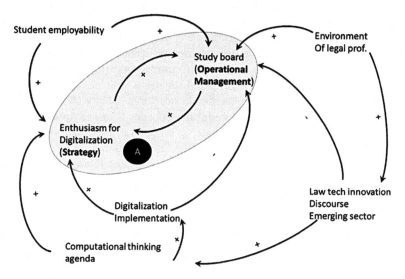

Fig. 4 Distinctions and boundaries within a university law department

choices (and tensions) to be managed elsewhere in the system. In understanding this complexity between different groups or entities, cybernetics provides a useful concept in 'variety'. Variety is not information or messages: it is the range of possible states that can be generated by a system. This means that the relations between the different boundaries is a relation between different sets of states. It also means that something happens at the interface between boundaries and arrows which converts one set of states into another.

The process of conversion of one kind of variety to another is called 'transduction' (Beer 1981; Simondon et al. 2017). The boundary of any distinction converts the variety of its environment into the variety of its internal organization, and that its operations internally can contribute to making its environment more habitable. In biological terms, we talk about the construction of 'niches' in which organisms survive. Each entity creates the conditions of its existence. Each entity's actions towards this can conflict with other organisms, with the net result being internal tension and organisational sclerosis.

6   Liminal Dynamics

- Human problems arise in the conflicts between distinctions;
- Psychotherapy is an approach to adjusting the processes of distinction-making to resolve conflicts;
- Articulating deep distinctions through dialogue or research activities can change the ways that processes upholding distinctions in conflict with one another can be reorganised.

The most obvious difficulty in researching education is that the educational system is very hard to change, and while research is voluminous, merely writing about educational phenomena rarely creates change. Indeed, discourse can feed self-reinforcing dynamics: education is a tangle of competing narratives whose conflicts appear to stabilise each other. Networks of distinctions which define themselves in opposition to one another produce ultrastable structures (Ashby 1960). Even when fundamental change in the context of education occurs – for example, through the rise of the web, or now perhaps, AI – those for whom a new technology is a liberation cause those who see it as a threat to defend their position more strongly. For all the potential transformative effects of the web, it is remarkable that students continue to study a uniform curriculum, complete the same assessment tasks, sit in rows facing the teacher (either in lecture rooms, or now on Zoom), enrol in September and graduate in July. Meanwhile the disruption caused by new tools and practices is damped through the invention of new policy. In this light, the aggregate of institutional change appears small (Beer 1994b). Yet at an individual level, if values did not change there would be no learning: there is always development in the light of conversation with others set against the noise of institutional and personal life in a technological context.

Marion Milner talked about the 'human problem of schools' (1938/2018) in studying the effects of the complex dynamics of school in 1938 on the psychic life of the students, teachers, and parents. These complex dynamics are the aggregate result of attempts to resolve problems, where many of these problems are generated by education itself. This is (as Illich noted 1971) a form of 'iatrogenic' ('healer-induced') sickness in the education system, which is particularly noticeable with current approaches to technology. Making a similar point, the cybernetician Heinz Von Foerster (a friend of Illich) summed this up: 'we have, hopefully only temporarily, relinquished our responsibility to ask for a technology that will solve existent problems. Instead we have allowed existent technology to create problems it can solve' (von Foerster 1984).

Among the problems education creates which it attempts to solve are: how to know assessment is fair, how to tell success from failure, how to codify status (certification), how to classify knowledge (reductionism), the time learning takes, how to know what's true, how to know who to trust, and how to meet people who might have similar interests to yourself. Each of these introduces new organizational problems – how to organize people, knowledge, time, resources, prestige and rank, buildings, and finances. All of these are far removed from education's regulatory function of ensuring the intergenerational transfer of knowledge.

What the postdigital perspective brings to this is inspection of the dynamics whereby the system's behaviour produces new problems. Why, for example, do we see the intellectual tribalism in education described by Becher and Trowler (2001)? Even in education research departments, we see the competing sociological paradigms (Burrell and Morgan 1979) of 'functionalism', 'phenomenology' or 'critical theory'. As Becher says, each tribe distinguishes itself from the others, even 'going to war' with each other. Much of the discourse is dominated by defence or attack of one tribal position against another. This, I suggest, is a matter about value dynamics, not values themselves. Only when the dynamics of value are considered is it possible to inspect the underlying institutional pathologies that they give rise to.

Milner (1938/2018) was postdigital in her outlook long before computers appeared. Her approach was about understanding the value dynamics between teachers, students, and parents in a girls' school in the 1930s. She engaged in many strategies to understand and intervene with the children, parents and teachers in the school with the aim of trying to provide greater capacity for individuals to process the complexity of their environment. She put much emphasis on listening, noting that (with regard to the children):

> Much of the time now spent in exhortation is fruitless; and that the same amount of time given to the attempt to understand what is happening would, very often, make it possible for difficult girls to become co-operative rather than passively or actively resistant. It seems also to be true that very often it is not necessary to do anything; the implicit change in relationship that results when the adult is sympathetically aware of the child's difficulties is in itself sufficient. (Milner 1938/2018: 290)

Being 'sympathetically aware of the child's difficulties' was something that Milner's psychotherapeutic training provided her with a coherent theoretical frame for examining value dynamics. Milner (1938/2018) adopted a similar philosophy to that espoused by Read's 'Education Through Art' (2021), and she used a variety of imaginative techniques to tease-out the tacit knowledge from the children. For example, drawing on some techniques of psychological projection, she developed an innovative 'postcard sorting' game she devised to identify the interests of the children, and in her interviews with the children, she would ask about their daydreams, and where their anxieties lay. This was a process of connecting the tacit domain of understanding with the expressed desires of the children.

Milner's (1938/2018) use of projective techniques placed particular emphasis on creativity and expression in education. In both schools and universities, her work was aligned with other psychotherapeutic approaches to art education (particularly Ehrenzweig 1967) with an emphasis on the role of making as an expressive engagement with the environment. This, she suggests, assists in the rebalancing of inner psychic forces. This emphasis on psychotherapy, art, and expression was a way of loosening the distinctions and values that individuals make.

7   Individuation

- The maintenance of the distinction of 'self' is a motivating force in human behaviour;
- Individuation is a name given to the process whereby selves become whole rather than split;
- In split selves distinctions and values contradict each other, but nevertheless maintain each other in a mutually reinforcing conflict.

The boundary of the personal 'self' and the boundaries within the education system are very different, but they share similar dynamics. The personal self contains ambitions, dreams, practical concerns, and relationships. The dynamics between these components and their organization has an impact on the adaptability of individuals, which in turn impacts on the practices and problems of the institutions in which they work. In Freudian psychodynamics, the self which is articulated and operates at a practical day-to-day level is shaped by the superego, which bears upon the subconscious to ensure that behaviour fits norms. However, this can lead to splits in personality between the dynamics of the ego/subconscious and those of the superego.

At an organisational level, problems arise from these dynamics in individuals – particularly those individuals in positions of power. Most approaches to organizational consultancy and systems theory focus on changing the psychodynamics of key actors (for example, Checkland 1981; Beer 1994a; Engeström et al. 2007). If there is an objective to this kind of organizational therapy, it is to find a way in which individual psychodynamics and organizational dynamics can better tune with one another. In a context of fast-moving technology, where it is difficult to codify practices, this balance between individual psychodynamics and organizational dynamics becomes more important, otherwise the institution will rely on levels of codification and bureaucracy and lose adaptive flexibility.

In the modern world, the construction of self always occurs in the context of technologies. This point was emphasized by Gilbert Simondon et al. (2017) who used the same word from psychotherapy, 'individuation', to describe the process by which any entity – a person, an organism, or a tool – becomes concrete. Simondon points to the distinction-making processes made by the individual in a world of technical objects. Many of these distinction-making processes lie at the interfaces between humans, machines, and institutions. Simondon's connection between technology and the construction of self through individuation presents an important opportunity for postdigital research. If the construction of self is partly dependent on the engagement with technology, then it means that intervention with technology can become a tool [rather like Milner's (1938/2018) and Read's (2021) uses of art as a therapy], for changing the way selves are constructed.

From a research perspective, a lot depends on having a good model of the research situation, and that means having a model of the distinctions that people make – and specifically, the value distinctions that are made. As a Jungian analyst trying to determine the behaviour, motivation and feelings of students, teachers, parents and managers, Milner's (1938/2018) method was designed to tease out the distinctions that her research participants make; she is interested in ways in which those distinctions might be changed, and in the ways that a change at one level leads to a change at other levels.

But if we model the distinctions that a person makes, it is not a list of those distinctions or values that is required, but an understanding of the dynamics whereby those distinctions and values (and not others) are maintained. In considering this, we have to consider that all distinctions arise through relations, and so the postdigital approach is to fundamentally focus on the betweenness of education.

8 The Logic of Postdigital Betweenness

- At the boundary of the self, processes convert energy from the environment into physiological structures, producing expectations and dreams while physiological structures create energy through communication and organization;
- Relations between transduction processes can get tangled and can be untangled.

The postdigital lens situates technology as contextual. and observes that the effects of technology must be an increasing uncertainty and in the contexts of education. A shifting context means a flux in the ways values arise in the dance between the external context of education and the internal processes of a body. Investigation as to how this might work was one of the key themes in early cybernetics which gave rise to neural networks in the 1940s through the work of Warren McCulloch (2016). In recent years, the work of Solms (2021) and Friston (2020) developed dynamic processes drawing on Freud and Strachey's (1966) description of energy dynamics. This work also draws on cybernetic ideas.

In the 1940s, the relationship between mechanical systems with feedback and biological systems was a central concern. Interest in what became known as neural networks developed alongside cybernetics, and indeed the concept of the network itself. What kind of logic did a neural net possess? Drawing on a stream of work in psychology from psychophysics (Fechner 1966; Weber 2020; Thurstone 1927) where nineteenth- and early twentieth-century psychology attempted to understand the relationship between external stimuli and internal perception, McCulloch (2016) presented a cybernetic model of the internal perceptual system. He considered the way that the brain consisted of neurons wired together in an interconnected (what he called 'heterarchical') fashion, arguing that this meant that the Aristotelian idea that logic was a matter of 'true' and 'false' with nothing in-between (the 'Law of the Excluded Middle') did not reflect the physiology of cognition. He saw perception as a circular process involving circuits that ran partly within the body through the nervous system, and then through environmental stimuli which were picked up by physiological sensors. This circularity was presented in a diagram in which he sought to explain the circular neural logic (Fig. 5).

Figure 5 shows an adaptation of McCulloch's (2016) diagram detailing four loops. Each loop is labelled A, B, C, and D. Each loop represents a circuit within the body (the heavy line) and a circuit in the environment (the dotted line). Each loop has a sensor, an amplifier and attenuator, and the outputs of each attenuator/amplifier are connected to next loop, and the system is circularly connected via the line that connects the outermost loop to the innermost loop.

McCulloch's (2016) question when examining this setup was: What kind of a logic does it possess? He noted that the system's complex dynamics could systemically show a contradiction in expressing that A > B, B > C, while C > A. The value of any particular loop being greater than any other loop was dependent on all the other value loops. If it is then assumed that the environment within which this 'value' system operates is highly fluid, then the conditions under which any value is stabilized is both highly complex (involving many loops), and highly sensitive to

Fig. 5 McCulloch's
(1945) model of nervous
circuits

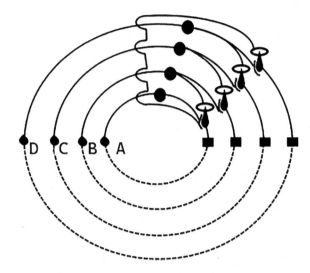

environmental change. Indeed the only way that such a system could occupy stable
states is if, in its environment, there existed another perceptual system of similar
complexity (i.e. another person).

When Milner (1938/2018) was investigating the ways in which her research participants were making distinctions, she was trying to get a feel for how this dynamic
of value was operating so that she could intervene with it by stimulating the perceptual circuits with external stimuli (postcard sorting, artistic activities, questioning
about daydreams, etc). If these loops of distinction-making are considered in the
context of other loops of distinction making operations at the level of the institution,
the research space becomes a search for effective interventions to reorganize the
ways values propagate through the whole system.

McCulloch's (2016) model of perception was simplistic, but a more thoroughly
specified model was developed by Beer (1994a) to analyse the distinction-making
processes within institutions. McCulloch was Beer's mentor, and McCulloch's
ideas had a deep influence on Beer's understanding of business and social organisations. What was apparent was that McCulloch's diagrams represent an indeterminate social system within which there were undecidable propositions which
somehow stabilized in a social context. This aspect of undecidability and the management of complexity found a form of expression in Beer's (1994a) understanding
of the relationship between institutions and their environment. Beer's metaphor for
doing this remained physiological, but rather than consider the neural activity of
perception, Beer expanded the metaphor to consider the different components of a
physiological system: heart, liver, kidneys, brain, etc. – and the associated physiological regulating mechanisms between them. Social institutions too had different
components which operated together for the maintenance of viability of the whole.

A second important step in expanding this model to understand societies and
institutions was to consider that the essential systemic behaviour concerned the
management not of individual values, but of the variety of possible values a system

could express. Different components of a physiological system, or an educational system have different amounts of variety, and these imbalances of variety have to be managed in order to maintain sustainable relationships between the components.

The most obvious example of variety management concerns the relationship between an organism and its environment. All organisms have less complexity than their natural environments – so how can any organism manage its relation with complexity that otherwise might appear to overwhelm them? In terms of variety, the organism has two basic options for action: it can attenuate those aspects of environmental variety which are not relevant to it; and it can take action to amplify its own variety so as to create a part of the environment that suits its own existence – a 'niche'. The result is that the organism maintains its boundary with which, as with any boundary, there is always a question as to what belongs within the boundary and what doesn't. Beer (1994a) argued that a higher-order system is required to deal with this uncertainty and to steer the organism's adaptive processes as the environment changes. This higher-level system he called a metasystem, and Beer argued that complex multi-component systems like bodies and corporations consisted of functional components performing different levels of regulation – some at the operational level, some at the meta-systemic level (see Fig. 6).

Technology interferes with ways of perceiving the world. Taking into account the model that McCulloch (2016) presents together with Beer's (1994a) model of institutional organization, it is possible to model the ways in which perceptual changes can lead to changes in values, which in turn can have effects on the structural organization of institutions. The possession of a rich model like this can help situate the interventions that are made to improve things. The results from some explicitly postdigital interventions in the light of these kinds of models have been promising (Johnson et al. 2020, 2022a, b, c).

Milner (1938/2018) didn't have these kind of cybernetic models to situate her interventions, but she did have a psychodynamic model which led her to direct her research practice in schools. There are strong similarities between the Freudian

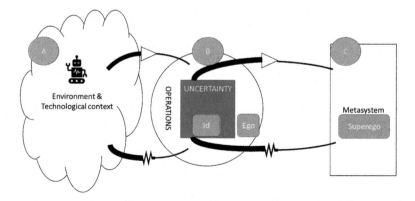

Fig. 6 Diagram of the relationship between environment, operations, and metasystem adapted from Beer (1981)

psychodynamic model (Freud and Strachey 1966) and Beer's (1994a) model: as Fig. 6 indicates, both feature uncertainty (Freudian Id), an outward set of operations engaging with the world (Ego), and a higher-level system that seeks to steer those operations according to social expectations (Superego). The Superego's role is particularly interesting, because as Talcott Parsons (in Sills 1968) observed, Freud's invention of the superego was a recognition that 'the expression of instinctual need was regulated by the society's moral standards—often, but in no simple sense always, in conflict with instinctual needs—and that these standards were introjected into the personality itself, becoming components of its structure'.

This is where a dynamic of value begins, and from this starting point, it is possible to conceive, as Milner did (1938/2018), of ways of working within a system to adjust the dynamics so as to help individuals deal with their inner and outer conflicts in the course of being able to facilitate psychotherapeutic processes.

9   Conclusion: Good Regulators and Models of Good Regulators

As Morin (2001) notes, human beings are the only possible good regulators of the transfer of knowledge from one generation to the next, but the regulatory function necessitates a deeper understanding of what he calls the 'individual ↔ society ↔ species' relationship. But good regulators are constructed in a society, and they must have a good model of the system they are trying to regulate. If the society in which the regulator is made prevents the regulator from developing a good model, then we will have bad regulators. It seems that our present educational system is a bad regulator which is likely to get worse. With increasingly powerful machine intelligence which will amplify individual capability even more, it is hard not to think that the existing technology will no longer be able to withstand the challenge of technology.

The fundamental problem is the system's inability to process the variety of society in a world where that variety is being amplified by technologies. The education system's attenuative approach will lead to more bias, more inequality, and less adaptability. It is also not helped by the fact that educational research is also attenuative. Ironically, this is even true of critical research which highlights the pathology of attenuative education!

I have made three fundamental proposals for how a postdigital research approach can address this. Firstly, I suggest that unlike conventional educational research, postdigital research should be catalytic, not attenuative. The fundamental relationship between researcher and research context is inverted, and the researcher seeks to discover existing mechanisms latent in institutional structures which, through careful and targeted support, can be activated to produce new ways of working. I have suggested that this catalytic process is essentially a middle-out process.

Secondly, I have suggested that germane to this middle-out process is the focus on uncertainty, and the production of order from noise. This throws the spotlight on what the attenuative system discards, not on what it selects.

Finally, at the heart of this process is the acknowledgement that within a context of increasing technological complexity and capability, our technology of education – in whatever form it takes – must tackle the fundamental process of engagement with underlying tacit and subconscious knowledge. The increasing fluidity of our technological world means that distinctions will become less clear, necessitating tacit engagement as a way to come to deeper knowledge. Collaborative, dialogical, practical, and performative scenarios for learning are going to become increasingly important in engendering good judgement and fine distinction-making in a world where it will be increasingly difficult to rely on established norms and rules.

Behind the fluidity of our knowledge sit tacit assumptions that motivate behaviour. These deep distinctions concern fundamental values about which only engagement and challenge is able to explicate and orchestrate reconfigurations of value. New technological possibilities will arise which will enable deeper inspection of tacit knowledge and values. It is for us to construct a good enough model of our changing environment so that we can anticipate what is likely to come next.

References

Andersen, C. U., Cox, G., & Papadopoulos, G. (2014). Postdigital research—editorial. *A Peer-Reviewed Journal About, 3*(1), 5–7. https://doi.org/10.7146/aprja.v3i1.116067.

ANPA. (n.d.). Alternative Natural Philosophy Association. https://anpa.onl. Accessed 17 April 2023.

Ashby, W. R. (1960). The Brain as Regulator. *Nature, 186*(4722), 413–413. https://doi.org/10.1038/186413a0.

Ashby, W. R. (2015). *Introduction To Cybernetics*. Eastford, CT: Martino Fine Books.

Barnett, R. (2014). *Thinking and Rethinking the University*. Abingdon: Routledge.

Becher, T., & Trowler, P. (2001). *Academic Tribes and Territories*. Maidenhead: Open University Press.

Beer, S. (1981). *Brain of the Firm*. Chichester and New York: John Wiley & Sons.

Beer, S. (1993). *Designing Freedom*. Toronto: House of Anansi.

Beer, S. (1994a). *Beyond Dispute*. Chichester and New York: John Wiley & Sons.

Beer, S. (1994b). *Platform for change: a message from Stafford Beer*. Chichester and New York: John Wiley and Sons.

Biesta, G. (2017). *The Rediscovery of Teaching*. New York: Routledge.

Biggs, J. B., & Tang, C. S.-K. (2011). *Teaching for Quality Learning at University: What the Student Does*. 4th Ed. Maidenhead and New York: Mcgraw-Hill and Open University Press.

Bourdieu, P., Passeron, J. C., Nice, R., & Bottomore, T. B. (2014). *Reproduction in education, society, and culture*. Los Angeles, CA: Sage.

Bridle, J. (2018). *New dark age: technology, knowledge and the end of the future*. London, UK and Brooklyn, NY: Verso.

Burrell, G., & Morgan, G. (1979). *Sociological Paradigms and Organisational Analysis: elements of the sociology of corporate life*. London: Routledge.

Checkland, P. (1981). *Systems Thinking, Systems Practice*. Chichester and New York: John Wiley and Sons.

Claxton, G. (2002). *Building learning power : helping young people become better learners*. Bristol: TLO.

Claxton, G. (2009). *What's the point of school?: rediscovering the heart of education*. Richmond: Oneworld.

Club of Remy. (n.d.). Really-relevant Emergency Mindfully-minding You. https://www.clubofremy.org/. Accessed 17 April 2023.

Damasio, A. R. (2019). *The strange order of things: life, feeling, and the making of cultures*. New York: Vintage Books.

Eden, C., & Ackermann, F. (2013). *Making Strategy*. London: SAGE Publications.

Ehrenzweig, A. (1967). *The Hidden Order of Art*. London: Weidenfeld & Nicolson.

Engeström, Y., Miettinen, R., & Punamäki, R-L. (2007). *Perspectives on activity theory*. Cambridge: Cambridge University Press.

Fechner, G. T. (1966). *Elements of Psychophysics*. New York: Holt, Rinehart and Winston.

Freud, S., & Strachey, J. (1966). *Project for a scientific psychology (1950 [1895])*. London: Hogarth Press.

Friston, K. J. (2020). The importance of being precise: Commentary on 'New Project for a Scientific Psychology: General Scheme' by Mark Solms. *Neuropsychoanalysis*, 22(1–2), 57–61. https://doi.org/10.1080/15294145.2021.1878610.

Illich, I. (1971). *Deschooling society*. London: Marion Boyars.

Jandrić, P., MacKenzie, A., & Knox, J. (2022). Postdigital Research: Genealogies, Challenges, and Future Perspectives. *Postdigital Science and Education*. https://doi.org/10.1007/s42438-022-00306-3.

Johnson, M. W., Rodriguez-Arciniegas, S., & Kataeva, A. N. (2020). Comparative judgement and the visualisation of construct formation in a personal learning environment. *Interactive Learning Environments*. https://doi.org/10.1080/10494820.2020.1799030.

Johnson, M. W., Maitland, E., Torday, J., & Fiedler, S. H. D. (2022a). Reconceiving the Digital Network: From Cells to Selves. In M. A. Peters, P. Jandrić, & S. Hayes (Eds.), *Bioinformational Philosophy and Postdigital Knowledge Ecologies* (pp. 39–58). Cham: Springer. https://doi.org/10.1007/978-3-030-95006-4_3.

Johnson, M. W., Alavi, K., & Holm-Janas, V. (2022b). Communicative Musicality, Learning and Energy: A Holographic Analysis of Sound Online and in the Classroom. *Postdigital Science and Education*. https://doi.org/10.1007/s42438-022-00355-8.

Johnson, M. W., Suvorova, E. A., & Karelina, A. A. (2022c). Digitalization and Uncertainty in the University: Coherence and Collegiality Through a Metacurriculum. *Postdigital Science and Education*, 4(3), 772–792. https://doi.org/10.1007/s42438-022-00324-1.

Kafai, Y. B., & Resnick, M. (1996). *Constructionism in practice: designing, thinking, and learning in a digital world*. Mahwah, NJ: Lawrence Erlbaum Associates.

Kelly, G. A. (1963). *Theory of Personality: the psychology of personal constructs*. New York: W. W. Norton.

Land, R., Meyer, J. H. F., Flanagan, M. T., & Springerlink (2016). *Threshold Concepts in Practice*. Rotterdam: Sense.

Laurillard, D. (2013). *Rethinking University Teaching*. London: Routledge. https://doi.org/10.4324/9781315012940.

Leydesdorff, L. (2021). *The Evolutionary Dynamics of Discursive Knowledge*. Cham: Springer. https://doi.org/10.1007/978-3-030-59951-5.

Magni, G. (2017). Indigenous knowledge and implications for the sustainable development agenda. *European Journal of Education*, 52(4), 437–447. https://doi.org/10.1111/ejed.12238.

McCulloch, W. S. (1945). A heterarchy of values determined by the topology of nervous nets. *The Bulletin of Mathematical Biophysics*, 7(2), 89–93. https://doi.org/10.1007/bf02478457.

McCulloch, W. S. (2016). *Embodiments of mind*. Cambridge, MA: The MIT Press.

Millgram, E. (2015). *The great endarkenment: philosophy for an age of hyperspecialization.* Oxford and New York: Oxford University Press.

Milner, M. (1938/2018). *The Human Problem in Schools.* London: Routledge.

Mingers, J. (2006). *Realising Systems Thinking: Knowledge and Action in Management Science.* New York: Springer. https://doi.org/10.1007/0-387-29841-X.

Morin, E. (2001). *Seven complex lessons in education for the future.* Paris: UNESCO.

Takeuchi, H., & Nonaka, I. (1995). *The knowledge-creating company: How Japanese companies create the dynamics of innovation.* New York: Oxford University Press.

Thurstone, L. L. (1927). A law of comparative judgment. *Psychological Review, 34*(4), 273–286. https://doi.org/10.1037/h0070288.

Polanyi, M., & Nye, M. J. (2015). *Personal knowledge: towards a post-critical philosophy.* Chicago, IL: University of Chicago Press.

Read, H. (2021). *Education Through Art.* Melbourne: Hassell Street Press.

Robinson, K. (2011). *Out of our minds: learning to be creative.* Hoboken, NJ: John Wiley and Sons.

Rousseau, J.-J. (1966). *Emile.* New York: Teachers College Press.

Seth, A. (2021). *BEING YOU: a new science of consciousness.* London: Dutton.

Sills, D. L. (Ed.). (1968). *International encyclopedia of the social sciences. Vol. 11[-12].* New York and London: Macmillan Company and The Free Press.

Simondon, G., Malaspina, C., & Rogove, J. (2017). *On the mode of existence of technical objects.* Minneapolis, MN: University of Minnesota Press.

Solms, M. (2021). *The hidden spring: a journey to the source of consciousness.* New York: W.W. Norton and Company.

Spencer-Brown, G. (2011). *Laws of form.* Leipzig: Bohmeier.

Ulanowicz, R. E. (2009). *A Third Window.* West Conshohocken, PA: Templeton Foundation Press.

Ulrich, W. (2000). Reflective Practice in the Civil Society: The contribution of critically systemic thinking. *Reflective Practice, 1*(2), 247–268. https://doi.org/10.1080/713693151.

Von Foerster, H. (1984). *Observing Systems.* Seaside, CA: Intersystems.

Von Foerster, H. (2003). *Understanding understanding: Essays on cybernetics and cognition.* New York: Springer. https://doi.org/10.1007/b97451.

Weber, E. H. (2020). *E. H. Weber on The Tactile Senses.* London: Psychology Press.

Part III
Postdigital Sensibilities

Postdigital Research in Education: Towards Vulnerable Method and Praxis

Michael Jopling

1 Introduction

This chapter takes a simple approach to complex issues. It brings together two terms: postdigital and vulnerability, in order to apply them to the process, aims and praxis of conducting research in education. There are a number of justifications for this. One is their increasing ubiquity, which suggests that both postdigital and vulnerability capture something of the essence and texture of our context. Bringing them together may help us to see both terms in different lights and explore the challenging nature of our times and their potential for transformation. Another reason is their conceptual overlap. The terms share an openness to uncertainty and possibility, to what Benjamin (1979: 243) in a different context called 'the spark of contingency', which are applicable to our work as researchers, educators, and education researchers. This is reflected in the very notion of the postdigital, which is notoriously and explicitly resistant to definition. Jandrić et al.'s (2018: 895) ground-clearing declaration points the way in its assertion that: 'The postdigital is hard to define; messy; unpredictable; digital and analog; technological and non-technological; biological and informational. The postdigital is both a rupture in our existing theories and their continuation.'

These notions of messiness and unpredictability are particularly important. The elements of combination and problematising combination (e.g., of the technological and the non-technological) also help justify the chapter's commingling of the postdigital and the vulnerable. This reflects the indivisibility signalled in Knox's (2019: 368) identification in the more specific context of critical educational research of the need explicitly to address 'the increasing entanglement of digital technology in capitalism and capitalist society, in which data has become a valuable resource, and

M. Jopling (✉)
University of Brighton, Brighton, UK
e-mail: M.Jopling@brighton.ac.uk

education itself has become a site for its associated entrepreneurialism'. Knox's use of the word 'entanglement' emphasises the fact that research needs to examine the human subjectivities involved as well as the (supposedly) objective rationalities at play (Ritzer 2018; Hayes 2021) in order to reflect and understand the messiness that such rationalities deny. This hybridity is key: Lewis (2020: 265) also reminds us of the 'always already' commingling of the analogue and the digital and the increasingly false opposition between the digital and the 'real'.

Cramer's (2015: 12) early claim that the postdigital describes 'either a contemporary disenchantment with digital information systems and media gadgets, or a period in which our fascination with these systems and gadgets has become historical' is also relevant, although the messianic terms in which some aspects of digital innovation are still described suggests this historicity has not always been achieved. These issues are helpfully problematised elsewhere in this book in Ralston's (2023) notion of 'postdigital parity, which kicks away 'the ladder that permanently hierarchizes the digital over the predigital' and 'promises to establish symmetry between humans and machines, the predigital and the digital, as a baseline from which to formulate judgments about appropriate valuation or prioritization'.

Bringing together vulnerability and method in a postdigital context encourages us to trace how developments such as the datafication of so much of our work in education and elsewhere and the blurring of the human and the digital have increased our sense of precarity to the extent that we all experience them but at the same time remain paradoxically complicit in the demonisation of the vulnerable. This chapter suggests that as postdigital and educational researchers, as human beings, we might address the uncertainty captured in the postdigital by accessing, rather than denying, our vulnerability and integrating it into our praxis as researchers. As well as allowing us to understand, and potentially improve, our situation, this may go some way towards countering the neoliberal concentration on the depersonalised achievement of expected progress, outcomes, and impact, so that we can also learn from exploring the living narratives and experiences (Hayes 2021) of learners, teachers, and researchers. Finally, it should be emphasised that the theoretical framework for a method presented here is intended to be emergent and developmental. As such, the chapter should be regarded as a conceptual experiment, which outlines only one of many possible approaches that could be proposed for postdigital education research.

2   Mess and Uncertainty

Despite attempts to rationalise education, symbolised most clearly perhaps in the incorporation of digital technologies into educational governance through an increased reliance on measurement and metrification and the emerging adaptations collected in the term 'precision education' (Williamson 2019), education (and by extension education research) remains a messy business. It is also worth noting that after the (non-)definitional statement quoted above, Jandrić et al. (2018: 895) go on to add that 'such messiness seems to be inherent to the contemporary human condition'. Similar thoughts are expressed in Reader's (2021: 156) assertion in relation to postdigital humans that '[t]he boundaries are blurred, messy and complex, and the challenge is to keep track of developments which are already well underway', which catches the urgency of the need to remain cognisant of the speed of change.

This highlights the ambiguity of the 'post' in the postdigital in that, as the dialogues collected in Jandrić et al. (2019) claim, it signals 'a critical holding to account of the broad cultural understanding that the term "digital" has come to represent' (166), including its association with ecological crisis, and 'keeps us hopeful that new possibilities remain' (169). This note of hope amidst crisis might remind us of the paradoxical force of Benjamin's (2015: 265) description of the historical materialist's task of 'blasting a specific life out of the era or a specific work out of the lifework. As a result of this method the lifework is preserved and at the same time cancelled.' This note of ambiguity suggests that it makes sense to regard the 'post' of postdigital in similar ways to the 'post' in 'post-punk' music and culture. Butt et al. (2016: 12) emphasise the dynamic nature of this development: 'the shift into post-punk didn't involve a simple setting-aside of [those] rules, it entailed a constant renegotiation'. They go on to quote Green Gartside of Scritti Politti's comment that 'he wanted to make a music that was as uncertain and as unsure as he felt. Post-punk invented ways to dramatize that uncertainty'. This impression of uncertainty has only been heightened 40 or so years later.

Uncertainty also points towards Slater's (2022: 151) identification of a tension in 'prevailing perspectives about contemporary education', created by 'the incongruity between the proliferation of affirmative concepts in both academic and public discourse about education and the deteriorating political, economic, and ecological conditions globally'. Deteriorating conditions are something with which the postdigital has been extensively concerned, but the examples he offers of affirmative concepts, which are said to be opposed to deficit-based neoliberal explanations of inequalities and disadvantages, include grit, resilience, and character-building, concepts which also run the neoliberal risk of locating the responsibility for overcoming disadvantage in the individual. In addressing these issues, Slater (2022) uses the figure of the conjuncture, not in Hall and Massey's (2010: 55) sense of contradictions 'fus[ing] in a ruptural unity', but as a catastrophic conjuncture in which neoliberal capitalism is exhausted but alternatives are not yet available. The question of the extent to which vulnerability can function as a response and possible means of examining this catastrophe, as well as interrogating these affirmative concepts, in and through education research, also influenced the development of this chapter.

Finally, it is worth acknowledging the relevance in this context of Law's (2004) exploration of mess in social science research. He rejects the desire for stability, certainty, and generality in favour of an aspiration '[t]o live more in and through slow method, or vulnerable method, or quiet method. Multiple method, Uncertain method. Diverse method.' (Law 2004: 11) This preference for combining vulnerability, uncertainty, and diversity in approaching research would appear to have the potential to allow us to explore the situation in which we find ourselves authentically and fruitfully. To this, I would add Halberstam's notion of low theory, which tries to locate all the in-between spaces that save us from being snared by the hooks of hegemony and speared by the seductions of the gift shop. But it also makes its peace with the possibility that alternatives dwell in the murky waters of a counterintuitive, often impossibly dark and negative realm of critique and refusal. (Halberstam 2011: 2)

The appeal to high and low culture, theory and knowledge allows access to the hybridity already identified and the possibility of answers to Law's (2004: 63) provocative question: 'How to think the in-between?'

Boyd (2021: 22) is in similar territory when she explicitly describes the entangled nature of learning in online classrooms as 'messy' to indicate that 'the approach is not perfect, but it also suggests a degree of playfulness', a characterisation which we should take seriously. In the same edited collection, Buchanan (2021: 124) suggests that postdigital theory 'provides a useful, multidimensional lens for looking at teaching, one that goes beyond looking at the effectiveness of specific teaching and learning practices' to incorporate the digital and the analogue, the material and the social. Jandrić et al. (2019: 166) remind us that the postdigital is about dragging the digital into the mud: 'rubbing its nose in the complexities of everyday practice, such as managing a class of 7-year-olds working on tablets' and the messiness and openness to contingency of daily learning and teaching should not be underestimated. They go on to suggest that educational research and practice must also inhabit the postdigital age paranoically, which 'means that pedagogy has to always be sceptical, searching and uncertain' (Jandrić et al. 2019: 180).

This gestures towards issue of trust and holding your nerve in relinquishing control, which returns us to Boyd (2021: 22): 'The key lies in admitting uncertainty, so students can see that staff members are also unsure of the answer. It shows that learning to puzzle out the answer together, to embrace uncertainty, 'not-knowing', and 'not-yetness' is acceptable.' For learning and pedagogy we can also read research methodology. This openness to risk, which requires courage for anyone working in neoliberalised schools or universities, is captured in Tauritz's (2016 in Boyd 2021) notion of 'uncertainty competences'. It also points towards the notion of vulnerability.

3   (Re)Conceptualising Vulnerability in and for Postdigital Times

Law's (2004) inclusion of 'vulnerable method' in his brief taxonomy of approaches may look like an aside, but it also offers a potential way of approaching research in postdigital contexts. Vulnerability is closely tied to uncertainty. In the context of teacher education, Dale and Frye (2009: 124) suggest that teachers should remain learners in order to 'experience the joys and the delights as well as the discomforts and tensions of vulnerability and uncertainty'. This echoes Larrivee's (2000) observation that openness to uncertainty in addressing a problem is an important part of developing a reflective approach to teaching. It also parallels Gilson's (2011) concept of 'epistemic vulnerability', which involves remaining open to learning, being wrong and accepting uncertainty, and Fonagy and Allison's (2014) notion of 'epistemic trust', which they also present as a precondition of both learning and developing effective relationships. Thus, before outlining what a postdigital vulnerable method framework might look like, it is important briefly to trace the growing interest in vulnerability in education and other areas of social policy, as well as critical theory more widely, in recent years.

It is almost ten years since Brown (2014) identified a 'vulnerability *Zeitgeist*' and the ubiquity of the term has only increased since (Jopling and Vincent 2020). This may be in part due to the 'return to vulnerability' which has been seen in feminist, psychological, and critical theory over a similar period, drawing in particular on Judith Butler's work (Murphy 2012; Sudenkaarne 2018). Honkasalo (2018: 14) explicitly identified the distance between these conceptualisations of vulnerability, which has not led to definitional or operational clarity, and claimed that in social policy it 'has gained an instrumental meaning that is a pale and narrow version compared to its existential and ethical origins'. Vulnerable method has the potential to allow us to draw on all of these conceptual sources and, as with the postdigital, turn the semantic polyvalence to our advantage.

In neoliberal, market-oriented social systems, the policy discourse of vulnerability has tended to concern itself with what Somers (2008) described as a 'conversion narrative'. This denies what Cutter et al. (2003) and Strindberg et al. (2020) term 'social vulnerability', recasting social and structural marginalisation in terms of personal responsibility, failure, and blame, in which interventions are imposed to address and overcome the deficiencies of individuals (McLeod 2012; Farrugia et al. 2015). Brunila et al. (2018: 115) have demonstrated how this process of individualisation has in turn infected what they call the 'vulnerabilizing' discourses of psychology, psychiatry, and self-help, which assume that 'young people's inherent vulnerability takes a specific psycho-emotional form', the responsibility for which is the responsibility of each young person. This therapisation of young people's experiences reduces their capacity to participate in society (Brunila 2012; Ecclestone and Hayes 2019) and the interventions that are implemented to support them tend to avoid addressing social factors or questions (Ecclestone and Rawdin 2016).

There are obvious parallels with how digitalisation and technologisation have been used to place the responsibility for learning on the individual in the same neoliberal education and social systems. As Jandrić and Hayes (2020: 287) emphasise, this has had a disproportionately negative effect on children and young people from disadvantaged backgrounds and not achieved the intended gains in social mobility: 'Such examples exist alongside a varied constellation of who does, or does not, have access to the social and economic currency the digital may bring, before contemplating what a "postdigital" era could alter'.

Growing interest in the convergence between the postdigital and the biodigital (Peters et al. 2022) is also relevant here in that the reconfigurations involved in 'biologizing the digital' may not only exacerbate existing disadvantages but also create new vulnerabilities. More than thirty years ago, Donna Haraway (1991) actively opposed the need to remain vulnerable with fantasies of overcoming weakness and death:

> Immunity and invulnerability are intersecting concepts, a matter of consequence in a nuclear culture unable to accommodate the experience of death and finitude within available liberal discourse on the collective and personal individual. Life is a window of vulnerability. It seems a mistake to close it. The perfection of the fully defended, 'victorious' self is a chilling fantasy. (Haraway 1991: 224)

This has some resonance with the notion of 'autoimmune vulnerability', which Naas (2006) developed out of late period Derrida. As Drichel (2013: 63) emphasises: 'Although "autoimmune vulnerability" necessarily risks being traumatized by an external threat it cannot foresee, it avoids the anxious defense of a projective anticipation of future threats: an anticipation that effectively amounts to a canceling out of temporality.' Playing with Spivak's (1990) description of deconstruction as 'a radical acceptance of vulnerability', she posits autoimmunity as the constitutional vulnerability that is vital for survival.

This has unsettling implications for our biodigital, (almost) post-pandemic times, when we consider unsettling developments such as the 'vulnerability scores' used to ration Covid-19 treatment in April 2020 – the higher the score, the less likely patients were to be treated (Bennett and Jopling 2022). Drichel's position is paralleled to some extent by Braidotti's (2019: 312) exploration of posthuman knowledge, in which she states that '[t]he emphasis falls not so much on vulnerability as a foundational condition, as on the embodied and embedded subjects' capacity to turn it into a generative force'. Approaching Visker's notion of the 'trauma which heals' (Braidotti cited in Drichel 2013: 53), she suggests that this is achieved through co-producing conditions and practices that 'transform the negative instance, including hurt and pain' (Braidotti 2019: 312). This notion of co-production is important.

This all stands in opposition to the ways in which the individualising dynamic we have already noted 'turns vulnerability from an existential condition, and sometimes debilitating effect or symptom of difficult life experiences, social and economic change or oppression and inequality, into an ontological characteristic' (Ecclestone 2012: 475). It also hides the fact that interdependent policy discourses of vulnerability and marginalisation create 'systems of power and privilege that interact to produce webs of advantages and disadvantages' (Fineman 2008: 16), just as the use of an algorithm to produce A Level results for students in England in 2020 demonstrated how technology can embed and extend inequalities that already exist (Eubanks 2018; Hayes 2021). The 'dark character' of vulnerability (Honkasalo 2018) which has resulted, emphasising risk and suffering, has often led to a preoccupation with making individuals (again) resistant through fostering invulnerability and resilience in individuals. Despite Slater's (2022) inclusion of such attributes among his affirmative concepts, Bernasconi (2018) suggests this has only led to vulnerabilities being exacerbated.

Rather than resorting to instrumental notions of building resilience, we might better draw on the less restricted conceptualisations of vulnerability which see it as part of the 'fragile and contingent nature of personhood' in which we are 'all vulnerable in some respect' (Beckett 2006: 3). On this model, vulnerability becomes a 'universal' dimension of human experience and identity rather than the property of particular marginalised groups' (McLeod 2012: 22). Gilson (2011: 310) asserts that 'vulner*ability* is not just a condition that limits us but one that can *enable* us' (emphases in original), revealing the 'ambivalent potentiality' (Murphy 2012: 86) that underlies it, which conceptualisations that only emphasise the extreme positions of negativity or openness fail to acknowledge. Murphy (2012: 9) follows Shildrick (2002) in being motivated to 'reconfigure vulnerability, not as an intrinsic quality of an existing subject, but as an inalienable condition of becoming'. Similarly, Luna (2009: 129) warns against viewing vulnerability as a 'permanent and categorical condition', preferring a more intersectional approach in which it is regarded as 'layered and inessential', affected by the complex entanglement of multiple variables.

In this way, we might come to understand vulnerability as involving conflict and tension between universal experience, social attribution, and individual coping. This follows Honkasalo (2018: 4) in seeing that vulnerability is 'about being exposed and about relations' and Fineman (2008: 9) in using it as a 'heuristic device' with which to examine the experiences of both individuals characterised as 'vulnerable' and those who support and engage with them, including researchers. As Law (2004: 63) underlines, there is no need to choose between singularity and pluralism: 'Something in between is a possibility.'

If vulnerable method involves the researcher in part admitting and accessing their own vulnerability, this also requires them to reconceptualise how teachers, academics and other practitioners in education should regard vulnerability. The research that explores vulnerability in teachers in schools has also been influenced by the negative, individualised approach to vulnerability already described. For example, Kelchtermans' (1996: 312) influential work approaches vulnerability as a structural issue 'when teachers feel powerless or politically ineffective in the micropolitical struggles about their desired workplace conditions', rather than as a primarily emotional or experiential condition. This largely remains the case, particularly among school leaders (Berkovich and Eyal 2015; Jopling and Harness 2022), although in a later study, Kelchtermans (2005) inched towards a more nuanced view by suggesting that vulnerability should be both endured and 'embraced' by teachers.

A more radical perspective can be found in Bullough's (2005: 23) study of teachability and vulnerability in which he anticipated Gilson (2011) and others in asserting that '[t]o be vulnerable is to be capable of being hurt, but to be invulnerable, if such a state is possible, is to limit the potential for learning'. He suggests that it is important that the 'burden of vulnerability' does not become too great for teachers, preventing them, or their students, from taking risks (that word again). In a revision of the paper, he added that this is most likely to occur 'within a committed professional community and least likely in isolation' (Bullough 2019: 117). This has important implications for teachers and other professionals.

Similarly, Salvatore and McVarish (2014: 49) suggest that 'vulnerability in the classroom helps to establish a constructivist mindset, one that allows all participants in the room to learn'. This moves us towards a more active, activist view of vulnerability, which is central to Ruck Simmonds' (2007) notion of 'critical vulnerability'. Drawing on Freire and focusing on school leaders, Ruck Simmonds (2007: 84) describes this as an act of resistance: 'To be critically vulnerable, therefore, implies a conscious recognition and willingness to transform society, and its institutions, into places where equity is experienced rather than considered.' For her, critical vulnerability is a radically open approach, which involves cultivating strategic risk-taking, reflective self-interrogation, creativity, and community-building. They could act as useful elements of a framework for vulnerable method.

The only example I have found of anyone explicitly exploring vulnerability in a postdigital context is Lee's (2021) autoethnographic account of embracing authenticity and vulnerability in online PhD studies. Fascinatingly, Lee demonstrates vulnerability and considerable honesty in tracing how she helped students to build a community, writing of how they were given multiple opportunities to overcome the fear of being 'real and vulnerable' (Lee 2021: 80), which involved taking the risk to open themselves up to each other. It is interesting that, while the class demonstrates many of the features of a positive, open approach to vulnerability, the lingering negativity of the dominant neoliberal conceptualisations can still be detected. The students are described as 'key helpers in creating a vulnerability-tolerant culture in the module' (Lee 2021: 76).

The point is here is not to criticise the account. After all, its outcomes seem to have been largely positive, but to draw attention to the enduring effects of neoliberal discourse, in which negative conceptualisations of vulnerability seem (at least initially) to have exacerbated the challenges of establishing an authentic learning community. However, before it can be suggested that adopting vulnerable method into both the autoethnographic and pedagogic approaches described may have been beneficial, the framework for that method needs to be outlined.

4   Towards a Framework for Vulnerable Method

The use of 'towards' in academic writing has always seemed to me like a dishonest sleight of hand, or a failure of nerve. Its use here is therefore a little ironic and intended both to signal the tentativeness of proposing a 'method' in this context and a reflection of the need to embed vulnerability into that method. The framework, which has been derived from the preceding analysis of vulnerability theory in a postdigital context, should by no means be regarded as definitive, but rather like an early beta version, to be refined through reflexive application in research. In this way, the framework reflects aspects of postdigital positionality (Hayes 2021: 10), which enables us to 'examine individual experiences in postdigital society' and reflexively consider their implications for understanding ourselves and others.

In fact, admitting vulnerability can be seen as a way of enabling us to examine the complexities of our identities and entanglements with technologies, as well as exploring the complex interactions between humans and technologies in policy, research, and practice. In the spirit of honesty and vulnerability, I acknowledge the influence on the thinking behind and development of this chapter of Hayes' (2021) work and the (postdigital) dialogue and collaboration in which we have been involved in relation to a range of projects and issues in recent years. She describes postdigital positionality as being: 'personal, collective and inclusive of all, because everyone can contribute to what this means as lived experience in their context' (Hayes 2021: 63). The framework presented here is suggested as a potential means of achieving at least some of these goals.

However, there is a danger of making this all sound rather straightforward. Sudenkaarne (2018: 87) follows Luna (2009) in arguing for a flexible, complex understanding of vulnerability because 'the most serious shortcoming of the rigid vulnerability approach is to treat vulnerability as a label affixed to a particular sub-population' and suggests its value to research:

> The layered approach to vulnerability proves helpful at a conceptual level: when identifying relevant layers in relation to a research subject, the research situation, and the context by drawing from lived experience. At a practical level it is helpful when designing ways to eliminate or diminish a layer of vulnerability. This makes it an interesting crossdisciplinary tool. (Sudenkaarne 2018: 87–88)

Drawing on this perspective, the prototypical elements of the framework are presented here first, followed by a brief exposition of how they might be used in the context of postdigital education research. As always, these elements should be regarded as functioning interdependently and dynamically. Thus, vulnerable method might be:

- Praxis-oriented and reflexive.
- Relational and collaborative.
- Radically multiple.
- Emancipatory, focused on the becoming, being and developing of learners, teachers, and humans in a postdigital context.

4.1 Praxis-Oriented and Reflexive

In an early intervention, Andersen et al. (2014: 5) suggested that the postdigital should address 'how [it] potentially acts as a framework for practice-based research that relate[s] to material and historical conditions'. Its subsequent conceptual development has done nothing to diminish the importance of focusing on practice, which is nothing new of course. The challenge is for researchers to gain an understanding of the postdigital context and the challenges it presents them as educators and researchers and integrate this into their approaches to conducting research with others.

Reflexivity relates to the importance of integrating a vulnerable openness to the uncertainty that postdigital advances in areas such as artificial intelligence or organic computing have only increased. This will require the researcher to remain open to contingency in a way that funded research often does not allow, enacting what Barthes (1981: 8) calls 'a desperate resistance to any reductive system' and Tauritz's (2016 in Boyd 2021) 'uncertainty competences'. It also has parallels with Ruck Simmonds' (2007) emphasis on self-interrogation and requires us to maintain a position 'in between' (Law 2004) the universal and the individual, conscious of the overlap between and interdependence of these different perspectives.

4.2 Relational and Collaborative

Judith Butler's (2009: 3) description of 'precariousness' as an existential condition, which is affected by, but also (like Barthes) potentially resistant to, socio-economic notions of precarity, is linked to her perspective on vulnerability, which she regards as 'based on social relations, and ... contextually contingent', rather than a disempowering ontological condition. The relational perspective is closely related to an individual's sense of agency, which 'arises from the social, political, and cultural dynamics of a specific time and place' (Honkasalo 2018: 13), and is an important part of how researchers and teachers work with vulnerable young people, as well as with colleagues and technologies.

Examples of this kind of approach include postdigital dialogue, which is intended to promote collaboration and constructive critique (Jandrić et al. 2019), and the trialectic of we-think, we-learn and we-act, concepts underlying a form of collective intelligence which 'the postdigital context has somewhat transformed ... and created a new dynamic between them' (Jandrić 2019: 278). This stands in opposition to Berardi's (2011: 46) warning that 'the future becomes a threat when the collective imagination becomes incapable of seeing possible alternatives to trends leading to devastation, increased poverty and violence'. It would also draw on Braidotti's (2019) emphasis on co-production and Ruck Simmonds' (2007) community-building.

4.3 Radically Multiple

This calls back to Law's (2004: 61) desire for multiple and diverse methods, which 'implies that the different realities overlap and interfere with one another' but also Hayes' (2021: 204) urging us to find 'new, personal and plural starting points from which to teach', and also by implication research, in order to explore a range of experiences in postdigital contexts. Ulmer (2017) has identified the possibilities that are potentially offered by posthumanism, which decentre the role of humans in research. It rejects the idea that we are the only species capable of creating knowledge 'and instead creates openings for other forms/things/objects/ beings/phenomenon to know' (Ulmer 2017: 834). This further opens the category of the vulnerable and forces the researcher take risks and creatively reconsider their approach to research in the light of the uncertainty with which they are faced (Vannini 2015).

Boyd (2021) has also explored in detail the value of rethinking place-based approaches in online classrooms, integrating digital approaches into place-based opportunities for research. As she demonstrates, this involves adapting to unanticipated circumstances and encounters and modelling that adaptability to students and colleagues. Bringing these notions together, it is also likely that universities will be decentred as places of research as (post)digital and hybrid approaches offer new opportunities to participate in and conduct research, including enabling those often marginalised to engage with and lead research.

These kinds of multiple approaches also require research to reconcile and further problematise both individualising notions of vulnerability, often associated with stigmatisation, and perspectives which see it as part of a universal condition. This requires an 'in between' approach to accessing our vulnerability, seeing it as part of both a universal condition and our individual identity.

4.4   Emancipatory

Finally, the emancipatory element of the method has a strong ethical dimension, encompassing the need for postdigital research to examine how datafication can entrench and deepen disadvantages and vulnerabilities, for example. It involves exploring in detail new ways in which researchers and the subjects of their research can move through the cycle of becoming, being and developing as learners, teachers, researchers, and/or humans in the postdigital context and the implications for individual and collective emancipation. The call to reclaim the digital sphere as a commons through a postdigital critical pedagogy (Jandrić et al. 2019; Jandrić and Knox 2022) needs to be extended into a postdigital critical research method as part of its resistance to neoliberalism and the development of more democratic, emancipatory methods.

5   Testing the Framework Retrospectively: Two Research Examples

There is a risk that all this has become too abstract, so I will briefly work through some of these issues and characteristics with reference to two recent research projects in which I have been involved in England. One had an explicitly postdigital focus, the second addressed issues of vulnerability. The first project, Extending Human Data Interaction (HDI) Theory, was funded by the UK's Engineering and Physical Research Council (EPSRC) in 2021. It involved a systematic, interdisciplinary literature review of HDI, which informed two online dialogues involving participants from universities, local government, charities, and social enterprises working on issues such as digital poverty, inclusion, disadvantage and lifelong learning (Hayes et al. 2022). The online meetings were structured around short presentations from 10 speakers and around 30 participants took part in each discussion (the totals fluctuated as individuals, and their Internet connections, came and went). The outcomes of these dialogues are collected in an edited book (Hayes et al. 2023).

The second project, Birmingham Lives, was funded by the Birmingham Children's Partnership (part of Birmingham City Council) in 2020–21. It explored the experiences of 'vulnerable' young people and families who had been supported by social and other support services in the city. Thirteen narrative case studies were developed through long interviews, conducted online or by phone in the first phase of the pandemic, focusing on their everyday lives, key events and challenges (educational or otherwise) and how they coped with them. The approach was broadly participatory with the participants identifying key incidents and producing their narrative in partnership with a researcher. One of the case studies is presented in Jopling and Zimmermann (2023). The research was conducted digitally because of restrictions related to the pandemic, but neither the digital nor the pandemic were the explicit focus of the research.

Viewed in retrospect, both projects drew on aspects of the vulnerable method framework. However, the explicitly postdigital focus of the HDI project perhaps demonstrates best the relevance of the framework in this context. The approach we adopted was dialogue- and place-based, engaging regional partners in universities, local government, the third sector and social enterprises to discuss issues around digital skills development and human-data interaction online. The approach involved open dialogue, lightly facilitated by the research team, and the edited academic book which has resulted (Hayes et al. 2023) has allowed a range of voices, some of which are not commonly reflected in academic writing, to come together in varying registers as a form of postdigital dialogue. This required us as researchers to approach the dialogue openly, minimising our expectations and accepting the uncertainty of what would emerge. The range of voices and experiences allowed a focus on practice (and praxis), with the edited collection enabling the collaborative relationships established to become visible, alongside some elements of co-production. However, not all participants felt able to write for the book and it would have perhaps been beneficial to explore different, more radical ways of sharing what we (all) learned from the process and involving marginalised voices much more. There are also questions about how emancipatory such a time-limited project can be.

In contrast, the Birmingham Lives project was much closer to 'traditional' research, involving intensive participatory work with families and young people, which was forced online by the pandemic. The vulnerability of the research participants resulted in at least some of the research team empathising with them and their experiences, accessing their own sense of vulnerability, but the limited time available to develop the participatory approach made it less collaborative and relational than we would have liked. The constraints imposed by the project's funder, as well as the inexperience of some of the researchers, also limited our ability to be innovative in our approach and address in depth the effects of the postdigital world on participants during periods of lockdown. Participants were more open and honest in telling their narratives and experiences, which integrated aspects of the digital into their place-based accounts, than the funder was willing to allow us to be in representing their perspectives. They were constrained by well-motivated concerns about the participants' vulnerability and lack of anonymity, but also by worries about the effect their narratives would have on demotivated colleagues working in social services. This meant that opportunities were lost to effect change, exacerbated by the instability of the funding organisation (local government) during a time of uncertainty. It may be that building vulnerable and postdigital approaches, notably postdigital dialogue, into the research design more explicitly would have made a difference.

6 Conclusion: Towards Postdigital Vulnerability

In the face of a postdigital world of big data and performative education, we are called on as researchers to develop methods and approaches which allow us both to examine and resist the claims and objectives on which this world is founded. It is the contention of this chapter that a more open conceptualisation of vulnerability, integrated into research method and praxis, is one means of exploring the challenges and potentials created by our postdigital context. Bringing together the notions of the postdigital and vulnerability may represent a way to do this because they strengthen each other, helping to counter the demonisation of vulnerability and the vulnerable, which is central to neoliberalism's blame culture (Farrugia et al. 2015), and to ground the postdigital in everyday realities: the (post)digital mud (Jandrić et al. 2019) and com-post (Sinclair and Hayes 2019), in which learning, teaching and research develop. This is where Law's (2004) notion of the 'in between' is helpful, not as a form of synthesis or 'third way', but as a way of opening research and research methods to uncertainty and indeterminacy.

There are also some parallels with Ralston's (2023) call for postdigital parity, symmetry, and a 'perspective-bridging rationale', but these ideas are extended via the radically 'ambivalent potentiality' that Murphy (2012) locates in vulnerability. This calls back not only to Benjamin's (1979) openness to contingency, but also his paradoxical impulse, already cited, to understand history through both preserving and cancelling it (Benjamin 2015), which is given an unsettling resonance in our current context of culture war and climate crisis.

The extent of the challenge is demonstrated in Brunila et al.'s (2018) discussion of another convergence of the postdigital-biodigital and the vulnerable. Like Williamson (2019), they describe the shift from psychology-based knowledge to behavioural genetics as 'precision education governance', which aims to use scientific engineering to instil or eradicate certain traits or vulnerabilities from birth. The intention is to increase individuals' capacity to learn, train, and be employed. Their concern is that this ethos of vulnerability, which they regard as part of neoliberal rationality, tends to 'frame ideas of young people's subjectivity as diminished and psycho-emotionally deviant, even in the school context' (Brunila et al. 2018: 115). This has the effect of both ignoring and restricting their capability and sense of political agency. The goal is to make young people 'more learnable, manageable and reliable', but runs the risk of wearing them out through subordination and restriction (Brunila et al. 2018: 118).

The kind of method outlined in this chapter, with its emphasis on praxis, reflexion, collaboration, and emancipation, stands in opposition to this restrictive impulse, which denies access to the uncertainty, contingency and messiness that both the postdigital and what I have called 'in between' conceptualisations of vulnerability afford and enable. In the battle for the future, it is proposed that adopting at least elements of the kind of approach to postdigital research in education and other areas outlined in this chapter might allow us to accept and access our postdigital vulnerability as researchers in order to understand our context and challenge, problematise and resist the kinds of dangers and extensions of neoliberalism that Brunila et al. (2018) highlight before it is too late.

References

Andersen, C. U., Cox, G., & Papadopoulos, G. (2014). Editorial: Postdigital Research. *A Peer-Reviewed Journal About, 3*(1), 5–7. https://doi.org/10.7146/aprja.v3i1.116067.
Barthes, R. (1981). *Camera Lucida: Reflections on Photography*. Berkeley, CA: University of California Press.
Beckett, A. E. (2006). *Citizenship and vulnerability: Disability and issues of social engagement*. Basingstoke: Palgrave Macmillan. https://doi.org/10.1057/9780230501294.
Benjamin, W. (1979). *One-Way Street and Other Writings*. London: Verso.
Benjamin, W. (2015). Theses on the Philosophy of History. In H. Arendt (Ed.), *Illuminations: Essays and Reflections* (pp. 253–264). New York: Shocken.
Bennett, P., & Jopling, M. (2022). The global pandemic did not take place: cancellation, denial and the normal new. In M. A. Peters, P. Jandrić, & S. Hayes (Eds.), *Bioinformational Philosophy and Postdigital Knowledge Ecologies* (pp. 301–317). Cham: Springer. https://doi.org/10.1007/978-3-030-95006-4_16.
Berardi, F. (2011). *After the Future*. Edinburgh: AK Press.
Berkovich, I., & Eyal O. (2015). Educational Leaders and Emotions: An International Review of Empirical Evidence 1992–2012. *Review of Educational Research, 85*(1), 129–167. https://doi.org/10.3102/0034654314550046.
Bernasconi, R. (2018). Levinas, Social Vulnerability, and the Logic of South African Racism. *Suomen Antropologi, 43*(3), 91–101. https://doi.org/10.30676/jfas.v43i3.82735.
Boyd, S. (2021). Taking Time to Get Messy Outside the Online Classroom. In T. Fawns, G. Aitken, & D. Jones (Eds.), *Online Postgraduate Education in a Postdigital World* (pp. 21–38). Cham: Springer. https://doi.org/10.1007/978-3-030-77673-2_2.
Braidotti, R. (2019). *Posthuman Knowledge*. Cambridge: Polity Press.
Brown, K. (2014). Questioning the 'Vulnerability zeitgeist': Care and Control Practices with 'Vulnerable' Young People. *Social Policy & Society, 13*(3), 231–241. https://doi.org/10.1017/S1474746413000535.
Brunila, K. (2012). From risk to resilience. *Education Inquiry, 3*(3), 451–464. https://doi.org/10.3402/edui.v3i3.22046.
Brunila, K., Mertanen, K., Tiainen, K., Kurki, T., Masoud, A., Mäkelä, K., & Ikävalko, E. (2018). Vulnerabilizing Young people: Interrupting the ethos of vulnerability, the neoliberal rationality,

and the precision education governance. *Suomen Antropologi, 43*(3), 113–120. https://doi.org/10.30676/jfas.v43i3.82737.

Buchanan, R. (2021). Networked professional learning in the postdigital age: Asking critical questions of postgraduate education. In T. Fawns, G. Aitken, & D. Jones (Eds.), *Online Postgraduate Education in a Postdigital World* (pp. 121–138). Cham: Springer. https://doi.org/10.1007/978-3-030-77673-2_7.

Bullough, R. V. (2005). Teacher vulnerability and teachability: A case study of a mentor and two interns. *Teacher Education Quality, 32*(2), 23–39.

Bullough, R. V. (2019). *Essays on Teaching Education and the Inner Drama of Teaching*. Bingley: Emerald.

Butler, J. (2009). *Frames of War. When is Life Grievable?* London: Verso.

Butt, G., Eshun, K., & Fisher, M. (2016) Introduction. In G. Butt, K. Eshun, & M. Fisher (Eds.), *Post-Punk Then and Now* (pp. 8–24). London: Repeater.

Cramer, F. (2015). What is 'post-digital'? In D. M. Berry & M. Dieter (Eds.), *Postdigital aesthetics: Art, computation and design* (pp. 12–26). New York: Palgrave Macmillan. https://doi.org/10.1057/9781137437204_2.

Cutter, S. L., Boruff, B., & Lynn Shirley, W. (2003). Social vulnerability to environmental hazards. *Social Science Quarterly, 84*(2), 242–261. https://doi.org/10.1111/1540-6237.8402002.

Dale, M., & Frye, E.M. (2009). Vulnerability and the love of learning as necessities for wise teacher education. *Journal of Teacher Education 60*(2), 123–130. https://doi.org/10.1177/0022487108329.

Drichel, S. (2013). Towards a "radical acceptance of vulnerability": Postcolonialism and Deconstruction. *SubStance, 42*(3), 46–66. https://doi.org/10.1353/sub.2013.0034.

Ecclestone, K. (2012). From emotional and psychological well-being to character education: challenging policy discourses of behavioural science and 'vulnerability'. *Research Papers in Education, 27*(4), 463–480. https://doi.org/10.1080/02671522.2012.690241.

Ecclestone, K., & Hayes, D. (2019). *The Dangerous Rise of Therapeutic Education*. 2nd Ed. London: Routledge.

Ecclestone, K., & Rawdin, C. (2016). Reinforcing the 'diminished' subject? The implications of the 'vulnerability zeitgeist' for well-being in educational settings. *Cambridge Journal of Education, 46*(3), 377–393. https://doi.org/10.1080/0305764X.2015.1120707.

Eubanks, V. (2018). *Automating inequality: How high-tech tools profile, police and punish the poor*. New York: St. Martin's Press.

Farrugia, D., Smyth, J., & Harrison, T. (2015). 'Vulnerable', 'At-Risk', 'Disengaged': Regional Young People. In K. te Riele & R. Gorur (Eds.) *Interrogating Conceptions of 'Vulnerable Youth' in Theory, Policy and Practice. Innovations and Controversies* (pp. 165–180). Rotterdam: Sense.

Fineman, M. (2008). The Vulnerable Subject: Anchoring Equality in the Human Condition. *Yale Journal of Law & Feminism, 20*(1), 1–23.

Fonagy, P., & Allison, E. (2014). The role of mentalizing and epistemic trust in the therapeutic relationship. *Psychotherapy, 51*(3), 372–380. https://doi.org/10.1037/a0036505.

Gilson, E. (2011). Vulnerability, Ignorance, and Oppression. *Hypatia, 26*(2), 308–332. https://doi.org/10.1111/j.1527-2001.2010.01158.x.

Halberstam, J. (2011). *The Queer Art of Failure*. Durham, NC: Duke University Press.

Hall, S., & Massey, D. (2010) Interpreting the Crisis. *Soundings, 44*, 57–71. https://doi.org/10.3898/136266210791036791.

Harraway, D. J. (1991). *Simians, Cyborgs and Women: The Reinvention of Nature*. New York: Routledge.

Hayes, S. (2021). *Postdigital Positionality: Developing powerful inclusive narratives for learning, teaching, research and policy in higher education*. Leiden: Brill.

Hayes, S., Connor, S., Johnson, M., & Jopling, M. (2022). Connecting cross-sector community voices: data, disadvantage, and postdigital inclusion. *Postdigital Science and Education 4*(2), 237–246. https://doi.org/10.1007/s42438-021-00251-7.

Hayes, S., Connor, S., Jopling, M, & Johnson, M. (Eds.). (2023). *Human Data Interaction, Disadvantage and Skills in the Community: Enabling Cross-Sector Environments for Postdigital Inclusion*. Cham: Springer.

Honkasalo, M-L. (2018). Vulnerability and Inquiring into Relationality. *Suomen Antropologi, 3*(3), 1–21. https://doi.org/10.30676/jfas.v43i3.82725.

Jandrić, P. (2019). We-Think, We-Learn, We-Act: the Trialectic of Postdigital Collective Intelligence. *Postdigital Science and Education, 1*(2), 257–279. https://doi.org/10.1007/s42438-019-00055-w.

Jandrić, P., & Hayes, S. (2020). Postdigital We-Learn. *Studies in Philosophy of Education, 39*(3), 285–297. https://doi.org/10.1007/s11217-020-09711-2.

Jandrić, P., & Knox, J. (2022). The Postdigital Turn: Philosophy, Education, Research. *Policy Futures in Education, 20*(7), 780–795. https://doi.org/10.1177/2F14782103211062713.

Jandrić, P., Knox, J., Besley, T, Ryberg, T., Suoranta, J., & Hayes, S. (2018). Postdigital Science and Education. *Educational Philosophy and Theory, 50*(10), 893–899. https://doi.org/10.1080/00131857.2018.1454000.

Jandrić, P., Ryberg, T., Knox, J., Lacković, N., Hayes, S., Suoranta, J., Smith, M., Steketee, A., Peters, M. A., McLaren, P., Ford, D. R., Asher, G., McGregor, C., Stewart, G., Williamson, B., & Gibbons, A. (2019). Postdigital Dialogue. *Postdigital Science and Education, 1*(1), 163–189. https://doi.org/10.1007/s42438-018-0011-x.

Jopling, M., & Harness, O. (2022). Embracing vulnerability: How has Covid-19 affected the pressures school leaders in Northern England face and how they deal with them? *Journal of Educational Administration and History, 54*(1), 69–84. https://doi.org/10.1080/00220620.2021.1997945.

Jopling, M., & Vincent, S. (2020). Vulnerable families: policy, practice and social justice. In R. Papa (Ed.), *Springer Handbook on Promoting Social Justice in Education* (pp. 1–22). Cham: Springer. https://doi.org/10.1007/978-3-030-14625-2_2.

Jopling, M., & Zimmermann, D. (2023). Mental health, wellbeing and the 'vulnerable educational context' in schools in England and Germany. *Research Papers in Education*.

Kelchtermans, G. (1996). Teacher Vulnerability: understanding its moral and political roots. *Cambridge Journal of Education, 26*(3), 307–323. https://doi.org/10.1080/0305764960260302.

Kelchtermans, G. (2005). Teachers' emotions in educational reforms: Self-understanding, vulnerable commitment and micropolitical literacy. *Teaching and Teacher Education, 21*(8), 995–1006. https://doi.org/10.1016/j.tate.2005.06.009.

Knox, J. (2019). What does the 'Postdigital' mean for education? Three critical perspectives on the digital, with implications for educational research and practice. *Postdigital Science and Education, 1*(2), 357–370. https://doi.org/10.1007/s42438-019-00045-y.

Larrivee, B. (2000). Transforming Teaching Practice: becoming the critically reflective teacher. *Reflective Practice, 1*(3), 293–307. https://doi.org/10.1080/713693162.

Law, J. (2004). *After Method: Mess in Social Science Research*. Abingdon: Routledge.

Lee, K. (2021). Embracing Authenticity and Vulnerability in Online PhD Studies: The Self and a Community. In T. Fawns, G. Aitken, & D. Jones (Eds.), *Online Postgraduate Education in a Postdigital World* (pp. 63–84). Cham: Springer. https://doi.org/10.1007/978-3-030-77673-2_4.

Lewis, T. E. (2020). Everything you always wanted to know about being postdigital but were afraid to ask a giant squid. *Postdigital Science and Education, 2*(2), 265–266. https://doi.org/10.1007/s42438-019-00082-7.

Luna, F. (2009). Elucidating the Concept of Vulnerability: Layers Not Labels. *International Journal of Feminist Approaches to Bioethics, 2*(1), 121–139. https://doi.org/10.3138/ijfab.2.1.121.

McLeod, J. (2012). Vulnerability and the neo-liberal youth citizen: a view from Australia. *Comparative Education, 48*(1), 11–26. https://doi.org/10.1080/03050068.2011.637760.

Murphy, A. V. (2012). *Violence and the Philosophical Imaginary*. Albany, NY: State University of New York Press.

Naas, M. (2006). 'One Nation . . . Indivisible': Jacques Derrida on the Autoimmunity of Democracy and the Sovereignty of God. *Research in Phenomenology, 36*, 15–44.

Peters, M. A., Jandrić, P., & Hayes, S. (2022). Postdigital-Biodigital: An Emerging Configuration. In M. A. Peters, P. Jandrić, & S. Hayes (Eds.), *Bionformational Philosophy and Postdigital Knowledge Ecologies* (pp. 205–222). Cham: Springer. https://doi.org/10.1007/978-3-030-95006-4_11.

Ralston, S. J. (2023). Towards a theory of postdigital parity. In P. Jandrić, A. MacKenzie, & J. Knox (Eds.), *Postdigital Research: Genealogies, Challenges, and Future Perspectives.* Cham: Springer. https://doi.org/10.1007/978-3-031-31299-1_3.

Reader, J. (2021). Postdigital Humans: Algorithmic Imagination? In M. Savin-Baden (Ed.), *Postdigital Humans: Transitions, Transformations and Transcendence* (pp. 155–168). Cham: Springer. https://doi.org/10.1007/978-3-030-65592-1_10.

Ritzer, G. (2018). *The McDonaldization of society: Into the digital age.* 9th Ed. New York: Sage.

Ruck Simmonds, M. (2007). Critical Vulnerability: An Imperative Approach to Educational Leadership. *Journal of Thought, 42*(1/2), 79–97.

Salvatore, J., & McVarish, J. (2014). Vulnerability: A Metalogue. *Counterpoints, 380,* 47–59.

Shildrick, M. (2002). *Embodying the Monster: Encounters with the Vulnerable Self.* London: Sage.

Sinclair, C., & Hayes, S. (2019). Between the post and the com-post: Examining the postdigital 'work' of a prefix. *Postdigital Science and Education, 1*(1), 119–131. https://doi.org/10.1007/s42438-018-0017-4.

Slater, G. B. (2022). The Precarious Subject of Neoliberalism: Resilient Life in the Catastrophic Conjuncture. In K. Saltman & N. Nguyen (Eds.), *Handbook of Critical Approaches to Policy and Politics in Education.* London: Routledge.

Somers, M. (2008). *Genealogies of citizenship: Markets, statelessness, and right to have rights.* New York: Cambridge University Press.

Spivak, G. C. (1990). *The Post-Colonial Critic: Interviews, Strategies, Dialogues.* London: Routledge.

Strindberg, J., Horton, P., & Thornberg, R. (2020). Coolness and social vulnerability: Swedish pupils' reflections on participant roles in school bullying. *Research Papers in Education, 35*(5), 603–622. https://doi.org/10.1080/02671522.2019.1615114.

Sudenkaarne, T. (2018). Queering Vulnerability: A Layered Bioethical Approach. *Suomen Antropologi, 43*(3), 73–90. https://doi.org/10.1016/j.jemep.2018.06.004.

Tauritz, R. L. (2016). A pedagogy for uncertain times. In J. Hindson & W. Lambrechts (Eds.), *Trends in ESD research and innovation* (pp. 90–105). Leuven: ENSI.

Ulmer, J. B. (2017). Posthumanism as research methodology: inquiry in the Anthropocene. *International Journal of Qualitative Studies in Education, 30*(9), 832–848. https://doi.org/10.1080/09518398.2017.1336806.

Vannini, P. (2015). Non-representational ethnography: New ways of animating lifeworlds. *Cultural geographies, 22*(2), 317–327. https://doi.org/10.1177/1474474014555657.

Williamson, B. (2019). Digital policy sociology: Software and science in data-intensive precision education, *Critical Studies in Education, 62*(3), 354–370. https://doi.org/10.1080/17508487.2019.1691030.

Caring Cuts: Unfolding Methodological Sensibilities in Researching Postdigital Worlds

Sara Mörtsell ⓘ and Karin Gunnarsson ⓘ

1 Introduction

This chapter sets out to answer the call to engage with the 'curious dance of episte-mology and methodology' in postdigital scholarship (Jandrić et al. 2022). In order to do that, we will engage with methodological questions that add vital ontological groundings onto this dance. This dancing engagement is carried out with inspiration from the now well-established theoretical framework within education labelled feminist posthumanism, material feminisms, and Actor-Network Theory (ANT). Within this framework, epistemology, ontology, and methodology are interdependently enacted which means that knowledge practices cannot be separated from world-making practices. By assuming epistemology-ontology entanglement, we will enter the engagement with the postdigital in this chapter by addressing two key notions offered from feminist thinking within ANT and posthumanism: *care* and *cuts*. The configuration of these two notions, we argue, raises vital methodological questions onto postdigital research that will be discussed in this chapter. For example, the questions concern the co-constructions of empirical material, researcher position, and research ethics.

By introducing caring cuts, the ambition for this chapter is then to spark up a conversation between three vivid 'post'-approaches; posthumanism, postqualitative research, and postdigital research. The postdigital has injected lively debates and much-needed theorising on the relationship of education and digital technology.

S. Mörtsell (✉)
Faculty of Education and Business Studies, University of Gävle, Gävle, Sweden

Department of Education, Umeå University, Umeå, Sweden
e-mail: sara.mortsell@hig.se

K. Gunnarsson
Department of Education, Stockholm University, Stockholm, Sweden
e-mail: karin.gunnarsson@edu.su.se

P. Jandrić et al. (eds.), *Postdigital Research*, Postdigital Science and Education, https://doi.org/10.1007/978-3-031-31299-1_10

Nevertheless, the difficulty of defining what the postdigital is and entails has been repeatedly stressed in these conversations. Instead, the postdigital is understood on the basis of its messiness and moving matter (Jandrić et al. 2018, 2022; Knox 2019). With this in mind, the postdigital is approached in this chapter with a sensibility of acknowledging and resting in that very messiness. This means that mess and indeterminacy of the digital is not there to be solved by clarification or to be set right but is assumed as an ontological condition. This assumption makes possible explorations that push and rupture digital-educational relationalities.

Posthumanist theory and postqualitiative methodology, described in more detail below, have nurtured a long-standing interest in the 'posts'. For example, spearheaded by Haraway, the prefix 'post' marks an examination into the problematics of purified phenomena, e.g., the human and the digital, as has been taken up in the emerging postdigital scholarship (Sinclair and Hayes 2019: 24). In sharing overlapping interests into interrogating knowledge politics in research methods, feminist methodological sensibilities have inspired attention to the empirical matters of how research methodologies enact educational realities of what it is to teach, learn, and research in these realities. Furthermore, in this methodological space, matters of *care* have been explored and, importantly, connected to the research apparatus as a mode of attention that enacts exclusions and *cuts* that shape research objects (Barad 2007; Puig de la Bellacasa 2017).

The aim of this chapter is then to explore how these post-approaches, posthumanism, postqualitative and postdigital research can reconceptualise each other's methodologies. This means that our concern is how postdigital worlds are made researchable. Therefore, we propose 'caring cuts' as a productive endeavour to include within methodological sensibilities. Moreover, we explore its potentiality through materialised methodological examples.

In elaborating on this, we begin with situating the chapter's concern as informed by two strands of research: educational posthumanism and postdigital education. After that, we give the outline for the ontology of relational materialism and the concepts of *care* and *cut*, before introducing the configuration of *caring cuts*. Then follows the exploration of how caring cuts contribute to methodological sensibilities as it is put to work on more-than-digital empirical research events. The chapter concludes with a discussion, in which the potentiality of caring cuts is highlighted.

2 Researching Postdigital Worlds

There are two strands of educational research that are of great concern for situating this chapter and to which we will pay specific attention here. The first one is educational research working with posthumanist theories and the second one is research considering the postdigital. This brief review of educational research is set to address is the theoretical and methodological inspiration it carries toward the notion of caring cuts.

2.1   Educational Posthumanist Research

Within educational research, a range of posthumanist approaches has gained great interest over the last decade. Although quite heterogenous, this body of work shares the ontological groundings of *relational materialisms*. Altogether, they strive for reorientations of subject-centred conceptions of knowledge, and thereby comprehend both teaching and research as collective and performative sociomaterial doings (Gunnarsson 2021; Juelskjær 2020; Lenz Taguchi and Eriksson 2021). With related theoretical takes, the co-producing features of spatial, material, and affective aspects are addressed. Accordingly, this research raises questions concerning the agential characteristics of bodies, affectivity, technology, things and in addition how this can be explored.

To give a glimpse of this extensive field, there are theoretical-empirical studies with specific relevance to this chapter in their focus on digital educational technology. For example, Bodén (2016) explores how the digital registration of school absenteeism is not a stable or neutral recorder of reality, but rather takes part in producing school absenteeism itself. In similar terms, Mörtsell (2022) highlights the sociomaterial and ritual devices that produce attendability within pandemic school closure. Thompson (2016) explores 'digital doings' in restless assemblages of online learning with contract workers in Kenya, Rwanda, and Canada. Concerned with digital health technologies as unreducible to totalizing notions of power or control, Rich and Lupton (2022) examine biopedagogies with students to explore the more-than-human forces and tensions. On basis of its empirical orientation, this research emphasises the unpredictive and heterogenous relationality of the digital in educational practices, albeit not explicitly so in postdigital terminology.

As an interwoven movement within this educational posthumanism, a specific interest in methodological questions has taken hold. Herein, *postqualitative research* has been introduced with the ambition of both embracing and extending more traditional qualitative approaches by troubling separations of epistemology, ontology, and methodology (e.g. Murris 2020; Renold and Ivinson 2022). This methodological approach emphasises how knowledge is a performative practice taking place together with the world and therefore pushes for experimentation and creativity. By stressing co-producing and interfering aspects of research, collaboration and engagement with those whom the research concerns become a vital ambition. This means acknowledging how research is a relational doing including co-becomings of theory, researcher, participants, research objects, and sites (Gunnarsson and Bodén 2021). Moreover, by urging for *methodological sensibility* the manifold of relations involved compels additional and inventive research methods. This means not to identify the 'right' approach or the 'best' way to conduct research, but rather to consider how to intervene as well as account for the co-constitutive effects of doing research. The methodological sensibilities urge attention for how certain actors become powerful in the web of relations that are made researchable (Lenz Taguchi et al. 2020).

2.2 Postdigital Education

The second strand of research that informs the concerns of this chapter comes from postdigital scholarship in education. As for its theoretical contribution to digital educational technology research, postdigital debates have gained traction on the premises of calling out technological determinism and the limitations of instrumentalism, the belief that technologies are not neutral tools (e.g., Jandrić and Knox 2022). This emerging body of work takes the postdigital to be messy and unpredictable and notoriously resisting any attempts at settling on a definition. It gives the postdigital a certain creative openness to a range of theoretical approaches and methodologies. Nonetheless, there are two main theoretical underpinnings; one is critically emphasising the regulatory and disciplinary powers of digital technology and another is informed by posthumanism emphasising sociomaterial relationalities and their materialisations (Jandrić et al. 2018, 2022; Knox 2019).

An early influential piece to inspire postdigital thinking was Negroponte's Wired article from the 1990s 'Beyond the Digital'. He based his proposal on how a blindness to plastics had developed since the 1960s and suggested that a future beyond the digital would involve a blindness to 'the big deal' of the digital. In techno-optimistic terms, Negroponte (1998) predicted that '[l]ike air and drinking water, being digital will be noticed only by its absence, not its presence'. Current scholarship engaged in the postdigital turn has maintained a forward-looking curiosity into possible futures of the postdigital, e.g., postdigital ecopedagogies (Jandrić and Ford 2022). Others have been less preoccupied with a chronological coming 'after' the digital in favour of developing critical sensibilities for interrogating the digital. For example, postdigital scholarships on education have scrutinised the digital discourses of innovation, automation, and enhancement (Knox 2019; Wagener-Böck et al. 2022).

The messy heterogeneity of the postdigital has been examined as digital-analog and bioinformational relationalities in postdigital scholarship, which has severely troubled any simplified notions of a bounded digital category. For example, one major lesson from the pandemic, including the various forms of pandemic education, was our fragile biological existence and its entanglement with information. This added insights into the postdigital that concerned not only the digital-analog dichotomy but a richer plethora of digital relations that has been influential in the postdigital turn (Jandrić and Knox 2022).

2.3 More-Than-Digital Methodologies

This review of educational posthumanism, including postqualitative research, and postdigital research, shows that they raise related questions and concerns. Not least do they all attract the prefix post. What has been emphasised within educational posthumanism and postqualitative research, is how adding the prefix 'post' does not imply a rupture with either humanism or qualitative approaches. Rather, these post-approaches are entangled with, build upon, and strive for pushing the possible (Gunnarsson and Bodén 2021; Lather and Pierre 2013; Murris 2020). In line with Sinclair and Hayes (2019), we see that the prefix contributes to the rejection of binaries and highlights urgent questions of our time. Accordingly, we find energy in the 'com-post' as acknowledging interdependent relationalities emphasised in all three (com)posts included here.

Informed by the methodological sensibilities of post-approaches in education described above, we are less concerned with a definition of the postdigital and instead find that a guiding notion for this chapter can be conceptualised as 'more-than-digital' relations (e.g., Rich and Lupton 2022). In other words, more-than-digital relations are constituted in the indeterminate webs of relations that are the ontological conditions of becoming, as outlined below. This ontological assumption of relational materialism, that relationality is all there is, sets up the methodologies developed in feminist post-approaches to respond to the issue of how to research the messiness of postdigital worlds.

For postdigital scholarship, the methodological sensibilities of post-approaches present the question: how are worlds enacted of our care and particular curiosity for the digital? This is one of the methodological questions that this chapter explores with the configuration of *caring cuts*. By tapping into this ontology of relational materialism put forth by ANT and posthumanism, caring cuts are explored with how postdigital research practices are done and how they enact and amplify post-digital worlds.

3   Unfolding Relational Materialism

The exploration of *caring cuts* is here done within the vein of posthumanisms and especially ANT. This means deploying an ontology of relational materialism that includes a shift from anthropocentric privilege towards decentering the human by focusing on relations and gatherings. These relations include not only the social but also materiality in the constructions of reality. Here meaning and matter, language, and reality are considered interconnected with no fixed boundaries (Gunnarsson 2018). This builds on the ontological postulation of 'world-making entanglements' (Haraway 2008: 4), which implies that human and non-human relations are mutually constituted.

Within such interdependency, relations are what co-shape us as well as the rest of the world and therefore 'make us responsible in unpredictable ways for which worlds take shape' (Haraway 2008: 36). This responsibility has a distributed character and is enacted within sociomaterial gatherings, or with another word, *assemblages*. The concept assemblage addresses the messy reciprocity of how entities both come together and are constituted within these entanglements. This means that entities gain their characteristics and become stabilised within the gatherings of the assemblage. Hence, assemblages put forward how realities are indeterminate, contingent, and emergent matters that constantly can be done differently (Gorur 2011). How the world comes to matter is then an empirical, as well as an epistemological and ontological responsibility.

Given the ontology of relational materialism, methodological traditions in post-approaches challenge the separation of theory and practice since they are always mutually and relationally constituted of each other. This means that thinking, for example about caring cuts in the case of this chapter, cannot be done in the abstract (Law and Lin 2020). We accommodate this by first introducing caring cuts in this section and then carrying on the unfolding of the concept with the messiness of empirical research events.

The generative research examples work as sociomaterial events that help reconceptualise and disrupt methodological endeavours. As such, engaging with relational materialism 'encourages an attentiveness to the many everyday mundane actors' (Bodén et al. 2019: 6) where caring cuts open up specific potentialities, that will be further outlined below.

3.1 Matters of Care: Non-innocent and Generative Potentials

Care has a long history of being addressed by scholars within different disciplines and theoretical approaches. In exploring methodologies for postdigital research, we turn to the work on care from feminist ANT scholars like Annmarie Mol (2008) and María Puig de la Bellacasa (2017). They have insisted that care and technology are vital to each other. For example, the mundane care practices that get us through the day inevitably embed technology; eating, washing, making purchases, etc. Equally, technology demands care and maintenance. This is an important challenge to the technology-care binary in which care and care practices become devalued or neglected. It calls for an expanded frame of technology in which care matters and counts for its success. In other words, accounting for technology should consider how care becomes enacted; neglected or made expendable. For this chapter, this thinking makes care a way of entering the more-than-digital. Furthermore, this has implications for methodological sensibilities with technology. Mol (2008: 50) says: 'Technologies do not subject themselves to what we wish them to do, but interfere with who we are.'

In turning this thinking onto the topic of care and methodology, Puig de la Bellacasa's (2017) *Matters of care: Speculative ethics in more than human worlds* has been influential. In this book, she takes on a classic question from science and technology studies (STS), namely how researchers become involved in making the world. This is done in conversation with Bruno Latour's (2004) proposal on *matters of concern* which is expanded by adding care to knowledge politics, as *matters of care*. Puig de la Bellacasa argues that articulating research problems is more than a matter of concern; it is also a gathering of trouble, worry, and care that, importantly, effects how researchers account for the life of things. Therefore, her reasoning goes, we must not neglect '(our) intervention and involvement, and let's say ethicopolitical commitment and obligations, as an essential part of the politics of knowledge production' (Puig de la Bellacasa 2017: 40). Attending to care can reveal oppressive and objectifying relations in the process of making knowable and researchable the objects that we care for.

Taking this intervention of care to technoscience and ecology, the two combined fields in Puig de la Bellacasa's work, means to resist oppositional thinking that reduces things, i.e. *matters of care*, to (human) domination. For the field of education research, it implies that digital technologies increasingly entangle schooling in more-than digital assemblages of not only data but also thermoplastics, affects, minerals, markets, and so on. The caution to this that Puig de la Bellacasa (2017: 45) raises with matters of care is that detaching and demonising some part of, for example, school-technology assemblages render us irresponsible in 'looking after their possible transformation'. With this, she speaks on the corrosive effect of critical approaches as they dismantle rather than add and enrich relationalities (Martin et al. 2015). Configured this way as *matters of care*, care becomes a gatherer that mobilises ethical and practical engagements with knowledge production that creatively looks for and articulates other possible realities.

By foregrounding the fragility of things, Puig de la Bellacasa (2017) and Mol (2008) articulate that care is vital and active as it makes livable worlds possible and life more bearable. At the same time, the relationality of care implicates a double movement in that it is enacted of the arrangements of fragile and vulnerable matters. Thus, care is relationally entangled with digital aspects of the fabric of life. It troubles the aforementioned technology-care binary that has dominated Western thought throughout the twentieth century. The dichotomy has rendered gendered and hierarchical structures of, for example, public-domestic in notorious disregard for the value of care (Martin et al. 2015; Mol et al. 2010).

The generative relationality of care has been addressed by feminist thinking as a 'willingness to respond' and a responsibility in the becoming of things (Martin et al. 2015). This assumption of care should not be mistaken for a wholesome moral disposition. Firstly, since care is understood relationally it is enacted in specific more-than-human relationalities that ontologically achieve the capacity for different responses, being responsible is not only an individual matter. Secondly, this research has emphasised the non-innocent entanglements of care. Care is a selective and affectively charged mode of attention, which means that it involves neglect of other things and enacts exclusions, ambivalence, and unsettling tensions (Martin et al. 2015; Puig de la Bellacasa 2017).

3.2 Cuts as the Temporary Manifestation of Matter

We will now turn to the companion notion within the caring cuts configuration, that of *cuts*. Within posthumanist research, the notion of cut has a significant ontological and methodological position. As such, cuts are necessary doings to make the world knowable within its indeterminate character. In other words, what this notion puts forward is how an indeterminate world, shaped in webs of relations (Law and Lin 2020), is constantly being done within the processes of ordering, manifesting, and categorizing. Here, the work of what posthumanist philosopher Karen Barad calls *agential cuts* gives additional contributions.

Grounded in feminist and queer quantum field theory, Barad (2007: 340) argues that 'agential cut enacts determinate boundaries, properties, and meanings'. This means that cutting is a boundary-making process that both makes the world come to matter and makes the world meaningful. By emphasising its relational and material character, cuts put forward how research never can be done from a distance but rather involves a relational experiment with messy and fluid co-becomings. As Haraway puts it; research and the researcher are always 'finite and dirty, not transcendent and clean' (Haraway 2004: 236).

What is important to stress is how cuts are not done in isolation or as fixed and final doings. Instead, they are iteratively enacted in relation to the material and discursive conditions of the specific practice in a reciprocal relation of also being part of creating these conditions (Barad 2007:107). Cuts are enacted within a 'larger material arrangement of which "we" are a "part"' (Barad 2007: 178). Then, it is crucial to acknowledge where or when the cutting is made, how it is done, and what effects it carries.

With the notion of cuts, the distributed and temporary separation or selection of what to care for becomes emphasised. As Puig de la Bellacasa (2017: 78) writes '[w]e cannot possibly care for everything, not everything can count in a world, not everything is relevant in a world'. Hence, the notion of cuts helps us acknowledge that what we care for counts for what in turn becomes produced. Accordingly, what makes the doing of cuts so vital is that it not only concerns divisions and separations but, also is a matter of co-constituting and interfering with what is being explored. This gives the doings of cuts a double move of simultaneously disconnecting and connecting.

In the work of Barad, this double move is to be understood as '[o]ne move - cutting together-apart' (Barad 2014: 176). What then becomes emphasised is how cuts separate things and at the same time, create new relations and connections. As such, cuts become immensely ethical acts since they involve collective and iterative ruptures of the world's becoming (Barad 2014). Therefore, we mean that connecting cuts with care highlights the responsibilities that inevitably come with doing research.

3.3   Caring Cuts: Sensibilities of the Making of Researchable Worlds

In elaborating on *care* and *cuts*, there are also questions about how they inform each other and invite methodological sensibilities. Configuring care and cuts as *caring cuts* addresses how that which is concerned for, found interesting, or regarded as important has material and worldly ethical effects. With a reconfigured concept such as *caring cuts*, familiar research events, technologies, and practices can potentially fall into other (rather than 'new') relationalities with one another (Murris 2020: 10).

In the work of Puig de la Bellacasa (2017), 'critical cuts' is briefly mentioned in relation to care as a way of stressing the vital and interfering character of research in a similar vein to caring cuts. However, although we agree that cuts are critical, we find that *caring cuts* becomes a configuration that affords embracing the messiness of how knowledge production involves attachment, curiosity, and uncertainty. Moreover, caring cuts opens up for the researcher's distributed responsibility in the becoming of things. In doing so, the discussion has links to Baradian cuts:

> Not only do we become able to cut in a certain way because of our own attachments— because we care for some things more than others—but also to produce a caring account. Critical cuts don't merely expose or produce conflict, they also foster caring relations. (Puig de la Bellacasa 2017: 62)

Here, Puig de la Bellacasa describes how cuts become enacted of the attachments of the larger arrangements of, for example, research, not as an individual act. Furthermore, care is vital to how cuts enact what is assembled and not. Part of a research assemblage is also the account, the story told from the research. The research account is enacted of the cuts that care entails. It emphasises that the research account is part of the research assemblage, not in a linear relationship of following from preceding methods merely reflecting a passive world. It has wordly and ethical effects. Puig de la Bellacasa argues that this double movement of cuts in research makes possible the generation of care.

Furthermore, we put *caring cuts* in conversation with the recent ANT interest in *care-ful* research articulated by John Law and colleagues Vicky Singleton and Wenyuan Lin. Care-ful research is a way of tending to (caring for) how divisions are made in research practices and their generation of power. Building on ANT and relational materialism, it is an 'after method'-approach to method assemblages and an alternative to thinking about research design (Law 2022; Law and Lin 2020; Law and Singleton 2013). In relation to care-ful research, *caring cuts* conceptualises the idea that what concerns researchers also structures how we notice the world and how we think it should be. This entails that knowledge production foster, among other things, a creative generation of care. Adhering to the logic of care means that 'gathering knowledge is not a matter of providing better maps *of* reality, but of crafting more bearable ways of living *with*, or *in*, reality' (Mol 2008: 46) (emphasis in the original). The configuration of *caring cuts* stresses that research practices are co-constituted of epistemology-ontology entanglements.

The configuration of *caring cuts* puts emphasis on caring for the cuts that enact researchable worlds. Left unattended, repeated cuts can become dominating and consolidate dichotomies in educational realities. By accentuating that the mundane is lively and surprising, Law and Lin (2020: 6) articulate that '[u]nless we are careful, most materials disappear into the background even when they are crucial to the associations of the social'. Caring cuts raise the question; how messy is the digital if the digital is kept intact as objects by/of/within research practices? The relational materialism of ANT and posthumanism affords caring cuts with the potential to contribute to methodological sensibilities of more-than-digital worlds in education.

4 Methodological Sensibilities: Putting Caring Cuts to Work

In this section, *caring cuts* is put to work to explore its potential in postdigital methodologies. We do so by plugging in the concept to empirical research events from our own practices on more-than-digital methodologies that situate specifics of postdigital research practices. We explore how analytic assemblages are shaped and enacted of caring cuts. The explorations have been informed by our ethnographic and collaborative engagements with theory, research, and educational practices. The empirical events we present and analyse are from doing research within the Covid-19 pandemic that amplified unpredictive care while digital technologies were not merely instruments of teaching or research desires that solved and assisted in neutral ways. The first empirical event is presented with a vignette, and the second is a screenshot.

4.1 Example 1: Trust and Modest Interruptions with Research Technologies

Due to the pandemic and the fact that no outsiders are allowed to visit the school, our collaboration with teachers is being moved to Zoom. Five teachers are participating, and we are three researchers; two run the workshop and I attend mainly to document. I'm sitting at home in my workroom in front of two computer screens, one showing zoom and one with memory notes. For sound quality I use headphones. When the workshop starts, I tell the participants that I am recording the audio and taking notes. I turn on the recorder and place it on my desk next to the screens. I also start to write what is happening. After about 15 minutes, I realise that the sound that has been recorded is only what I said and foremost the clatter from the keyboard.

In this event, it emerges how mundane and perhaps even trivial research practices involve vital co-producers. Despite trying hard to set up a proper research setting and do everything right, the situation nevertheless becomes a failure. It turns into a vibrant acknowledgment of the sociomaterial gatherings of doing research. Here, the failure puts forward an intimate sense of trust and interdependency on the technical devices. As recognised within ANT research, failures and breakdowns tend to blur the boundaries of 'what material and human actors can accomplish' (Bodén et al. 2019). Furthermore, they disrupt and expand the things that are important and what to care for, as this event addresses how 'our machines are disturbingly lively, and we ourselves frighteningly inert' (Haraway 1991:152).

As such, this event becomes a reminder not to 'stop with people and talk, don't stop with devices or technologies, and don't stop with texts' (Law and Lin 2020:7) but rather to forefront relations and assemblages where we all – researcher, headphones, recorder, etc. are co-constructed. This raises questions about what/who we become within the assemblage. Who or what become trustworthy? Whom and what are to be documented?

Within this event, the complex relationalities of computer, headphones, and recorder create a cut where foremost the clicks from the keyboard are documented. The voices of the participants that initially were regarded as most important become excluded. This also creates new relations, and new subjects, and shifts positions of centre and background. As such, it raises a range of methodological and analytical questions. When the recorder primarily documents the clicking, does it assist us in broadening attention towards the multiple relations going on in the research practice? The click of the keyboard as fingers type what is heard from the participants through electronic headphones and Wi-Fi connection, should it be noticed in research? Where do we draw the lines for what is considered valuable?

Additionally, the example evokes questions about the mundane methods for empirical work such as field notes and sound recordings. What becomes vital is how the recorder produced feelings of trust such as doing research and documenting the practice correctly. However, within the failure taking place, the fragility and vulnerabilities of the actors become materialised shifting the relation onto uncertainty. It unfolds how putting trust in the recorder as a neutral and stable technology capable of caring for the documentation of the situation is at the same time part of producing the situation within the research assemblage. Following Haraway (1991: 90), there is no unmediated or passive way of documenting practices, but only specific possibilities 'with a wonderfully detailed, active, partial way of organizing worlds'. This means that together with field notes and a recorder, transformative fragments of a practice are co-produced as empirical material. Thereby empirical material is regarded as active and partial engagements where the body, as well as the recorder, become responsive and performative research technologies (Gunnarsson 2018).

As Mol (2008) insists, all technologies, recorders as well as field notes, are never neutral or stable. They may be strategic, ordering the practice in a certain manner, but still leaky and transformative, interdependent on how caring cuts are enacted. This urges research practices to carefully address, in terms of paying attention to, the collectively and interdependent cuttings going on. Caring cuts, then, are relational obligations of interfering with unpredictable and moving practices (Puig de la Bellacasa 2017:61). In other words, caring cuts involve paying careful attention to the involved situated ambivalences and vulnerabilities of the things we study as well as those things that become ignored (Gunnarsson 2023). Accordingly, working with caring cuts affords critical attention to how knowledge-producing practices are interferences and reorderings with material consequences.

This example puts forward how what becomes produced as empirical material is defined by agential cuts. Moreover, the transformative character of knowledge production where '[t]hings that look solid aren't because the relations that make them up are processes' (Law and Lin 2020: 8). Importantly, these processes are involved in interfering, excluding, and privileging. Even though it might be modest interruptions, putting caring cuts to work in relation to the example above meant embracing the everyday messiness of doing research that might guide towards 'another kind of world and worldliness' (Haraway 2004: 234).

4.2 Example 2: Uneventful Research Events with Educational Technology

In ethnographic engagements with an upper secondary school in Sweden during the pandemic school closure, the following event took place while clicking and exploring the features of the school's Microsoft Team. A screenshot was captured with the researcher's computer (Fig. 1).

The event initially provoked the question of how to accommodate digital technology in research. In other words, it was a struggle to care about Teams. It presented as mute with presumptive ideas about education (assignments, points, and other features) that appeared altogether uneventful. On top of that, the display was a folly mixture of the researcher's account and anticipated graded assignments. Not only was it uneventful, but it was also not meaningful. As the pandemic put pressure on teachers and students at this school, and everywhere else, it seemed fair to question the value of researching Teams (this way). We cannot possibly care for everything. The encounter did not seem to achieve capacity for response. So, how can this researcher-school technology encounter render the researcher responsible?

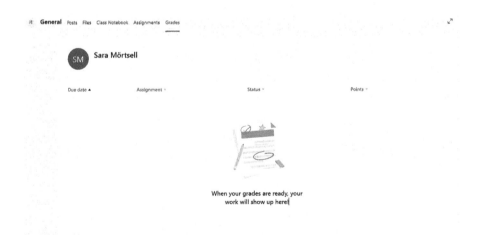

Fig. 1 Screenshot of Microsoft Teams displayed on the researcher's computer screen. Used with permission from Microsoft

The screenshot is 'folly' as long as it is mobilised only of meaning-making endeavours and capturing data. Research narrated and practiced as capture and discovery enact the 'pull of a linear narrative' (Juelskjær 2013: 760). In this narration of research practices, the screenshot is rendered meaningless and the only available position for it is as discarded data. In other words, the screenshot appears too messy for a linear research practice. The question is how the screenshot event can be reconfigured to foster caring relations that connect. What happens in the uneventful? Interestingly, following Puig de la Bellacasa, the unexciting is replete with care:

> Focusing on everydayness, on the uneventful, is a way of noticing care's ordinary doings, the domestic unimpressive ways in which we get through the day, without which no event would be possible. While events are those breaks that make a difference, marking a before and after that gets recorded in history, care, in spite of all the work of political reclaiming, in spite of its hegemonic marketization, remains associated with the unexciting, blended with the dullness of the everyday, with an uneventful temporality. (Puig de la Bellacasa 2017: 117–18)

The finger-keyboard coordination of taking the screenshot, and carefully naming and storing the file in a list of other files took part in turning something uneventful into a recorded event. The cut enacted an empirical material as a recording in history, a bounded entity manifested in spacetime, yet still ambivalent with the uneventful.

Noticing what makes this uneventful event possible means becoming sensitised to the multiple agencies involved in its ontological doings and enlarging the scope included while continuing the decentring of the human. Haraway (2008) asks researchers to consider the ontological choreography of the natureculture phenomena that make up our concerns. Post-approaches in education have responded by taking inquiries beyond the narrow face-to-face scale of, in this case, the researcher-screen to involve the event as simultaneously played out on molecular and planetary scales (Lenz Taguchi and Eriksson 2021). This begs the question: how is the screenshot of Teams co-constituted of multiple scales?

The encounter is a more-than-human effect of distributed agencies across scales that entangle the research event with data, protocols, thermoplastics, energy, rare-earth elements (REE), etc. They co-constitute the enactment of material durability that stabilises the event. However, this enlarged scope of spatio-temporal arrangements also discloses vulnerabilities and brevity. Material durability is not naturally enduring. Multiple scales, which do not stop at the face-to-face, bring into the picture an eventful temporality also in digital things, as argued by media geologists, whose science also become enrolled in the expanded research assemblage (Emejulu and McGregor 2019; Taffel 2022).

In terms of the spatio-temporal distribution that these assembled associations are brought into being of, pasts and futures meet in the uneventful research event. The boundaries that make up the screenshot are at the same time its connections to geological processes in the past and discarded wastes of the future. It brings to light that the more familiar, at least to postdigital research, story/world of education as living with digital data simultaneously harbours a story/world of education as living with minerals. REE purification and processing sites are associated with cancerous deaths (Taffel 2022). There is also the violent extraction, exploitation, and associated conflicts of mining minerals (Emejulu and McGregor 2019). The world is a more-than-digital problem. It raises questions about what other matters of care also demand and call for scholarly attention. To echo Mol's (2008) logic of care, what knowledge practices can craft more bearable ways of living in this reality?

The omnipresent fact of the screen made it dominating and stable, pushing the work done that produced the screen into the background. The accomplishment of vital actors was erased. But by engaging with the screenshot, it became part of a researchable event that transformed the Teams screenshot as vital empirical material worth caring for and taking into account. Albeit not in an expected way but by responding differently. It raises the question of how the researcher becomes co-constructed in the process. In the movement from a matter of fact to matters of care, the digital became a lively set of heterogeneous associations, and the object screenshot of Teams was not as safely bounded or atomistic as it appeared before.

The uneventful and collateral aspects of research practices call attention to how erasures are constantly involved in knowledge production. For example, the digital as a category does a lot of erasing work when it becomes attached to devices and platforms. However, it is not the work of language alone, which can easily be corrected with a prefix like 'post'. Erasures also happen in the material arrangements as they unimpress us with how things are taken care of. Caring cuts involve a relational obligation to bring care into the picture of neglected things to affect the life of things (Puig de la Bellacasa 2017).

With care-ful sensibilities (Law and Lin 2020) and research accounts that weave human and non-human storylines (Thompson and Adams 2020), a digital device can transform from an insular individual/private worry/concern into also becoming a collective problem for a field of research in education, other disciplines, corporations, developers, teaching, policy, manufacturing, etc.

5 Caring Cuts for Thinking/Researching/Doing Digital Worlds Anew

This chapter has explored the configuration of *caring cuts* within postdigital research. To unfold methodological sensibilities, the question that post-approaches and *caring cuts* raise in the encounter with postdigital research is – how are worlds made by our care and particular curiosity for the digital?

Working with caring cuts on empirical research events has made possible attention to how knowledge production is inevitably untidy and non-innocent. Furthermore, caring cuts creatively points to the mundane and ambivalent practices of research. For instance, a sound recorder is vulnerable to failure while at the same time calling for trust in its ability for a partial organisation of empirical fragments. In research assemblages, things, concepts, literature, body, and recording technologies co-constitute researchable worlds. Caring cuts highlight that the assemblage is brought into being of cuts, ignorance, and neglect, with material and ethical effects. Some things become valued and amplified, others are ignored. With caring cuts, modest interruptions suggest a methodological sensibility of not too hastily putting things 'right' but acknowledging that other worlds are possible.

The mundane practices of research also take place in the uneventful and unexpected. Caring cuts lay bare the anthropocentric notion that something can be uneventful. Liveliness is rather taking place across distributed scales that decentre human privilege. The cut performed *of* the event separates a before and after and at the same time brings pasts and futures together. Here, caring cuts offers the potential for engaging with material vulnerabilities and erasures. It generates questions for knowledge production about how to collectively make more bearable postdigital worlds. The potential of caring cuts comes in how it conceptualises ways of noticing, thinking, and researching more-than-digital relations anew.

This chapter started on the note of engaging with ontology in the curious dance of epistemology and methodology. The ontological engagement with the postdigital, informed by posthumanism and ANT, means to approach research practices as world-making, not only as a knowledge-making practice. When (post)digital technologies are centred and privileged by our anthropocentric research methods, their vital vulnerabilities become at the same time ignored and subordinated. In the enactment of such a cut, the relational ontology of the digital is neglected, and as it becomes stabilised it is only noticed by its absence or failure.

Negroponte's (1998) proposal ironically serves as a caution for a postdigital scholarship that plastics, air, and water should *not* be neglected. Caring cuts can help address the potential and ethics involved here, in the unnoticeable presence of the digital. Postdigital research problems can foster care and attention for the digital that does not passively wait at a distance for it to break or decay to be noticed. Therefore, caring cuts point to the creative potential of engaging with the ontology of the postdigital. Bringing attention to this cut makes possible an exploration of how care-ful postdigital research is and can be.

Jandrić et al. (2022) raise the issue of responsibility on part of a postdigital scholarship. Taking that as an invitation to care, we have done so in this chapter by relating and stressing the concerns of postdigital research with that of relational materialism. This ontology of posthumanism and ANT affords the engagement with feminist thinking on *care* and *cut*. The configuration of *caring cuts*, we propose, opens up multiple and ethical more-than-digital relations. Thus, the chapter's contribution is the argument that, on the one hand, post-approaches to education can learn from postdigital scholarship to take better care of the (more-than) digital relations.

On the other hand, postdigital research can learn from post-approaches that there are methodological sensibilities that might afford to challenge anthropocentric care for digital matters in education. As such, methodological sensibilities can be vital for acknowledging transformations of human-technology relations. Postdigital scholarship shows capacities to take these thorny matters beyond a mere critique into new commitments to building alternatives, in times when it is desperately needed (Law 2022).

We would like to end by leaving the reader with a few questions. What cuts have been enacted in this sociomaterial account of caring cuts? What have we ignored? How carefully is it possible to engage with postdigital worlds?

References

Barad, K. (2007). *Meeting the universe halfway: quantum physics and the entanglement of matter and meaning*. Durham, NC: Duke University Press.
Barad, K. (2014). Diffracting Diffraction: Cutting Together-Apart. *Parallax, 20*(3), 168–187. https://doi.org/10.1080/13534645.2014.927623.
Bodén, L. (2016). Present absences: Exploring the posthumanist entanglements of school absenteeism. PhD Thesis. Linköping: Linköping University. http://liu.diva-portal.org/smash/record.jsf?pid=diva2%3A951239&dswid=-2263. Accessed 20 December 2022.
Bodén, L., Lenz Taguchi, H., Moberg, E., & Taylor, C. A. (2019). Relational Materialism. In G. Noblit (Ed.), *Oxford Research Encyclopedia of Education*. Oxford: Oxford University Press. https://doi.org/10.1093/acrefore/9780190264093.013.789.
Emejulu, A., & McGregor, C. (2019). Towards a radical digital citizenship in digital education. *Critical Studies in Education, 60*(1), 131–147. https://doi.org/10.1080/17508487.2016.1234494.
Gorur, R. (2011). Policy as Assemblage. *European Educational Research Journal, 10*(4), 611–622. https://doi.org/10.2304/eerj.2011.10.4.611.
Gunnarsson, K. (2018). Responding with care: A careful critical approach within educational health promotion. *Reconceptualizing Educational Research Methodology, 9*(1). https://doi.org/10.7577/rerm.2699.
Gunnarsson, K. (2021). How to expand the boundaries: feminist posthumanist elaborations on change in education. *Reconceptualizing Educational Research Methodology, 12*(1). https://doi.org/10.7577/rerm.4245.
Gunnarsson, K. (2023). Care and feminist posthumanisms. In M. L. Rasmussen & L. Allen (Eds.), *The Palgrave Encyclopedia of Sexuality Education*. Cham: Palgrave Macmillan. https://doi.org/10.1007/978-3-030-95352-2.
Gunnarsson, K., & Bodén, L. (2021). *Introduktion till postkvalitativ metodologi*. Stockholm: Stockholm University Press. https://doi.org/10.16993/bbh.
Haraway, D. (1991). *Simians, Cyborgs, and Women: The Reinvention of Nature*. New York: Routledge. https://doi.org/10.4324/9780203873106.
Haraway, D. (2004). *The Haraway reader*. New York: Routledge.
Haraway, D. (2008). *When species meet*. Minneapolis, MN: University of Minnesota Press.
Jandrić, P., & Ford, D. R. (2022). Postdigital Ecopedagogies: Genealogies, Contradictions, and Possible Futures. *Postdigital Science and Education, 4*(3), 692–710. https://doi.org/10.1007/s42438-020-00207-3.
Jandrić, P., & Knox, J. (2022). The postdigital turn: Philosophy, education, research. *Policy Futures in Education, 20*(7), 780–795. https://doi.org/10.1177/14782103211062713.
Jandrić, P., Knox, J., Besley, T., Ryberg, T., Suoranta, J., & Hayes, S. (2018). Postdigital science and education. *Educational Philosophy and Theory, 50*(10), 893–899. https://doi.org/10.1080/00131857.2018.1454000.
Jandrić, P., MacKenzie, A., & Knox, J. (2022). Postdigital Research: Genealogies, Challenges, and Future Perspectives. *Postdigital Science and Education*. https://doi.org/10.1007/s42438-022-00306-3.
Juelskjær, M. (2013). Gendered subjectivities of spacetimematter. *Gender and Education, 25*(6), 754–768. https://doi.org/10.1080/09540253.2013.831812.

Juelskjær, M. (2020). Mattering pedagogy in precarious times of (un)learning. Matter: *Journal of New Materialist Research, 1*(1). https://doi.org/10.1344/jnmr.v1i1.30067.

Knox, J. (2019). What Does the 'Postdigital' Mean for Education? Three Critical Perspectives on the Digital, with Implications for Educational Research and Practice. *Postdigital Science and Education, 1*(2), 357–370. https://doi.org/10.1007/s42438-019-00045-y.

Lather, P., & Pierre, E. A. S. (2013). Post-qualitative research. *International Journal of Qualitative Studies in Education, 26*(6), 629–633. https://doi.org/10.1080/09518398.2013.788752.

Latour, B. (2004). Why Has Critique Run out of Steam? From Matters of Fact to Matters of Concern. *Critical Inquiry, 30*(2), 225–248. https://doi.org/10.1086/421123.

Law, J. (2022). From After Method to care-ful research (a foreword). In C. Addey & N. Piattoeva (Eds.), *Intimate Accounts of Education Policy Research: The Practice of Methods* (pp. xvi–xx). Abingdon and New York: Routledge.

Law, J., & Lin, W. (2020). Care-ful Research: Sensibilities from STS. http://heterogeneities. net/publications/LawLin2020CarefulResearchSensibilitiesFromSTS.pdf. Accessed 20 December 2022.

Law, J., & Singleton, V. (2013). ANT and Politics: Working in and on the World. *Qualitative Sociology, 36*(4), 485–502. https://doi.org/10.1007/s11133-013-9263-7.

Lenz Taguchi, H., & Eriksson, C. (2021). Posthumanism/New Materialism: The Child, Childhood, and Education. In N. J. Yelland, L. Peters, M. Tesar, & M. S. Pérez (Eds.), *The SAGE Handbook of Global Childhoods* (pp. 165–178). London: SAGE.

Lenz Taguchi, H., Semenec, P., & Diaz-Diaz, C. (2020). Interview with Hillevi Lenz Taguchi. In C. Diaz-Diaz & P. Semenec (Eds.), *Posthumanist and New Materialist Methodologies: Research After the Child* (pp. 33–46). Singapore: Springer. https://doi.org/10.1007/ 978-981-15-2708-1_4.

Martin, A., Myers, N., & Viseu, A. (2015). The politics of care in technoscience. *Social Studies of Science, 45*(5), 625–641. https://doi.org/10.1177/0306312715602073.

Mol, A. (2008). *The Logic of Care: Health and the Problem of Patient Choice.* London: Routledge. https://doi.org/10.4324/9780203927076.

Mol, A., Moser, I., & Pols, J. (2010). Care: putting practice into theory. In A. Mol, I. Moser, & J. Pols (Eds.), *Care in practice: on tinkering in clinics, homes and farms* (pp. 7–25). Bielefeld: Transcript.

Mörtsell, S. (2022). Sociomaterial explorations of attendance practices in 'schooling without schools'. *Learning, Media and Technology, 47*(4), 1–12. https://doi.org/10.1080/17439884. 2022.2039939.

Murris, K. (Ed.). (2020). *Navigating the Postqualitative, New Materialist and Critical Posthumanist Terrain Across Disciplines: An Introductory Guide.* London: Routledge. https:// doi.org/10.4324/9781003041177.

Negroponte, N. (1998). Beyond digital. Wired. https://web.media.mit.edu/~nicholas/Wired/ WIRED6-12.html. Accessed 1 November 2022.

Puig de la Bellacasa, M. (2017). *Matters of care: Speculative ethics in more than human worlds.* Minneapolis, MN: University of Minnesota Press.

Renold, E., & Ivinson, G. (2022). Posthuman co-production: becoming response-able with what matters. *Qualitative Research Journal, 22*(1), 108–128. https://doi.org/10.1108/ QRJ-01-2021-0005.

Rich, E., & Lupton, D. (2022). Rethinking digital biopedagogies: How sociomaterial relations shape English secondary students' digital health practices. *Social Science & Medicine, 311*, 115348. https://doi.org/10.1016/j.socscimed.2022.115348.

Sinclair, C., & Hayes, S. (2019). Between the Post and the Com-Post: Examining the Postdigital 'Work' of a Prefix. *Postdigital Science and Education, 1*(1), 119–131. https://doi.org/10.1007/ s42438-018-0017-4.

Taffel, S. (2022). AirPods and the earth: Digital technologies, planned obsolescence and the Capitalocene. *Environment and Planning E: Nature and Space.* https://doi. org/10.1177/25148486221076136.

Thompson, T. L. (2016). Digital doings: curating work–learning practices and ecologies. *Learning, Media and Technology, 41*(3), 480–500. https://doi.org/10.1080/17439884.2015.1064957.

Thompson, T. L., & Adams, C. (2020). Accountabilities of posthuman research. *Explorations in Media Ecology, 19*(3), 337–349. https://doi.org/10.1386/eme_00050_7.

Wagener-Böck, N., Macgilchrist, F., Rabenstein, K., & Bock, A. (2022). From Automation to Symmation: Ethnographic Perspectives on What Happens in Front of the Screen. *Postdigital Science and Education*. https://doi.org/10.1007/s42438-022-00350-z.

Vestigial Research for Postdigital Pataphysics

Peter B. Hyland and Tyson E. Lewis

1 Introduction

Digital research, simply put, concerns counting. As Florian Cramer argues (2015), digital comes from the digits of the hand and can thus refer broadly to any research concerned with discernibility, distinction, discreteness, and/or differentiation. The digital therefore has a long genealogy that stretches beyond obvious references to computational systems, including games, textiles and weaving, and other premodern artifacts, objects, and machines (Galloway 2021). On this broad interpretation, the digital in research is actually redundant as *all* modern, Western, scientific research is digital insofar is it concerns discretization of lived experience into datapoints. It thus follows that postdigital is a term that refers not simply to the undeniable implosion of the digital, biological, and cultural spheres but also to the *uncomputable* nature of these implosions. Indeed, as the ability of cybernetics to gather data on every aspect of our lives, the resulting 'big data' sets become increasingly unwieldy and incalculable (hence the impossibility of making accurate predictions, despite the surplus of data).

In this chapter, we argue that the terrain of postdigital research is precisely the terrain of the uncomputable. For us, the beginning point for thinking through the uncomputable dimension of the postdigital condition is in the French theoretical interest in expenditure, first theorized by pataphysician Alfred Jarry and then taken up by Georges Bataille. For instance, in his iconic essay 'The Notion of Expenditure', Bataille (2017) argues that a defining feature of social structure is unproductive

P. B. Hyland (✉) · T. E. Lewis
University of North Texas, Denton, TX, USA
e-mail: peter.hyland@unt.edu; tyson.lewis@unt.edu

P. Jandrić et al. (eds.), *Postdigital Research*, Postdigital Science and Education,
https://doi.org/10.1007/978-3-031-31299-1_11

expenditure that cannot be counted or accounted for (cannot be made fully operative or functional). If Bataille is correct then society was first and foremost postdigital before it was ever digital! This claim is similar to that made by Andrew Feenberg (2019) who argued that the postdigital might very well predate the digital and thus, paradoxically, be thought of as the *predigital*.

Although a turn to Bataille can clarify the unique terrain of postdigital research, it poses a serious problem as well: what are the research techniques that would allow us to experiment with on and through the postdigital without subjecting it to digital forms of differentiation, computation, and calculability? Methods of digital research are all, in some way, geared toward transforming experience into discrete data points that can be aggregated and disaggregated in order to measure and predict, and to subject postdigital experiences, objects, and relations to these same methods would be to destroy the very experiences, objects, and relations that are of interest and concern. As such, we cannot fall back on digital methods in order to understand something about the postdigital condition. Instead, we suggest a new turn toward pataphysical research creation techniques as a way of accessing the postdigitial without thereby destroying it.[1]

Throughout the rest of this chapter, we will outline two ways in which pataphysical research creation techniques differ significantly from the metaphysics of Western, digital research. First, the pataphysical dimension of postdigital research emphasizes nonknowledge through the exploration of exceptional states.[2] Patapysical research creation techniques appropriate the form of the 'rule' found in most digital culture but subvert the ends of such rules, releasing rule-bound procedures from their role in calculation and discretization. Instead, rules open themselves up to releasing exceptions, or what Bataille (2017) would call expenditure.

Second, pataphysical research creation techniques augment the body of the researcher in a strikingly different way from computationally determined research methods, the former producing vestigial organs (unproductive expenditures of the ecstatic body, as Bataille would say) and the latter producing utilitarian, productive organs (for a hierarchically organized, visually oriented body). We then conclude with a brief turn toward David Cronenberg's student film *Crimes of the Future* (1970) as an example of pataphysical research creation into the noneconomic, non-utilitarian surplus of postdigital reality.

---

[1] Research creation, in this chapter, refers to pataphysical, arts-based research that renders inoperative divisions between science and art, producing useless expenditure or excess (Tavin, Tavin, and Ryynänen 2019; Lewis 2020).

[2] The themes of nonknowledge against the transparency and calculability of knowledge in relation to anti-capitalist, postdigital research has been introduced in the work of Ford, Swenson, and Fosher (2022). The present essay is, in many ways, a restaging of these themes with regards to Bataille.

2   The Postdigital as Expenditure

For Alfred Jarry writing in the late nineteenth century, Western metaphysics concerns the existence of the general or typical conditions that make possible reality whereas pataphysics concerns the investigation into the 'laws of exceptions' that resist any generalization (Jarry 1996: 21). Science, as the operationalized and instrumentalized embodiment of Western metaphysical assumptions, presupposes as its gold standard, generalizability and verifiability, yet the pataphysical pursuit of the exception challenges these scientific standards. The exception is precisely that which cannot be generalized (it remains a singular event, eruption, or performance) and fails to be verified (as it cannot be repeated within a controlled setting). Pataphysics thus embraces what science would otherwise reject as nonsense, statistically unimportant, or simply anomalous/monstrous.

Jarry's emphasis on the exception has been inherited by a number of French thinkers (think of Deleuze's notion of desire, Lacan's notion of the Real, Kristeva's abject, or Lyotard's notion of the sublime). Even if the influence is oblique, one cannot miss Jarry's imprint on figures such as Georges Bataille and his deep and penetrating analysis of expenditure.[3] In 'The Notion of Expenditure' Bataille (2017) directly draws upon the ethnographic work of Marcel Mauss (2016) and his analysis of the structure of the gift—best exemplified in potlatch—in order to critique the Western, classical economic theory of utilitarianism. Whereas utilitarian economics focuses on the calculation of pleasure over pain, Mauss discovered in Pacific Northwest potlatch an excess of exchange that was not predicated on any notion of personal benefit. Instead, there was an excessive exchange of gifts between groups that produced a series of obligations leading to ever increasingly high levels of gift giving bent on humiliating the other through sheer volume. Instead of amassing wealth, these were displays of epic loss, expenditure, and sacrifice that were absolutely uncalculatable according to any utilitarian scale of pleasure or pain.

For Bataille (2017), Mauss's (2016) theory revealed an essential truth about society obscured by the rationalistic approach to exchange found in Western economic sciences: exchange and consumption are not about production and acquisition so much as non-economic expenditure. Opposed to any utilitarian theory of the human being defined by needs, Bataille argues that an individual is 'not simply a stomach to fill, but an excess of energy to be squandered' (2017: 334). The problem with utilitarianist economics is that existence is 'not a problem of production and the distribution of products' but rather concerns the question of the 'excess energy of workers' (2017: 334), which falls outside of any economic calculus. In other words,

---

[3] It is important to note that even if Bataille (2017) does not cite pataphysics *per se*, Jarry's (1996) aesthetic concerns with the occult, ritual, and pornography certainly contributed to Bataille's explorations into tabooed erotica, not to mention their shared concern with sovereign power. Furthermore, Bataille's friend and collaborator Raymond Queneau was a well-known pataphysical writer.

expenditure is an expression of pure sacrifice without orientation toward any measurable end (pleasure, profit, utility, etc.).

To summarize, life is not defined in terms of *productive* and *calculable* social activity. Missing from this picture are a series of important events that cannot easily be dismissed as mere exceptions to the utilitarian rule: catastrophes, depressions, orgiastic states, revolutions, all of which are expenditures of such loss that they *break* any utilitarian scale that attempts to measure them in terms of pleasure and pain, gains and losses, positives and negatives. Such events cannot be disaggregated into discrete unites of measure. Indeed, these events and phenomena fall within the realm of the sacred, which, for Bataille, is the exceptional world of inutilious and exhaustive expenditures. In this sense, the sacred stands opposed to not only utilitarian economic theory but also to institutionalized religion, both of which attempt to mitigate the radically disruptive potential of unproductive, impractical, uncomputational surplus.

Digital research concerns itself with what Bataille calls 'productive activity' or activity that 'serves as a means to the end of production' (1997: 169). Postdigital research, on the other hand (or perhaps this turn of phrase is inadequate at this point because hands imply digits and thus an accounting of what is *on* the other hand), concerns 'unconditional expenditure' of 'unproductive forms' in which loss and sacrifice must be as great as possible. The unconditional means that there are no utilitarian laws that place limits on how much will be lost and there is no calculation capable of measuring its outcomes (whatever they might be). The postdigital therefore has no ends orienting it beyond its own massive expenditure (massive in the sense of the mathematical sublime).

Bataille includes in his eclectic list of expenditures the purchasing of jewels, cultic sacrifices, games (especially those which end in death), certain forms of art, and revolution as unproductive forms of social life. We would also add to the list study practices (Lewis and Hyland 2022), which are the unproductive expenditure of learning insofar as the studier sacrifices a great deal (in terms of social life, time, and career) in order to obsessively and addictively dwell on the rituals of thinking (the results of which cannot be measured in any utilitarian calculation and which do not have any endpoint in sight). In short, expenditures such as potlatch are already postdigital precisely because they are uncomputable.

Within Western utilitarian economic theory and practice (re: digital sciences), expenditure is 'rediscover[ed] on the scale of irreducible needs through the efforts of those who push the consequences of current rationalist conceptions as far as they will go' (Bataille 1997: 176), to the point where expenditure itself is sacrificed (a sacrifice of the sacrifice!). Its only remaining expression is, for Bataille, in moments when the bourgeois investment in utilitarian economics breaks apart in a moment of class struggle, also known as revolution. Revolution—the ultimate postdigital event—has been either (a) villainized by bourgeois economists interested in ameliorating working conditions through calculated reforms (increasing profits while decreasing the pain of workers through minimal wage increases) or (b) has been betrayed by so called 'scientific Marxism' which attempts to compute it according to irrefutable economic laws. In both cases, the error lies in faith entrusted to *digital* research and theory imposed upon postdigital phenomena. Digital research concerns the secular, whereas postdigital research concerns the sacred (re: the absolutely accursed share of society which has no value, no function, no employment, and no end).

At this point we can thus posit the question of the specific *techniques* of postdigital research that can help us touch, contact, conjure up, and study phenomena of (sacred) expenditure. Bataille's own approach to such topics as perversion, festivals, ritual, and sacrifice offer some important reference points. For instance, he focuses his attention on studying precisely those phenomena that digital research either (a) dismisses as statistical anomalies or (b) attempts to digitize by imposing its methods of analysis to otherwise unanalyzable and uncomputational exceptions. According to Bataille, bourgeois society—with its utilitarian economics and Catholic institutions—attempts to suppress the excessive (by making it 'work' to achieve profit or salvation), yet we might argue that increasingly, this is impossible. Indeed, theorists have argued that we live in a historical moment in which the exception has become the rule, and the law has been suspended, thus making possible the appearance of sacrifice on a mass scale (Agamben 1999).[4] Various cybernetic attempts to quarantine the exceptional, rationalize it, or control it only demonstrate the growing inadequacies of such digitalizing approaches to contain the increasing levels of expenditure that define political, social, and economic realities. Despite the continual functioning of cybernetic surveillance systems, acts of terrorism continue to 'surprise' us precisely because such events are uncomputable surpluses.

Thus, we live in postdigital times in which the explosive nature of the expenditure has become the norm to the point where the division Bataille himself pointed out between the productive and unproductive differences in social phenomena cannot hold. Everything is sacred. This means that the postdigital is not a specialization so much as a much needed and urgent study of expenditure on a global scale. Second, Bataille's philosophical writing style does not submit expenditure to overly rational presentation (in the form of logical proofs or carefully plotted, evidentiary claims) but instead attempts to poetically convey an intuitive sense of the uncomputable dimensions of a phenomenon. The key here is that the uncomputable can never be fully present in writing, can never be fully calculated, but this does not mean that it cannot be figured through certain techniques of writing. In this sense, the form of the writing is the content (thus, in a postdigital way, imploding the discrete difference between form and content). These are starting points, but in the next section we hope to elaborate further.

---

[4] While Agamben (2020) ultimately rejected Bataille's politics as neo-fascist (even if Bataille resolutely stood against all forms of political, social, and military servility to fascist dictators), it is unquestionable that Agamben's treatment of sovereign power, states of exception, the sacred, and so forth are in dialogue with both Jarry and Bataille.

3 Protocols for Nonknowledge

Digital research utilizes discretization to produce accurate models for predictive purposes. It attempts to control for variability and minimizes contingencies in order to discover consistent patterns through computational programs, rules, and games. Postdigital research of expenditures focuses on phenomena that lack coherent models and thus cannot generate consistent patterns. The former concerns the accounting of what can be counted whereas the latter concerns the eruption of the discounted. In this section, we argue that postdigital research draws from pataphysical inheritances in two senses. Drawing on the work of Jarry (1996), we see pataphysics as comprised of the following key dimensions: it is a science that pursues nonknowledge of exceptions in order to discover/produce/create impossible solutions. The linguistic experiments of the Oulipo pataphysical group[5] (which include figures such as Raymond Queneau, Georges Perec, and Italio Calvino) in the 1960s has taken up Jarry's eccentric mix of science, mathematics, and literary experimentation. For Bataille, the way to research expenditure was through ritualistic enactments (more religious than anything else) while for Oulipo, such expenditure was the product of playful appropriations of mathematical and logistical formulizations. In both cases—ritual and mathematical—protocols, or sets of constraints (Lewis and Hyland 2022), were used to ignite swerves leading from knowledge to nonknowledge.

Ritual, for Bataille's antireligious religion might be thought of as an impractical practice for rendering inoperative the ends guiding bodies, actions, and thought within society. Bataille's secret society named Acéphale—which lasted for less than 3 years (beginning in 1937 and ending in 1939)—enacted a series of complex, nocturnal rituals meant to evoke exceptional states of Dioysian ecstasy and revery existing in surplus of diurnal, socially normative pressures to conform. For instance, initiates of Acéphale would receive an envelope containing instructions giving the day and time for a rendezvous in the forest of Marly (usually at either the ruins of the fortress of Montjoie or a famous oak tree struck by lightning). The instructions might also include a number of other procedural details meant to separate the individual participant from his/her worldly habits and everyday state of mind in which social norms are taken as necessary (rather than contingent). Here we cite a description of an initiation ritual into the secret society Acéphale written by Patrick Waldberg:

> As soon as I arrived in Paris I was taken by Bataille up to the balcony of the building where he was living, at 76 bis rue de Rennes. It was dusk. He turned me to face the east, in other words towards the night, and made me take an oath of silence. The initiation I was to undergo was due to take place a few days later. To this end he gave me a timetable and the drawing of a map. On the appointed date, the night of the new moon, I was told to take the train from Saint-Lazare station to Saint-Nom-la-Bretèche. If in the course of the journey I

---

[5] Affiliated with the Collège de 'Pataphysique, which was founded in 1948 by devotees of Alfred Jarry, the Oulipo group combines and exagerates constraints found in poetry and mathematics to produce unexpected, playful, and often absurdist writing techniques (see Motte 1986).

happened to come across any people I knew, I was advised to ignore them, just as, after we got off the train and while we were following the path through the forest, if the same people were also on that path our instructions were to keep our distance and remain silent. The long walk along sunken paths, steeped in the damp smell of the trees, took us in pitch darkness to the foot of an oak that had been struck by lightning, on the edge of an étoile, where soon enough there gathered a dozen still and silent shadows. After a short while someone lit a torch. Bataille, standing at the foot of the tree, took an enamelled dish out of a bag and put a few pieces of sulphur on it, which he then set alight. As the blue flame sputtered, smoke rose up and wafted towards us in suffocating gusts. The person holding the torch came and stood on my right as one of the other officiants walked towards me, face on. He was holding a dagger identical to the one brandished by the headless man in the effigy of Acéphale. Bataille took my left hand... the person holding the dagger pressed its tip into my forearm and made a cut several centimetres long, although I did not feel the slightest pain... Someone then tied a handkerchief around the wound, my shift and jacket sleeves were rolled back down again and the torch was put out. (Waldberg in Bataille 2017: 330)

Similar ritual enactments took place every month on the night of the new moon, and were meant to 'establish new rules for living' (Bataille 2017: 330). The intervening time was divided into two periods: periods of tension in which members of the community were required to remain silent and had to avoid seeing one another and periods of license which included every excess. These ritualistic experiments on the self and on community were always to invoke the explosive point of indistinction between life and death (ecstasy) in opposition to the servility imposed by the Christian Church and Fascism (both of which attempt to appropriate expenditure for the conservation of their own institutional or dictatorial forms of power).

With the Second World War looming and with the breakup of Acéphale, Bataille continued ritual practice, this time in the form of meditation. While the details remain obscure, Bataille does describe successive meditative practices, starting with meditation on peace followed by a second meditative concentration on a poem with an insistent rhythm. Next, Bataille would concentrate on visual representations of cosmic annihilation. After several further steps, Bataille would conclude by meditating on grotesque images of extreme Chinese torture. In sum, the practice was meant to produce a breach in Bataille's psyche (an existential decapitation, perhaps) (Bruno 1963). In terms of postdigital research, it is important to note how much Bataille struggled to interrupt, suspend, and render inoperative instrumental ways of thinking about the body and life in general. While digital culture turns toward mediation and new agism to 'optimize' one's happiness or to make one more productive at work, Bataille turned toward meditation as a way to explode the constraints of the self and expose the self to an unbearable cosmic expenditure beyond the horizon of utility (economic calculation) or spiritual salvation (religious indoctrination).

While Bataille drifted more toward occult mysticism and religion (certainly religion that would be considered anti-religious by Christian standards[6]), pataphysical research into expenditure can also take on a more 'scientific' or 'mathematical'

---

[6] Interestingly, Bataille (2017: 326) defines his religion as nothing more than the 'act of laughing (or tears, or erotic stimulation) in the precise sense that laughter (like tears or erotic stimulation) represents the defeat of everything that had sought to impose its permanence'.

guises. Jarry (1996) refers to pataphysics as the science of the exceptional whose meaning and function rest beyond computation (utilitarian or otherwise). At the same time, Jarry proposed mathematical proof of God's existence and used up-to-date scientific research to create blueprints for an absurdist time machine. In this sense, Jarry did not turn his back on science or mathematics (as in Bataille's occultist practices) so much as he playfully engaged with them in decisively uncomputational ways. Instead of surrealism—with its rejection of all forms of rules for the free, uninhibited play of the unconscious—pataphysicians such as the Oulipians opted for what might be called *surrationalism* (Bök 2001: 64), which attempts to produce exceptions out of the systematic use of computational and algorithmic constraints.

Key here is the difference between rule and constraint. As Marcel Bénabou clarifies, 'people accept the rule, they tolerate technique, but they refuse constraint' (1986: 41). Rules are accepted as natural to those who use them (and are used by them!) on a daily basis, but a constraint is rejected as a 'superfluous redoubling of the exigencies of technique' therefore becoming 'exaggerative and excessive' (1986: 41). Instead of rejecting the definition of constraint as the unnecessary and gratuitous redoubling of the rule, Bénabou accepts it without the attending disgust and contempt. Precisely by redoubling the rule, the constraint becomes a technique for researching inutilious and uncomputable expenditures.

Games of constraint have several effects. First, they demonstrate the limits of rules, releasing the rule from its functional role in digital computation. Second, such games demonstrate the virtual potentiality present within rules yet constrained by their computational function. Third, they distract the research from both the pressures of professional rule-following and the trap of inspiration (which is overly dependent on the mystery of individual genius or creativity for artistic production). Like Jarry (1996), Oulipian writers and artists were inspired by ancient geometry and forgotten/obscure literary forms while also inventing new, experimental sets of constraints that pushed beyond the very same traditions. In both cases, the constraints of displacement, substitution, addition, subtraction, multiplication, division, deduction, and contraction produce swerve effects on multiple phonetic, syntactical, grammatical, and lexical levels. The dark freedom of excessive expenditure is not born from mere chaos but rather through the (mystical: Bataille or surrational: pataphysical) use of constraints which push rules to their point of maximal absurdity.

Examples of some of the more famous Oulipo, pataphysical constraints include the lipogram (writing that excludes a particular letter), recurrent literature (writing that contains a rule that enables one to pursue the production of the text to infinity or until exhaustion), and the S + 7 method (writing that replaces each substantive with the seventh following it in a given dictionary). As these examples demonstrate, for Oulipo there is no distinction between poetry and mathematical formulization. For this reason, pataphysical experimentation is inherently postdigital. It accepts that no clear distinctions are possible any longer between the arts and the sciences, between creation and code. Oulipo does not deny this, but rather maximizes the constraints already at work within language in order to create radical swerves within yet beyond the very same codified communication systems. Even if computers are used to calculate combinatorials for pataphysical experimentation, for the Oulipo writer Italio Calvino (1986), the aid of the computer is decisively postdigital insofar as it unleashes a strange, unanticipated, sometimes ludicrous set of combinatorials that often times heighten the effects of absurdity, paradox, and useless expenditure.

Whereas digital research can produce productive knowledge that functions within society to make improvements, poetry and the arts can be thought of as post-digital research for producing nonknowledge beyond socially accepted norms and linguistic rules (defining the proper vs. the improper). Knowledge is, according to Bataille, a 'stable domain' where 'one recognizes oneself, where one recovers one-self' (2001: 133). The stability of knowledge means that it can act as a consistent ground, an ontological foundation, for defining, measuring, and assessing phenomena. For Bataille, nonknowledge is unemployable within such a utilitarian framework. With nonknowledge, there is 'no guarantee of stability' (2001: 133). It reveals that the foundation of knowledge always includes an excess or uncomputable expenditure found at the very limit of the knowable.

There are two implications of Bataille's argument. First, nonknowledge is not the opposite of knowledge (antiknowledge). Instead, it is the outside of knowledge *inside* of knowledge. It is the expenditure of knowledge that knowledge does not know about itself (error, cannot compute!). Second, if research remains within the boundaries of what can be counted (and thus counted on as reassuringly stable), then such research enslaves us to what falls within the limits of good and common sense. Bataille's thus warns that 'at the base of all knowledge there is a servility' (2001: 129). There is therefore an ethical injunction at the heart of postdigital research: rebel against knowledge in the name of experimental freedom!

Embracing nonknowledge means playing with the limits of knowledge by using ritualistic and surrational games. These games might utilize rules and procedures familiar to digital research, but for Bataille, the game becomes what is 'the undefinable, what thought cannot conceive' (2001: 131)—an engine or machine for producing what cannot be thought (nonknowledge). In this way, the game (of exceptional constraints rather than normative rules) is at the edge of knowledge, pointing toward its surplus.

Poetic games in particular have a capacity to invoke a senseless sense of knowledge. Bataille writes, '[a]ll communication among men is rich with garbage' (2001: 5). While digital research attempts to clean up communication (reducing interference or glitches so as to produce maximally functional, logically consistent systems or precise, replicable results), postdigital research not only accepts the existence of such garbage (useless excess) but actually allows it to exist and even finds joy in its unproductive production. It is scuzzy research, glitchy research that pushes programs, rules, and games to the point where they breakdown communication to reveal states of nonknowledge that are equal parts exceptional and particular (non-replicable and irreducible). In this way, programs and games (in both ritualistic and quasi-scientific guises) can be retooled as techniques in what Bataille refers to as 'a struggle against the spell in which useful language holds us' (2001: 16). They can be deployed to 'interrogate the limits of being' (2001: 16), or the waste that is sacrificed by the digital in the name of consistency, security, employability, and productivity. Poetry is trash, waste, but for this very reason it is precious and fragile, needing the special attention of the postdigital researcher.

Nonknowledge, to use pataphysical language, offers up only 'imaginary solutions' (Jarry 1996: 22). Imaginary solutions are not perceived as real solutions within digital research because they are not statistically valid (they concern outliers and accidents). Nor do they lend themselves to rational reforms of existing systems. Take for instance Jarry's (1996) space-time machine in the novel *Exploits & Opinions of Dr. Faustroll, Pataphysician* as an 'imaginary solution' to Dr. Faustroll's problem with local law officials trying to deliver a warrant for his arrest. Imaginary solutions demonstrate the limits of existing social systems, epistemologies, and ontologies, pushing the digital to the postdigital horizon. They are also imaginary in the sense that it is unclear what end (if any) they serve. Digital research is guided by specific ends defined in advance by the economics of utility, but postdigital research does not have such firm foundations against which it can define its progress (or regress). Because it is unclear what kind of instrument Dr. Faustroll's solution actually *is*, the concept of 'solution' is resolutely separated from the question of instrumentality underlying any utilitarian economic or ethical theory (and their ends). How do we evaluate Dr. Faustroll's attempts at escape? How do we measure its success or failure? These questions seem to be rendered inoperative in the face of the postdigital, pataphysical world opened up by Dr. Faustroll's experimentation.

4   The Acéphalic Researcher

Digital research uses various technologies (such as microscopes and telescopes) to improve upon, extend, and intensify the range and scope of the finite capacities of the human body to perceive the world. For Merleau-Ponty, the human body is defined by a certain horizon that sets spatial and temporal limits. Within a given situation, the body strains to achieve what Merleau-Ponty refers to as 'maximal grip' (2012: 248) or the optimal conditions for perceiving a phenomenon/achieving an equilibrium between the body and its environment. Digital science enables the body to extend the range of what it can grip maximally. What can be seen and then thought about through the microscope or the telescope is increased exponentially, as is the number of phenomena that can be quantified and calculated. Indeed, a central aspect of digitalization is the discretization of experience. The technologies of digital research finetune discretionary capacities, enabling research to count on infinitely small and infinitely vast scales, resulting in undermining objects (reducing them to parts or even particles to be counted).

One can almost think of digital technologies as providing prosthetic organs/limbs for achieving ever greater abilities to see and calculate the world. Through various prosthetic additions to the body, finer and finer discriminations appear as affordances for counting and calculating. Result: the pixelization of the world. Before the advent of computer screens, scientific grids and algorithmic tables produced through technologically enhanced research transformed phenomena into digital databanks ready for extraction. The prosthetic here is not merely to make a fragmented body whole again, but rather to enrich what a body can do in order to radically alter the firmness of its grip on the world and its phenomena.

In particular, it would seem that Western digital science has first and foremost privileged the head, and in particular the eye, for prosthetic enhancement. Although mind and body have been thought of as separate in Western philosophy, sight has also been historically associated with mind, hence the intuitive familiarity of phrases such as 'I see what you mean'. Making the hierarchy of the senses in Western digital science clear, philosopher Michel Serres writes, 'many philosophers refer to sight; few to hearing; fewer still place their trust in the tactile, or olfactory' (2008: 26). Philosophy invests in vision as superior and uniquely connected to mind/thought/ cognition precisely because of its discretion: it can view the world from a distance without becoming entangled with the world. Vision produces what Donna Haraway might refer to as the 'God Trick' (1988) of Western digital science: that it has unmediated, transparent access to the world *as it really is*. Bataille undercuts this association between the human, the mind, and the eye. He writes, '[t]oo long has human life served as head and reason for the universe' identifying the hierarchical organization of the body as a sign of 'servitude' (2017: 125). Instead, the human must escape the head 'like a condemned man escaping from prison' (2017: 125).

Postdigital research into expenditure must produce a different kind of body. Digital research is predicated on maximal grip through heightened utility and accuracy of vision via prosthetic enhancement. Yet the postdigital is not concerned with discretization so much as with nondiscretionary expenditures. Postdigital research would need to intentionally interrupt, suspend, and render inoperative the body's tendencies toward maximal grip, creating an inoperative rupture in what a body can do, sense, perceive. What we are after here is not prosthetic enhancement so much as the production of vestigial limbs, or limbs that do not have clear functions, that do not seem to have utility, that themselves are bodily expenditures without clear functionality.

Postdigital research's first tactic is to cut off the head to create an acéphalic body. Once freed from the tyranny of the head, the body can then experiment with nonexisting organs, vestigial organs that are unproductive and nonfunctional. For Bataille, the acéphalic body was the symbol of his secret society of the same name. The severed body was a symbol for the death of god, and by extension, the secular God Trick of Western digital research. Instead, he concentrated on the body without eyes or ears as a site for research into expenditure. Interestingly, in André Masson's rendition of Acephallus for the journal *Acéphale 2*,[7] there is no longer a focus on the head but on the stomach, which has growing on it (or in it) a strange, vestigial organ that looks like a labyrinth.

The labyrinth for Bataille was a central image of expenditure. Unlike a maze, the labyrinth has no solution, but was rather a perpetual problem, a place where

---

[7] See https://thesacredconspiracy.com/contributors/georges-bataille/programme-from-acephale-2/. Accessed 14 December 2022.

monsters dwell. One does not escape from a labyrinth, but rather falls deeper and deeper inside its mystery. Describing Acephallus, Bataille writes, 'his stomach is the labyrinth in which he himself has become lost, and I along with him, and there I rediscover myself as him, in other words the monster' (2017: 125). In other words, the pathways of the labyrinth cannot be calculated, an escape route cannot be charted. Instead of solutions, one discovers the monster that one always already is (a nonhuman human form that undermines the supposed dignity of the human 'man' and the optics of reason).

The vestigial organ of labyrinthian flesh is a metamorphosis that makes it impossible to disentangle 'man' from 'monster'. If the vestigial body of the postdigital researcher studies labyrinthian expenditures that have no escape/no exist, then so too the body takes on (grows) labyrinthian organs that are as mysterious as the phenomena which are to be studied. In other words, Bataille points the way toward the insight that research affects what is researched, but also, loops back to affect the researcher. Indeed, another symbol for Bataille of the labyrinth is the serpent devouring itself (*ouroboros* in Greek magic and, later, alchemy). In this sense, it is important to once again turn to Masson's drawing to highlight how the headless figure's left foot merges with a billowing cloud drifting above a cavernous landscape. The body of acephalous man is increasingly indistinguishable from elemental forces of nature, blurring the very distinctions upon which digital calculation rests.

The labyrinthian, vestigial organs of the postdigital researcher are not telescopes or microscopes (they do not produce small or far seeing), indeed such organs are not scopic at all. They are haptic organs, allowing one to touch upon sticky, gooey, slimy, opaque, nondenumerable expenditures of a dark world invisible to sight. It does not open these phenomena up to knowledge (which necessitates discretization) but rather opens up the body to a field of nonknoweldges (which are uncomputational exceptions, functionless, unemployable surpluses).

Nonknowledge, for Bataille, is uniquely connected to myth (as a secret, living art), or perhaps the dark arts of conjuring up a nonfunctionalized, uncomputational, inutilous form of life. Thus, we find it a mistake when theorists of research creation such as Charles Garoian (2014) focus on the arts as prosthetic limbs. The underlying assumption of prosthesis is increased utility, maximal grip, and improved functionality. An underlying instrumentalism manifests itself when Garoian writes, 'prosthetic interconnections, distortions, displacements, and mutual interactions within the representational space of art make creative and political agency possible within social space' (2014: 15). Against abstract (digital) space, the space of prosthetically enhanced, embodied interconnections paves the way for 'critical citizenship and possibilities for social democracy' (2014: 18–19).

Research creation is thus put in the service of political ends. The nonknowledge of prosthetic experimentation with supplemental expenditure is subtly transformed into knowledge for social democracy. But what is unique and vital about certain arts is precisely how they produce disutility, minimal grip, and ineffectiveness. While Garoian's theory of artistic prosthetics emphasizes unforeseen connections and filiations between eccentric parts, the theory, on our view, is *too operative* and thus misses the ruptural qualities of pataphysical expenditure which likewise make the body multiply, mutate, and disperse itself but this time through *impotent* iterations that lack the certainty of ends (such as the reassurances of political agency for social democracy). Such (anti)production is not nihilistic but rather places the body in proximity to the kinds of nonknowledge which produce the queer joy of self-dispensation (in which self and world die and are reborn as an-archic monsters).

So, what exactly does the vestigial body of the acephalic researcher 'do' in and through such 'undoings'? For Bataille, nonknowledge is uncomputable. It is nondiscretizable and nondenumerable, therefore existing on the dark side of knowledge as its accused share. What happens in the darkness of nonknowledge cannot be verified through digitalization (cannot be counted on, cannot be accounted for, cannot be counted *at all*). We cannot make sense of it without destroying it (as nonknowledge is fragile and fleeting). For these reasons, the *body* of the postdigital researcher is of absolute importance in the process of playing surrational games. 'I think', ponders Bataille, 'it is impossible to talk about nonknowledge other than in the experience that we make of it' (2001: 137). Stated differently, intensified affective flows of the body (and its experience) indicate the emergence of nonknowledge. Bataille observes, 'the sudden invasion of the unknown can, depending on the case, have laughter, tears, and not only laughter or tears, but other reactions as well' (2001: 136).

Laughter and tears—comedy, anguish, terror, and ecstasy—are the affective clues that indicate the presence of nonknowledge. Tears and laughter convulse the body, making it uncontrollable by reason (one cannot talk one's self out of crying or laughing) and vestigial (incapable of continuing to work or function in a productive manner). They are, simply put the body in an unbound state of becoming. Indeed, we might say that laughter and tears cut off the head, rendering the body of the researcher acephalic. In this state, the researcher and the researched, inside and outside, subject and object are indistinguishable and thus actively engaged with postdigital becomings.

5   David Cronenberg: Images of Postdigital, Achephalic Research

To conclude, we will gesture toward a cinematic artifact that, in some sense, embodies the kind of postdigital, achephalic research we have outlined above. In no way is this artifact to be thought of as a 'model', as a model would transform a vestigial (and therefore useless) object into a productive teaching tool. Instead, think of our final example as a resolutely *inoperative example*, one that can never be actualized. In this sense, we offer the following as an impossible solution to the question of representing vestigial research.

Crimes of the Future (Cronenberg 1970), one of filmmaker David Cronenberg's earliest works, concerns the strange and tedious adventures of Adrian Tripod, director of a medical institute called the House of Skin. The film presents a dystopian

future where an uncanny disease has destroyed most of the world's female popula-
tion. Named after Antoine Rouge, the 'mad dermatologist' who discovered the disease, 'Rouge's Malady' causes the patient to secrete a substance named 'Rouge's
Foam' from the ears, nose, or nipples. The foam is a death marker, as it indicates the
late stages of the fatal disease, but it is also an alluring substance that invokes a
sensual experience for those who ingest it, which Tripod and other characters take
part in. Victims of the disease finally discharge a brown fluid from the mouth preceding death, which like Rouge's Foam, has a tantalizing quality. The House of Skin
treats sufferers of Rouge's Malady. Tripod himself was a disciple of Rouge, who
went into isolation when he contracted the malady and is presumed dead, and it is
suggested that the master's experiments may have spawned the disease. While this
may or may not be true, it is certain the disease originated, somehow, from cosmetics.
    The film follows Tripod as he navigates a series of institutions and corporations
in pursuit of the mystery of Rouge's Malady. These include the House of Skin,
Institute of Neo-Venereal Disease, Oceanic Podiatry Group, Metaphysical Import/
Export, and Gynecological Research Foundation. The bodily, sexual, and philosophical connotations these names call forth echo similar preoccupations seen
throughout the film. It is silent, except for Tripod's narration and an array of bizarre
noises that erupt throughout. The audio gurgles, clicks, rattles, drones, hisses, sput-
ters, hoots, croaks, howls, chirps, buzzes, pulses, and squawks for various durations
as Tripod tells his tale. His tone is highly mannered—serious, calm, erudite, and
contemplative, but with a vocal delivery that suggests something unnerving. Tripod's
language has a formal, baroque quality to it, and it tends toward the pseudo-
scientific. He remains dressed in black during the entire film, clad in a turtleneck
and long coat, wearing a pair of glasses with thin, octagonal frames. He is a pecu-
liar, mostly dispassionate figure, wandering a clinical, pandemic-stricken landscape
as he transitions from one weird professional appointment to the next.
    Modernist spaces—largely vacant, perhaps due to the impact of Rouge's
Malady—dominate the scenes. Buildings are imposing figures shaped from glass,
brick, and concrete, some in the brutalist style. Prim courtyards with large pavers
and manicured grasses comprise most of the outdoor settings. These features, combined with a minimalist approach to cinematography, create what film scholar
William Beard (2006: 16) calls the movie's 'oppressively antiseptic beauty', antiseptic in a clinical sense as well as in terms of impersonality. This antiseptic quality
contrasts with the mucky, haptic character of Rouge's Malady, so that the moments
of bodily emission feel particularly grotesque.
    While the film has a plot of sorts, it often seems intentionally aimless. The roving
Tripod moves from place to place without any identifiable motivation, other than a
vague compulsion to pursue the legacy of his vanished mentor. When we first
encounter him, Tripod states that the House of Skin 'is undeniably in decline'. Two
interns, seemingly the only other employees, have taken over operations, a situation
for which Tripod cannot account. They attend to the House's last remaining patient
in an odd fashion, chasing him around the courtyard, playing with a stereopticon,
and painting his fingernails. The patient eventually succumbs to the disease. When
Tripod finds him lifeless in the courtyard with brown fluid spilling from his mouth,

he kisses the patient deeply to savor the secretion. As the patient is his last link to the House, Tripod is now existentially adrift. Yearning for his mentor and confounded by the collapse of his vocation, he ventures out, encountering an array of bizarre characters and situations. Importantly, these episodes find Tripod engaged in, or privy to, research and assessments that are, we argue, fundamentally pataphysical.

Before we examine these instances, we must also note the film's tone and style. It is boring, in a radical sense. Long silences and minimal camera movements create a languorous pacing as the film proceeds. With a few exceptions, the color palette remains muted. Tripod's staid vocal delivery, which includes long pauses and slow verbalization, also serves to deaccelerate the film's perceived speed. Characters rarely talk to one another, and there is no captured audio when they do. Their interactions generally feel listless and hollow. While the plot includes disease, social ruin, eroticism, gender fluidity, strange behaviors, violence, and even pedophilia, one leaves the film feeling as if not much has happened, other than that one's time has been arrested for the hour-long duration. Rather than being indicative of a young director's lack of control over his medium, which Cronenberg's technical and artistic abilities would seem to belie, even at this early stage in his career, these features experiment with the viewer's attention. The film cultivates boredom to draw attention to attention itself, heightening the viewer's attunement to the transactions between perception and thought, ultimately forcing one to confront consciousness in its most basic form.

To be self-aware, and at the same time indifferent to that awareness, is to experience a paradox, or, at its most extreme, even a crisis, of being. Paradoxes are immune to computation, and here boredom presents itself as a strategy that disrupts the rules of cinema, edging the film into a pataphysical zone. An early, noteworthy scene suggests Cronenberg's intentions. As Tripod, in a close-up shot, watches his ill-fated patient through a window at the House of Skin, he inexplicably removes his glasses, slowly licks the inside of each lens, and returns them to his face. On the one hand, the act is a conflation of the senses—taste, touch, and vision—preparing the audience for the sensuality of Rouge's Foam, but it also presages how attention and visual perception will be challenged by the film itself, much in the same way silence and erratic noise challenge one's auditory perception. The licking of the lenses is also perhaps a comment on the director's 'vision', as expressed through the camera lens. Put another way, Cronenberg, like Bataille, seeks to remove the head of the viewer (and director) to manifest nonknowledge.

The audience's boredom mirrors Tripod's own in the face of his mentor's disappearance. He is in some sense coming to terms with a world that no longer interests him, thus his almost aimless transition between employers and his general detachment from others. People and their actions are 'opaque' to him, as are seemingly his own. The film cannot be described as entertaining, educational, humorous, moving, or really even provocative, despite the fact that it culminates in the kidnapping of a young girl, whose pubescence will be artificially induced for the purpose of insemination and research, or, more accurately, rape. Here we find the inutilious aspect of Cronenberg's endeavor.

The entire film is useless, unproductive expenditure. It does not *do* anything, in the sense of traditional cinema. The sacrifice here is that of the viewer's invest-ment—emotional, intellectual, and temporal—in the productive experience of mov-iegoing, where some sort of pleasure exchange, through the machinations of entertainment, is expected. What is to be gained by watching such a film? How does one measure its effects? Is it even possible to do so? No, because the film itself is a vestigial organ that defies classification and purpose, demonstrating nonknowledge through the actions of it characters as well as through the film's formal composition, mode of storytelling, means of representation, and position as an unstable object of interpretation.

During his various visits and employments, Tripod encounters situations and engages in practices that are pataphysical in nature. His first destination after leav-ing the House of Skin is the Institute of Neo-Venereal Disease, where he finds a former colleague receiving treatment for a sexual disease he has contracted from his own patient. It is important to note that, time and again, the ethical boundaries between clinician and patient break down. While at the House of Skin, Tripod crawls next to his patient's bed and reaches over his chest to extract Rouge's Foam from his nipple, which he licks from his fingers in the subsequent scene, clearly not typical or appropriate behavior for a health care provider. Similarly, it is suggested that Tripod's former colleague has slept with his patient, resulting in his condition. More severely, Tripod conspires to violate the young girl toward the film's end, in the name of some obscure 'research'. While certainly disturbing, these transgres-sions speak to the extent to which Tripod and his companions have detached from general experience and embraced states of exception. They also underscore the absolute need to apply an ethical framework when engaging in pataphysical under-takings, a theme we return to in the conclusion of this chapter.

We learn that the illness Tripod's colleague has contracted causes him 'to create puzzling organs, each one very complex, very perfect, unique, yet seemingly with-out function'. As these vestigial organs are removed, new ones grow to replace them. A nurse intimates that the disease may be 'a form of creative cancer'. The extracted organs are kept in jars, and the colleague becomes 'melancholy' when they are not near him. The colleague's body is caught up in perpetual expenditure, extending itself through the generation of nonproductive parts. This excess bears resemblance to Rouge's Foam in that they both represent the inability to contain an abundance. Fluids overflow through orifices; useless organs germinate, crowd the body, and must be removed. These manifestations are incomputable, resistant to the methods of those who study them.

The true cause of Rouge's Malady remains a mystery, as does that of the 'cre-ative cancer'. Rather than providing any real treatment for these conditions, those administering care to the afflicted seem more mesmerized by their illnesses than driven to attain a cure. They have entered the acéphalic labyrinth in pursuit of the nonknowledge that will deliver them from their state of torpor, or exaggerate it to such an extreme that an ontological rupture occurs. In the film's final moments, as he appears to prepare to rape his young victim, we see her licking foam from her fingers, a signal of her impending death, and Tripod remarks that he 'senses the presence of Antoine Rouge'. Perhaps Rouge is the beast at the labyrinth's center, the man/monster that both creates and destroys.

Other pataphysical dealings take place in the film, surrational practices that comprise Tripod's job duties. At the Oceanic Podiatry Group, he is charged with enacting a ritualistic technique meant to 'reverse the psychic relapse, now so common, which can occur under intense genetic pressure'. It is unclear what this means exactly. The technique itself requires one partner to lie on the ground as another partner stands above. The vertical administers a series of manipulations to the legs and feet of the horizontal, flexing joints this way and that. Shoes and socks are eventually removed, and the standing party places the underside of the other's foot on his forehead. There is no detectable utility to these absurdist motions, yet *something* is happening. The technique is somewhat intimate, in so far as two bodies physically engage with one another, but it is also an awkward engagement that breaks laws governing normal, social behavior, a ritual that renders community standards inoperative. Such violation does not seem to bother the story's characters, who take to this fetishistic routine with vigor. Rather, the audience's community is problematized by behaviors that would be discounted in 'real life'.

Rules for living are redoubled, and constraints develop as typical modes of interaction are exaggerated. Instead of shaking hands in greeting, two strangers play a sophisticated, technical, and public form of footsie. Improper actions are treated as ordinary, necessary even to Tripod's impenetrable research. The film, the vestigial organ, pulls the audience into the realm of the sacred, where norms are rendered inoperative by the film's constraints. There are the constraints that the characters encounter and cultivate throughout the plotline, but the film itself can be understood as the product of a protocol enacted by the director, consciously or otherwise, which might be summarized in the following way:

1. Create a film that does not seek to entertain.
2. Allow only a single character to speak.
3. Use no other sounds, except those that seem unnatural or out of place.
4. Emphasize the uninteresting aspects of what would otherwise be interesting (such as erotic temptations or murders).

These criteria could, depending on the director, result in very different forms of cinema. The protocol essentially forces the audience to confront, remain sensitive to, and ultimately reorder expectations for perception and pleasure when engaging with film.

Crimes of the Future (Cronenberg 1970) is difficult to sit through even for those used to art house productions. It is easy to discount, which is entirely the point. The title gives an indication that laws will be broken. The characters certainly break the laws of the world in which they exist. There are murders and sexual exploitation and abuse. As he plans to kidnap and rape his young subject, Tripod describes his co-conspirators as 'heterosexual pedophiles, a group specifically outlawed, though increasingly pervasive nonetheless'. While difficult to fully ascertain, the film's world does have an ethical framework, which Tripod and his companions intentionally violate. But are these the only crimes the movie presents? Are there not violations of the laws governing our traditional viewing experiences?

The film's protocol seeks to behead the audience for the purposes of postdigital, acephalic research into the phenomena of attention and pleasure exchange. The resulting vestigial organ, the movie itself, is a pataphysical object that refuses to obey the laws of cinema, instead offering constraints that encourage the play of nonknowledge. There is no other way to gain the experience afforded by *Crimes of the Future* (Cronenberg 1970) than through the pataphysical means it articulates and embodies. How else could it be done? The Hollywood blockbuster gets metricized in various ways—money earned, seats filled, markets engaged, demographics reached, streams obtained, awards won, etc. Popular websites such as Rotten Tomatoes assign a film's quality a numeric rating. *Crimes of the Future* is a foreign body within such an environment. Investigating its purpose requires a completely different strategy, a different method, one that leads to the labyrinth from which the researcher will not escape.

6 Conclusion

In sum, we can formalize pataphysical techniques for postdigital, research creation as follows:

1. Write protocols that render inoperative defining habits, ways of thinking/acting/behaving so as to insert a division/gap between participants and expected social, political, economic, educational, aesthetic norms, values, expectations.

   (a) Ritualistic, impractical practices or surrational rules.

2. Cut off the head of the researcher in order to experience various states of expenditure in terms of perceptual, cognitive, erotic, and intra-relational dynamics with self and world

   (a) What personal and institutional limits are revealed by the expenditure?
   (b) What kinds of vestigial organs and/or surplus affects emerge (states of ecstatic laughter, horror, terror, anguish, radical boredom)? What new uses beyond computation and functionality become possible when vestigial organs bloom?

3. Record the resulting nonknowledge that emerges through processes of vestigial (excessive, impractical, uncomputational) use.

   (a) Nonknowledge cannot be clearly communicated or digitally calculated, instead it must be poetically conjured, obliquely hinted at, circumspectly rendered (always rigorously, given the nature of the phenomenon).

We also suggest that underlying this technique is a special pataphysical ethics. As *Crimes of the Future* (Cronenberg 1970) indicates, pataphysical experimentation with postdigital expenditures is a *crime* and enacts various *crimes* against certain individuals. In the film, various women and children are abused, revealing the dangers of pataphysical research and the cruelty it might embody, especially against the least privileged. But there is another crime at stake in the film, and that is the very nature of expenditure itself which transgresses laws of utility and functionality in the name of nonknowledge. Can these two levels of criminality be separated or are they co-determining? Our wager is that, in the last analysis, perhaps *Crimes of the Future* did not go far enough to suspend the existing exploitation of women and children already part of the operative law, and thus did not fully embody an exceptional state.

In this sense, we cannot retreat from the crimes committed in *Crimes of the Future* (Cronenberg 1970) by simply reinstating a utilitarian ethical calculation (which would be a move back to the digital). Instead, any pataphysical ethic must remain outside the law, must remain in the field of nonknowledge, and thus embrace expenditure. Such an ethic would be be an *imaginary* solution to the question of exploitation, meaning it would not yet have a fully functional formulation that could guide actions with certainty or guarantee. Rather, it would be a headless ethic that would fully embrace the *risks* that emerge when laws, habits, norms, and values (especially those supporting exclusion, exploitation, and marginalization) are rendered inoperative, and when the laws of sacrifice are sacrificed. In this sense, the experiment of *Crimes in the Future* (Cronenberg 1970) was not experimental/ exceptional enough precisely because it ultimately falls back on an unconscious reliance upon existing forms of exploitation in order to produce nonknowledge. Yet a pataphysically impossible ethic would push for more risks, would push research to a horizon in which even the sacrifice necessary for expenditure is sacrificed. This would be research truly full of laughter.

References

Agamben, G. (1999). *Homo Sacer: Sovereign Power and Bare Life*. Stanford, CA: Stanford University Press.

Agamben, G. (2020). Bataille and the Paradox of Sovereignty. *Journal of Italian Philosophy, 3,* 247-253.

Bataille, G. (1997). *The Bataille Reader*. Eds. F. Botting & S. Wilson. New York: Routledge.

Bataille, G. (2001). *The Unfinished System of Nonknowledge*. Minneapolis, MN: University of Minnesota Press.

Bataille, G. (2017). *The Sacred Conspiracy: The Internal Papers of the Secret Society of Acéphale and Lectures to the College of Sociology*. Eds. M. Galletti & A. Brotchie. London: Atlas Press.

Beard, W. (2006). *The Artist as Monster: The Cinema of David Cronenberg*. Toronto: University of Toronto Press.

Bénabou, M. (1986). Rules and Constraint. In W. F. Motte, Jr. (Ed.), *Oulipo: A Primer of Potential Literature* (pp. 40-47). Lincoln, NE: Dalkey Archive Press.

Bök, C. (2001). *Pataphysics: The Poetics of an Imaginary Science*. Evanston, IL: Northwestern University Press.

Bruno, J. (1963). Les Techniques d'illumination chez Georges Bataille. *Critique, August-September,* 195–196.

Calvino, I. (1986). Prose and Anticombinatorics, In W. F. Motte, Jr. (Ed.), *Oulipo: A Primer of Potential Literature* (pp. 143-152). Lincoln, NE: Dalkey Archive Press.

Cramer, F. (2015). What is 'post-digital'? In D. M. Berry & M. Dieter (Eds.), *Postdigital aesthetics: Art, computation and design* (pp. 12–26). New York: Palgrave Macmillan. https://doi.org/10.1057/9781137437204_2.

Cronenberg, D. (1970). *Crimes of the Future* [Motion Picture]. Emergent Films Ltd.

Feenberg, A. (2019). Postdigital or Predigital? *Postdigital Science and Education, 1*(1), 8-9. https://doi.org/10.1007/s42438-018-0027-2.

Ford, D. R., Swenson, K, & Fosher, M. (2022). From the Knowable and Transparent Individual to the Secret Thought of Individuation: An Anti-Capitalist Postdigital Ecopedagogy. In P. Jandrić & D. R. Ford (Eds.), *Postdigital Ecopedagogies: Genealogies, Contradictions, and Possible Futures* (pp. 43-57). Cham: Springer. https://doi.org/10.1007/978-3-030-97262-2_3.

Galloway, A. R. (2021). *Play and Politics in the Long Digital Age*. London: Verso.

Garoian, C. (2014). *The Prosthetic Pedagogy of Art: Embodied Research and Practice*. New York: SUNY Press.

Haraway, D. (1988). Situated Knoweldges: The Science Question in Feminism and the Privilege of Partial Perspective. *Feminist Studies, 14*(3), 575-599.

Jarry, A. (1996). *Exploits & Opinions of Dr. Faustroll, pataphysician*. Boston, MA: Exact Change.

Lewis, T. E. (2020). Defining a 'Pataphysical Stance for Arts-Based Research. *Studies in Art Education, 61*(3), 220-229. https://doi.org/10.1080/00393541.2020.1778436.

Lewis, T. E., & Hyland, P. (2022). *Studious Drift: Movements and Protocols for a Postdigital Education*. Minneapolis, MN: University of Minnesota Press.

Mauss, M. (2016). *The Gift*. London: HAU Publisher.

Merleau-Ponty, M. (2012). *Phenomenology of Perception*. New York: Routledge.

Motte, W. F. Jr. (Ed.). (1986). *Oulipo: A Primer of Potential Literature*. Lincoln, NE: Dalkey Archive Press.

Serres, M. (2008). *The Five Senses: A Philosophy of Mingled Minds*. London: Continuum.

Tavin, K., Mallio-Tavin, M, & Ryynänen (Eds.) (2019). *Art, Excess, and Education: Historical and Discursive Contexts*. Cham: Palgrave Macmillan. https://doi.org/10.1007/978-3-030-21828-7.

Part IV
Postdigital Agencies

Postdigital Research and Human Agency

John Reader

1 Introduction

One of the unresolved tensions in postdigital research is that of the role of human agency (Jandrić et al. 2018). At one extreme (as paralleled by Reader 2022a) is a determinism which suggests that human agency is in danger of being severely limited either by the technology itself or the companies in control of its development. At the other extreme is the view that the technology is of no more than instrumental significance and is simply to be shaped by autonomous human activity. This chapter will explore other options which lie between these two extremes and propose philosophical resources that can further illuminate this dynamic. Two main examples will be presented: that of the Metaverse and that of developments in robot technology.

In their book *Everyday Data Cultures* Burgess et al. (2022: 15) talk about the 'technological sublime'. This is the interpretation that Big Tech is in complete control of future developments to the point where human agency becomes almost superfluous. A danger of Big Critique such as that of Zuboff in her *Surveillance Capitalism* (2019) is that of effective collusion with the interpretation that human agency has no role to play but is replaced by some form of almost magical process representing the external forces of good and evil (Burgess et al. 2022: 15). This serves the interests of Big Tech and suggests that Artificial Intelligence, for instance, can do everything that it is claimed it can do. By contrast, Burgess et al. (2022) present examples of everyday individuals, communities, and organisations resisting and challenging this deterministic dominance through subversive and alternative practices.

J. Reader (✉)
William Temple Foundation, Rochdale, UK

Oxford Centre for Mission Studies, Oxford, UK

© The Author(s), under exclusive license to Springer Nature
Switzerland AG 2023
P. Jandrić et al. (eds.), *Postdigital Research*, Postdigital Science and Education,
https://doi.org/10.1007/978-3-031-31299-1_12

2   The Metaverse

The first example of Big Tech's deterministic discourse is that of the Metaverse illustrated by how financial institutions such as KPMG[1] are engaging with this. For instance, retailers are now purchasing 'virtual property' in the various alternatives. There are also examples of how education is now functioning in the virtual world such as MOOCs and 'Futurelearn' with the Open University.[2]

What could well seem like the ultimate test of the argument emerges from contemporary discussions about virtual and augmented reality (VR and AR). If either or both detach humans from their physical existence as in what I have termed disincarnation (Reader 2022b) then it would strengthen the case for resisting further developments of digital technology. The publication which presents the arguments in favour of VR and AR in great philosophical detail is *Reality+: Virtual Worlds and the Problems of Philosophy* (Chalmers 2022). Although there is a speculative element to much of his material it nevertheless describes accurately both the mechanisms and the potential consequences of such developments. Chalmers' central thesis is that virtual reality is genuine reality, neither illusion nor fiction (2022: xvii). He suggests that living in virtual reality can be good and he suggests can be the location for a fully meaningful life. It is also possible that we are already living in virtual reality. The crucial proposal though is that living in virtual reality does not represent a form of escapism but can instead be the route to a genuine life.

Much as one might admire the logic of Chalmers' (2022) arguments, the conclusion that this is not a form of escapism is surely the most controversial and disturbing. Abandoning one's physical existence for a virtual or augmented one will, for instance, create or exacerbate the disconnections with the environment that rest at the heart of the ecological crisis. This does not seem to bother Chalmers in the least, and he even talks about the justification for abandoning a degraded external world in order to lead a better life in the virtual one. The concern is that the future he anticipates is far more than science fiction and could indeed be closer to the present than we realise. In which case, there are huge moral and practical issues about our relationship with the nonhuman world to be examined immediately.

There is far more to Chalmers' (2022) book than can be covered here, but a couple of chapters represent the problems which will be encountered. He argues, for instance, that augmented reality could be a technology we will all be using in a decade or two (Chalmers 2022: 225). It could enable communication with friends in faraway places. It could navigate using built-in maps and recognise people using facial recognition. It could also bring historical locations to life by augmenting them with scenes from the past. This reality augments our minds by extending our brains with new capabilities. Will what we see however be an illusion or will it be real?

---

[1] See https://home.kpmg/xx/en/home/insights/2022/04/the-future-of-the-metaverse.html. Accessed 12 September 2022.

[2] See https://www.futurelearn.com/partners/the-open-university. Accessed 12 September 2022.

As with virtual reality this is where things get complicated. Thanks to brain-stimulation technology, we can smell or taste virtual objects. With haptic technology they can even be touched and felt. This being the case there is a physical dimension to the virtual experience that is not the case when it is merely augmented. Is this then an incarnational aspect of VR? If so, what are the implications for our care of the nonhuman which is the planet on which we exist? Why would we bother with this if a different sort of reality were now to be available?

The other question relevant to this discussion is whether or not it is possible to lead a good life in virtual reality (Chalmers 2022: Chap. 17). Faced with the choice whether to enter such a world one might well decide against it.

> The reality machine is simply an escapist fantasy. Life in a virtual world doesn't mean anything: at best, its like spending one's life at the movies or playing video games. You should stay in the physical world where you can have real experiences and where you might be able to make a real difference. (Chalmers 2022: 311)

Chalmers of course argues against this that life in the virtual world can have the same sort of value as life in the nonvirtual world. If the latter turns out to be bad, it won't be because it is virtual, but for some other reason just as in physical reality.

This seems to deny the importance of human life as embedded in that external reality, let alone ignore any sense of responsibility for what happens to the nonhuman components of that external world. The planet can burn up around us, but as long as individuals can retreat into their virtual worlds then all is well. Chalmers (2022: 322) argues that there may come a point where an attachment to the physical will be seen as a novelty or a fetish. Virtual reality may become where many people choose to live out their lives, as even relationships with other humans will be possible in this sphere. This will be no more a form of escapism than is emigration (Chalmers 2022: 323).

It is clear that this approach risks abandoning the challenges facing humans in our relationships with the nonvirtual nonhumans we think of as the natural world and is an ultimate form of disincarnation, even though there may be an element of the physical available in some way. It is however an important argument to consider as what Chalmers (2022) is talking about is potentially on the horizon – a known unknown – and unless this is brought to the surface now then any critical discussion of the issues may be lost by default. The question then is what alternatives can be developed that counter the potentially damaging impacts of the disconnections that have been identified in both the environmental and digital domains.

The problem with Chalmers' (2022) concept of the Metaverse is that it rests on a false positivity based on a concept of 'full presence' which denies that real presence also involves absence, and that the relationship between the positive and the negative cannot be reduced to a matter of resolving deficits. Cotton's *Virtual Reality: Empathy and Ethics* (2021), for instance provides good examples of how VR is being used to address awareness of disturbing international situations. The problem with this is that the presentations are still being framed according to a particular perspective and work on the assumption that addressing deficits in knowledge will encourage more appropriate responses. So rather than there being simply difference there is a deficit of information and if this is remedied then appropriate responses will follow. The impact of this is to diminish attention on alternatives which may indeed be the better path to pursue.

3 Difference, Determination, and Opposition

A philosophical counter to the danger of assuming a notion of full presence comes from Esposito's *Politics and Negation: For an Affirmative Philosophy* (2019), particularly his sections on 'Difference; Determination; and Opposition'. Esposito builds on Deleuze (1994) to provide a positive and affirmative concept of difference and argue that a full positivity or understanding of presence presupposes absence and difference. Hence his discussions of disjunctive synthesis; Spinoza on good and evil; Nietzsche on heath and illness. Each provide a positive approach to negation and the importance of keeping alive the alternatives.

The references to Deleuze (1994) are central to this argument and emerge from his discussion on Plato which is where the problem of the negative first takes shape. In attempting to differentiate the opposite from the different, Plato distinguishes between the negation of the attribute which is necessary for speech, and negation of the subject which makes it impossible. He does this by situating non-being inside being, by modelling it as difference. This leads Deleuze (1994) to provide a solution to the main problem of his own philosophy which is how to reconcile the presence of the negative within the primacy of affirmation. The answer, as suggested by Plato, is that 'non' as in the expression 'non-being' can express something other than the pure negative. This would liberate difference from its dependence on negation. By doing this Deleuze (1994) hopes to escape the alternative in which Western thought seems to be stuck: either there is no non-being and negation is illusory, or there is non-being, which puts the negative in being and grounds negation.

Both the idea that being is a positive reality without tensions and the idea that being is posited from non-being are equally wrong. There is a third possibility which is that of affirmative difference. Being is also non-being but this non-being is not negative. Deleuze's concept of difference here is not that of either Heidegger or Derrida as it is affirmative. Each 'different' is in itself and not in relation to the other. Difference therefore corresponds to singularity, and, in the same way, each single instance can be understood in its own right and therefore as different from all others. This leads into Deleuze's (1994) concept of the disjunctive synthesis.

In a similar vein to Deleuze's notion of difference, one can separate disjunction from exclusion and incorporate it into an affirmative semantics. Once disjunction is separated from a theological context it can take on a positive interpretation. Two things can be affirmed because of their divergence rather than despite it. For things to be different in themselves, taken individually, means that they differ not only from the others but also from themselves. This is the crucial point as it suggests there is no such thing as pure or complete presence but that all presence also contains absence or difference. This is how a synthesis can be disjunctive as it puts its terms in relation without making them identical, but instead by differentiating them. It is their distance that enables them to communicate. Each thing therefore is defined by the infinite multiplicity of its modes. This is one element of an alternative ontology derived from Deleuze (1994) that holds open a creative tension between presence and absence.

A second affirmative mode of negation is that of determination, and, once again, Deleuze (1988) is a key figure interpreting Spinoza's philosophy as one of pure affirmation. Central to this is the difference between the concepts of determination and distinction. While determination is necessarily negative, distinction is always positive. Deleuze (1988) suggests that this cannot be the whole picture however as it still locates determination solely on the side of the negative. Even though to determine something is to limit it through something else which necessarily negates its absoluteness, it is not the case that this is always and exclusively negative.

Is 'finite' the same as negative? Determining and limiting are ways of setting boundaries and creating an identity, but don't have to be equated with negation. To be finite means to be determined by another finite being, just as a thing is determined by another thing, which is determined in turn by another thing, but this is to grant that thing existence and thus also to affirm it. What this suggests then is that other possibilities remain open so once again there is not a full, pure, or complete presence, but rather that element of absence which enables the new to emerge.

The final argument relates to the concept of opposition, where, once again, one encounters the polarity between the positive and the negative. Esposito (2019: 188) examines this in the context of recent discussions about immunization, which has resonances because of the Covid-19 pandemic. The term immunity is etymologically linked to that of community so that a person who is 'immune' is one who owes nothing to and is exempt from the burden of inter-relating to a specific community. This individual does not share a common fate with those around. The negative value of this, however, also relates to modes of action as well as to status.

Someone or something is safeguarded from a greater harm or negative by means of a lesser negative. Both Plato's *pharmakon* [deployed by both Derrida (2013: 75) and Stiegler (2013: 37)] and St Paul's *katechon*, are figures of immunity. 'There is no such thing as a harmless remedy.' (Derrida 2013: 102) Vaccinations work on this principle often by introducing a harmful element in order to trigger an immune response. Rather than being a simple exclusion, or negative, it implements a sort of exclusionary inclusion. The strategy requires a coming to terms with the adversary. The negative is modulated rather than eliminated. Thus the immune system is constitutive of the community rather than being superimposed upon it.

> For there to be difference, or change, a subjective identity is required that can differentiate or alter itself. From this point of view, one can conclude that only the process of immunization allows us to think, in a reversed cone, of something like our being in common. (Esposito 2019: 197)

This is opposition as affirmative difference and negation and rests upon the understanding that there is always already an internal other which challenges the view of a full and pure presence. Without this one cannot see how alternatives can become possible.

I argue that in the non-virtual world we can talk meaningfully about the difference between what is real and what is illusion. In the virtual world of the Metaverse, however, one cannot do this as there is only 'the virtual' or illusion and no other reality with which to compare it. This therefore constitutes a mistaken 'full presence' which excludes difference and absence. Using Esposito (2019) on Deleuze (1988, 1994) (and critical of Heidegger and Derrida 2013) one can construct a critical engagement with the Metaverse and VR generally similar to comments on AI as dependent on algorithms that also produce a limited and restricted view of reality. Hence deploying VR in research and education reproduces these limitations.

4 The Logic of Incarnation

Another counter to the notion that there can be a 'full presence' comes from a more theological source. In *The Nicene Option: An Incarnational Phenomenology* James K. A. Smith (2021: 171) proposes that the logic of incarnation is to be preferred to what he calls the logic of determination that he identifies in the work of Derrida, even though he argues that Derrida's early work contains elements of the logic of incarnation. Smith traces these arguments back to different theological interpretations of Plato which, as for Deleuze (1994), remains an orienting and fundamental theme for reflection. Smith argues that Derrida's (1973) account of language can be interpreted as incarnational in that he sees it as constituted by both presence and absence – a manifestation that both announces and conceal. It is this incarnational account of language that provides the condition for theology itself.

What lies behind this discussion is the central question of how the interior experience of an encounter with the divine can be articulated by the public mechanism of language. '[T]he interiority and privacy of the God-relation is incommensurate with language which is exterior and public. With respect to the "making present" of language, such an incommensurate interiority must remain absent.' (Smith 2021: 175) But then how can one speak of God, or reveal one's interior experience to others? Is the theologian condemned to silence? What is required is an account of language analogous to the incarnation itself which is a mode of manifestation that both makes God present to the immanence of human perception but also retains the transcendence of the Wholly Other. Smith (2021: 175) calls this a non-reductive manifestation. In terms of the digital and what it is capable of communicating, under what conditions is this either reductive or non-reductive? Does it reduce either the human or the divine to pure presence thus obscuring or so diminishing absence as to distort or misrepresent?

Assuming that humans are made in the image of God, this concept of a non-reductive manifestation applies equally to the human as to the divine. If human dignity it to be protected, then it needs to counter the potentially reductive impacts of the digital upon any sense of the deeper self. Reducing the interpretation of the human will have a damaging impact upon notions of human freedom and agency. If humans participate fully in the incarnation then there needs to be a resistance to that 'pure presence' offered by the digital and the acknowledgement of a presence which is both immanent and transcendent, incomplete, always in process and dynamic.

Taking the philosophical argument further, Smith (2021) examines Derrida's critique of Husserl (Derrida 1973; Husserl 1970) because it appears that the latter was pursuing the concept of a pure presence, one in which materiality and embodiment constitute a contamination. This would be a metaphysical assumption that clashes with the concept of incarnation which clearly incorporates notions of the material and embodiment. Derrida (1973) challenges this, proposing instead that the terms require greater nuance and differentiation, so there is both absence and nonpresence as distinguished from presence; also alterity and otherness, and then transcendence itself (Smith 2021: 177).

Husserl's (1970) idea of a full or pure presence excludes these other possibilities, and Derrida (1973) is seeking a non-reductive account. 'In other words, Derrida seeks to demonstrate a more holistic, incarnational account of the relation between body and soul, presence and absence, immanence and transcendence.' (Smith 2021: 179) Whereas for Husserl communication represents a loss of pure presence, for Derrida this is a mistaken form of Platonism and the intertwining of presence and absence, ideality and materiality, is inescapable and constitutes the very conditions of language, discourse, and communication. Manifestation is both an announcement and a concealment, a making present which contains an element of absence or transcendence. Language operates as does the incarnation.

If language operates in the same way as incarnation, then it allows for confession and testimony by the individual within theological discourse. It also acknowledges in the wider believing community that which remains beyond articulation, the inevitably failed attempts to express the Wholly Other. Full presence is seen as a mistaken understanding to be replaced by real presence which includes an absence, excess, or remainder which remains transcendent.

If it can be shown that aspects of the Metaverse and forms of VR and AR compromise this dynamic by presenting an equivalent of the pure presence rather than the real presence of an incarnational approach, thus ignoring or even destroying the elements of absence and excess which are demanded by an understanding of human dignity and indeed of the divine itself, then there are grounds for critique. It is the interpretation of the incarnation which can lead to further research.

5   Robot Rights

The second example comes from current discussions about robot rights. Once again there is a tension between a determinism where there will be no alternative to the technology functioning independently of human agency and the other extreme of robots being no more than another technology to be deployed and shaped by human activity. Of particular importance is Darling's *The New Breed: How to Think about Robots* (2022) where she argues that questions of design, implementation, and future developments are in the hands of human agents. This contrasts much of the

Sci-Fi influenced discourse which suggests robot takeovers and artificial intelligence will outstrip that of humans. Taking the examples of how humans both in the past and in the present relate to the nonhumans of animals provide some clues to how and why relationships between humans and robots will develop.

According to Darling (2022: 150), humans are capable of a wide variety of relationships including complex and unequal social relationships and emotional connections with animals. These are effortlessly diverse and may 1 day include robots. It is clear that robots are now entering new spaces inhabited by humans. Comparing robots with humans, however, leads to a false determinism, for instance the interpretation that this will lead inevitably to automating human jobs and friendships. Darling's view is that this will depend on how we design and implement the technology.

Animals have supplemented but they have not replaced humans. Darling is not saying that relationships with robots will be the same, but she takes this as a useful and illuminating analogy. There is in fact no agreed definition of robots, but she is dealing only with physical robots. Obviously, this is an image of robots heavily influenced by both Sci-Fi and popular culture. Robots differ from humans in important ways, tending to be used for tasks that are dirty, dull, and dangerous. One could argue that humans in fact are underrated, as robots are less able to cope with complex areas and unanticipated occurrences. So is the objective of replacing humans by robots a feasible or appropriate target?

Darling (2022) suggests that it is better to enable the supplementary aspects of the human robot relationships. She offers further examples of human partnerships with animals such as dogs being sent into space and the canary in the coalmine (Darling 2022: 26). Even when it comes to the domestication of animals, similar relationships are in play hence her conclusion that robots are better suited to support human flourishing rather than replacing humans.

In terms of presence or absence we need to acknowledge that there are problems of defining intelligence, sentience, and indeed consciousness, so applying these terms to the nonhuman is problematic (Darling 2022: 41). It is also the case that the Western view of robots is not the only one as we see from the example of Japan (Darling 2022: 47). Do robots even have to look like humans? Darling argues that we don't need humanoid robots such as Data from Star Trek. Darling (2022: 65) also argues that it not possible to program ethical rules into robots.

In terms of robot presence through companionship, Darling provides evidence of robots being missed by humans. If this is a form of anthropomorphism, one might ask why is it humans project onto the nonhuman other? (Darling 2022:93). What is it that we are missing or requiring in addition to the straightforwardly human? Perhaps it is that physical robots trigger our perception of movement (Darling 2022: 97), hence we tend to see robots as agents rather than objects. Given that humans have negotiated relationships with the nonhuman in the shape of animals before, why not now with robots? (Darling 2022: 111).

In the area of animal rights, sentience, consciousness, and intelligence don't have agreed definitions. When it comes to the vexed issue of robot rights, therefore, it is not easy to come to straightforward interpretations of what these would look like

(Darling 2022: 180). One way to approach this is through this dimension of relationships and this might involve considering the question of damage to humans. Do we damage ourselves if we treat robots harmfully or disrespectfully and does that then become a justification for attributing some sort of rights to the nonhuman? Humans are not consistent in how we develop and handle the diverse relationships that Darling (2022) describes, but then what is perhaps required is a wider understanding of empathy. Darling (2022) agrees with Mark Coeckelbergh (2022) that we need less emphasis upon the rational and more consistency in our relatedness.

The debate about robot rights forms around what characteristics or properties of both humans and nonhumans are relevant to this discussion. For instance: who is/ are the subject(s) of human rights (HR) and how are these to be defined? This raises questions about properties and characteristics and the danger of reducing individuals to categories by producing 'legal subjects' who become more distant from actual people as a result. Habermasian and Kantian definitions of the 'rational individual' need to be critiqued and/or supplemented by other dimensions of what it is to be/ become human such as the affective, the unconscious and what I have called the pre-autonomous (Reader 2005). Who is 'the other' of HR and how can this 'otherness' be articulated and defined?

If the talk about robot rights (RR) as an attempt to expand HR into another area, that of the nonhuman, then it is instructive to examine how earlier examples of this expansion have functioned, hence the value of Darling's (2022) work. One could also refer to David Attenborough's *A Life on our Planet* (2022) and his account of encountering gorillas in their natural habitat for the first time while filming for the BBC in 1978 and then later with whales and the impact this had not only on him but on the wider public (Darling 2022 also offers this example). Encountering 'the other' directly and through the mediation of social media has changed the public perception of and approach to the non-human and raised the issue of rights needed to protect these species. One assumes it is only a matter of time before something similar occurs with robots or forms of AI. But what would it mean, and will it be appropriate to transpose the discourse of HR to RR unless there is perceived to be some threat to 'robots' requiring legal status and protection? Will it also be a case of 'encountering the other in need' or rather a concern for the impact of developing human non-human relationships on humans themselves?

This leads into the debate about properties and characteristics. Can robots be defined according to certain properties such as consciousness, sentience, or intelligence and can they be subject to moral judgements accordingly? This approach would rest upon a particular ontology and thus subject to controversy. At this point I will introduce alternative ontologies building upon the proposal of Braidotti (2020: 101) that there is a continuum or spectrum of the human-nonhuman challenging the humanist interpretation of the human subject and arguing for a 'Vital Materialism'. This will move into discussions of New Materialism as in my *Theology and New Materialism* (Reader 2017) and the concept of distributed agency [see Bennett's *Vibrant Matter: A Political Ecology of Things* (2010)] plus discussion of assemblages of the human and the nonhuman and indeed the flat or lumpy ontology of

Bryant in *The Democracy of Objects* (2011). Harman's (2010) work within Object Oriented Ontology about the essential withdrawal of objects is also relevant.

6   Robot Agency

It is clear from Darling's (2022) approach that a key question is how to understand relationships between humans and robots, given that there are many different types of robots and that all the definitions in these debates are contested. When it comes to analyzing the issue of robot rights, deciding questions of both human and robot agency is critical. Darling is concerned that attributing too much agency to robots might detract from the responsibility that should rightly be attributed to humans, so achieving some sort of balance between the two becomes important. Once again, we are in the realm of full or partial presence with both the human and the nonhuman.

This debate has been pursued by Coeckelbergh (2022) and Gunkel (2018) but largely in terms of the moral standing of robots. Like Darling (2022), they are aware that despite the more obvious view that robots are simply machines, humans still sometimes treat them as more than this and attribute human characteristics to them.

> By contrast, David Gunkel and I have consistently asserted that it makes sense and is philo-sophically interesting to at least *ask* (and criticize) the question regarding robots' moral standing. For example, inspired by Emmanuel Levinas, Gunkel has asked whether robots can be given rights or be considered as an 'other' deserving of dignity – that is, appeal to our ethical responsibility. (Coeckelbergh 2022: 150) (emphasis from the original)

Rather than pursuing the properties approach to robots which gets into the vexed questions about consciousness and sentience, both authors prefer to follow a more relational path. This path requires being more cautious about what we think we know about the moral standing of other entities. It also emphasizes that our language about entities and our relations with entities shape how we think about them. One might suggest that this applies as much to our relationships with other humans. If one questions the concept of full presence in the human realm, then this caution and modesty become highly appropriate. As we now engage with social interactions with robots, it seems that the boundaries between ourselves and some robots are becoming blurred, and this may require developing a more nuanced ontology. One possible candidate for this is the concept of distributed agency.

7   Distributed Agency

Emerging from New Materialism, Bennett's *Vibrant Matter* (2010) deals explicitly with the question of human agency. Chapter 2 looks at the example of a power blackout which took place on Thursday 14 August 2003, affecting 50 million people in North America. What Bennett is trying to establish is a theory of distributed agency by looking at the electrical power grid as an agentic assemblage. In other words, it is the actions of the configurations and convergences of the human and the nonhuman which form the agency involved rather than simply those of humans *per se*. This raises questions of intentionality and indeed of human will or subjectivity as clearly Bennett is arguing that the human alone cannot account for what actually happened. It also poses the issues of moral responsibility and political accountability. Bennett (2010) employs two philosophical concepts in the process.

The first concept is Spinoza's concept of affective bodies (1996), putting this to work in order to establish a vital materialism. Bodies enhance their power in or as heterogeneous assemblages in combination with the nonhuman as well as with other humans. This suggests that the idea of agency as traditionally referred to becomes distributed across an ontologically heterogeneous field rather than being a capacity localized in a human body or in a collective produced only by human efforts. The second is Deleuze and Guattari's notion of an assemblage (2008). Since this also forms a central plank of DeLanda's (2009) theory, it requires more detailed description. Bennett says:

> Assemblages are ad hoc groupings of diverse elements, of vibrant materials of all sorts. Assemblages are living, throbbing confederations that are able to function despite the persistent presence of energies that confound them from within. … Assemblages are not governed by any central head: no one materiality has sufficient competence to determine consistently the trajectory or impact of the group. The effects generated by an assemblage are, rather, emergent properties, emergent in that their ability to make something happen. … is distinct from the sum of the vital force of each materiality considered alone. (Bennett 2010: 20)

While each member of the assemblage has a certain vital force, there is only an agency within the whole collective, that being an open-ended entity. The electrical power grid, it is argued, is a good example of this, in that the various elements work together and that some of these, while they include humans and their constructions, also include some very active and powerful nonhumans such as electrons, trees, wind, fire, and electromagnetic fields.

To the vital materialist the electrical grid is understood as a volatile mix of coal, sweat, electromagnetic fields, computer programmes, electron streams, profit motives, heat, lifestyles, nuclear fuel, plastic, static, legislation, water, economic theory, and so on, all of which are actants, to use Latourian terminology. The actual details of the power blackout are of less interest than what Bennett (2010) makes out of the event, but one grasps the picture she is painting of a whole series of different but interrelated components and activities, all of which contributed in some way or another to what happened that day.

Distributed agency then, based on this example, refuses to posit a subject as the root cause of the event. Instead, there is a swarm of vitalities at play, and the task is to identify these vitalities and the relationships between them. Where does intentionality fit into this? Bennett (2010) does not deny that intentionality was part of the picture but argues that it was less definitive of outcomes than might be assumed as so many other factors were in play. She says that the idea of purpose or trajectory of intention is normal when it comes to moral judgements but refers instead to

Derrida's notion of messianicity as a way of taking account of the unexpected which happened in this instance (Derrida and Vattimo 1998: 17) Even the notion of causality is difficult to apply here as it was never clear what was the overall explanation of the blackout. One does have a slight suspicion that this example plays directly into Bennett's (2010) required interpretation, and that matters might be more clear-cut in other instances.

What are Bennett's (2010) conclusions about human agency? She would prefer to talk about the agency of assemblages as this better represents the combination of elements within which the human operates as just another component. Bennett argues:

> No one really knows what human agency is, or what humans are doing when they are said to perform as agents. In the face of every analysis, human agency remains something of a mystery. If we do not know just how it is that human agency operates, how can we be so sure that the processes through which nonhumans make their mark are qualitatively different? (Bennett 2010: 21)

Clearly, this has implications for the questions of moral responsibility and political accountability. If one cannot factor human will and intentionality into the equation, how can such judgements be made? Bennett suggests that there is such human agency only as part of a distribution of responsibilities and that the notions of autonomy and strong responsibility are empirically false. 'A theory of vibrant matter presents individuals as simply incapable of bearing *full* responsibility for their effects.' (Bennett 2010: 22) (emphasis from the original)

One of the concerns of Bennett's (2010) approach is that it risks downplaying the role of human agency. However, one could argue that rather than diminishing the role of the human, Bennett's approach actually adds to it in creative and dynamic ways. Coeckelbergh (2022: 129) refers to this approach in relation to the debate about autonomous vehicles: 'one could argue that while artificial systems such as self-driving cars do not have full-blown moral responsibility, responsibility is distributed or shared within a network of human and nonhuman agents'. Such a network includes the engineers, the operator/driver, and the artificial system itself. However, it is not clear how the vehicle can be held morally responsible while it lacks moral and personal autonomy. Furthermore, according to more Kantian moral theories, following rules is not a moral activity in itself. What happens when the vehicle encounters unexpected or unanticipated circumstances and the human factor is more like to be required?

A second concern is that, at some stage in the future, robots may appear as if they can be responsible moral agents, displaying, as Coeckelbergh (2022: 130) says, some 'virtual' responsibility. Even with humans, appearances are all we have to go on: although we can look into their eyes, we cannot look into their minds and know for certain that they are moral and responsible agents. So what if robots could perform responsibly? Evidence from within the field suggests that this is not the case at the moment, but it raises the question of how certain we can be when attributing moral responsibility to any agent, human or nonhuman. In a model of distributed agency, one might have to assume some sort of hierarchy with humans taking a greater share of the moral responsibility. The complexities involved in this encourage Coeckelbergh (2022: 133) to conclude that 'it seems wise to avoid developing and widely deploying fully automated robots and systems that no longer enable humans to control, know, and answer for what machines do'.

Having pointed out some of the limitations of a distributed agency approach, one could argue that it has the advantage of not assuming a full presence but rather acknowledges that humans and nonhumans can operate as co-agents under certain circumstances. This is not to be equated with the ideas of deficit or of loss of agency, but instead emphasizes the positive role of difference, where absence enables becoming in the Deleuzian sense and it is possible to avoid the two extremes of determinism and instrumentalism. What it does require is a further development of a nuanced ontology as will now be presented.

8   An Alternative Ontology

The most promising alternative to the distributed agency approach, and one which was examined in *A Philosophy of Christian Materialism* (Bake et al. 2015: 89ff) is that of a flat ontology, and what has become known as Object Oriented Ontology (OOO). A major source of this is Bryant's *The Democracy of Objects* (2011). The main characteristics of a flat ontology are as follows. First, it rejects any ontology of transcendence or presence that privileges one sort of entity as origin of the others and as fully present to itself. Second, it signifies that the world or the universe does not exist – i.e., there is no super object that gathers all others into a single harmonious unity. Then, it refuses to privilege the subject-object, human-world relationship as a form of metaphysical relationship different in kind from other relations between objects, or as a relationship that is implicitly included in all object-object relations. Finally, and perhaps most significantly, it proposes that all entities are on an equal ontological footing (Bryant 2011: Chap. 6).

Why is any of this relevant? With OOO things are always on the move and entangled in ways that can never finally be unravelled. The challenge then is always that of assembling, gathering, or reassembling. What we need to examine are the ever shifting and developing assemblages of not only the human, but also human and nonhuman relationships, and indeed the nonhuman relations with other nonhuman objects.

Other aspects of this approach are that in scientific research one creates closed systems artificially in order to carry out experiments. Then one must avoid the epistemic fallacy of equating being with access to being. This means there is a link to the work of Harman (2010) and Speculative Realism and the notion of an object-orientated 'Weird Realism' arguing against the correlationism that equates being with access (human) to being rather than focussing on being as it is for itself. Although this begins to sound highly theoretical, the point is that if one is to understand digital technologies as they are in themselves rather than simply as they are for human beings, then something like this approach becomes necessary. What is required is an ontology that can cater for the possibilities of the technologies relating to each other externally to any relationships with humans: machines talking to or communicating with machines if you like, which is clearly now an aspect of the smart technologies being developed. Then there also needs to be consideration of endo-relations (those within the object itself) as well as exo-relations (those with other objects).

According to Harman's (2010) version of this theory, all objects withdraw and are never fully open to manifestation, as they are always in excess of any specific manifestation. One can never fully know what it is to be that other object or being. This begins to sound at least similar to an apophatic approach to the divine where it is argued that there is always that more or excess of God which cannot be known or directly experienced by humans. It could also be true for our relationships with each other, and indeed within ourselves, where the 'other' is never fully manifest to us or subject to our total knowledge, experience, or awareness. An even more challenging aspect of this approach is that with a theory of equal being, or a totally flat ontology, there is no hierarchy. What are the implications of this for understandings of the nonhuman? If there is no privileged position for the human or the human – nonhuman relationship, what are the consequences of this approach?

Objects are only selectively related to their environment and on their own terms: they are nested and then perturbed or irritated, therefore never fully related. This has critical political implications as we tend to concentrate solely on content or ideas in order to bring about change. A more appropriate response would be to focus on the material practices and structures in order to find or search out practical means of making connections or to look for the resonances between different objects.

So what is the value of this alternative ontology? It provides an ontological justification for the approach of gathering and reassembling both in terms of objects and their relations (and non-relations) to each other. It challenges a privilege of relationship between the human and nonhuman, raising implications for approaches to both the postdigital and environmental concerns. It also poses questions of practical politics and ethics suggesting that change will not come about until or unless connections or resonances can be made at a material level and not simply as a matter of content or pure theory.

9 Assemblages

Taking this alternative ontology as a base line, the next step is to examine the concept of assemblages as the appropriate means of analysing the various sets of relationships identified as essential for an understanding of configurations of the postdigital. In order to pursue this in a critical manner, I will refer to Harman's critique of DeLanda in *Towards Speculative Realism* (2010: 182ff).

DeLanda (2009) rejects any absolute distinction between micro and macro levels of explanation so all entities are intermediate zones, positioned somewhere in a chain of ascending and descending assemblages, that are partially but not totally interlinked. An assemblage is not therefore a seamless whole, but neither is it a mere aggregate, without properties that are more than the sum of its parts. Although this is a 'flat' ontology, this is not the flatness of a single immanent plane where all is continuum. DeLanda is a philosopher of the much maligned 'deep and hidden'. Assemblages are never fully actualized; they cannot even be partly actualized, given DeLanda's view. Instead of an accessible layer of the world where everything is fully actualized and fully powerless vis-à-vis other actualities, and a deeper unactualized layer of continuum, we find a duality at each and every layer of the world. Hence individual entities have a non-actualized reality, and that reality belongs to each entity alone, not to a continuum prior to all autonomous things (Harman 2010: 183–184).

An assemblage must exceed any relational effect that it has on other portions of the world, given its independence from any particular effects it might have in the world at large. Along with being an assemblage, an entity is also an emergence: it is something more than all the clusters and aggregates and is not a bundle of properties glued together through the habit of customary conjunction. Entities withhold themselves from their relations with the outer world insofar as they are never fully actualized and withhold themselves from their own pieces by exceeding those parts and forming a new reality.

DeLanda develops 4 criteria for assemblages in *A New Philosophy of Society* (2009). First, an assemblage tends to have retroactive effects on its parts. Second, an assemblage may be characterized by redundant causation, so a number of factors could have brought it into being. Third, as assemblage has causal power, so an emergent assemblage might have causal effects on entities other than its own parts as well. Finally, an assemblage will have the ability to generate new parts. Harman's (2010) problem with these 4 criteria is that they focus on what an assemblage does rather than what it is, so 3 of them are symptoms of a new assemblage rather than features of the assemblage itself. Redundant causation is the different one. Is it the case, however, that entities have intrinsic properties? DeLanda (2009) wants at all costs to avoid the concept of essence. To arrive at his flat ontology, DeLanda has to make all individuals into singularities and never fully actualized. He can do this with species but less so with genus, so he talks instead about possibility spaces and phase spaces. But are there such things as universal singularities?

Harman has problems with the theory at this stage and instead wants to develop a philosophy closely related to DeLanda's but different on certain key points. One of these points is there will be a danger of assuming an ontology of individuals who will be cut off from their own histories and indeed also cut off from each other (Harman 2010: 190). This makes it difficult to construct a coherent concept of agency and therefore more difficult to accept. One notes that Harman wants to keep DeLanda separate from Latour and Whitehead, despite the fact that they all reject the notion of substance. For the school of dynamic becoming, the problem with substance is its excessive rigidity and fixity, so for DeLanda, substance is always too specific. But, for a relational philosopher such as Latour, the problem with substance is its insufficient rigidity. Substance pretends to hide behind all specific determinations and endure though shifting states of affairs when in fact it should be

thoroughly defined by them. Latour and Whitehead require entities to be fully articulated in an instant, even if this occasion must immediately perish.

For DeLanda, however, how can there be a real continuum if we accept that the
real means that which is never fully actualized? If real individuals are defined by
their non-relational or trans-relational character, how can they relate to anything
else at all? (Harman 2010: 194). This was the problem raised by Islamic and French
Occasionalists, who reserved for God not only the power of creation, but the power
of any causal relation at all. Hume inverted this by having the human mind playing
the role of God. In both cases, one privileged entity is allowed a magical transgres-
sion beyond the ban that radical realism places on relationality. Neither of these
options can work for DeLanda's version of realism since the human mind is never a
necessary ingredient in any interaction and God doesn't appear at all. DeLanda
needs a sort of 'local occasionalism' in which entities are somehow equipped for
mutual interaction despite their non-relational character.

Moving to one of the discussions between Harman and DeLanda in *The Rise of
Realism* (2017), DeLanda wants to abandon the concept of essence but Harman is
not so keen. Harman argues that the real object has an essence simply because it
must have a certain consistency to remain what it is regardless of the extrinsic relations in which it is involved. So an individual cat has an essence rather than just
being a copy of some Platonic form of a cat. This serves to explain the enduring
identity of mind-independent objects. The problem, as ever, is what constitutes this
essence and what is non-essential in terms of properties, potentialities, and propen-
sities? How does this relate to the capacity of assemblages or entities to relate to
other entities? Do nonhuman entities only relate at their surfaces?

DeLanda goes on to talk about 'events' in addition to objects, the point being that
mind-independent realities possess a variety of significant time scales such as the
geological for instance and the (to us) slow movement of tectonic plates. DeLanda
talks about tendencies and capacities (DeLanda and Harman 2017: 60). Enduring
properties are the basis of dispositions, but the latter are what prevents us from
apprehending an object in its entirety simply by perceiving its properties. But dispositions are real, though if not manifested are not actual. This is ontologically
controversial. What is absolutely critical to be gained from these debates though is
that realist ontologies that are all process and no product must be rejected. In other
words, there must remain some aspect of being that is more than just assemblage in
process.

10   Conclusion

I have been arguing that postdigital research needs to steer a path between two
extreme understandings of human agency, the deterministic and the instrumental.
While the first allows no scope for creative but critical human-nonhuman interactions, the second treats such interactions as purely external with the digital being no
more than another technology to be shaped rather than one that itself shapes the

human. Two examples of these dynamics have been examined. The first is that of the Metaverse as a significant development of virtual reality which has both commercial and psychological implications, and the second is the controversial area of robot rights which draws on issues both legal and philosophical.

In both examples, the problems of assuming a full presence were highlighted as these risk a form of determinism and then also the dangers of equating partial presence with a deficit or lack which underplay the positive role of absence as a component of agency. As a counter to Chalmer's (2022) book on the Metaverse I presented Esposito's (2019) work which deploys the concepts of difference, determination, and opposition drawing on Deleuze (1994) to argue for the concept of an affirmative presence which stands alongside any form of absence.

In the realm of robot rights, Darling's (2022) suggestion that there are parallels between human-animal relationships and human-robot relationships revealed that empathy is essential for crossing these boundaries. Distributed agency was examined as a related alternative and then taken further to propose a more nuanced ontology drawing on the work of Bryant (2011), Harman (2010), and (DeLanda 2009; DeLanda and Harman 2017) to construct a more appropriate basis for human-nonhuman relationships. This interpretation of a flat ontology recognising that there is always that which withdraws from full presence while maintaining the integrity of relationships between objects, both human and nonhuman, avoids both the deterministic and the instrumental understandings of agency. Drawing also upon debates about incarnation it has been argued that both presence and absence are essential for understanding such agency. Postdigital research will benefit from this philosophical approach as it tackles the role of both human and nonhuman agents.

References

Attenborough, D. (2022). *A Life on Our Planet: My Witness statement and a vision for the Future.* London: Penguin Random House.

Baker, C., James, T., & Reader, J. (2015). *A Philosophy of Christian Materialism: Entangled Fidelities and the Public Good.* Farnham: Ashgate.

Bennett, J. (2010). *Vibrant Matter: A Political Ecology of Things.* Durham, NC: Duke University Press.

Braidotti, R. (2020). *Posthuman Knowledge.* Cambridge, UK: Polity Press.

Bryant, L. R. (2011). *The Democracy of Objects.* Ann Arbor, MI: Open Humanities Press.

Burgess, J., Albury, K., McCosker, A., & Wilken, R. (2022). *Everyday Data Cultures.* Cambridge: Polity.

Chalmers, D. J. (2022). *Reality+: Virtual Worlds and the Problems of Philosophy.* London: Penguin Random House.

Coeckelbergh, M. (2022). *Robot Ethics.* London: The MIT Press.

Cotton, M. (2021). *Virtual Reality, Empathy and Ethics.* Cham: Palgrave Macmillan.

Darling, K. (2022). *The New Breed: How to Think about Robots.* London: Penguin Random House.

DeLanda, M. (2009). *A New Philosophy of Society: Assemblage Theory and Social Complexity.* London: Continuum.

DeLanda, M., & Harman, G. (2017). *The Rise of Realism.* Cambridge: Polity Press.

Deleuze, G. (1988). *Spinoza: A Practical Philosophy.* San Francisco, CA: City Light Books.

Deleuze, G. (1994). *Difference and Repetition.* New York: Columbia University Press.

Deleuze, G., & Guattari, F. (2008). *A Thousand Plateaus.* London: Continuum.

Derrida, J. (1973). *Speech and Phenomena.* Evanston, IL: Northwestern University Press.

Derrida, J. (2013). *Dissemination.* London: Bloomsbury Academic.

Derrida, J., & Vattimo, G. (Eds.). (1998). *Religion.* Cambridge: Polity Press.

Esposito, R. (2019). *Politics and Negation: For an Affirmative Philosophy.* Cambridge: Polity Press.

Gunkel, D. (2018). *Robot Rights.* Cambridge, MA: The MIT Press.

Harman, G. (2010). *Towards Speculative Realism: Essays and Lectures.* Ropley: Zero Books.

Husserl, E. (1970). *Logical Investigations.* Milton Park: Routledge.

Jandrić, P., Knox, J., Besley, T., Ryberg, T., Suoranta, J., & Hayes, S. (2018). Postdigital Science and Education. *Educational Philosophy and Theory, 50*(10), 893-899. https://doi.org/10.108 0/00131857.2018.1454000.

Reader, J. (2005). *Blurred Encounters: A Reasoned Practice of Faith.* Vale of Glamorgan, Wales: Aureus Publishing.

Reader, J. (2017). *Theology and New Materialism: Spaces of Faithful Dissent.* Cham: Palgrave Macmillan. https://doi.org/10.1007/978-3-319-54511-0.

Reader, J. (2022a). Divine Becoming in the Postdigital. In M. Savin-Baden & J. Reader (Eds.), *Postdigital Theologies: Technology, Belief, and Practice* (pp. 59-73). Cham: Springer. https://doi.org/10.1007/978-3-031-09405-7_4.

Reader, J. (2022b). *The Digital and the Environmental: Disinhibition; Disincarnation and Deceleration.* Rochdale, UK: Temple Ethical Futures Tract.

Smith, J. K. A. (2021). *The Nicene Option: An Incarnational Phenomenology.* Waco, TX: Baylor University Press.

de Spinoza, B. (1996). *Ethics.* London: Penguin.

Stiegler, B. (2013). *What Makes Life Worth Living: On Pharmacology.* Cambridge: Polity Press.

Zuboff, S. (2019). *The Age of Surveillance Capitalism: The Fight for a Human Future at the New Frontier of Power.* London: Profile Books Ltd.

Researching With, On, In and Through the Postdigital: Accounting for More-Than-Humanness

Terrie Lynn Thompson

1 Introduction

There is a growing and wide range of scholarship interested in things, and how things and humans co-constitutively enact everyday actions and practices. Such perspectives include post/more-than/trans-humanism, Actor Network Theory (ANT), Science and Technology Studies (STS), postphenomenology, media ecology, new feminist materialisms, material anthropology, the Anthropocene, agential realism, and object-oriented philosophy. Postdigital theorizing is part of this nuanced philosophical and methodological endeavour and has a particular interest in the digital.

I draw on more-than-human sensibilities to explore what postdigital research might entail methodologically and theoretically. I endeavour to untangle three knots. First, how can more nuanced attuning to the co-mingling of humans and technologies enable researchers to move beyond familiar and persistent binaries perceived as unproductive? Can such binaries ever be generative? Second, given how thinking, doing and being in new ways are closely tied, how do researchers and theorists in the postdigital space attune to their own *more-than-humanness*? Third, how does this attuning contribute to the value, credibility, quality, and politics of postdigital inspired research and accounts of these inquiries?

Influenced by popular culture, Cramer (2014: 13) explains that terms such as post-punk, post-feminism, or postcolonialism describe 'more subtle cultural shifts and ongoing mutations' moreso than signal an 'inevitable linear progression of cultural and intellectual history'. In this sense, the postdigital is 'the state of affairs after the initial upheaval caused by the computerisation and global digital networking of communication, technical infrastructures, markets and geopolitics' (Cramer 2014: 13).

T. L. Thompson (✉)
University of Stirling, Stirling, UK
e-mail: terrielynn.thompson@stir.ac.uk

P. Jandrić et al. (eds.), *Postdigital Research*, Postdigital Science and Education,
https://doi.org/10.1007/978-3-031-31299-1_13

231

Similarly, the notion of the *post*human does not mean we are no longer human. Posthumanism and more-than-humanism is about 're-visioning the human *beyond* some of the anthropocentric constraints of humanism, and about questioning and transgressing some of our most prized dichotomies of thought including subject and object … human and machine' (Adams and Thompson 2016: 4) (emphasis in original). I gravitate to the term more-than-human, which as Whatmore (2002) advocates, may more clearly point to what is beyond the human rather than what comes after the human. Note that I use the terms posthuman and more-than-human interchangeably in this chapter.

It is through these sorts of theoretical moves, interested in the relational ontologies of human and the digital, that researchers can attune to and critique dominant technology discourses in ways that are provocative, generative, and reflective of possibilities for the *togetherness* of human-digital working and living. Digital-human relations are marked by complexities, ambiguities, and struggles that create rich opportunities for research, albeit not always a straightforward task. It is through more nuanced attuning to how digital entities co-mingle with other elements that researchers may move beyond binaried thinking: the first knot I will address. In this unsettled terrain, postdigital thinking joins with other philosophical perspectives to challenge binaries such as digital and analog, technological and non-technological, biological and informational, online and offline, virtual and real, old and new media (Jandrić et al. 2018; Magilchrist 2021). Cramer (in Cramer and Jandrić 2021: 971) explains that the postdigital is a 'perspective that finds the distinction between "digital" and "non-digital" to be less clear than it seems when it is rigorously inspected, and also less useful and relevant than it often seems'.

More-than-human sensibilities attempt to stand outside such binaries by finding ways to talk 'about the social-and-the-technical, all in one breath' (Law 1990: 8). To do so is to 'question the givenness of the differential categories of "human" and 'nonhuman", examining the practices through which these differential boundaries are stabilized and destabilized' (Barad 2003: 808). Similar to Gourlay (2021: 15), my interest is in the digital and digitally-mediated practices, which I do not see as 'existing in a separate and clear binary with the analogue, or nondigital'.

However, such framings do not mean ignoring various forms and impacts of digital presences and absences. As Pink (2022: 749) emphasizes, digital technologies have a 'historicity, materiality, and many existing imagined futures, which form part of the ways in which they inhabit experiential and imaginable environments relationally with people, other species, and other things'. Important in its own right, the digital needs to be brought out of the background: not as singular things but as assemblages, intertwined with other things and people. Working to blur binaries through a more relational and material ontology, it is nevertheless important to look at political moves that sometimes work to sustain such distinctions.

The different ontologies and epistemologies of more-than-human perspectives demand new methods: to *think, do,* and *be* differently is closely tied (Adams and Thompson 2016: 6). One question that frames this chapter (and the second knot) is how researchers attune to their own more-than-humanness. Attuning is a process of deliberate noticing and wondering mixed in with a sense of freedom to ask questions of the digital things of interest and the contexts in which they are employed and help to enact. Micro and macro analysis is meshed together to make visible layers, multiplicities, movements, the politics of assemblages, and presences/absences. Influenced by sociomaterial perspectives such as ANT and new materialisms, the intent is to see the digital not in the abstract or in isolation but in the unfoldings and part of the doings of everyday practices and bodies – including those of the researcher.

The third knot considers how this sort of attuning may contribute to the credibility and politics of postdigital inspired research. Cathy Adams and I put forward three possible dynamics to help to assess the value and quality of more-than-human inquiry, asking whether such accounts: (1) explain or make evident how the researcher speaks *with* things (in other words, how researchers attune to their own more-than-humanness); (2) weave and fuse human and nonhuman storylines; and (3) acknowledge the liveliness of posthuman research work in the performativity of difference (Thompson and Adams 2020). These dynamics are not meant as some sort of definitive checklist of what constitutes a good post/more-than humanist account, but rather ideas that may open a space for continuing to discuss these questions. They are openings that I further untangle here in an effort to extend work on accountabilities in ways that sustain the conceptual 'elasticity and capaciousness' of the postdigtal (Jandrić et al. 2022: 5). I will be focusing primarily on the first of these three, although they are inter-related.

This chapter works in the spaces between theoretical and methodological innovation. Consistent with more-than-human scholarship, there is movement across theorizing and data: developing the theoretical through the empirical and vice versa. These moves entail deliberate noticings to see the digital not in the abstract or in isolation, but in the micro-workings of everyday practices. Undertaking this up-close noticing is not the exclusive domain of academic researchers. Citizens are bombarded with a bewildering array of narratives about new technologies such as Artificial Intelligence (AI), machine learning, algorithms, and data-bodies. Policy makers and organizations across all sectors are wrestling with complex ethical issues, questions, and trying to draft the necessary moral and legal frameworks which will benefit society. Practitioners, therefore, often have an interest in attuning to various digital systems and devices that populate their work and workplaces.

This work includes using postdigital and more-than-human concepts and methods for exploring practices in ways that cultivate critical sensibilities and questions for better understanding how working, living, and learning practices are changing. Gourlay (2021: 19) argues that posthuman framing does not lead us 'into a rarefied world of high theory and fantasy', but rather can bring us 'right "back down to earth", by anchoring our attention as researchers, theorists, and practitioners in the fine-grained, detailed "nitty gritty" of the everyday *as it unfolds*, in a mesh of bodies nonhuman actors, and technologies' (emphasis in original).

In the next section I introduce data from a research project in which more-than-human research sensibilities and methods were used to study digitally-mediated work practices: specifically, how professional agency, expertise, and accountability are being re-distributed between human and nonhuman actors through the increasing use of automated and assisted decision-making in professional work. Several approaches were employed to facilitate this sort of attuning. Of interest is how the participants (i.e., practitioner-researchers) noticed and questioned their own more-than-humanness as they attuned to the digital mediation of their everyday work practices. I draw on this data to help explore the ontological and epistemological shifts of more-than-human and postdigital research. I conclude with thoughts on how such purposeful noticing may contribute to the credibility and quality of postdigital inspired research and speculate on the ways that more diffractive approaches to writing and analysis may help to explore the complexities of human-digital relations.

2 Methodological Assemblings

Participants in the study were post-graduate students enrolled in one of two online courses: Digital Leadership and Professional Practices or Work & Leadership in the Age of AI. All were professional workers: primarily teachers in the former module and in the latter, workers, managers, leaders, and entrepreneurs in sectors including human resources, public services, law, computing science and engineering, sales, health and social care. Through ongoing conversations, discussions, and writings (and re-writings) in the online space, data was co-produced over two years by the researchers and the 18 participants who consented to participate in this research.

One focus in these modules is to work with professional practitioners to: (1) develop methods of attuning to how they work with AI and advanced data systems that help to enact automated and assisted decision-making (AADM); and (2) build capabilities to interrogate AI-Data systems and the advice these generate. Throughout this process, participants explored ways they attuned to their own more-than-humanness, and it is this aspect of the data that informs this chapter. Ethical approval was granted for this research and pseudonyms are used in this chapter.

The study and the courses reflect a postdigital research ethos. Much of the mainstream discourse reinforces binaries of human vs. machine, worker vs. AI, and human vs. artificial intelligence and agency which creates divisiveness and a 'we vs. them/it' stance. To move forward, current thinking emphasizes the need to attend to how AI systems and humans work and become *together*: to blur these binaries (e.g., Lupton 2020; Nerland and Hasu 2020; Thompson and Graham 2021).

Conceptually, a more-than-human perspective avoids simplistic deterministic stances and views work practices as distributed across complex assemblages and changes to work as unfolding through social and material (digital) relations and negotiations. There is a pressing need to understand AI and data-driven systems based on the day-to-day experiences of workers. This includes how decision-making processes are being automated in work practices and where worker input and agency is critically needed, how responsibility and accountability for these algorithmic-influenced decisions are being re-distributed, and how workers come to trust these systems and address ethical dilemmas. Attuning to these sorts of interactions is riddled with complexities and practicalities.

Therefore, an assemblage of methods influenced by more-than-human sensibilities was employed to generate the noticing and description necessary for micro-analysis. This assemblage aligns with Lenz Taguchi and St. Pierre's (2017: 643) call to do research enabled by an 'ethico-onto-epistemological arrangement that *does not begin with the cogito* of pre-existing, formalized, systematized, instrumental empirical social science research methodologies commonly used in educational and social science' (emphasis in original). What follows is a brief overview of the assemblage of methodological intentions and approaches, including technography, interviewing objects, situated logging, and descriptive anecdoting.

Bucher's (2016) technographic methods emphasize the importance of observing technologies-in-use as a way to examine the interplay between digital technologies (such as algorithms) and people. Importantly, this approach orients the research towards encounters with the 'seemingly obscure and hidden' (Bucher 2016: 82) by attending to specific and situated practices (e.g., Gherardi 2019). Bucher (2016: 82) explains that 'algorithms seem to pose some serious conceptual, epistemological, and methodological challenges when it comes to actually studying and knowing them' and notes that there has been a tendency in social science and humanities to frame the 'secretive nature of a proprietary algorithm as a profound epistemic problem' (85). However, she argues that there are 'many ways of knowing algorithms ... besides opening the black box and reading the exact coded instructions telling the machine what to do' (Bucher 2016: 84).

Cellard (2022: 799) also suggests ways to re-frame the black box narrative towards a focus on day-to-day practices, maintaining that because algorithms both enact, and are enacted, in day-to-day practices, they become knowable by examining human-digital engagement with 'materiality, appearance, ... and the always contingent description of technical processes' through what she refers to as the *surfaces* of devices. Focusing on the algorithm as enacted, Cellard (2022) argues, disrupts the transparency metaphor, which extols the 'inner workings of the algorithm—the fetish of code (Chun 2011)' (799), instead seeing that 'the interior and exterior of an algorithm are not set apart by the device' (810).

To bring these digitally-mediated situated work practices to the fore and further theorise the performative relations between AI, bodies, and specific work practices, other conceptually-imbued methodologies were employed. Heuristics for *interviewing objects* (Adams and Thompson 2016) were used, such as following the actors, listening for the invitational quality of things, and anecdoting. The notion of interviewing objects is focused on attuning and is a way of 'speaking with things': making visible and questioning relevant digital objects found in one's research-work practice. The eight heuristics continue to evolve (e.g., earlier versions include Adams and Thompson 2011; Thompson and Adams 2013). The heuristics draw from ANT, postphenomenology, critical media studies, posthumanism, philosophy of technology, and new materialisms. The scholarship in these, and related areas, provides rich terrain for finding other innovative and vibrant approaches. Although the phrase 'interviewing objects' may imply a focus on just 'things', object interviews examine how the work of enacting specific practices is distributed across assemblages of human and nonhuman actors. For example, Groten (2020: 264) writes about object interviews as a form of reciprocity as he researched the music sample (recorded sounds) and sampling technology:

> I was not simply viewing the [music] sample along with different theoretical paradigms, or observing how the sample interacts ecologically with the other things of a composition workflow, I was palpating how such a seemingly innocuous object of music acts upon us to redefine the notion of a musician itself. (Groten 2020: 264)

These methods are a form of slow research (Law and Singleton 2012) characterized by less hurried looking, puzzling, and untangling as the researcher shifts from observation to description. In his writings on how to interview a plant, Hartigan (2017: 260) writes about this shift as he conducted his research in public botanical gardens, noting that 'the concentrated attention insects devote to the plants highlights how little attention humans pay to them, even in a place dedicated to their display'. In my study, situated logging approaches (adapting Friggo 2016) were used to enable workers (i.e., participants) to notice and record their interactions with AI and data systems throughout their workday (interactions which may otherwise fade into the background). It can start with a simple interview question: Describe how a particular digital technology appeared, showed up or was given in a particular work practice. What happened?

Situated logging is a way workers can document their in-situ interactions with AADM systems through short fieldnotes and reflections, followed by iterative co-production, with the researchers and other participants in the online spaces of the courses, to then develop these fieldnotes into AI-work anecdotes: short descriptive accounts that depict specific micro-encounters between them and their digital surround. As close-up accounts of material-discursive-affective practices, anecdotes were analysed to foreground changes to decision-making practices and the impact on professional agency. They became a way to think *with* and *through* practices rather than *about* them. Continuing to draw on the object interview heuristics, as well as other concepts and questions, prompted further noticings and analysis. In addition to anecdotes, the participants also generated academic texts: discussion forum and blog postings, critical commentaries in the assignment, collaborative digital artefacts, speculative fictions, and reflective writings. These texts created the corpus of data in this study. Through the process of attuning to, describing, and analysing the digital-mediation of work practices, these workers (participants in this study) became practitioner-researchers.

Of interest in this chapter are the anecdotes, which emerge in the untangling of the first two knots outlined in the Introduction. Adams and Thompson (2016) explain that anecdotes are descriptive accounts which tell detailed and provocative stories. They are a way to gather data, they are data, and anecdoting is a form of analysis. More-than-human anecdotes describe interactions between people and things and in so doing, they illustrate how specific practices are enacted and unfold. Distinctive about these more-than-human anecdotes is the way they work to weave together human and nonhuman storylines. Although different researchers may describe this kind of writing differently, it is evident across more-than-human scholarship (e.g., Decuypere 2019; Fenwick 2014; Introna 2014; Ireland 2020; Michael 2000, Taylor and Gannon 2018; Wernimont 2019; Wilson and De Paoli 2019). See also Michael (2012) and Stronge and Michael (2012) for further elaboration of the anecdote and van Manen's (1997) work on writing about lived experiences. Common across this diverse range of literature is a determination to generate descriptive texts that create vibrant accounts of the complexities of practices 'in the making' that highlight the entangling of human and digital assemblages: an attempt to enact a sense of co-constitution rather than reify familiar binaries.

The methodologies described are not methods merely picked up and employed. These methodologies are informed by, and help to enact, more-than-human sensibilities in the doing of research. Such theoretical and methodological moves help to attune to and recognize the deep intertwining of bodies and technologies. Indeed, by working in the spaces between theoretical and methodological innovation, this research may enact a form of *concept as method*. Influenced by Barad's work, de Freitas (2017: 741) states that the concept is 'neither a universal ideal *instantiated* in the material plane nor a social construct *abstracted from* the material plane'; there is no 'ontological dualism between matter and meaning—concepts are material, and matter is conceptual' (emphasis in original). Positioning concepts as 'working material assemblages', de Freitas (2017: 741) asserts, makes possible the pedagogy of the concept.

Lenz Taguchi (2016: 214) refers to Colebrook's invitation to 'begin to think of concepts as methods' which facilitates a 'pedagogical process of learning *from* and *with* the concept' (emphasis in original). Engaging more explicitly with concepts as pedagogy creates openings for postdigital research to unfold as a lively conversation between theory and methods. For example, the methodological assemblings described above unfold by pulling at more-than-human sensibilities in ways that enact conceptual-material methodologies. Transgressing prescriptive methodologies can be made possible by recognizing the materiality of conceptual work. And by asking, as Lenz Taguchi and St. Pierre (2017: 646) suggest, 'what new thought can make the concept appear with a different radiance, ambiance, vibration, or tone?'. Such a question is, in part, what the methodology in this study attempted to do as professional workers attuned to, engaged with, and questioned their own more-than-humanness. In this way, the concepts of more-than-humanness and postdigital realities served as pedagogies, instances of how researchers reorient thinking (aka Lenz Taguchi and St. Pierre 2017).

3   Attuning to More-Than-Humanness

Participants in this study attuned to what they started to refer to as their *digital coworkers*. They generated anecdotes. The work they did to research, write, and analyze these deeply descriptive accounts of specific encounters was done to foreground how a particular AI system was assisting or automating their professional decision-making. Their analysis of the anecdotes informed critical discussions of how labour, and in particular, agency, expertise, judgment, responsibility, and accountability are being re-distributed across AI-human systems. In this section, the texts generated and analysed in this project offer glimpses into the ways in which these participants became practitioner-researchers as they began to attune to their more-than-humanness: who-what they become with the things of their work. In other words, how they were learning 'how to think beyond one's *selbstständig* or standing-on-one's-ness in order to reckon with the complex ecologies of human and nonhuman' actors (Thompson and Adams 2020: 340).

Attuning to their own more-than-humanness unfolded in different ways and degrees. An initial analysis of this data generates three aspects to this attuning work. First, the data speaks to a sense of 'getting to know' each other: the overtures made by the worker and the digital systems as they noticed them anew. Second, is a re-thinking of understandings of human-digital relations and practices in more speculative and provisional ways, albeit often layered with caveats. Third, there were indications of moving towards a *becoming with* the things of their working practices, although the pull of humanist orientations and language is still evident.

3.1   Taking Your AI Out for Coffee: Possible Overtures?

The idea of taking your AI out for coffee emerged from discussions with the participants. Attuning activities were designed to enable them to notice and describe their AI interactions in everyday work: making these interactions more visible as well as surface the work that various digital actors (and associated labyrinth of other actors) did. Although these workers engage with many of these systems daily, once they started the deliberate process of noticing they found surprises. And hence the idea of getting to know their AI systems better – taking their AI out for coffee in a way they might do with a new human colleague.

Noticing is not always as straightforward as it sounds. The first challenge was to recognize whether the digital technologies with which they worked were, in fact, AI-Data systems. Not surprising given the current rhetoric around AI and data, there was a tendency to think of AI-Data systems in a homogeneous way and confusion as to what digital platforms contain AI and further, act to consume, process and represent data, which may then inform decisions made either by humans or decisions taken automatically by the technologies themselves. How some of these systems fade into the background was also noted. One of the participants, Emma, reports her initial struggle to separate the work of specific AI-Data systems in her workplace from her daily work; Mila noted that she tended not to 'consciously register' her daily interactions with multiple digital systems that surround her at home or in the workplace. Once these workers noticed particular interactions with a digital system, its complexity started to surface.

Object interviews encourage paying attention to what workers see, hear, click and the overtures that such systems extend: menu drop down options, error messages, sounds, recommendations, thumbnails, and prompts. Some warn and sound alarms: It may be 'a sea of red': 'The display lit up like a warning flag, new errors scrolling and falling quickly down the screen' and at other times relief from the 'visual yelling of bright red flashes as the tool shouts at me to get moving and fix a critical incident' (Sarah). Other overtures entice: 'Ping! The familiar sound of that digital distraction – an email has landed in my inbox and at the bottom right of my screen, I am lured in by the colourful imagery and bold text "Match-Up Talent"' (Avi).

Rich accounts arose when practitioner-researchers lingered in those moments when their curiosity was piqued. For some, this was a departure from seeing the technology as a tool and instead as some 'thing' they needed or wanted to work with. At times, this seemed to be about exploring and playing with the software to 'see what happens when I click on this …', or to question 'how did the system arrive at this conclusion?', or to work backwards to try to influence the outputs by changing the data inputs, filters, and the range of settings that are changeable in order to generate different recommendations, data, or pronouncements.

The Social Selling Index (SSI) on LinkedIn generated a lively discussion as several participants tried to figure out how scores were generated and what data they were based on, what the scores actually mean and how to interpret them, and the power of these scores amongst the LinkedIn community. Some, such as Chris, wonder if these scores are strategically generated in order to encourage the user to purchase LI Pro or Premium: 'If a score of 80% is the highest you can get without paying for their service, is the SSI a valuable metric or a LI sales tool?'. Questions were raised about what overtures SSI encouraged from human workers: 'Is the SSI is a ruse to sucker in those users that feel the need to be at a higher score or the competitive user that wants to be at the top?' (Jimmy). The SSI enacted multiple performances as it was also seen as part of having a strong public profile. Jimmy adds: 'As my post today is already receiving good traction I expect my score to shift again within the next week. … Whilst I continue to search for my next career opportunity I'm safe knowing that my profile is high and I am at the forefront of my next employers mind.' For others, the assumptions the SSI seemed to be making were both confusing and comical. Julie writes:

> I looked at mine. … Its not something I've worked on, but now I see that in order to do better I need to 'engage with insights' – whatever that means. …I am also interested that it assumes I am a sales professional in HE, which I'm not ... and the comparison with others in my network might be considered really depressing!

3.2 Re-Thinking Human-Digital Relations: More Speculative and Provisional?

The data tells stories that foreground re-thinking understandings of human-digital relations and practices. Some in more open, speculative, and provisional ways and some laden with caveats. Throughout the data, there is a sense of often uneasy alliances with these more sophisticated AI-Data systems. Some of these digital systems are regarded as *co-workers* and others do not seem to earn that label. Throughout, there are indications of workers *becoming with* the digital technologies they work with daily. But there are often cautions around trust; concerns about lack of transparency, understanding, capabilities; and/or a sense of fear, uneasiness, and unwanted surveillance. The data conveys considerable struggle and questioning.

For example, the tussle between expectations and acceptance of AI compared to human contributions was pronounced. Amelie posts:

> The widespread acceptance of the human paraprofessional in education (such as administrative and teaching assistants) does not extend to our AI co-workers. The fear that decomposed tasks may become automated and undertaken by machines seems to be perceived as a direct threat to the 'craft' of the teacher as this suggests an easier and increasingly rapid move towards alternative models of production and distribution of professional knowledge (aka Susskind and Susskind 2015).

There was a sense of wanting to negotiate with the technology, as expressed on one of the collaboratively produced digital artefacts:

> When making these decisions, humans look for the same qualities of trust, transparency and shared responsibility with their human colleagues as they do with their nonhuman AI-Data co-workers. Just as you need to negotiate with a colleague to reach a decision, we need to develop methods of negotiation with technology.

Others considered the reasons that algorithmic decision making is not more transparent by wrestling with tensions between trust and power on a more macro-level. For example, Chris observes:

> A platform's need to protect its intellectual property from competitive eyes restricts the insights that might help its users gain trust. Perhaps the complexity and work that is being done by AI developers and providers is less visible and therefore downplayed: issues of integrity, safety and security are placed firmly in the 'just trust me' background by internet-appliance providers. The literature also seems to skip the more subtle attributes of systems to focus on their observable poke-twitch responses.

Reflexive work by participants attempts to articulate how they were impacted and affected by the materiality of their human-AI-data interactions that became more evident through the attuning done in their object interviews, anecdoting, and speculative fictions. Present in the data are tentacles of imaginaries, aspirations, social narratives, criticality, frustrations: possibilities and openness to the 'not yet' alongside concerns of the 'not yet' and absences. 'Are there better ways to do our work?' was one imaginary that these practitioner-researchers circled around (especially evident in the speculative fictions). Olivia elaborates:

> Given the way some data is held in such high regard – often completely obliterating teacher judgement, professional opinion, observations – does this suggest that in the interplay between professionals and their AI co-workers, the AI is more highly regarded? But what if there was a better way to 'assemble' this knowledge? We have so much going on in our heads and so much data being gathered. Perhaps AI is better at organising that output? How do we collate and bring this knowledge together in the best ways?

Some of the object interviews highlights different and more active expectations of workers. For example, Josephine comments: 'If we dwell on the negatives and the faults and don't take the responsibility to trust and further explore AI systems used in education we will not be using them to their full purpose and they then become a burden rather than co-worker.' At times, the discussions tilted towards an off-loading of responsibility to the individual to be more proactive, receptive, and capable vis a vis new technologies. In a subsequent posting, Josephine adds: 'All too often we hear of professionals finding the fault with AI systems only to further discover their lack of knowledge on the working of the system and some of the time this is due to their fears of working with these systems.'

3.3   Becoming with: Articulating More-Than-Humanness?

In this research, there was a sense of moving towards *becoming with* digital systems: of beginning to see the co-constitutive nature of practices. In other words, how working human bodies *become* 'in tandem with the erratic, nonhuman temporality of the technological assemblage of which they have become an inseparable part' (Hatfield 2020: 178). Abby explains (emphasis in original data):

> Writing the anecdotes pushed me out of my comfort zone as I had to challenge myself to attempt to speak *with* and not just *about* the technologies. But by doing this, it revealed new insights about the human-technology entanglements. This prompted a change to how I go about everyday tasks, as I now find myself thinking more deeply about what the technology is 'saying' and how it situates itself in my surroundings.

Mila notes more sensorial relations with digital technologies as well as increased patience and curiosities about intra-actions, adding:

> Imagining YouTube or a ChatBot as more than a bunch of coded algorithms, posthumanism is a promising way to shift professionals' perspective. Tailored anecdotes sharing personal everyday conversations with technologies that surround us is an interesting approach to develop a shared responsibility for a better bond between human and AI beings.

As these practitioner-researchers started to engage with more-than-human theorizing, one of the first things they came to quickly realize is fraught nature of our current use of language. It seemed very easy to slip into deterministic modes that simplify and over/under-exaggerate the role and presences (and sometimes the power) of digital technologies. There was speculation that perhaps our current words and terms are inadequate and limit possibilities for re-conceptualizing human-digital relations: 'Perhaps we need a new language to describe our relationship with AI' (Lucie).

Re-considering their relationship and authoring of human-digital encounters generated debate. Amelie comments how she naturally assumed ownership of what she called 'my' entanglements and that she needs to think more inclusively:

> Human-thing entanglements were something I focused on from a somewhat self-centred angle. What are *my* entanglements? How am I involved in these entanglements? The exploration of the humble spreadsheet made me realise that complexity isn't based on the attributes of the actor, but rather the socio-material factors.

This is not easy work. Despite insights that emerged by attuning to objects, and better recognizing and understanding how the work that goes on in our world is performed through human-thing partnerships, it is difficult to step away from the prevailing humanist discourse. The practitioner-researchers found that the process of anecdoting (in which the anecdotes are both a form of data gathering and data analysis as well as data) was very much an iterative undertaking as comments from the tutors highlight. For example, Julie notes:

> It is true that some of the literature talks in terms of a binary/polarised representation of AI and automated data systems. Is this what you found in practice? You might raise your level of critique by challenging the binary – thinking more in terms of a spectrum (shades of grey rather than black and white).

St. Pierre (2013) cautions that although materialist *epistemologies* are not new, the *ontological* turn seems to be more difficult. Despite the innovative strides in posthumanist theorizing and research over the last 20 years, much qualitative inquiry continues to be firmly rooted in anthropocentric, humanist ontologies. The way these practitioner-researchers continually played with concepts (such as more-than-human, digital co-workers, agency as distributed, becoming with, assemblings of human and digital actors, attuning to the invitational quality things, cyborgs and hybridic entities) foregrounded attempts to re-orient thinking. In this respect, these participants were encountering and engaging with the conceptual as material which makes the pedagogy of the concept possible.

In so doing, research work can move beyond a listing of the things of interest in a more-than-human research account and instead orient towards gestures of 'how various human–nonhuman entanglements come into view, open themselves up to more critical questioning and act on – and with – the researcher' (Thompson and Adams 2020: 340). This too is a way of becoming with the things of their work-research that are close and entangled. Groten (2020: 264) describes how he becomes the 'sampling-human' with his Zoom H4N (digital audio recorder) as they become co-authors of music: 'In following the actors, I enjoyed the insight into the sampling composer as a hybridic entity … who arises from the hyphenated space between person and thing – between human and digital recorder.'

This section offered glimpses into how more-than-human methodological assemblings encouraged practitioner-researchers to attune to their own more-than-humanness and to question what it means ontologically: exploring the first and second knots introduced at the outset. How researchers do this is complex work. The literature offers several innovative ways to encourage attuning work and although not a linear process, the data in this study suggests it perhaps begins by 'getting to know' the other as the overtures made by the worker and the digital systems are noticed anew. These noticings may create a space to re-think understandings of human-digital relations and practices in more speculative and provisional ways. These deliberate research practices open up possibilities of recognizing and commenting critically on how workers and researchers become with the things of their working practices. In the final section I explore the implications of attuning work to the quality and credibility of postdigital / more-than-human research.

4 Conclusion

This chapter set out to examine three knots: How can more nuanced attuning to the co-mingling of humans and technologies enable researchers to move beyond persistent binaries and can such binaries be generative? How do researchers and theorists attune to their own *more-than-humanness*? How does this attuning contribute to the value, credibility, quality, and politics of postdigital inspired research and accounts of these inquiries? These are not three separate knots, as the process of untangling them in this chapter illustrates. In this section, I move in, out, and between these knots.

Jandrić et al. (2022: 5) suggest that the notion of the postdigital is not well served by paradigmatic and methodological enclosure and prescriptions: it is a 'guiding idea, rather than an absolute or definitively bounded concept'. Yet, the distinctiveness of this guiding idea makes it timely to consider the possibilities and boundaries of the growing body of theorization, empirical work, and innovations in research methods amalgamating in this area.

The contribution of this chapter to this endeavour is to use more-than-human sensibilities to explore what postdigital research and thinking might entail methodologically and theoretically and the ontological shifts it evokes. I focus on how researchers attune to their more-than-humanness: one of the knots untangled in this chapter and one of three dynamics Cathy Adams and I put forward as important in assessing the value and credibility of more-than-human inspired inquiry (Thompson and Adams 2020). This focus may offer insights to the call to researchers by Jandrić et al. (2022: 5) 'to take a stand on what we mean by quality, credible, trustworthy postdigital research'.

It seemed that a starting point for these practitioner-researchers was to first attune to the presences and absences of specific digital actors in their work practices. A process that entailed shining a spotlight on these digital systems, bringing them out of the background, being curious about what they do and how, and untangling the many connections these digital things have with other actors. It was in these moments of deliberately noticing and seeing the digital (and its entourage) as *other* or *otherwise* or *otherness* – somehow distinct from them – that helped to move these researchers beyond the mere functionality of technologies and into what Ihde (1990: 100) refers to as 'quasi-otherness'. The binary made more visible but in a more nuanced way. The temporary holding of the digital as other was generative: efforts to 'see' its presences and absences in situated practices helped to highlight the inescapable intertwining of human and nonhuman actors. There was a sense of conceptually pulling the digital out and then placing it back 'within' assemblages in which the relational materiality had now become more apparent.

Perhaps exploring at the edges of these binaries can be productive: another knot explored in this chapter. *Binary-boundary* work started to draw attention to how binaries persist in instrumental and divisive ways as well as illuminate the politics of assemblages that sustain these distinctions. Barad (2007) states that to unsettle humanist assumptions, efforts must be given to boundary-making practices (material and discursive) that delineate human from other (414) and not presume 'sets of well-worn binaries in advance' (30).

There were inklings of this work in the data. Lucie questions: 'When reflecting on transparency and trust in the workplace why are we often keen to distinguish our human actions from technology?'. Problematics noted: 'The binary nature of attitudes towards AI coupled with an increasing social proclivity for polarised debate becomes dangerous tinder which may well cause "lack of understanding" and "active resistance" to burn together in the same fire' (Amelie). There was a sense that such binaries create obstacles: 'This "us and them" attitude or othering of AI systems is not helpful when we consider the place of AI as a co-worker' (Collaborative Digital Artefact). However, even with such insights, binaries are not always easily transgressed. The deep entanglement between researchers and their digital surround seems to generate attempts to erase, work across, *and* reify human-digital binaries and boundaries.

These critical questions are a way of noticing: a stepping-stone from 'getting to know the other' towards being able to articulate and wonder about how what goes on in the world is a co-constitutive achievement. This is a significant ontological shift and perhaps a hallmark of strong postdigital research. Questioning if the term 'postdigital' is necessary, Magilchrist (2021: 665) concludes that it might not be, but that 'words do things' and the postdigital flags 'the attempt to overcome a troublesome binary that still dominates public and academic discussions of technology and education'. Perhaps this positioning is a way of achieving what Masschelein (2010: 44–45) describes as e-ducating the gaze: 'not about becoming *conscious or aware*, but about becoming *attentive*, about paying *attention*. … displacing one's gaze so that one can see differently' (emphasis in original).

The methodological assemblings in this data generated anecdotes, critical analytical texts, and reflective writings. It was in the anecdotes that describe actual practices where there was a stronger sense of a blurring of binaries and the dynamics of the co-constitutive made more visible. Although challenging, this sort of writing encourages a meshing of human and nonhuman storylines. Indeed, the nature of the ontological shifts implicated in moves towards more-than-human sensibilities may become more achievable when the focus is 'not on things already made but on things in the making' (St. Pierre 2018: 604). Exploring 'things in the making' is what anecdoting does. Similar to St. Pierre's (2018: 605) thoughts on writing postqualitatively, anecdoting 'is adventure, experimentation, pushing through toward … a different world'. It is a different way of relating to what is present and what could be (Masschelein 2010). Emphasized here is the importance of attuning to the particular and specific of the everyday as it unfolds—relating to the tangling of digital and human.

Perhaps the work of anecdoting or other forms of descriptive analytical postdigital writing is an organic move towards more diffractive readings of the researcher's digitally-mediated practices: a natural way to weave together human and nonhuman storylines. Diffractive approaches may help to explore the complexities of these ongoing, fluid, and negotiated engagements. Barad (2007: 72) draws from Haraway's (1997) work to emphasize how the methodology of reflexivity is caught up in 'geometries of sameness' whereas diffraction is a relational ontology offering a sense of overlap, bending, and spreading. Bozalek and Zembylas (2017) suggest that diffraction is 'a way of troubling dualisms' (117) as subjects and objects are 'read through one another as entanglements' (116).

Notions of diffractive writing and analysis, displacing one's gaze, and finding new ways to write about 'practices in the making' are not just ways to work with more-than-human or postdigital sensibilities. They may also be important means to hold such research to account, further elaborating the ways that researchers can attune to and explore their own more-than-humanness in the doing of research. The gathering of ideas here may serve to open up a space for continued discussion on how postdigital research can enact credibility, rigour, and trustworthiness.

References

Adams, C., & Thompson, T. L. (2011). Interviewing Objects: Including Educational Technologies as Qualitative Research Participants. *International Journal of Qualitative Studies in Education, 24*(6), 733–750. https://doi.org/10.1080/09518398.2010.529849.

Adams C., & Thompson, T. L. (2016). *Researching a Posthuman World: Interviews with Digital Objects*. London: Palgrave Macmillan. https://doi.org/10.1057/978-1-137-57162-5.

Barad, K. (2003). Posthumanist Performativity: Toward an Understanding of How Matter Comes to Matter. *Signs: Journal of Women in Culture and Society, 28*(3), 801–831. https://doi.org/10.1086/345321.

Barad, K. (2007). *Meeting the Universe Halfway: Quantum Physics and the Entanglement of Matter and Meaning*. Durham, NC: Duke University Press. https://doi.org/10.1215/9780822388128.

Bozalek, V., & Zembylas, M. (2017). Diffraction or Reflection? Sketching the Contours of Two Methodologies in Educational Research. *International Journal of Qualitative Studies in Education, 30*(2), 111–127. https://doi.org/10.1080/09518398.2016.1201166.

Bucher, T. (2016). Neither Black nor Box: Ways of Knowing Algorithms. In S. Kubitschko & A. Kaun (Eds.), *Innovative Methods in Media and Communication Research* (pp. 81–98). Cham: Palgrave. https://doi.org/10.1007/978-3-319-40700-5_5.

Cellard, L. (2022). Surfacing Algorithms: An Inventive Method for Accountability, *Qualitative Inquiry, 28*(7), 798–813. https://doi.org/10.1177/10778004221097055.

Cramer, F. (2014). What is 'Post-Digital'? *APRJA, 3*(1), 11–24. https://doi.org/10.1057/9781137437204_2.

Cramer, F., & Jandrić, P. (2021). Postdigital: A Term That Sucks but Is Useful. *Postdigital Science and Education, 3*(3), 966–989. https://doi.org/10.1007/s42438-021-00225-9.

de Freitas, E. (2017). Karen Barad's Quantum Ontology and Posthuman Ethics: Rethinking the Concept of Relationality. *Qualitative Inquiry, 23*(9), 741–748. https://doi.org/10.1177/1077800417725359.

Decuypere, M. (2019). Researching Educational Apps: Ecologies, Technologies, Subjectivities and Learning Regimes. *Learning, Media and Technology, 44*(4), 414–429. https://doi.org/1 0.1080/17439884.2019.1667824.

Fenwick, T. (2014). Knowledge Circulations in Inter-Para/Professional Practice: A Sociomaterial Enquiry. *Journal of Vocational Education & Training, 66*(3), 264–280. https://doi.org/10.108 0/13636820.2014.917695.

Frigo, A. (2016). As We Should Think? Lifelogging as a Re-Emerging Method. In S. Kubitschko & A. Kaun (Eds.), *Innovative Methods in Media and Communication Research* (pp. 139–159). Cham: Palgrave. https://doi.org/10.1007/978-3-319-40700-5_8.

Gherardi, S. (2019). *How to Conduct a Practice-Based Study: Problems and Methods.* 2nd Ed. Cheltenham: Edward Elgar Publishing. https://doi.org/10.4337/9781788973564.

Gourlay, L. (2021). *Posthumanism and the Digital University: Texts, Bodies and Materialities.* London: Bloomsbury Academic.

Groten, S. (2020). Interviewing the Musical Sample. *Explorations in Media Ecology, 19*(3), 255–266. https://doi.org/10.1386/eme_00045_1.

Haraway, D. (1997). *Modest_Witness@Second_Millennium. FemaleMan©_Meets_OncoMouse™: Feminism and Technoscience.* New York: Routledge.

Hartigan, J., Jr. (2017). *Care of the species: Races of corn and the science of plant bio-diversity.* Minneapolis, MN: University of Minnesota Press. https://doi.org/10.5749/minnesota/9780816685301.003.0010.

Hatfield, J. E. (2020). How Data Haunt. *New media & society, 22*(1), 177–188. https://doi.org/10.1177/1461444819880585.

Ihde, D. (1990). *Technology and the Lifeworld: From Garden to Earth.* Bloomington, IN: Indiana University Press.

Ireland, A. (2020). A Posthuman Ecology of Simulated Human Patients: Eidolons, Empathy and Fidelity in the Uncanny Embodiment of Nursing Practice. *Explorations in Media Ecology, 19*(3), 299–318. https://doi.org/10.1386/eme_00048_1.

Introna, L. D. (2014). Towards a Post-Human Intra-Actional Account of Sociomaterial Agency (and Morality). In P. Kroes & P-P. Verbeek (Eds.), *The Moral Status of Technical Artefacts* (pp. 31–53). Dordrecht: Springer. https://doi.org/10.1007/978-94-007-7914-3_3.

Jandrić, P., Knox, J., Besley, T., Ryberg, T., Suoranta, J., & Hayes, S. (2018). Postdigital Science and Education. *Educational Philosophy and Theory, 50*(10), 893–899. https://doi.org/10.108 0/00131857.2018.1454000.

Jandrić, P., MacKenzie, A., & Knox, J. (2022). Postdigital Research: Genealogies, Challenges, and Future perspectives. *Postdigital Science and Education.* https://doi.org/10.1007/s42438-022-00306-3.

Law, J. (1990). Introduction: Monsters, Machines and Sociotechnical Relations. *Sociological Review, 38*(1), 1–23. https://doi.org/10.1111/j.1467-954X.1990.tb03346.x.

Law, J., & Singleton, V. (2012). ANT and Politics. Working In and On the World. http://www.sv.uio.no/sai/english/research/projects/newcomers/publications/working-papers-web/ant-and-politics.pdf. Accessed 1 December 2022.

Lenz Taguchi, H. (2016). "The Concept as Method": Tracing-and-Mapping the Problem of the Neuro(n) in the Field of Education. *Cultural Studies ↔ Critical Methodologies, 16*(2), 213–223. https://doi.org/10.1177/1532708616634726.

Lenz Taguchi, H., & St. Pierre, E. A. (2017). Using Concept as Method in Educational and Social Science Inquiry. *Qualitative Inquiry, 23*(9), 643–648. https://doi.org/10.1177/1077800417732634.

Lupton, D. (2020). *Data Selves: More-Than-Human Perspectives.* Cambridge: Polity.

Macgilchrist, F. (2021). Theories of Postdigital Heterogeneity: Implications for Research on Education and datafication. *Postdigital Science and Education, 3*(3), 660–667. https://doi.org/10.1007/s42438-021-00232-w.

Masschelein, J. (2010) E-ducating the Gaze: The Idea of a Poor Pedagogy. *Ethics and Education, 5*(1), 43–53. https://doi.org/10.1080/17449641003590621.

Michael, M. (2000). *Reconnecting Culture, Technology and Nature: From Society to Heterogeneity*. London: Routledge. https://doi.org/10.4324/9780203135334.

Michael, M. (2012). Anecdote. In C. Lury & N. Wakeford (Eds.), *Inventive Methods: The Happening of the Social* (pp. 25–35). Abingdon: Routledge.

Nerland, M., & Hasu, M. (2020). Challenging the Belief in Simple Solutions: The Need for Epistemic Practices in Professional Work. *Medical Education, 55*(1), 65–71. https://doi.org/10.1111/medu.14294.

Pink, S. (2022). Methods for Researching Automated Futures. *Qualitative Inquiry, 28*(7), 747–753. https://doi.org/10.1177/10778004221096845.

St. Pierre, E. A. (2013). The Posts Continue: Becoming. *International Journal of Qualitative Studies in Education, 26*(6), 646–657. https://doi.org/10.1080/09518398.2013.788754.

St. Pierre, E. A. (2018). Writing Post Qualitative Inquiry. *Qualitative Inquiry, 24*(9), 603–608. https://doi.org/10.1177/1077800417734567.

Stronge, P., & Michael, M. (2012). Suggestion and Satisfaction: On the Actual Occasion of Agency. In J-H. Passock, B. Peuker, & M. Schillmeier (Eds.), *Agency Without Actors? New Approaches to Collective Action* (pp. 15–30). Abingdon: Routledge.

Susskind, R., & Susskind, D. (2015). *The Future of the Professions: How Technology will transform the Work of Human Experts*. Oxford: Oxford University Press.

Taylor, C. A., & Gannon, S. (2018). Doing Time and Motion Diffractively: Academic Life Everywhere and All the Time. *International Journal of Qualitative Studies in Education, 31*(6), 465–486. https://doi.org/10.1080/09518398.2017.1422286.

Thompson, T. L., & Adams, C. (2013). Speaking with Things: Encoded Researchers, Social Data, and Other Posthuman Concoctions. *Distinktion: Scandinavian Journal of Social Theory, 14*(3), 342–361. https://doi.org/10.1080/1600910X.2013.838182.

Thompson, T. L., & Adams, C. (2020). Accountabilities of Posthuman Research. *Explorations in Media Ecology, 19*(3), 337–349. https://doi.org/10.1386/eme_00050_7.

Thompson, T. L., & Graham, B. (2021). A More-than-Human Approach to Researching AI at Work: Alternative Narratives for AI and Networked Learning. In N. Bonderup Dohn, J.J. Hansen, S.B. Hansen, T. Ryberg, & M. de Laat (Eds.), *Conceptualizing and Innovating Education and Work with Networked Learning* (pp. 171–188). Cham: Springer. https://doi.org/10.1007/978-3-030-85241-2_10.

van Manen, M. (1997). *Researching Lived Experience: Human Science for an Action Sensitive Pedagogy*. 2nd Ed. London, ON: Althouse Press.

Wernimont, J. (2019). *Numbered Lives: Life and Death in Quantum Media*. Cambridge, MA: MIT Press.

Whatmore, S. (2002). *Hybrid Geographies: Natures Cultures Spaces*. London: Sage. https://doi.org/10.4135/9781446219713.

Wilson, A., & De Paoli, S. (2019). On the Ethical and Political Agency of Online Reputation Systems. *First Monday, 24*(2). https://doi.org/10.5210/fm.v24i2.9393.

Collective Writing: The Continuous Struggle for Meaning-Making

Petar Jandrić ⓘ, Timothy W. Luke, Sean Sturm ⓘ, Peter McLaren,
Liz Jackson ⓘ, Alison MacKenzie ⓘ, Marek Tesar ⓘ,
Georgina Tuari Stewart ⓘ, Peter Roberts ⓘ, Sandra Abegglen ⓘ, Tom Burns ⓘ,
Sandra Sinfield, Sarah Hayes ⓘ, Jimmy Jaldemark ⓘ, Michael A. Peters,
Christine Sinclair ⓘ, and Andrew Gibbons ⓘ

1 Introduction: Herding Cats, Building Narratives (Petar Jandrić)

In 2016, Michael Peters invited me to write a 500-word contribution for the collectively authored paper 'Toward a Philosophy of Academic Publishing' (Peters et al. 2016). For me, collective writing was a new concept; I took a leap of faith, wrote my contribution, and eagerly waited to see what Michael would make of the article. I

P. Jandrić (✉)
Zagreb University of Applied Sciences, Zagreb, Croatia

University of Wolverhampton, Wolverhampton, UK
e-mail: pjandric@tvz.hr

T. W. Luke
Virginia Polytechnic Institute and State University, Blacksburg, VA, USA
e-mail: twluke@vt.edu

S. Sturm
Faculty of Education and Social Work, University of Auckland, Auckland, New Zealand
e-mail: s.sturm@auckland.ac.nz

P. McLaren
Chapman University, Orange, CA, USA

Northeast Normal University, Changchun, China

L. Jackson
The Education University of Hong Kong, Ting Kok, Hong Kong
e-mail: lizjackson@eduhk.hk

A. MacKenzie
Queen's University Belfast, Belfast, UK
e-mail: a.mackenzie@qub.ac.uk

P. Jandrić et al. (eds.), *Postdigital Research*, Postdigital Science and Education,
https://doi.org/10.1007/978-3-031-31299-1_14

249

had so many questions. What does it mean to write together? How can we combine people's diverse ideas and strands of thinking into a coherent whole? To explore these questions, I emulated Michael's collective methodology and took the lead on a few collectively written articles including 'Collective Writing: An Inquiry into Praxis' (Jandrić et al. 2017) and 'Postdigital Dialogue' (Jandrić et al. 2019).

That article has indicated some possible directions for answering my questions and made it painfully obvious that no academic article, no matter how elaborate, can provide definitive answers. However, it was comforting to learn that I am not alone in asking these questions. Soon after, Michael founded the Editors' Collective[1] — a community of academic editors and authors interested in collective approaches to knowledge-making and dissemination. Our small community immediately began to rapidly expand, creating a torrent of collectively written articles on topics from academic publishing (Peters et al. 2016) to the arts (Peters et al. 2018).

---

[1] See https://editorscollective.org.nz/. Accessed 17 January 2023.

M. Tesar
Faculty of Education, University of Auckland, Auckland, New Zealand
e-mail: m.tesar@auckland.ac.nz

G. T. Stewart
Auckland University of Technology, Auckland, Aotearoa, New Zealand
e-mail: georgina.stewart@aut.ac.nz

P. Roberts
University of Canterbury, Christchurch, New Zealand
e-mail: peter.roberts@canterbury.ac.nz

S. Abegglen
University of Calgary, Calgary, AB, Canada
e-mail: sandra.abegglen@ucalgary.ca

T. Burns · S. Sinfield
London Metropolitan University, London, UK
e-mail: t.burns@londonmet.ac.uk; s.sinfield@londonmet.ac.uk

S. Hayes
University of Wolverhampton, Wolverhampton, UK
e-mail: sarah.hayes@wlv.ac.uk

J. Jaldemark
Department of Education, Mid Sweden University, Sundsvall, Sweden
e-mail: jimmy.jaldemark@miun.se

M. A. Peters
Beijing Normal University, Beijing, China
e-mail: mpeters@bnu.edu.cn

C. Sinclair
University of Edinburgh, Edinburgh, UK
e-mail: christine.sinclair@ed.ac.uk

A. Gibbons
School of Education, Auckland University of Technology, Auckland, New Zealand
e-mail: agibbons@aut.ac.nz

In the intervening few years since, almost twenty mainstream academic journals have started to publish collective writings, and the community has produced so many articles that it became increasingly hard to keep track of them. Michael's original concept has somehow become the norm; most of these articles are collections of 500-word contributions on the theme, with an introduction and conclusion by article instigators, often followed up by open review. It is probably too pretentious to say that Michael has started a new genre of academic writing, yet he did instigate a significant body of specific types of articles that have entered the mainstream extremely quickly.

In 2021, I was not at all surprised when Michael invited me to co-edit the book *The Methodology and Philosophy of Collective Writing*: *An Educational Philosophy and Theory Reader, Volume X* (Peters et al. 2021a). As the subtitle says, this is a collectively edited collection of the Editors' Collective's previously published collectively authored articles. It was only when we started to curate this book that I realised how many articles our community has published over these few short years. As we did our best to select the most relevant articles for our intended narrative, we felt almost guilty that we needed to skip so many important contributions due to obvious space limitations. Soon after our book was published, it was collectively reviewed by Sandra Abegglen, Tom Burns, and Sandra Sinfield. Their review was extremely positive, yet they wrote a comment that indicates an important gap in our work:

> Picking up the book, we expected a collection of arguments that would constitute a sort of manifesto on collective academic writing. However, opening the pages, it became clear that this is not that. Rather, it is a patchwork text, bringing together and re-presenting previously published articles of various kinds. … This leaves readers to map their own journey through the text and to draw their own conclusions on the potential of collective scholarly writing. (Abegglen et al. 2022)

Openness has so many virtues (Peters and Roberts 2011; Peters 2014; Jandrić 2018), yet it does not arrive without its own problems. In our age of viral modernity, when there is more published content than any human being can read (see Peters et al. 2020a, b, c, d; Peters et al. 2021b), we urgently need sources that are open to access and open to human understanding. This conclusion does not apply only to (scholarly) books and articles; it is just as relevant for image, film, databases, and other sources of information.

Reading our book (Peters et al. 2021a) and Abegglen, Burns, and Sinfield's (2022) review, I identified two urgent areas for expansion of our collective work: methodology and synthesis. I emailed Michael: 'Let's do something about this!' Michael agreed (his exact response is in the Conclusion), and we started working on the idea for this chapter.

1.1 Methodology

To an extent, the community has experimented with the design of collective articles. For instance, *Postdigital Science and Education* has published collectively written pairs of articles (where the first article is provoking the second) (Networked

Learning Editorial Collective 2021; Networked Learning Editorial Collective et al. 2021), collectively produced visual articles, where images are as important as text (Pfohl et al. 2021; Jandrić et al. 2020, 2021), collective responses to collective writings (MacKenzie et al. 2021), and so on. Yet Michael's original design: one provocation, a patchwork of 500-word responses (with or without visuals), has stubbornly stuck with the community.

Given the standard length of academic articles, most of these articles are co-written by 20 or so authors. Some articles, such as Jandrić et al.'s Covid-19 responses (2020, 2021, 2022) may go up to 80 + authors, resulting in very long (150 + pages) reads. Most of these articles have been co-written using emails, resulting in limited opportunities for interaction between the contributors. These factors bring about certain consequences, some of which have become visible only at scale. To mention just one: reading and making sense of a collective article consisting of ten or twenty 500-word contributions is an exciting experience; reading and making sense of a 150-page article or a 350-page book consisting of 500-word contributions is very hard!

1.2   Synthesis

Most collectively written articles have a different publishing trajectory from standard academic articles. Leading authors typically contact journal editors before the article is made, looking for expressions of interest and help in conceptualisation. More often than not, they also ask for some 'good' examples. Yet collective writing arrives in so many shapes and hues, and results in such different articles, that it is very hard to help those who want to instigate a new collective piece!

Supporting the development of collective articles as editor of *Postdigital Science and Education*, I feel an urgent need for a synthesis piece that could be used as a point of departure. Of course, ideas about collective writings cannot be systematized in one chapter. Yet, at the very least, an overview of current issues pertaining to collective writing, and a list of sources, would be very beneficial for further development of the field.

1.3   Herding Cats, Building Narratives

In this chapter, we addressed the question of methodology by developing a slightly different collaborative process for collective writing. While we retained Michael's original 500-word limit for individual contributions (old habits die hard!), we also developed a 9-week process in which all co-authors use a shared document to engage with the text, with plenty of opportunity for mutual review, criticism, under/ over writing, and so on. We allowed contributors to choose their role (author or reviewer), and we involved reviewers from the ideational stage one (see Appendix 1).

We addressed the question of synthesis in a collective literature review, resulting in a long list of publications written collectively or written about collective writing. While our list will never be complete, many heads are better than one, and this resulted in a long list of titles that could save a lot of browsing to those interested in the theme (see Appendix 2).

In our contributions, we tried to cover as many different aspects of collective writing as we reasonably could. While the many faces of collective writing just cannot be all covered in any single chapter, our contributions do point out some of our main concerns at our postdigital historical moment.

It would be pretentious, and plainly wrong, to claim that this chapter is a one-stop resource for the theory and practice of collective writing. This is also a writing experiment, and one that merely takes our previous experiments one tiny step further. This time, however, we took special care to focus on the current issues in collective writing, expose our methodology in detail (Appendix 1), and offer a comprehensive reading list (Appendix 2). The struggle for collective meaning-making continues, and we hope that our small contribution will build at least a tiny steppingstone for future collective writers.

2   Praxis and Methodology of Collective Writing (Timothy W. Luke)

The praxis and methodology of collective writing are, and have been, to a certain degree, embedded in 'writing collectives' for decades, if not centuries. Within many professions, like accounting, law, or science, the methods of presentation for book-keeping, contractual agreements, or research reports often are always already indrafts due to the logic of spreadsheets, legal sufficiency, or empirical persuasion. The content of financial statements, legal documents, and experimental results – due to professional norms, procedural brevity, or empirical reports – flow through conduits of convention that are stylised to the point that such writing often begins within or upon practically stylised authorial armatures. The next collective writer fills in contingent blanks, completes highly regulated expressive utterances, and adds insights in accord with those regarded as 'insightful contributions' adding to the writing collectives' expectations of correct communicative sufficiency. The preliminary balances, initial briefs, or first reports intermix the thinking of networked professionals-of-practice, rapidly and methodically, practising professional praxis, even through handwritten and print documents.

In one register, continuously drilled dictates for collective writing standardize many documents intentionally around fixed presentational media or favoured formats, which are subconsciously adopted via the normalisation of default spreadsheet configurations, conventionalised formbooks, or routineised experimental scientific communication styles. The traffic built-up between authors and audiences endorses such material, operational, or rhetorical collective writing work-ups as pre-writs for the works that writing collectives generate, as much or more than the post-writs contributed by reviewers, printers, editors, or critics who all regulate the qualities and quantities of collective written work. The elements of individual voice, unique perspective, and original contribution are expected, but their presentation must be performed elegantly in concord with each aspect of these staging media, support staff, and styled standards.

In another register, new value-added, fresh insights, elegant arguments, or new contributions will be expressed, but often only to the extent they resonate inventively within the collective conventions authors must twirl effectively to trigger the recognition of real advances among the audience. Collective writing by writing collectives stabilises the bar for brilliance as well as banality behind, between or beneath these generative guardrails, which can both release or retard the liberatory potential of new writing collectives joining collective writing exchanges. How much the communicative channels add to, or possibly take away from, the communicated content are questions open to the collective writers to accept or reject, amend or forget, and improve or tolerate in the processes of writing collectively. Quite likely, the inescapable measure of hidden agendas, invisible networks, or latent prejudices with regard to content, style, and tone cannot easily be avoided. So their positive and negative elements can be retained as ur-textual anchors holding such experimental texts closer enough to float their shared, but never quite identical, communicative aspirations for writing collectively. Collective writing aims to organise diversity rather than replicate uniformity.

Fluid new thoughts circulate in fixed embedded channels, since university training approaches such professional communication as necessarily crafted for commercial, industrial, and organisational reception (Barnett and Bengtsen 2017). More occupations are generating such quasi-legislated standards of collective expression as professional correct cultural work. The growing expectations that academe have continuously improved capacities to 'add value' evolving in unison with standards of performance in non-academic communities being open to incorporating such 'valued additions' to maintain standards of effectiveness, profitability, or service evince new facets of the socialisation of knowledge (Peters 2021). Many conventions 'make writing academic', but these reworked practices of theory suggest that academic conventions are being pushed to display performative payoffs beyond those of rehearsing the 'normal science' traditional academic communication, continuity, and craft (Molinari 2022). Cultural workers of many types are teachers, and their cultural work often teaches most daringly at a distance through their activities as men and women of letters whose collective writings provide networks to form coalitions for learning how to contribute to, benefit from, or join with these many writing collectives (Freire 1997).

In such collaborative writing collectives, the normality of collective writing too often occluded by common professional methodological, ideological, or ethical assumptions about who can say/write as well as what, when, or why they are authorised to guide themselves in such communicative acts. Thinking and writing together can come naturally to these writing collectives. They often unconsciously presume they have the professional prerogative to guide not only themselves but also lead others by addressing those without their credentialed privileges and powers. In many ways, these experiments are an inventive assault on the traditional architecture of 'learning through writing', because they pit the collective writers' well-trained capacities to write in the normalised fashion of their disciplines to flip the 'infotecture' of normalised individual writing to begin 'learning through unwriting' those conventions (Couples and Luke 1998). As this happens, the writing collective can face, and then by-pass, overcome, or reframe 'the trained incapacity' that years of cultivated craft have ingrained in their acting and thinking (Kahn 1979).

No one may be identified as 'being in charge', but their will to contribute to, steer forward, or express openly thoughts and feelings among themselves and for themselves as collective writers gives 'a lead' for other collectives to follow. Some 'quality checking' may go out the window, but audience reception, government censors, public acceptance, social movements, or underdeveloped misinterpretation soon will emerge in response to those who dare to collectively write perhaps about individual troubles/social problems (Luke 1999). Writing collectives are always linked to many more non-writing collectives that soon will engage in a range of 'quality checks', running from wild enthusiasm, utter neglect, and heated argument to mild amusement, nasty blowback, and baffled hesitation. Hence, collective writing begins testing its own pedagogy in 'writing collectively' by virtue of 'relearning in unwriting individually' beyond existing individual disciplinary norms in fresh networks of research testing new communicative infotectural forms.

3   Openness to Collective Writing; Collective Writing as Openness... (Sean Sturm)

Collective writing is a 'writing device' (Callon 2002) that embodies a certain openness to the *outside* of academic writing and, perhaps, if we take the lead of Michel Foucault's 'The Thought of the Outside' (1998), to the outside of writing itself, which, for him, is trans-subjective and transgressive.

Collective writing, as the term suggests, implies an openness to both the *collective* and, in turn, *writing*. Its openness to the collective is an openness to *the multiple*, which takes at least two forms. First, it involves an openness to dissensus, to the co-existence of multiple positions and perspectives, not only because it allows multiple authors to write together – and perhaps to express themselves in a way that stretches their usual field of research, mode of collaboration, or style – but also because it allows for a collective authorial position or perspective to be expressed that can be dissensual (diverse) rather than consensual (unified), in particular, for example, when the resulting text takes a more or less 'patchworked' form that allows for the 'voices' or 'threads' of the text to remain relatively distinct (see Guttorm et al. 2015 on the problem of research collaboration as a humanist construct).

Second, it involves an openness to what Deleuze and Guattari (1987: 238) would call 'alliances', that is to say, symbioses or 'becomings' such as the kind of collective authorial perspective or position just described, which is, in fact, not just an alliance between human beings but also with technical 'beings' like the software and infrastructure through and with which the human beings interact (see Sturm in Peters et al. 2021b). Of course, the multiple positions and perspectives and the alliances that an openness to the multiple involve have more practical implications: it tends to foster both transdisciplinary collaboration (see Guattari 2015) and nonexclusive forms of intellectual property that move beyond 'intellectual monopoly' (Boldrin and Levine 2008), for example, through open access publishing.

This openness to the collective gives rise, in turn, to an openness to *writing*, which is an openness to the *writtenness* of the resulting text (see Sturm in Peters et al. 2020a). Firstly, collectively written texts, in particular, patchworked texts, have tended to involve parataxis, or a logic of juxtaposition that is open to multiple interpretation (see Hayles 1990 for parataxis as characteristic of both postmodern literature and informatic technology). And they have often involved textures that involve an openness to textual experimentation, for example, by juxtaposing prose and poetry (see, for example, the 'collaborative writing' (Wyatt et al. 2011) or 'postqualitative inquiry' (St. Pierre 2018 informed by the work of Deleuze and Guattari). Finally, they have often involved an openness to writing procedures, for example, the collage (Elbow 1999) or Surrealist *cadavre esquis* ('exquisite corpse', see Jandrić et al. 2020).

What collective writing's openness to the collective and writing thus offers is an openness to the outside, that is to say, an 'opening to the future' (Deleuze 1988: 89) that enables both resistance to, and transformation of, academic or disciplinary norms and practices of writing.

4 Collective Writing and Academic Labour (Peter McLaren)

One generative issue driving the imperatives of collective writing is that it should not be something forced on us by the academy. An analogy with the forced collectivization of the Soviet Union's agricultural sector during its 5-year plan or China's People's Communes during the Great Leap Forward is admittedly an 'apples and oranges' analogy, since this collective writing project is certainly not going to be the first step towards state ownership of our works nor will it bring about millions of deaths (unless from eye strain). It is doubtful that such world-historical tragedies like these will emerge from collective writing projects organised by a group of international transdisciplinary scholars (we are not being forced to join this collective, nor are we working under socialist distribution principles; private publishing has not been forbidden, and it is doubtful that any of us will be the victim of enforced pauperization or grow hungry as a result of our efforts).

While we are not compliant, defenceless, and self-censoring human beings, there are good reasons for volunteering to experiment with writing collectively. One reason is that critical-dialogical engagement deepens our understanding of issues that require intense deliberation today, such as the transformation of the university into an increasingly inhuman, digitised corporate monstrosity – the result of an advanced digitalisation of today's entire global economy and society which is utilizing fourth industrial revolution technologies to develop the rules of the 'social market economy' (which is better than predatory capitalism but still opposed to socialist economic systems), expedite its services, penetrate new foreign markets, and add leverage to its own survival. These technologies include Artificial Intelligence (AI) and the analysis of 'big data' (machine learning, automation and robotics, nano- and bio-technology, quantum and cloud computing, 3D printing, virtual reality, new forms of energy storage, etc.).

We cannot ignore the larger political context in which the university is reimagining its priorities under the renewed mandates of a global surveillance state whose digital realms are being repurposed to, for instance, 'tech wash' racism in the service of crime prevention and national security. This digital restructuring 'can be expected to result in a vast expansion of reduced-labour or laborless digital services, including all sorts of new telework arrangements, drone delivery, cash-free commerce, fintech (digitalised finance), tracking and other forms of surveillance, automated medical and legal services, and remote teaching involving pre-recorded instruction' (Robinson 2020). Robinson also notes that the 'post-pandemic global economy will now involve a more rapid and expansive application of digitalisation to every aspect of global society, including war and repression'. This will involve increased emotional manipulation, norm-setting, the weaponizing of political discourse, stigmatisation, and increased forms of cultural governance beyond the inherited repertoire of political gaslighting or what I call 'ideological grooming'.

Each historical (and therefore economic) epoch in the development of society has its own ideal of what constitutes collective work and adopts a certain morality surrounding that work. Different economic systems have different moral codes. In the bourgeois-capitalist university system, a significant emphasis is placed on whose name comes first in the publication of a collective research article, for instance. Publishing with more than one author is not always valued as much as single authorship. Systems of capitalist development that value private property have corresponding moral codes about shared and collective work. Hence, the need for rethinking academic labour in this new era of cognitive capitalism could strengthen our communal immune system by creating a new 'academic commons' that is not powered by value production and the commodity form, beginning with digital writing communes as a means of making postdigital science work in the interests of the oppressed, rather than reproducing the corporate guardians of the transnational capitalist class.

Collective writing could follow some of the ideas developed by Josh Winn (2015) and Mike Neary (2020), who have seen the value in converting the university from a neoliberal corporation to a worker-cooperative with teachers and students assuming the roles of producers working collectively, as protagonistic agents furthering the development of socialism for the commons, for the public good. The co-operative values that inform the new design of the university could be those that inform collective writing projects such as, equality, equity, solidarity, and concern for community (Winn 2015). In this way, co-constructing knowledge through collective writing becomes a 'red' pedagogical practice where the teaching–learning dialectic is at play, an act of red love that is directed at overcoming difference and defending humanity from its own barbarism. While I am not calling for collective writing to become an historical repository for our better angels, the current state of world affairs does call us to engage in more proactive participation in public discourses. I do believe that collective writing can enable the group to control the means of knowledge production and potentially produce new forms of social knowledge through a 'common ownership' form that transforms the distinction between 'public' and 'private' in order to create an 'academic commons' designed for the good of the community.

5   Collective Writing and Peer Co-production, Peer Review, and Peer Systems of Control (Liz Jackson)

Collective writing can be educational for authors, while leading to high-quality outputs that benefit from collective insights and perspectives in the first instance, prior to formal peer review processes. This is due to an essential feature of collective writing: peer co-production. Through co-production, the individual author fades from view in light of a different, socially influenced and collaborative collective voice. In truth, this individual voice is always a kind of myth that is perpetuated by a neoliberal academic culture that favours competitive, comparative metrics and standards, where each person is ranked and graded according to their apparently singular performance. In other words, academic knowledge always is incremental when considered at a broad scale. Meanwhile, at the individual level:

> As soon as we use a word, and expect it to be understood, we enter into an act of collaboration with both those who have used the word previously and those who are part of the same language community engaged in receiving that word, whether by listening or reading, in the here and now. (Jandrić et al. 2017: 88)

Through co-production, one instantly becomes accountable to co-authors. By 'accountable', I mean that they become positioned in a relationship of responsibility to co-authors, in contrast to more neoliberal, performative notions. This situation, and agreement to participate in collective writing, also immediately reflects back to the author an external view of their self and the relational, perspectival nature of their own knowledge, arguments, and claims to data. This kind of self-regulation of expression (to put it into a pedagogical language) encourages reflexivity and attempts at bridging divides through discourse. One is not alone in front of the computer screen, but always with others who will read their work, who become real embodied audiences to the work rather than anonymous, vaguely conceived peers.

Collective writing also has its own built-in peer review mechanism in that through the act of co-writing, one is subjected to others' instant, ongoing, dynamic 'criticism'. However, this is not the criticism of a reviewer who is hiding behind an anonymous identity – who can therefore criticise at will, without remorse, with little recourse from potentially upset, discouraged authors (Jackson et al. 2018). The peer reviewer who is a co-author and collaborator instead has already staked a claim to support the work and sees its value. Therefore, this reviewer has co-learning in mind first and foremost, and not only the responsibility of being a standard-bearer or arbiter in more abstract journal review processes. This peer reviewer aims to ensure meaning is understood by a broader audience: of two or more instead of one, initially. Through collaborative co-writing, each imprints their own understanding dialogically over time on others. Thus, there is an inbuilt internal review process of the ideas before a manuscript is submitted which can bolster the quality of the ideas and expression and the likelihood of a positive outcome through peer review.

The result is a kind of thought that is essentially collaborative, not additively different from just one person's writing, but qualitatively different, in terms of content and perspective. This instant and ongoing peer review function of engaging in collaboration enhances quality of expression and thought before a paper gets to the formal peer review stage. This can, in turn, also help to support more positive early results in the usual processes of peer review, thereby leading to a kind of enhanced peer control of ideas, so that collective authors are not as susceptible to having their hard work revisioned at the whim of less invested external reviewers in order to be published and shared more broadly.

Other modes of formal peer review can also be helpful in relation to the ideas presented here. For example, single-anonymous review, where the reviewer knows the identities of authors, can facilitate reviewers' more humane, constructive responses to authors, while reviews conducted by known reviewers for unknown authors can also lead to a more relational sense of collaborative, shared responsibility. Arguably, these are important innovations to more traditional double-anonymous approaches, which can lead to more supportive, collaborative modes of peer quality enhancement and control, echoing the main point of this section, that through knowing and relating to each other, processes of interpersonal reception, response, and feedback can be more constructive and productive than more individualistic approaches overall.

6 Collective Writing as a Form of Relational Epistemology Without Foundations (Alison MacKenzie)

Traditional epistemology theorised knowledge as emerging from an idealised, autonomous rational thinker in isolation from social and political relations (Descartes, Kant, and many white, male western philosophers). The acquisition of knowledge (via the written word – theses, philosophical tracts, mediations) was conveyed to other autonomous rational beings learning in isolation from others – the lone learner, in great universities and in the school system (which is why we demand silence in class when individual learning is taking place; a pedagogical approach that stimulates learning, apparently). So influential was this line of enlightenment thinking that it is still hard to disabuse educators of the idea that to be a genius is to think, experiment, and write alone. Learning, however, is a social and collaborative practice, as is collective writing if approached in the same spirit; and some highly influential philosophers and psychologists in education understood this, Dewey and Vygotsky, for example, even while those who cite these thinkers continue to think that teaching and learning is an individualistic endeavour.

In contrast to the autonomous rationalist tradition, thinkers from social epistemology begin with the premise that knowledge production, acquisition, and dissemination are social: knowers are socially situated but have unequal access to, and participation in, knowledge practices, whether in the creation, production, dissemination, or conveying of knowledge. This is a point that social epistemologists (and other thinkers, of course) and, especially, feminists have sought vigorously to tell us (Lorde 1984; hooks 1992; Alcoff 1996, 2010; Fricker 2007). That analysis applies to academic writing.

As other writers using different ideas in this collective chapter have touched upon (Jackson, Stewart, and Roberts, for example) our everyday epistemic practices of conveying knowledge to others and making sense of our social experiences can be blocked by unequal power relations. These relations are shaped by a number of epistemic and ethical constructs, and mechanisms. For example, credibility judgements about *who* the speaker/writer is (her social identity); the identity power of individuals qua members of a social class, which shapes who is believed or trusted, and why (junior versus senior academic); identity-prejudicial stereotypes which result in social and individual biases in our judgements of the speaker's/writer's credibility; the social imagination, in terms of how persons are constructed (good/ bad academics); and epistemic trustworthiness.

Academia can be plagued with what might be termed the vice of 'insensitivity' or being 'cognitively and affectively numbed to the lives of others' (Medina 2012). This vice means that, usually, epistemically advantaged people are inattentive to, unconcerned with, or disparaging of the experiences, problems, and aspirations of the disadvantaged or disfavoured. I am thinking of academics from the Marxist tradition; or research methods that seek to authentically include the voices of children (Burroughs and Tollefson 2016). The academically dominantly situated have the power to determine what is produced and published, particularly if they are editors, big names, reviewers of grant applications, etc.

Collaborative writing can be a form of epistemic resistance, a bulwark against such practices, and a process that can force us to acknowledge (again) that learning is social, collaborative, productive, and necessary. Transdisciplinarity, for example, a much-vaunted ideal in the academy, is not possible without collaboration and collaborative writing, most simply because our problems are too big, too complex, and too diverse (MacKenzie 2022) to be solved only by autonomous thinkers and lone writers writing from preferred standpoints (and see Peters et al. 2021c). As Jandrić et al. (2021: 75) suggest, 'collaborative writing is a thing of learning-by-doing' that can wrest academic writing from the dominant purview of the 'knowledge economy'. Collaborative writing offers opportunities for unequal epistemic practices to be disrupted and to grant epistemic credibility to academic voices who find themselves on the margins of neoliberal forces.

7 Collective Writing as Data (Marek Tesar)

Collective writing as data is an important subject that is often overlooked in the methodology and philosophy of collective writing. Collective writing is discussed as an experiment that moves away from the singular production of an academic article and opens up possibilities and opportunities for unexpected collaborations. It has become a part of a larger global ontological, intellectual, and conceptual project that has enabled us to connect diverse traditions and lines of thought.

Traditionally, data are often considered singular – owned by one author/researcher or research team. In contrast, if we are to think of collective writing as data, it opens up different, diverse and divergent conceptualisations of data. For example, there is a difference between data sets produced via collective writings and those, for instance, that are generated via systematic reviews. While systematic reviews produce answers to questions, collective writings produce new questions that we continue to ask ourselves.

It is important that we give attention to the notion of 'data'. Collective writing lets us examine and see data as something which radically reconceptualises our philosophical and pedagogical attention to the concept of 'data'. Collective writings are a great way that data can be organised and presented, and yet they do not lead to one expected solution or outcome. Perhaps we need to think of collective writing as a 'data encounter', rather than data mobilisation or data production. Collective writing presents and reflects a variety of ontological and epistemological stances, but it is not data-less; quite the opposite, data makes this scholarly practice of data production possible (see Koro-Ljungberg et al. 2017a, b, 2019).

If collective writing is data, then it is important to explore the axiological questions this raises. Data are not ethically neutral, they serve a particular argument, policy, or ideology, and the lead author of the collective writing carries a particular power over the data that are included, excluded, invited, rejected, or in other ways shaped into master or minor narratives. These data can be seen as part of the accountability discourse, which is important to include in our deliberations (Ford 2020).

What data are in collective writing and how collective writing acts as data is not easy to conceptualise. Providing a definition or a definitive answer would disrupt and counter the work that collective writing is trying to achieve. What is clear is the idea of data as productive, both as a 'noun' or as a 'verb' in collective writing, and the substance it represents. Collective writing as data has enabled us to produce critical and important texts that have addressed key challenges and performed ideas of social justice (Biesta et al. 2021). Furthermore, we need to look into the future to conceptualise what the future of collective writing as data may bring us (Tesar et al. 2021)?

Finally, within the philosophical purposes of collective writing, it is important to discuss ideas around concepts, knowledge, and information. While debating concepts and the production of new knowledge is part of collective writing, the dissemination of information is perhaps not so much. The idea for caring for collective writing and the care for the data that collective writing do carry, represent, and perform is critical (Ailwood 2022).

8   Repositories of Indigenous Knowledge and Identity (Georgina Tuari Stewart)

In 2013, the Philosophy of Education Society of Australasia (PESA) established a special interest group, the Indigenous Philosophy Group (IPG),[2] which became a catalyst for ongoing collaborations resulting in collective Indigenous articles and editorials. In these collective writing projects, we applied our experience of participating in the writing experiments of the Editorial Collective to working with our Indigenous (Māori, Pacific and 'others') networks of friends and existing collaborators, as our first collective editorial explained (Stewart et al. 2014). The unity that comes from being Indigenous, even across email, comes from understanding the undiscussable, without need to discuss it: the ambivalence and discomfort that inevitably comes along with being Indigenous, and which makes most Indigenous scholars extremely vulnerable in their workplaces – in ways from which academic seniority offers little protection.

The second group publication made a more extended self-examination of the intersection between 'indigenous' and 'philosophy' (Mika et al. 2018). Next, we took the theme of Indigenous responses to 'decolonization' (Martin et al. 2020). After that, we published an article on Indigenous responses to 'agnotology' (Proctor 2008; Stewart et al. 2021). The latest article (Stewart et al. 2022) considers all forms of colonisation from Indigenous viewpoints on both sides of the Tasman Sea.

As Māori and Pacific university scholars in Aotearoa New Zealand, we are often 'flying solo' in our teams or departments, and this is one of the paradoxes of our work. We are asked and expected to represent whole collectivities of our peoples on all sorts of matters in the university, including extremely embedded questions concerning teaching, learning, research, and knowledge, while often concomitantly speaking alone on a committee or in a staff meeting or teaching team. An attitude of 'one is enough' often seems to operate in regards to Māori and Pacific academic staff in local universities.

The notion that Māori and Pacific university students need to see role models in their lectures has supported a tendency to overload emerging Māori and Pacific academics with low-level, labour-intensive teaching duties, at the expense of supporting them to develop their research programmes. In terms of research, Māori and

---

[2] See https://pesa.org.au/about-us/indigenous-philosophy-group. Accessed 19 January 2023.

Pacific academics are often expected to provide a cultural 'imprimatur' to every research group and give advice almost on a 'walk-in' basis, frequently well beyond what is recognised on official workload records. In terms of academic citizenship, they may be expected to serve on many committees, with little thought given as to the reasonableness of such demands.

The sense of unity of purpose that comes from collective Indigenous philosophy writing projects may be unconventional in terms of traditional Māori and Pacific cultures, but is no less valuable in the current academic milieu.

9   Collective Writing as an Ethical System: Trust, Integrity, and Collegiality (Peter Roberts)

Trust and collegiality provide the ethical glue that holds academic entities together over the long term. Trust is a key educational virtue (Freire 1997; Haynes 2020), and an ethos of collegiality is vital if the ancient ideal of a community of scholars is to be upheld (Nussbaum 2010). We live in an age, however, where both trust and collegiality have been systematically undermined. A commitment to collegiality rubs against the grain of self-interested, competitive individualism, and appeals to the importance of trust – with responsibility – can fall on deaf ears in an institutional world structured by the language of accountability, performance, and measurement (Roberts 2022).

Accountability presupposes a lack of trust; it assumes that we cannot leave people to do their jobs well and must constantly monitor their activities to ensure that public money is being well spent. Accountability is based on satisfying formal procedural requirements, often within a hierarchical environment. It operates in a linear fashion (we speak of 'lines' of accountability) and it has an outward-facing orientation. *Being* accountable is not sufficient; we must *be seen* to be accountable. Responsibility, the partner of trust, relies more on inner conviction and is closely related to the notion of integrity. To conduct oneself with integrity is to *be* trustworthy and responsible. A spirit of collegiality both fosters the development of these qualities and is fostered by their prevalence among members of an academic group.

Collective writing can play its part in feeding the neoliberal academic machine, enhancing publication profiles, and generating further revenue through research assessment exercises. But it can also be quietly subversive, granting opportunities for scholars to be critical and creative in addressing controversial topics and themes, in the company of like-minded peers. This can be especially helpful for younger scholars who might otherwise feel reluctant to 'stick their necks out' because, as novices, it is not their place to do so, or for fear of being denied tenure or promotion. The work of new and emerging researchers can also sometimes not be given the attention it deserves simply because it takes time to establish credibility in a scholarly discipline or field. With collective writing efforts, a sense of shared responsibility towards others in the group can emerge. With larger collectives, the demands on a researcher's time are also more manageable than those imposed by substantial sole-authored projects, allowing scholars to contribute more widely to educational discussion than they might initially have envisaged.

Trust is necessary on the part of those who lead collective writing projects; trust not only in the capacity of their fellow authors to deliver contributions within specified timeframes but also in the process. Collectively composing an article requires a willingness to live with, and indeed celebrate, uncertainty. Lead authors can provide a sense of direction and purpose in the guidelines they issue for contributors, but exactly what the article becomes will always be unknown. With so many diverse voices contributing to a collective writing exercise, there is a potentially liberating unpredictability in determining what will be said, by whom, in what ways. There must be trust that what emerges will be worthwhile, adding something distinctive to existing scholarly conversations, but the risks associated with this process (e.g., some possible losses in coherence and cohesiveness) must also be recognised.

For work that appears in academic journals, the integrity of the process is, from a publisher's perspective, affirmed through peer review. But, here too, trust is paramount. Authors who accept invitations to contribute to collective articles often do so for collegial reasons – e.g., to support intellectual friends – and may be reluctant to offer their services again if the peer review process is destructive, debilitating, or mean-spirited. This is not to suggest that such experiences are common with collective writing; to the contrary, they are likely to be relatively rare, in part because many initiatives in this direction encourage a more open approach to reviewing. Equally, those who take on peer-reviewing tasks need some reassurance that their efforts in reading and responding will be appreciated and valued as an integral part of the composition process. Peer review, when undertaken promptly and constructively, is a vital form of service (to other scholars and to our fields of study) and will often demonstrably improve the quality of the work.

The face of academic communication is changing, and collective writing is likely to have a continuing presence in the new scholarly landscape. It may, however, evolve in some surprising ways, and all involved will want to keep an open mind in contemplating possibilities for the rigorous exchange of ideas in the future.

10 Collective Writing as an Emancipatory Practice (Sandra Abegglen, Tom Burns, Sandra Sinfield)

Collective writing, writing produced by a group, is distinct from single authorship (see Peters et al. 2021a) – and is by its very nature transgressive (hooks 1994). It crosses boundaries, especially those of academic acceptability. It challenges and disrupts the individualistic and competitive norms of higher education (Hall 2021) and troubles the notion of the monologic construction of ideas and knowledge (Giroux and Searls Giroux 2006). This alternative, collective academic practice is akin to critical pedagogy (Freire 1970), embodying and representing the idea that education should empower and allow all participants to regain their sense of humanity, to become academics on their own terms.

For Molinari (2022) academic writing is essentially about knowledge-making; it is social and open to interpretation: in research, in teaching and in learning. It is not about closure. Murray (1972), in the vein of Molinari, calls writing a 'process of discovery' – a way to learn about and evaluate the world as well as a method of communication. Together, these conceptualisations of writing suggest that successful academic writing practices are more than 'showing what you know': they are a way of learning, better facilitated when engaged in together. We are not empty vessels, but co-producers (Carey 2013) and social constructors (Burr 2015), with rich lived lives and empowered when in dialogue (Bakhtin 1981) with knowledge-claims and with each other.

Writing for exploration and in exchange facilitates agency and creative power (Creme 2003; Abegglen et al. 2021a): a more humane academia (Abegglen et al. 2020). In this sense, academic writing becomes thinking and action (Abegglen et al. 2017): the flow of ideas for crafting, composing, reformulating. Free writing (Elbow 1998), slow writing (DeSalvo 2014; Berg and Seeber 2016), and especially, collaborative writing (Gale and Bowstead 2013) radically transform notions of what writing, knowledge, and ownership 'is', what it can be and how it might be challenged, developed, applied, and enacted.

Collective writing is refractive, ludic. It disrupts the performative and the normative; the undisturbed, common sense and day-to-day pattern of (academic) thinking and acting. This is the way we three write together. We open a Google Doc and freewrite thoughts, ideas, observations, descriptions, opinions, and references. We write synchronously and asynchronously. We return frequently to our document – if you can ever leave this process – going over what we have contributed, finding patterns, inserting quotes, and making points. Instead of finding what we were already looking for, as Bowstead (in Gale and Bowstead 2013) says, we go where the writing takes us. We then edit – shift text around – cut and extend – and cut again. We engage in this sustained collaborative writing to produce a formal written piece that emerges from our joint playing with ideas, with our expertise and with our findings. As Elbow (1998: 28) states, '[p]roducing writing, then, is not so much like filling a basin or pool once, but rather getting water to keep flowing through till finally it runs clear'.

Experiencing the power and potential of exploratory collaborative writing for ourselves, we saw even more vividly that the teaching of writing within the academy is often flawed. If addressed at all, it is as an individual problem and in decontextualised moments that remove the point and the power of writing itself (Abegglen et al. 2019). Thus, we strongly advocate for writing to be an integral part of the curriculum – more than a skill to master or the formulaic production of the perfect answer. Writing as emancipatory practice creates the hermeneutic space that enables Students to come together and (also) to experience writing as a thinking process: writing to play with ideas and learn (Abegglen et al. 2021b).

As academics we need to make spaces in our classes – and in our schedules – for writing. Thinking that is shaped together – and over time. Thinking seeded perhaps by other creative activities such as collage or model making, thinking through drawing or making music. Collective writing can help students and faculty find their academic identity: we can become academic without losing ourselves but finding others in the process.

11 Collective Writing as Positionality (Sarah Hayes)

Often academics encourage their research students to add a *positionality statement* to a written thesis to acknowledge their identity amid the research process they have enacted. *Positionality* attends to the social or political context that creates researcher or writer identity, including their race, class, gender, sexuality, and ability status among other influences. A *positionality statement* recognises a constitutive process whereby our individual values flow through and potentially bias our writing, but our writing in turn, further shapes our identities. Positionality may form an integral part of a research/writing process, or become a last-minute comment, such as when a supervisor suggests an examiner may ask the student more about their positionality!

Positionality raises interesting questions in the context of collective writing, about firstly, the perceived 'ownership' of any given writing approach. For example, what aspects of collective writing would I 'claim' as influenced by my own identity, or by that of the others in this chapter? Each of our 'positions' can shift as we read the ideas shared by our co-authors. Yet there are other forms of collective writing where the identity of authors is less transparent. A university policy document is often written by a group, so can it ever be 'owned' by an institution that commissioned it? Can it ever be free of the identity, or bias, of contributors? Yet I have never yet noticed a reflexive *positionality statement* included in a policy…

Secondly, others have commented on the role of authority and the rules that may guide, but also inhibit, writing. Positionality though is not easily argued with by any authority; it is based on personal and intimate perceptions, elements that make it powerful, hard to imitate.

Thirdly, asking how the constitutive 'elements' in each writer's identity and context come to be identified is interesting too. In our postdigital society, key aspects of our identities, such as race, gender, or ability, are not isolated from data-driven Internet-based systems; they intersect with them. Each of us could be said to have a unique and fluid 'postdigital positionality' (Hayes 2021) as social media, algorithmic cultures, Internet of Things, or biodigital developments (Peters et al. 2021a, b, c, d) generate data that dialectically intertwines with our identities, circumstances, and locations. Torres-Olave and Lee (2019) suggest that positionality is constructed around identities that are complex and fluid, enmeshed in power relations, and contextually bound. Thus, positionality alters for writers too, as their work (and lives) cross geographical and digital boundaries, but also temporal ones, where we each try to make sense of accelerated experiences of writing to deadlines in globalised, capitalist society across different media (Hayes and Jandrić 2017).

So, how might positionality be understood and responded to in collective writing, across time, space, and physical and virtual locations, as we write and connect ideas? Is positionality in collective writing collaborative, individual, or both? When I led a Masters' course in Education, I asked participants to undertake a free writing task, sat together in a room. They wrote and commented on each other's handwritten texts. When such an exercise is conducted online how does this alter individual and collective positionality, if at all?

Recognising positionality in the postdigital contexts where we undertake collective writing can help to not only indicate that 'knowledge and voice are always located in time, space, and social power' (Barker and Jane 2016: 643) but to consider how knowledge and voice also become fragmented forms of *data*. If collective comments made by strangers on a topic in an online forum quickly become data, how does this differ when enacting a piece of collective writing? Is it a different shared ethos? What connects us, and what may divide us, as the narratives we write and comment on remain active online and gain independence from us, as the writers that first shared them? Perhaps the knowledge that our shared critically reflexive thinking and writing 'enables people to re-write their lived experiences' (Hayes and Jandrić 2017:16) is enough. We have co-authored a collective positionality that we have each experienced.

12 Collective Writing and the Collective Public Ownership of Production and Idea-Generation: Knowledge Socialism in Terms of Different Relationships Between the University and Society (Jimmy Jaldemark)

Collective writing is not a new idea; people have thought and written together for centuries. However, the last decade's sharp rise in the digital evolution of society in general and, more particularly, the advent of social computing through the Internet have afforded humans new possibilities to gather in groups and explicitly express their collective intelligence. With the rise of weblogs – quickly shortened to blogs – in the 1990s, the smart mobile digital devices, microblogs, and cloud-based networking in the 2000s changed the scenario for collective writing. This development, in turn, has paved the way for digital knowledge practices based on socialism.

Therefore, digital collective writing practices are forms of knowledge socialism (Peters et al. 2020a; Peters 2021). At least if writing is considered a collaborative practice – including collective ownership of the means of production – ideas are the means produced in the collective. However, in such an approach to knowledge socialism, collective writing and collaboratively produced and owned ideas link to membership in groups or organisations. Therefore, to create society-wide ownership of knowledge, groups or organisations must be linked in a larger structure to reach a societal level. From such reasoning, a conclusion is that collective writing can emerge on at least two levels: Type A on the group or organisational level and Type B on a societal level.

Building on the ideas of Barnett, collective writing as knowledge socialism embraces the relationship between the university and the society (Barnett and Bengtsen 2017; Jaldemark 2021; Peters et al. 2020a, b). Barnett discusses three modes of this relationship: the ivory tower, the factory, and the network. Analytically, these three modes are straightforward and distinct. Nevertheless, in reality, they might be mixed up and thrive in the same university.

The old-school ivory tower university does not bother to build any substantial relationship with the society. Therefore, society needs to find ways to disseminate and apply the knowledge produced. Collective writing focuses on issues that the university and its scholars think are critical, and the free mind reigns. Collective writing in terms of knowledge socialism is an internal matter for the scholars within the tower; in effect, collective writing of Type A.

In the factory, knowledge capitalism reigns, and research, teaching, and collaborative activities and initiatives start with and reflect ideas expressed in society. The knowledge produced results from the demands of public or private capital owners (Geoghegan and Pontikakis 2008). Therefore, knowledge socialism and collaborative writing in the factory mode need to focus on and relate to societal needs. Critical perspectives of knowledge are only necessary if it solves an externally expressed societal need and if it meets criteria set up by the philosophy of new public management. Ownership of the collective writing is a public affair belonging to society. Therefore, the factory mode links to Type B of collective writing.

The third mode – the networked university – is a hybrid between the university and society (Barnett and Bengtsen 2017). The networked mode emphasises a power balance between the internal knowledge barriers of the ivory tower and the demands from the capital owners in the factory; in effect, it affords another kind of knowledge socialism. Hybrid and networked knowledge practices can emerge, building on the free mind from the ivory tower and the vital link to society of the factory. This hybrid can create conditions for collective writing and collective public ownership of knowledge production to be shared between groups and organisations in society. The merging between the ivory tower and the factory can set up barriers to the thriving knowledge capitalism and new public management philosophies in the university. It could create conditions to brew knowledge socialism approaches based on merging Type A and Type B of collective writing.

13   Conclusion: Collective Writing, Openness, and Co(labor) ation: Collective Research, Writing, and Pedagogy in an Era of Knowledge Socialism (Michael A. Peters)

It is always a pleasure to work with Petar. He is inventive, thorough, collaborative, intelligent, and innovative. And we have worked together over the last few years being very productive over a range of books, topics, journals, and so on. Why I start by highlighting this relationship is because it is clearly the case that we have a genuine relationship that encourages us to work together and we spark off each other.

I have come to recognise it because it has happened to me more than once where a collaboration has turned into something special and different. Collective writing does not depend on this kind of relationship but it can encourage it and allow for it by putting scholars in touch with one another.

I developed these next comments in response to the helpful review of *The Methodology and Philosophy of Collective Writing* (Peters et al. 2021a) that Petar sent me (Abegglen et al. 2022). I responded immediately so the comments have a kind of immediacy.

I suggest that you and I co-edit a piece for your journal on collective writing that explores its epistemology and its experimental focus. In developing the *Educational Philosophy and Theory* (*EPAT*)[3] uses, I focused on the natural epistemological socialism of peer review, two concepts that structured first the philosophically implicit notion of the journal as a collection (of observations, experiments, reports, etc.), then much later the peer evaluation system that controlled the quality based on the concept of (Kantian) criticism.

The journal then emerged as (an alignment of) these two ideas that were moulded into an industrial system of knowledge production. The system was based on intellectual property with the Statue of Anne that returned author rights to the creator and grew up around the legal apparatus of rights and copyright, which was quickly re-appropriated by the publishers who reduced copyright (and creation) to a minimal payment with focus on rights for use and reuse. The industrial system also controlled the form of the article mass producing a standard peer review based loosely on the methodology of science and scientific report that eclipsed the author (writing in the third person) and subjective experience to imply an eye-of-god objectivity and that allowed an easily produced mass science.

Its crucial mechanism of peer review kicked in much later to shore up the modern scientific system but was, in fact, the basis and promise of its postmodern development for the control, assessment, and ranking of quality for the industrial system. Its radical purpose was silenced and deadened and used in the purpose of maintaining industrial system quality rather than in encouraging open criticism among peers. In the digital publishing ecosystem after 1992, peer review began to emphasise aspects of peer co-production and other forms of horizontal peer development that demonstrated different forms of collegiality, co(labor)ation, and collective intelligence.

The Methodology and Philosophy of Collective Writing (Peters et al. 2021a) is a historical record and a 'patchwork' – I like this concept because of its reference to women's work of 'patching' and 'patch-work' like much intellectual work. The Abegglen, Burns, and Sinfield (2022) review is well taken as is your suggestion that we do something together on extending the idea but collective writing as a line or argument is only one possibility that must be supplemented by the historical narrative of development, the control of academic labour, the channelling of academic writing and subjectivity, and the effacing of the implicit collective dimension of

---

[3] See https://www.tandfonline.com/toc/rept20/current. Accessed 19 January 2023.

knowledge inherent in language (and recognised by Russian formalists, Wittgenstein, the Swiss and French structuralists, the French poststructuralists).

So my response to the review is to thank Sandra, Tom and Sandra for raising a legitimate criticism and to agree with you about another carefully crafted piece that examines the argument for collective writing as part of an omnibus standard for collective writing as:

1. An argument (in standard linear form).
2. An historical narrative about publishing.
3. A praxis and methodology.
4. A philosophy based on openness – open form and multiple authors – making peer reviewing central.
5. A history of the concept of peer review and peer systems of control.
6. The emergence of peer co-production.
7. A form of relational epistemology without foundations.
8. A repository of collective subjectivity.
9. An ecosystem of new (and original) ideas (without foundations).
10. An ethical system – trust, integrity, and collegiality.
11. A pedagogy.
12. Copyleft system that can also recognise and value individual contributions to the system.
13. A form of knowledge socialism based on the collective public ownership of ideas.

My first foray in an instant response: let's do this in a carefully crafted way that should involve openness, critique, and review for the early stages to discuss codesign of the architecture, as well as its code and content.

One thing the review does not realise or recognise very well is the ways in which collective writing is but one of the methodologies of knowledge socialism which has strong conceptual and real-world overlaps to forms of peer co-production economy that includes learning, innovation, and science economies based on what I call 'the virtues of openness'. There is more than a kindred spirit with peer review and open peer review, but also with collective research, writing, and pedagogy, especially with forms of citizen science, which is one of the forms of public knowledge cultures. Surely this has to be one of our objectives to reinforce and strengthen the understanding of these relations?

The five stages of the collective creative process (needs work):

1. Collective ideation – the emergence of novel ideas through conversation, dialogue, discussion, and sharing that does not deplete use but enhances it.
2. The sequence and architecture of ideas in an aesthetic assemblage of text production.
3. The critical review and reevaluation of text.
4. The incorporation of critics and criticism – the under/over writing.
5. The editorial process as an iterative, spiral with a pragmatic response that represents community of inquiry.

We must also emphasise:

1. 'Arguments' and 'narratives' are different but can complement each other.
2. Technically arguments operate in logical space and narratives in historical or fictional space.
3. There are different forms of argument, most inferential but hardly linear.
4. Postmodern narrative fiction disrupts the old modernist linear narratives... to begin and end anywhere and to employ nonlinear, dynamic, and interactive storylines.
5. The 'patchwork' is a great epistemological device because most linear narratives are ideological and unable pragmatically to respond to disruptions or breaks.

We can expand this list; maybe see it as a matrix.

We can dress up collective writing in terms of existing theory – Wittgenstein, Pierce, Bakhtin, Foucault, etc., and more contemporary sources both literary and philosophical – but, to be honest, the source for my innovation was quite pragmatic as a journal editor. I detested the neoliberal regime of performativity that created neuroses and academic anxieties taking away the joy of collaboration and writing as well as impinging on scientific purposes. As I used to say to my students (in Peters and Jandrić 2018), the journal article is 'a dirty little industrial machine' based on a productionist metaphysics. I wanted a concept of the paper that tried to stretch and contest the genre. We *EPAT* Editors started by offering first a clear architecture of a theme or topic that others could then develop in their own ways. I must say I was lucky with my *EPAT* and PESA colleagues at that particular time, i.e., the last five or so years.

So the experiment of collective writing in *EPAT* was developed as a mildly subversive practice, and it had other benefits: it helped to democratise publishing; it disrupted the notion of academic author; it provided relief from the tedium of the academic article; it enabled more scholars to participate in a creative process of collective writing; it provided a model suitable for quick publishing where an opinion is required almost immediately. For me, it also allowed a form of academic journalism and a form of the journal that encouraged the development of expert judgement with 'fast reflection'. Perhaps most importantly, the *EPAT* experiment in collective writing has led to other innovations. *EPAT* now has a genre called collective writing, which has its own form of open review, and it has also been used successfully as a teaching and assessment methodology with Masters students. I have used it as such at Beijing Normal University over the last 3 years. Student feedback indicates that they enjoy collective writing and are greatly enthusiastic when it leads to a publication. I must also note that I like the idea of student-colleagues.

Collective writing, as we argued in the collection *Knowledge Socialism* (Peters et al. 2020a), is a form of collective intelligence that does not require consensus, and it is not based on the individual (ideationally, the whole is greater than the sum of its parts). The process is an emergent one, and there are synergies. It does rely on new technologies for making groups smarter, and there is an ethics of collective writing at stake, even though it has not yet been properly unpicked). Even at the small scale, collective writing is a form of self-organisation and collective adaptation at work. In this regard, there are some interesting philosophical issues to do with the group mind, with distributed cognition, coordination, and cooperation. In my view, there is much more to be understood in these terms and also in terms of devising new forms of feedback and cycles of criticism, as Petar has provided in this experiment. It is not the case as many scholars argue that, with collective intelligence, there is little to no centralised communication or control. Maybe it is useful to distinguish between architecture, code, and content. At the psychological level, it may be useful to recognise that cognition is not solitary, but is shaped by collective learning, practice, and memory.

This collective essay covers the ground nicely, and I am interested in seeing the interconnections, overlaps, and acknowledgement of both theoretical resources, but also properly acknowledge the sources for models of historical practice. My own approach, informed by Wittgenstein, Peirce, and Foucault (mostly) as a general background but also in relation to an editor's problem that takes seriously knowledge capitalism and the political economy of academic publishing, was to develop with my colleagues a vehicle that provides a change of writing practice that yet still requires further application, development, and innovation. In particular, a group of us see collective writing and develop it explicitly as a form of knowledge socialism.

Neither I nor they want to lay claim to any originality or theoretical privilege. I am sure that liberal, feminist, and postcolonial scholars, for example, have and might develop their own distinctive collective practices (e.g. the conscious-raising group that borrowed from Freire) that create intellectual solidarity and companionship, especially as we move further away from the German idealistic philosophy that helped to craft the modern notion of the academic author and academic writing, especially with new AI publishing technologies, automatic writing and editing, and data-driven autonomous science. I am still fascinated with the ideation phase of writing – the process of having an idea – and the collective thought experiment is a useful technique for group writing that ethically shapes our collective practice.

14   Review 1: Showing the Workings of Collaborative Writing (Christine Sinclair)

Too often, a journal reviewer struggles to work out what is going on in a piece of academic writing. That is certainly not the case with this collective chapter: the reviewers have been in at its birth and observed its development towards maturity. Reviewers have seen in real time how ongoing commentary and peer review supported authors to clarify and extend arguments. The origins and rationale for the chapter, along with its methods of production, have been made manifest in the Introduction, Conclusion, and Appendix 1. Moreover, the overarching topic of the chapter is itself about what is going on in collaborative writing. This is a chapter that shows its workings.

The reviewers of this chapter, then, are in an unusual position in that they are not presented with a previously unseen and supposedly finished work. This is not unprecedented in academic life; the familiarity with a postgraduate student's work can make it difficult for their supervisor to view that same work with an objective examiner's eye, and yet sometimes they are called on to do so. The peer reviewer's important role features strongly in the chapter, and the notion of 'co-learning with the reviewer' captures the combination of striving for shared understanding, offering of resources, and humility that should be a necessary part of this role, especially in a collaborative endeavour. A reviewer must make a personal synthesis of the chapter, offer a view on why it works or does not, and draw a conclusion about the next step (if any).

There is much woven into the fabric of this chapter. The underlying method of its production shows a guiding framework that was neither coercive nor constrained – a difficult trick, as anyone who has ever been in an 'enforced' collaborative writing process will testify.

With 'patchwork' writing, observation over an extended period brings concerns about how the pieces will eventually be stitched together and in which sequence. At one point, a contribution seemed to be in the wrong place, though it had great appeal with some well-crafted sentences. As I was still thinking about this, I encountered the expression 'parataxis' in the chapter, which was new to me but exactly fitted my line of thought. Behind the scenes, some re-sequencing followed. At that point, too, the line of reasoning in the chapter began to clarify for me. The chapter contains many enticing words and sentences, and I captured some themes around these and mapped them to the initial list for the chapter's architecture identified in the conclusion (see Fig. 1 for the themes and examples that emerged from this process).

Many of the chapter's enticing sentences did not make it to my personal synthesis of the chapter in Fig. 1. One of those supports a suitable conclusion about our openness to both the collective and its writing: we are indeed resisting and transforming traditional academic norms and practices. But I have nothing more to suggest at present. This is a valuable and well-written chapter, even if we say so ourselves.

15   Review 2: Good Game/Got Game/Game On/Game Over (Andrew Gibbons)

'Collective Writing: The Continuous Struggle for Meaning-Making' identifies a collective journey of discovery that recognises and is committed to the benefits of an openness to different approaches to writing, and methodological lessons that can be learned through and about collective writing. The methodological concern is perhaps made possible because of the experiments that led to the point of this collective work. As a reviewer and participant in some of those experiments, 'Collective Writing: The Continuous Struggle for Meaning-Making' has particular energy and

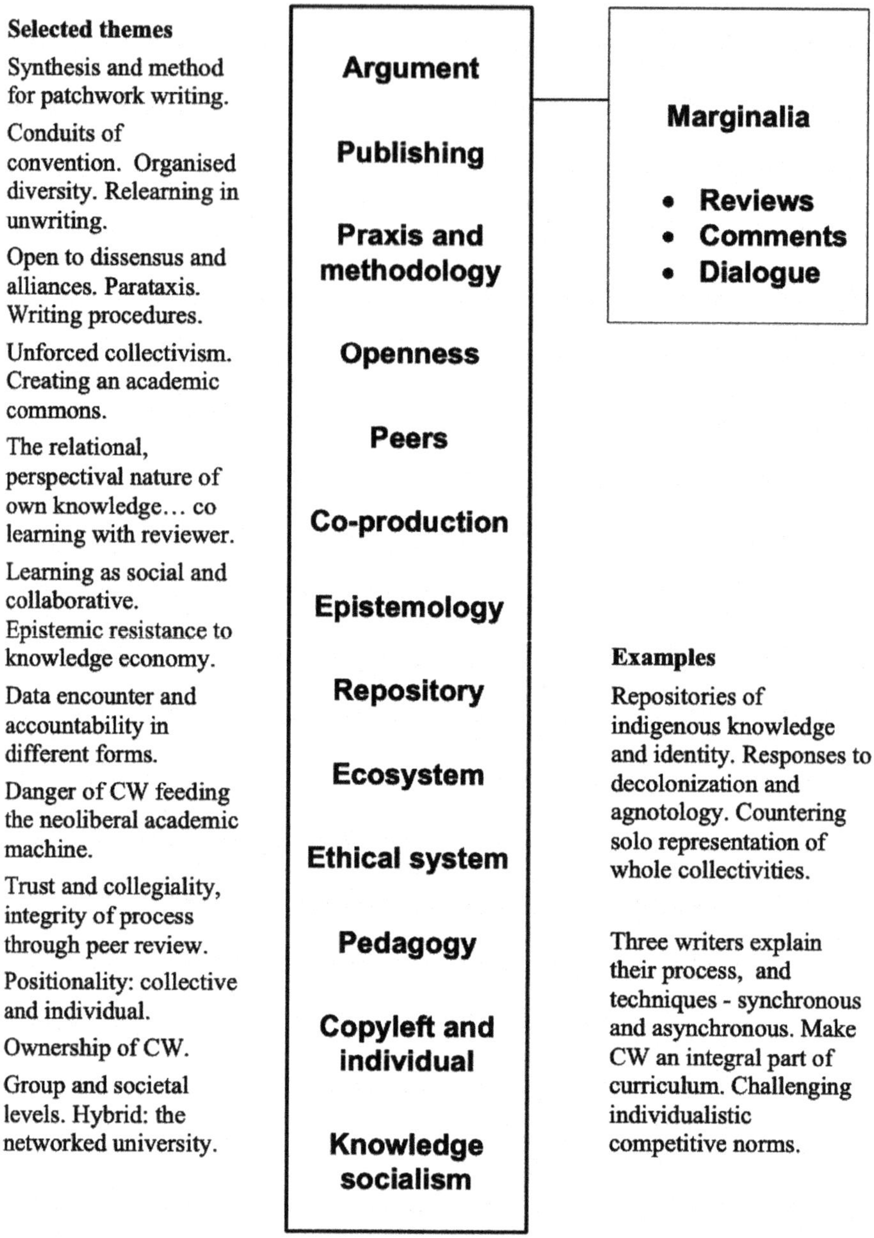

Selected themes

Synthesis and method for patchwork writing.

Conduits of convention. Organised diversity. Relearning in unwriting.

Open to dissensus and alliances. Parataxis. Writing procedures.

Unforced collectivism. Creating an academic commons.

The relational, perspectival nature of own knowledge… co learning with reviewer.

Learning as social and collaborative. Epistemic resistance to knowledge economy.

Data encounter and accountability in different forms.

Danger of CW feeding the neoliberal academic machine.

Trust and collegiality, integrity of process through peer review.

Positionality: collective and individual.

Ownership of CW.

Group and societal levels. Hybrid: the networked university.

| **Argument** |
| **Publishing** |
| **Praxis and methodology** |
| **Openness** |
| **Peers** |
| **Co-production** |
| **Epistemology** |
| **Repository** |
| **Ecosystem** |
| **Ethical system** |
| **Pedagogy** |
| **Copyleft and individual** |
| **Knowledge socialism** |

Marginalia

- **Reviews**
- **Comments**
- **Dialogue**

Examples

Repositories of indigenous knowledge and identity. Responses to decolonization and agnotology. Countering solo representation of whole collectivities.

Three writers explain their process, and techniques - synchronous and asynchronous. Make CW an integral part of curriculum. Challenging individualistic competitive norms.

Fig. 1 Our synthetic patchwork quilt (Christine Sinclair 2022) (CC BY NC SA 4.0)

substance in its coherence. The previous trials have created some sense of a need for a game plan. Trials and games come to mind in reviewing this collective work through a question, taking shape, about the practising of collective writing.

Thinking about practice (with connections to ludic experiences, and for writing as an integral part of the curriculum – although adding things to a curriculum can assess the fun 'write' out of them, more on that below) leads to thinking about the ways in which groups practise in different contexts (sports teams, bands, school of education early childhood bachelor's programme teams, and so on). Is it possible that the kind of collective writing that builds senses of purpose and connection and trust and openness and questioning with regard to collective writing might study traditions and developments in practising?

Practice leads to performance. It is clear in this piece that the performance is focused on collective writing; however, it is also focused on decolonization and higher education, and disciplinarity and labour and peer review and...

On practising and performing peer review, this experimentation with open peer review using shared documents online and structured in such a way as to involve reviewers in the collective from the 'stage of ideation' is great for the study of peer review because it creates alternate experiences of peer review that then feedback into questions of what, why, and how as well as, here, where, and when. Writing a review for a piece where the authors are openly commenting and reviewing as the piece grows obstructs some reviewerly intentions, but this is not a problem – just because it has been said does not mean it cannot be said again. And, perhaps, with that dimension of a reviewer's role taken up already, being in a sense watched by an audience as the writers work together collectively in this structured review process (I have not worked in a workshop with designers – I wonder whether there are some synergies with that design practice), the reviewer is untethered and can float else-where above the terrain of the piece, taking on different aspects of the horizon. And, perhaps most productively, now there is the possibility of engaging in peer review through review of the ephemeral comment functions of the authors with each other as they review themselves in the practice and performance of meaning making.

In 'Collective Writing: The Continuous Struggle for Meaning-Making', it is apparent that meaning-making is always a struggle and perhaps in part it is always a struggle because it is never not collective. The forgetfulness with regard that always collectiveness is perhaps the actual struggle... grappling with the collective conscious clutter that is produced by education systems and the production of par-ticular thinking subjects who lose a sense of the we that is the I (Gibbons and Craw 2018) – a struggle to remember something some institutions may not want us to remember. Stated clearly, and with impetus for the purpose of this collective work in both practice and performance: 'it is still hard to disabuse educators of the idea that to be a genius is to think, experiment and write alone'.

I am confident that there is an agreement that echo chamber practice fields would not offer much for collective writing without public performance. I am particularly keen to see how these collective experiments enter into different spaces of practice and performance, and the possibility of embedding curriculum experiences of col-lective writing. As an early childhood teacher educator, I see this work on collective writing as more than the theory and practice of collective writing; more than offer-ing up some ways and some substance, they challenge teacher education to dive into itself and pick away at the bones of what it does.

For early childhood student teachers engaged in the study of teaching as a collective practice, collective writing contributes to recognising the ideals of collective work and 'a certain morality surrounding that work', and challenging the ways in which constructions of their labour and their thinking is gendered in different ways and with different implications, challenging what it means to talk about, for instance, patching and patchwork in relation to gender, and perceptions of high and low-level scholarly work that are necessary for both exploitation and emancipation as and for teachers who work in early childhood care and education.

Acknowledgement This chapter was first published as Jandrić, P., Luke, T. W., Sturm, S., McLaren, P., Jackson, L., MacKenzie, A., Tesar, M., Stewart, G. T., Roberts, P., Abegglen, S., Burns, T., Sinfield, S., Hayes, S., Jaldemark, J., Peters, M. A., Sinclair, C., & Gibbons, A. (2022). Collective Writing: The Continuous Struggle for Meaning-Making. *Postdigital Science and Education.* https://doi.org/10.1007/s42438-022-00320-5. Before republishing, we slightly updated references and appendices.

Appendix 1 Workflow

Duration	Stage	Description	Tasks
1 week	Collective ideation and literature review.	Literature review and assessment of this work plan.	1. Check the list of all collectively written publications which will be published in the Appendix. 2. Add missing collectively written articles. 3. Assess this workflow; if needed, suggest changes.
1 week	The sequence and architecture of ideas.	Developing text structure and teaming up.	1. Check the provisional list of topics. Edit as you see fit – Delete, merge, change sequence, add more themes. 2. Add your name next to the topic you will write about. 3. Decide whether you want to author a contribution or review the chapter. If you want to serve as reviewer, write down your name in the appropriate place in the topics. Topics and reviews are allocated on a first-come-first-served basis. If there are more people interested in a topic or a reviewer position, we strongly encourage you to team up!
1 week	Writing up.	Writing up.	Write your 500-word entry.

Duration	Stage	Description	Tasks
1 week	Critical review and re-evaluation.	Peer review.	1. Review two sections of your choice. 2. Leave your reviewer feedback as a comment attached to the section title. 3. Edit reviewed text directly (if you please).
1 week	Revising round 1.	The under/over writing.	Implement reviewer comments to your section. Discuss feedback if needed.
1 week	Leading authors take over and produce the first draft.		
1 week	Revising round 2.	The under/over writing. Based on the first draft, reviewers write their reviews.	1. Authors: Read the whole chapter and your section in particular. Finalise your section. Offer your final feedback for the chapter. 2. Reviewers: Write up a 500-word review.
1 week	Leading authors take over and produce the final draft together with reviews.		
1 week	Authorisation.	The under/over writing.	Authors and reviewers: Make any last changes and authorise the final version.
Chapter sent to production			

Appendix 2 Reading List

Abegglen, S., Burns, T., & Sinfield, S. (2016). Utilising 'critical writing exercises' to foster critical thinking skills in first-year undergraduate students and prepare them for life outside university. *Double Helix, 4.* https://doi.org/10.37514/DBH-J.2016.4.1.06.

Abegglen, S., Burns, T., & Sinfield, S. (2017). 'Really free!': Strategic interventions to foster students' academic writing skills. *Journal of Educational Innovation, Partnership and Change, 3*(1), 251–255. https://doi.org/10.21100/jeipc.v3i1.589.

Abegglen, S., Burns, T., & Sinfield, S. (2018). Drawing as a way of knowing: Visual practices as the route to becoming academic. *Canadian Journal for Studies in Discourse and Writing/Rédactologie, 28*, 173–185. https://doi.org/10.31468/cjsdwr.600.

Abegglen, S., Burns, T., & Sinfield, S. (2021). Dialogic montage: Reflecting on playful practice in higher education. *Journal of Play in Adulthood, 3*(2), 82–95. https://doi.org/10.5920/jpa.843.

Abegglen, S., Burns, T., & Sinfield, S. (2021). Editorial: Collaboration in higher education: Partnering with students, colleagues and external stakeholders. *Journal of University Teaching & Learning Practice, 18*(7), 1–6. https://doi.org/10.53761/1.18.7.01.

Abegglen, S., Burns, T., & Sinfield, S. (2021). *Supporting student writing and other modes of learning and assessment: A staff guide*. Calgary: PRISM.

Abegglen, S., Burns, T., & Sinfield, S. (2022). Review of Michael A. Peters, Tina Besley, Marek Tesar, Liz Jackson, Petar Jandrić, Sonja Arndt, & Sean Sturm (2021). The Methodology and Philosophy of Collective Writing: An Educational Philosophy and Theory Reader Volume X. *Postdigital Science Education*. https://doi.org/10.1007/s42438-022-00310-7.

Abegglen, S., Burns, T., & Sinfield, S. (2022). Supporting university staff to develop student writing: Collaborative writing as a method of inquiry. *Journal of Learning Development in Higher Education, 23*. https://doi.org/10.47408/jldhe.vi23.839.

Abegglen, S., Burns, T., & Sinfield, S. (Eds.). (2021). Collaboration in higher education: Partnering with students, colleagues and external stakeholders. *Journal of University Teaching & Learning Practice, 18*(7), Special Issue. https://ro.uow.edu.au/jutlp/vol18/iss7/. Accessed 25 May 2022.

Abegglen, S., Burns, T., Middlebrook, D., & Sinfield, S. (2019). Disrupting academic reading: Unrolling the scroll. In L. Quinn (Ed.), *Re-imagining the curriculum: Spaces for disruption* (pp. 307–324). Stellenbosch: African Sun Media.

Ailwood, J., Lee, I-F., Arndt, S., Tesar, M., Aslanian, T., Gibbons, A., & Heimer, L. (2022). Communities of Care: A collective writing project on philosophies, politics, and pedagogies of care and education in the early years. *Policy Futures in Education*. https://doi.org/10.1177/14782103211064440.

Arndt, S., Asher, G., Knox, J., Ford, D. R., Hayes, S., Lăzăroiu, G., Jackson, L., Mañero Contreras, J., Buchanan, R., D'Olimpio, L., Smith, M., Suoranta, J., Pyyhtinen, O., Ryberg, T., Davidsen, J., Steketee, A., Mihăilă, R., Stewart, G., Dawson, M., Sinclair, C., & Peters, M. A. (2019). Between the blabbering noise of individuals or the silent dialogue of many: A collective response to 'Postdigital science and education' (Jandrić et al. 2018). *Postdigital Science and Education, 1*(1), 446–474. https://doi.org/10.1007/s42438-019-00037-y.

Arndt, S., Buchanan, R., Gibbons, A., Hung, R., Madjar, A., Novak, R., Orchard, J., Peters, M. A., Sturm, S., Tesar, M., & Hood, N. (2020). Collective writing: Introspective reflections on current experience. *Educational Philosophy and Theory*. https://doi.org/10.1080/00131857.2020.1824782.

Bayne, S., Evans, P., Ewins, R., Knox, J., Lamb, J., Macleod, H., O'Shea, C., Ross, J., Sheail, P., & Sinclair, C. (2020). *The Manifesto for Teaching Online*. Cambridge, MA: MIT Press.

Besley, T., Jackson, L., Peters, M. A., Devine, N., Mayo, C., Stewart, G. T., White, E. J., Stengel, B., Opiniano, G. A., Sturm, S., Legg, C., Tesar, M., & Arndt, S. (2022). Philosophers and professors behaving badly: Responses to 'named or nameless' by Besley, Jackson, & Peters. An EPAT collective writing project. *Educational Philosophy and Theory*. https://doi.org/10.1080/00131857.2021.2015322.

Biesta, G., Heugh, K., Cervinkova, H., Rasiński, L., Osborne, S., Forde, D., Wrench, A., Carter, J., Säfström, C. A., Soong, H., O'Keeffe, S., Paige, K., Rigney, L.-I., O'Toole, L., Hattam, R., Peters, M. A., & Tesar, M. (2021). Philosophy of education in a new key: publicness, social justice, and education: A South-North conversation. *Educational Philosophy and Theory*. https://doi.org/10.1080/0013185 7.2021.1929172.

Blumsztajn, A., Koopal, W., Rojahn, P., Schildermans, H., Thoilliez, B., Vlieghe, J., & Wortmann, K. (2022). Offline Memos for Online Teaching: A Collective Response to The Manifesto for Teaching Online (Bayne et al. 2020). *Postdigital Science and Education*, *4*(2), 259–270. https://doi.org/10.1007/s42438-022-00286-4.

Buchanan, R. A., Forster, D. J., Douglas, S., Nakar, S., Boon, H. J., Heath, T., Heyward, P., D'Olimpio, L., Ailwood, J., Eacott, S., Smith, S., Peters, M. A., & Tesar, M. (2021). Philosophy of Education in a New Key: exploring new ways of teaching and doing ethics in education in the twenty-first century. *Educational Philosophy and Theory*. https://doi.org/10.1080/00131857.2021.1880387.

Burns, T., & Sinfield, S. (2022). *Essential study skills: The complete guide to success at university*. 5th Ed. London: Sage.

Burns, T., Sinfield, S., & Abegglen, S. (2018). Case study 2: Cabinet of curiosity. *Journal of Writing in Creative Practice*, *11*(2), 211–215. https://doi.org/10.1386/jwcp.11.2.211_7.

Burns, T., Sinfield, S., & Abegglen, S. (2018). Case study 3: Games and board games. *Journal of Writing in Creative Practice*, *11*(2), 261–266. https://doi.org/10.1386/jwcp.11.2.261_7.

Burns, T., Sinfield, S., & Abegglen, S. (2018). Case study 4: Digital storytelling. *Journal of Writing in Creative Practice*, *11*(2), 275–278. https://doi.org/10.1386/jwcp.11.2.275_7.

Burns, T., Sinfield, S., & Abegglen, S. (2018). Case study 5: Multimodal exhibition. *Journal of Writing in Creative Practice*, *11*(2), 297–303. https://doi.org/10.1386/jwcp.11.2.297_7.

Burns, T., Sinfield, S., & Abegglen, S. (2018). Regenring academic writing. Case study 1: Collages. *Journal of Writing in Creative Practice*, *11*(2), 181–190. https://doi.org/10.1386/jwcp.11.2.181_1.

Cassidy, C., Christie, D., Coutts, N., Dunn, J., Sinclair, C., Skinner, N., & Wilson, A. (2008). Building communities of educational enquiry. *Oxford Review of Education*, *34*(2), 217–235. https://doi.org/10.1080/03054980701614945.

Claiborne, L. B., Cornforth, S., Crocket, K., & Manathunga, C. (2013). Exploring ethical difficulties in doctoral supervision: reflexive collaborative theorising around memory and practice. *Knowledge Cultures*, *1*(5), 39–49.

Cormier, D., Jandrić, P., Childs, M., Hall, R., White, D., Phipps, L., Truelove, I., Hayes, S., & Fawns, T. (2019). Ten Years of the Postdigital in the 52group: Reflections and Developments 2009–2019. *Postdigital Science and Education*, *1*(2), 475–506. https://doi.org/10.1007/s42438-019-00049-8.

Crinall, S., Rowbottom, E. C., Blom, X. P. M., & Blom, S. M. (2020). A place with no time: Re-conceptualising child–adult relations during 'homeschooling' in the 2020 pandemic. *Knowledge Cultures*, *8*(2), 65–81. https://doi.org/10.22381/KC82202010.

Czerniewicz, L., Agherdien, N., Badenhorst, J., Belluigi, D., Chambers, T., Chili, M., De Villiers, M., Felix, A., Gachago, D., Gokhale, C., Ivala, E., Kramm, N., Madiba, M., Mistri, G., Mgqwashu, E., Pallitt, N., Prinsloo, P., Solomon, K., Strydom, S., Swanepoel, M., Waghid, F., & Wissing, G. (2020). A Wake-Up Call: Equity, Inequality and Covid-19 Emergency Remote Teaching and Learning. *Postdigital Science and Education*, *2*(3), 946–967. https://doi.org/10.1007/s42438-020-00187-4.

Devine, N., Gresson, E., Olssen, M., Irwin, R., Coxon, E., Chueh, H., & Heraud, R. (2021). In Memoriam: Jim Marshall. *ACCESS: Contemporary Issues in Education*, *41*(1), 52–59. https://doi.org/10.46786/ac21.2779.

Gibbons, A., Cabral, M., & Moffett, C. (2021). Inter-galactic pedagogy, pedagogy inter-galactic: The first entries of the pedagogica intergalactica!. *Policy Futures in Education*. https://doi.org/10.1177/14782103211043979.

Gibbons, A., Peters, M. A., Delaune, A., Jandrić, P., Sojot, A. N., Kupferman, D. W., Tesar, M., Johansson, V., Cabral, M., Devine, N., & Hood, N. (2021). Infantasies: An EPAT collective project. *Educational Philosophy and Theory*, *53*(14), 1442–1453. https://doi.org/10.1080/00131857.2020.1860749.

Gibbons, A., Peters, M. A., Stewart, G. T., Tesar, M., Boland, N., Johansson, V., de Lautour, N., Devine, N., Hood, N., & Sturm, S. (2021). *Infantologies II: Songs of the cradle, Educational Philosophy and Theory*. https://doi.org/10.1080/00131857.2021.1906646.

Gibbons, A., Tesar, M., Arndt, S., Kupferman, D.W., Badenhorst, D., Jackson, L., Jandrić, P., & Peters, M. A. (2020). The Highway Robber's Road to Knowledge Socialism: A Collective Work on Collective Work. In M. A. Peters, T. Besley, P. Jandrić, & X. Zhu (Eds.) (2020). *Knowledge Socialism. The Rise of Peer Production: Collegiality, Collaboration, and Collective Intelligence* (pp. 301–325). Singapore: Springer. https://doi.org/10.1007/978-981-13-8126-3_15.

Hayes, S., Jopling, M., Hayes, D., Westwood, A., Tuckett, A., & Barnett, R. (2020). Raising regional academic voices (alongside data) in Higher Education (HE) debate. *Postdigital Science and Education*, *3*(2), 242–260. https://doi.org/10.1007/s42438-020-00131-6.

Hrastinski, S., Arkenback-Sundström, C., D. Olofsson, A., Ekström, S., Ericsson, E., Fransson, G., Jaldemark, J., Ryberg, T., Öberg, L-M., Fuentes, A., Gustafsson, U., Humble, N., Mozelius, P., Sundgren, M., & Utterberg, M. (2019). Critical Imaginaries and Reflections on Artificial Intelligence and Robots in Postdigital K-12 Education. *Postdigital Science and Education*, *1*(2), 427–445. https://doi.org/10.1007/s42438-019-00046-x.

Hung, R., Zhengmei, P., Kato, M., Nishihira, T., Okabe, M., Di, X., Kwak, D.-J., Hwang, K., Tschong, Y., Chien, C.-H., Peters, M. A., & Tesar, M. (2021). Philosophy of Education in a New Key: East Asia. *Educational Philosophy and Theory*, *53*(12), 1199–1214. https://doi.org/10.1080/00131857.2020.1772028.

Jackson, L., Alston, K., Bialystok, L., Blum, L., Burbules, N. C., Chinnery, A., Hansen, D. T., Hytten, K., Mayo, C., Norris, T., Stitzlein, S. M., Thompson, W. C., Waks, L., Peters, M. A., & Tesar, M. (2020). Philosophy of education in a

New Key: Snapshot 2020 from the United States and Canada. *Educational Philosophy and Theory*. https://doi.org/10.1080/00131857.2020.1821189.

Jackson, L., Peters, M. A., Benade, L., Devine, N., Arndt, S., Forster, D., Gibbons, A., Grierson, E., Jandrić, P., Lazaroiu, G., Locke, K., Mihaila, R., Stewart, G., Tesar, M., Roberts, & Ozoliņs, J. (2018). Is peer review in academic publishing still working?. *Open Review of Educational Research*, 5(1), 95–112. https://doi.org/10.1080/23265507.2018.1479139.

Jandrić, P., Bozkurt, A., McKee, M., Hayes, S. (2021b). Teaching in the Age of Covid-19 – A Longitudinal Study. *Postdigital Science and Education*, 3(3), 743–770. https://doi.org/10.1007/s42438-021-00252-6.

Jandrić, P., Devine, N., Jackson, L., Peters, M. A., Lăzăroiu, G., Mihăilă, R., Locke, K., Heraud, R., Gibbons, A., Grierson, E., Forster, D., White, J., Stewart, G., Tesar, M., Arndt, S., Brighouse, S., & Benade, L. (2017). Collective writing: An inquiry into praxis. *Knowledge Cultures*, 5(1), 85–109. https://doi.org/10.22381/KC5120177.

Jandrić, P., Fuentes Martinez, A., Reitz, C., Jackson, L., Grauslund, D., Hayes, D., Lukoko, H. O., Hogan, M., Mozelius, P., Arantes, J. A., Levinson, P., Ozoliņš, J., Kirylo, J. D., Carr, P. R., Hood, N., Tesar, M., Sturm, S., Abegglen, S., Burns, T., Sinfield, S., Stewart, G. T., Suoranta, J., Jaldemark, J., Gustafsson, U., Monzó, L. D., Batarelo Kokić, I., Kihwele, J. E., Wright, J., Kishore, P., Stewart, P. A., Bridges, S. M., Lodahl, M., Bryant, P., Kaur, K., Hollings, S., Brown, J. B., Steketee, A., Prinsloo, P., Hazzan, M. K., Jopling, M., Mañero, J., Gibbons, A., Pfohl, S., Humble, N., Davidsen, J., Ford, D. R., Sharma, N., Stockbridge, K., Pyyhtinen, O., Escaño, C., Achieng-Evensen, C., Rose, J., Irwin, J., Shukla, R., SooHoo, S., Truelove, I., Buchanan, R., Urvashi, S., White, E. J., Novak, R., Ryberg, T., Arndt, S., Redder, B., Mukherjee, M., Komolafe, B. F., Mallya, M., Devine, N., Sattarzadeh, S. D., & Hayes, S. (2022). Teaching in the Age of Covid-19—The New Normal. *Postdigital Science and Education*, 4(1), 877–1015. https://doi.org/10.1007/s42438-022-00332-1.

Jandrić, P., Hayes, D., Levinson, P., Lisberg Christensen, L., Lukoko, H. O., Kihwele, J. E., Brown, J. B., Reitz, C., Mozelius, P., Nejad, H. G., Fuentes Martinez, A., Arantes, J. A., Jackson, L., Gustafsson, U., Abegglen, S., Burns, T., Sinfield, S., Hogan, M., Kishore, P., Carr, P. R., Batarelo Kokić, I., Prinsloo, P., Grauslund, D., Steketee, A., Achieng-Evensen, C., Komolafe, B. F., Suoranta, J., Hood, N., Tesar, M., Rose, J., Humble, N., Kirylo, J. D., Mañero, J., Monzó, L. D., Lodahl, M., Jaldemark, J., Bridges, S. M., Sharma, N., Davidsen, J., Ozoliņš, J., Bryant, P., Escaño, C., Irwin, J., Kaur, K., Pfohl, S., Stockbridge, K., Ryberg, T., Pyyhtinen, O., SooHoo, S., Hazzan, M. K., Wright, J., Hollings, S., Arndt, S., Gibbons, A., Urvashi, S., Forster, D. J., Truelove, I., Mayo, P., Rikowski, G., Stewart, P. A., Jopling, M., Stewart, G. T., Buchanan, R., Devine, N., Shukla, R., Novak, R., Mallya, M., Biličić, E., Sturm, S., Sattarzadeh, S. D., Philip, A. P., Redder, B., White, E. J., Ford, D. R., Allen, Q., Mukherjee, M., & Hayes, S. (2021). Teaching in the Age of Covid-19 – 1 Year Later. *Postdigital Science and Education*, 3(3), 1073–1223. https://doi.org/10.1007/s42438-021-00243-7.

Jandrić, P., Hayes, D., Truelove, I., Levinson, P., Mayo, P., Ryberg, T., Monzó, L.D., Allen, Q., Stewart, P.A., Carr, P.R., Jackson, L., Bridges, S., Escaño, C., Grauslund, D., Mañero, J., Lukoko, H.O., Bryant, P., Fuentes Martinez, A., Gibbons, A., Sturm, S., Rose, J., Chuma, M.M., Biličić, E., Pfohl, S., Gustafsson, U., Arantes, J.A., Ford, D.R., Kihwele, J.E., Mozelius, P., Suoranta, J., Jurjević, L., Jurčević, M., Steketee, A., Irwin, J., White, E.J., Davidsen, J., Jaldemark, J., Abegglen, S., Burns, T., Sinfield, S., Kirylo, J.D., Batarelo Kokić, I., Stewart, G.T., Rikowski, G., Lisberg Christensen, L., Arndt, S., Pyyhtinen, O., Reitz, C., Lodahl, M., Humble, N., Buchanan, R., Forster, D.J., Kishore, P., Ozoliņš, J., Sharma, N., Urvashi, S., Nejad, H.G., Hood, N., Tesar, M., Wang, Y., Wright, J., Brown, J.B., Prinsloo, P., Kaur, K., Mukherjee, M., Novak, R., Shukla, R., Hollings, S., Konnerup, U., Mallya, M., Olorundare, A., Achieng-Evensen, C., Philip, A.P., Hazzan, M.K., Stockbridge, K., Komolafe, B.F., Bolanle, O.F., Hogan, M., Redder, B., Sattarzadeh, S.D., Jopling, M., SooHoo, S., Devine, N., & Hayes, S. (2020). Teaching in The Age of Covid-19. *Postdigital Science and Education*, 2(3), 1069–1230. https://doi.org/10.1007/s42438-020-00169-6.

Jandrić, P., Jaldemark. J., Hurley, Z., Bartram, B., Matthews, A., Jopling, M., Mañero, J., MacKenzie, A., Irwin, J., Rothmüller, N., Green, B., Ralston, S. J., Pyyhtinen, O., Hayes, S., Wright, J., Peters, M. A., & Tesar, M. (2021). Philosophy of education in a new key: Who remembers Greta Thunberg? Education and environment after the coronavirus. *Educational Philosophy and Theory*, 53(14), 1421–1441. https://doi.org/10.1080/00131857.2020.1811678.

Jandrić, P., Ryberg, T., Knox, J., Lacković, N., Hayes, S., Suoranta, J., Smith, M., Steketee, A., Peters, M. A., McLaren, P., Ford, D. R., Asher, G., McGregor, C., Stewart, G., Williamson, B., & Gibbons, A. (2019). Postdigital Dialogue. *Postdigital Science and Education*, 1(1), 163–189. https://doi.org/10.1007/s42438-018-0011-x.

Karamercan, O., Matapo, J., Kamenarac, O., Fa'avae, D. T. M., Arndt, S., Irwin, R., Kruger, F., Mika, C., Bassidou, M. Y. A., Tesar, M., & Del Monte, P. (2022). Engaging and developing community in digital spaces: Approaches from the Editorial Development Group. *Educational Philosophy and Theory*. https://doi.org/10.1080/00131857.2022.2041412.

Kato, M., Saito, N., Matsushita, R., Ueno, M., Izawa, S., Maruyama, Y., Sugita, H., Ono, F., Muroi, R., Miyazaki, Y., Yamana, J., Peters, M. A., & Tesar, M. (2020). Philosophy of Education in a New Key: Voices from Japan. *Educational Philosophy and Theory*. https://doi.org/10.1080/00131857.2020.1802819.

Koschmann, T., Hall, R. P., & Miyake, N. (Eds.). (2002). *CSCL 2; Carrying forward the conversation*. Abingdon: Routledge.

Locke, K., Gerlich, R., Godfery, M., Fraser, I., Robertson, G., & Roberts, A. (2017). The heart of the matter: A written presentation of the sixth annual Peter Fraser memorial lecture. *Knowledge Cultures*, 5(6), 25–44. https://doi.org/10.22381/KC5620173.

Longley, A., Sturm, S., & Yoon, C. (2021). Kindness as water in the university. *Knowledge Cultures*, 9(3), 184–205. https://doi.org/10.22381/kc93202111.

MacKenzie, A., Bacalja, A., Annamali, D., Panaretou, A., Girme, P., Cutajar, M., Abegglen, S., Evens, M., Neuhaus, F., Wilson, K., Psarikidou, K., Koole, M., Hrastinski, S., Sturm, S., Adachi, C., Schnaider, K., Bozkurt, A., Rapanta, C., Themelis, C., Thestrup, K., Gislev, T., Örtegren, A., Costello, C., Dishon, G., Hoechsmann, M., Bucio, J., Vadillo, G., Sánchez-Mendiola, M., Goetz, G., Gusso, H. L., Aldous Arantes, J., Kishore, P., Lodahl, M., Suoranta, J., Markauskaite, L., Mörtsell, S., O'Reilly, T., Reed, J., Bhatt, I., Brown, C., MacCallum, K., Ackermann, C., Alexander, C., Leah Payne, A., Bennett, R., Stone, C., Collier, A., Lohnes Watulak, S., Jandrić, P., Peters, M., & Gourlay, L. (2021). Dissolving the Dichotomies Between Online and Campus-Based Teaching: a Collective Response to The Manifesto for Teaching Online (Bayne et al. 2020) (2021). *Postdigital Science and Education*, 4(2), 271–329. https://doi.org/10.1007/s42438-021-00259-z.

Martin, B., Stewart, G., Watson, B. K. i., Silva, O. K., Teisina, J., Matapo, J., & Mika, C. (2020). Situating decolonisation: An Indigenous dilemma. *Educational Philosophy and Theory*, 52(3), 312–321. https://doi.org/10.1080/00131857.2019.1652164.

Mika, C., Stewart, G., Watson, K. i., Silva, K., Martin, B., Matapo, J., & Galuvao, A. (2018). What is indigenous research in philosophy of education? And what is PESA, from an indigenous perspective? *Educational Philosophy and Theory*, 50(8), 733–739. https://doi.org/10.1080/00131857.2017.1317042.

Networked Learning Editorial Collective (2021). Networked Learning: Inviting Redefinition. *Postdigital Science and Education*, 3(2), 312–325. https://doi.org/10.1007/s42438-020-00167-8.

Networked Learning Editorial Collective, Gourlay, L., Rodríguez-Illera, J. L., Barberà, E., Bali, M., Gachago, D., Pallitt, N., Jones, C., Bayne, S., Hansen, S. B., Hrastinski, S., Jaldemark, J., Themelis, C., Pischetola, M., Dirckinck-Holmfeld, L., Matthews, A., Gulson, K. N., Lee, K., Bligh, B., Thibaut, P.,Vermeulen, M., Nijland, F., Vrieling-Teunter, E., Scott, H., Thestrup, K., Gislev, T., Koole, M., Cutajar, M., Tickner, S., Rothmüller, N., Bozkurt, A., Fawns, T., Ross, J., Schnaider, K., Carvalho, L., Green, J. K., Hadžijusufović,M., Hayes, S., Czerniewicz, L., & Knox, J. (2021). Networked Learning in 2021: A Community Definition. *Postdigital Science and Education*, 3(2), 326–369. https://doi.org/10.1007/s42438-021-00222-y.

Orchard, J., Gaydon, P., Williams, K., Bennett, P., D'Olimpio, L., Çelik, R., Shah, Q., Neusiedl, C., Suissa, J., Peters, M. A., & Tesar, M. (2021). Philosophy of education in a new key: A 'Covid Collective' of the Philosophy of Education Society of Great Britain (PESGB), *Educational Philosophy and Theory*, 53(12), 1215–1228. https://doi.org/10.1080/00131857.2020.1838274.

Papastephanou, M., Zembylas, M., Bostad, I., Oral, S. B., Drousioti, K., Kouppanou, A., Strand, T., Wain, K., Peters, M. A., & Tesar, M. (2020). Philosophy of education in a new key: Education for justice now. *Educational Philosophy and Theory*. https://doi.org/10.1080/00131857.2020.1793539.

Peters, M. A. (2022). Educational Philosophies of Self-Cultivation: The Aesthetics of Collective Writing (关于修身的教育哲学:集体写作之美.Keynote address at the 2022 Annual Conference of Chinese Academy for Moral Education (全国德育学术委员会2021年年会), 16 April. Beijing: National Moral Education Academic Committee, School of Education of Capital Normal University, and Tian Jiabing Foundation.

Peters, M. A., Arndt, S., Tesar, M., Jackson, L., Hung, R., Mika, C., Ozolins, J. T., Teschers, C., Orchard, J., Buchanan, R., Madjar, A., Novak, R., Besley, T., Sturm, S., Roberts, P., & Gibbons. A. (2020). Philosophy of education in a new key. *Educational Philosophy and Theory*. https://doi.org/10.1080/00131857.2020.1759194.

Peters, M. A., Hollings, S., Zhang, M., Quainoo, E. A., Wang, H., Huang, Y., Zhou, S., Laimeche, A., Chunga, J. O., Ren, Z., Khomera, S. W., Zheng, W., Xu, R., Mou, C., & Green, B. (2021). The changing map of international student mobility. *ACCESS: Contemporary Issues in Education*, *41*(1), 7–28. https://doi.org/10.46786/ac21.7444.

Peters, M. A., Jandrić, P., Fuller, S., Means, A. J., Rider, S., Lăzăroiu, G., Hayes, S., Misiaszek, G. W., Tesar, M., McLaren, P., & Barnett, R. (2021). Public intellectuals in the age of viral modernity: An EPAT collective writing project. *Educational Philosophy and Theory*. https://doi.org/10.1080/00131857.2021.2010543.

Peters, M. A., Means, A., Neilson, D., Stewart, G. T., Jandrić, P., Sturm, S., Green, B., Ford; D. R., Fuller, S., Jackson, L., & Xue, E. (2022). 'After Brexit and AUKUS': A twitter-inspired collective article on changing world geopolitics and new multilateralism. *Educational Philosophy and Theory*. https://doi.org/10.1080/00131857.2022.2072289.

Peters, M. A., Oladele, O. M., Green, B., Samilo, A., Lv, H., Tosane, L. A., Wang, Y., Chunxiao, M., Chunga, J. O., Rulin, X., Ianina, T., Hollings, S., Barsoum Jusef, M. F., Jandrić, P., Sturm, S., Li, J., Xue, E., Jackson, L., & Tesar, M. (2020). Education in and for the Belt and Road Initiative: The Pedagogy of Collective Writing. *Educational Philosophy and Theory*, *52*(10), 1040–1063. https://doi.org/10.1080/00131857.2020.1718828.

Peters, M. A., Rizvi, F., McCulloch, G., Gibbs, P., Gorur, R., Hong, M., Hwang, Y., Zipin, L., Brennan, M., Robertson, S., Quay, J., Malbon, J., Taglietti, D., Barnett, R., Chengbing, W., McLaren, P., Apple, R., Papastephanou, M., Burbules, N., Jackson, L., Jalote, P., Kalantzis, M:, Cope, B., Fataar, A., Conroy, J., Misiaszek, G., Biesta, G., Jandrić, P., Choo, S., Apple, M., Stone, L., Tierney, R., Tesar, M., Besley, T., & Misiaszek, L. (2020): Reimagining the new pedagogical possibilities for universities post-Covid-19. *Educational Philosophy and Theory*. https://doi.org/10.1080/00131857.2020.1777655.

Peters, M. A., Tesar, M., Jackson, L., & Besley, T. (2020). *What comes after postmodernism in educational theory?* New York, NY: Routledge.

Peters, M. A., Tesar, M., Jackson, L., Besley, T., Jandrić, P., Arndt, S., & Sturm, S. (2021a). *The Methodology and Philosophy of Collective Writing: An Educational Philosophy and Theory Reader Volume X*. Abingdon and New York: Routledge.

Peters, M. A., Tesar, M., Jackson, L., Besley, T., Jandrić, P., Arndt, S., & Sturm, S. (2022). Exploring the Philosophy and Practice of Collective Writing. *Educational Philosophy and Theory*, *54*(7), 871–878. https://doi.org/10.1080/00131857.2020.1854731.

Peters, M. A., Wang, H., Ogunniran, M. O., Huang, Y., Green, B., Chunga, J. O., Quainoo, E. A., Ren, Z., Hollings, S., Mou, C., Khomera, S. W., Zhang, M., Zhou, S., Laimeche, A., Zheng, W., Xu, R., Jackson, L., & Hayes, S. (2020). China's Internationalised Higher Education During Covid-19: Collective Student Autoethnography. *Postdigital Science and Education*, *2*(3), 968–988. https://doi.org/10.1007/s42438-020-00128-1.

Peters, M. A., White, E. J., Besley, T., Locke, K., Redder, B., Novak, R., Gibbons, A., O'Neill, J., Tesar, M., & Sturm, S. (2021). Video ethics in educational research involving children: Literature review and critical discussion. *Educational Philosophy and Theory*, *53*(9), 863–880. https://doi.org/10.1080/00131857.2020.1717920.

Peters, M. A., White, E. J., Tesar, M., Gibbons, A., Arndt, S., Rutanen, N., Degotardi, S., Salamon, A., Browne, K., Redder, B., Charteris, J., Gould, K., Warren, A., Delaune, A., Kamenarac, O., Hood, N., & Sturm, S. (2020). Infantologies. An EPAT collective writing project. *Educational Philosophy and Theory*. https://doi.org/10.1080/00131857.2020.1835648.

Peters, M. A.; Jandrić, P; Irwin, R.; Locke, K.; Devine, N.; Heraud, R.; Gibbons, A.; Besley, T.; White, J.; Forster, D.; Jackson, L.; Grierson, E.; Mika, C.; Stewart, G.; Tesar, M.; Brighouse, S.; Arndt, S.; Lazariou, G.; Mihalia, R.; Bernade, L.; Legg, C.; Ozolins, J.; Roberts, P. (2016). Toward a Philosophy of Academic Publishing. *Educational Philosophy and Theory*, *48*(14), 1401–1425. https://doi.org/10.1080/00131857.2016.1240987.

Pfohl, S., Ayes, B., Turner, A., Amoo-Adare, E., Zecchin, M., & Borowski, M., Ito, K., Efeoglou, E., Moore, R., Wittig, M. D., Young, C., tujak, l., Thorne, A., Fletcher, B., Stevenson, D. E., Mañero, J., Maeso-Broncano, A., Mesías-Lema, J. M., Escaño, C., Hurley, Z., Spear, K., Brynjolson, N., Sanders, J. T., Lewis, T. E., & Blas, N. (2021). Simple, Dark, and Deep: Photographic Theorisations of As-Yet Schools. *Postdigital Science and Education*, *3*(3), 793–830. https://doi.org/10.1007/s42438-021-00233-9.

Reader, J., Jandrić, P., Peters, M. A., Barnett, R., Garbowski, M., Lipińska, V., Rider, S., Bhatt, I., Clarke, A., Hashemi, M., Bevan, A., Trozzo, E., Mackenzie, A., Aldern, J. J., Matias, C. E., Stewart, G. T., Mika, C., McLaren, P., Fawns, T., Knox, J., Savin-Baden, M., Jackson, L., Hood, N., Tesar, M., Fuller, S., & Baker, C. (2020). Enchantment – Disenchantment – Re-Enchantment: Postdigital Relationships Between Science, Philosophy, and Religion. *Postdigital Science & Education*, *3*(3), 934–965. https://doi.org/10.1007/s42438-020-00133-4.

Roth, K., Mollvik, L., Alshoufani, R., Adami, R., Dineen, K., Majlesi, F., Peters, M. A., & Tesar, M. (2020). Philosophy of education in a new key: Constraints and possibilities in present times with regard to dignity. *Educational Philosophy and Theory*. https://doi.org/10.1080/00131857.2020.1851189.

Sardoč, M., Coady, C. A. J., Bufacchi, V., Moghaddam, F. M., Cassam, Q., Silva, D., Miščević, N., Andrejč, G., Kodelja, Z., Vezjak, B., Peters, M. A., & Tesar, M. (2021). Philosophy of education in a new key: On radicalisation and violent extremism. *Educational Philosophy and Theory*. https://doi.org/10.1080/00131857.2020.1861937.

Smith, L. T., Maxwell, T. K., Puke, H., & Temara, P. (2016). Indigenous knowledge, methodology and mayhem: What is the role of methodology in producing Indigenous insights? A discussion from mātauranga Māori. *Knowledge Cultures*, 4(3), 131–156.

Stewart, G. T., Arndt, S., Besley, T., Devine, N., Forster D. J., Gibbons, A., Grierson, E., Jackson, L., Jandrić, P., Locke, K., Peters, M. A., & Tesar, M. (2017). Antipodean Theory for educational research. *Open Review of Educational Research*, 4(1), 61–74. https://doi.org/10.1080/23265507.2017.1337555.

Stewart, G. T., Hogarth, M., Sturm, S., & Martin, B. (2022). Colonisation of all forms. *Educational Philosophy and Theory*. https://doi.org/10.1080/00131857.2022.2040482.

Stewart, G. T., MacDonald, L., Matapo, J., Fa'avae, D. T. M., Watson, B. K. i., Akiu, R. K., Martin, B., Mika, C., & Sturm, S. (2021). Surviving academic Whiteness: Perspectives from the Pacific. *Educational Philosophy and Theory*. https://doi.org/10.1080/00131857.2021.2010542.

Stewart, G. T., Mika, C. T. H., Cooper, G., Bidois, V., & Hoskins, T. K. (2014). Introducing the Indigenous Philosophy Group (IPG). *Educational Philosophy and Theory*, 47(9), 851–855. https://doi.org/10.1080/00131857.2014.991540.

Sturm, S., Gibbons, A., & Peters, M. A. (2020). Pandemic education. *Knowledge Cultures*, 8(3), 7–12. https://doi.org/10.22381/KC8320201.

Tesar, M., Duhn, I., Nordstrom, S. N., Koro, M., Sparrman, A., Orrmalm, A., Boycott-Garnett, R., MacRae, C., Hackett, A., Kuntz, A. M., Trafí-Prats, L., Boldt, G., Rautio, P., Ulmer, J. B., Taguchi, H. L., Murris, K., Kohan, W. O., Gibbons, A., Arndt, S., & Malone, K. (2021). Infantmethodologies. *Educational Philosophy and Theory*. https://doi.org/10.1080/00131857.2021.2009340.

Tesar, M., Guerrero, M. R., Anttila, E., Newberry, J., Hellman, A., Wall, J., Santiago-Saamong, C. R., Bodén, L., Yu, H., Nanakida, A., Diaz-Diaz, C., Xu, Y., Trnka, S., Pacini-Ketchabaw, V., Nxumalo, F., Millei, Z., Malone, K., Arndt, S. (2021). Infantographies. *Educational Philosophy and Theory*. https://doi.org/10.1080/00131857.2021.2009341.

Tesar, M., Hytten, K., Hoskins, T. K., Rosiek, J., Jackson, A. Y., Hand, M., Roberts, P., Opiniano, G. A., Matapo, J., St. Pierre, E. A., Azada-Palacios, R., Kuby, C. R., Jones, A., Mazzei, L. A., Maruyama, Y., O'Donnell, A., Dixon-Román, E., Chengbing, E., Huang, Z., Chen, L., Peters, M. A., & Jackson, L. (2021). Philosophy of education in a new key: Future of philosophy of education. *Educational Philosophy and Theory*. https://doi.org/10.1080/00131857.2021.1946792.

Tesar, M., Peters, M. A., White, E. J., Arndt, S., Charteris, J., Fricker, A., Johansson, V., Sturm, S., Hood, N., & Madjar, A. (2021). Infanticides: The unspoken side of infantologies. *Educational Philosophy and Theory*. https://doi.org/10.1080/00131857.2020.1854730.

Tesar, M., Peters, M. A., White, E. J., Charteris, J., Delaune, A., Thraves, G., Westbrook, F., Devine, N., Stewart, G. T. (2021). Infantilisations. *Educational Philosophy and Theory*. https://doi.org/10.1080/00131857.2021.1933432.

Traxler, J., Connor, S., Hayes, S., & Jandrić, P. (2021). Futures Studies, Mobilities, and the Postdigital Condition: Contention or Complement. *Postdigital Science and Education*, *4*(2), 494–518. https://doi.org/10.1007/s42438-021-00245-5.

Varaki, S. B., Qamsari, A. S., Sefidkhosh, M., Sajjadi, S. M., Chaboki, R. M., Kalatehjafarabadi, T. J., Saffarheidari, H., Mohammadamini, M., Karimzadeh, O., Barkhordari, R., Zarghami-Hamrah, S., Peters, M. A., & Tesar, M. (2021). Philosophy of education in a new key: Reflection on higher education in Iran. *Educational Philosophy and Theory*. https://doi.org/10.1080/00131857.2021.1905517.

Waghid, Y., Davids, N., Mathebula, T., Terblanche, J., Higgs, P., Shawa, L., Manthalu, C. H., Waghid, Z., Ngwenya, C., Divala, J., Waghid, F., Peters, M. A., & Tesar, M. (2020). Philosophy of education in a new key: Cultivating a living philosophy of education to overcome coloniality and violence in African Universities. *Educational Philosophy and Theory*. https://doi.org/10.1080/00131857.2020.1793714.

Ward, A., Christ, R. C., Kuby, C. R., & Shear, S. B. (2018). Thinking with Klosterman's razor: Diffracting 'reviewer 2' and research wrongness. *Knowledge Cultures*, *6*(2), 28–50. https://doi.org/10.22381/KC6220183.

References

Abegglen, S., Burns, T., & Sinfield, S. (2017). "Really free!": Strategic interventions to foster students' academic writing skills. *Journal of Educational Innovation, Partnership and Change, 3*(1), 251–255. https://doi.org/10.21100/jeipc.v3i1.589.

Abegglen, S., Burns, T., & Sinfield, S. (2019). It's learning development, Jim – but not as we know it: academic literacies in third-space. *Journal of Learning Development in Higher Education, 15*. https://doi.org/10.47408/jldhe.v0i15.500.

Abegglen, S., Burns, T., & Sinfield, S. (2021a). Being fiercely alive and fiercely ourselves in higher education. In R. Toft Norgard, J. E. M. Solheim, & K. J. Bukholt (Eds.), *Playful higher education: Voices, activities, & co-creations from the PUP community* (pp. 110–113). Aarhus: Playful University Platform.

Abegglen, S., Burns, T., & Sinfield, S. (2021b). *Supporting student writing and other modes of learning and assessment: A staff guide.* Calgary: University of Calgary.

Abegglen, S., Burns, T., & Sinfield, S. (2022). Review of Michael A. Peters, Tina Besley, Marek Tesar, Liz Jackson, Petar Jandrić, Sonja Arndt, & Sean Sturm (2021). *The Methodology and Philosophy of Collective Writing: An Educational Philosophy and Theory Reader Volume X. Postdigital Science and Education.* https://doi.org/10.1007/s42438-022-00310-7.

Abegglen, S., Burns, T., Maier, S., & Sinfield, S. (2020). Global university, local issues: Taking a creative and humane approach to Learning and Teaching. In E. Sengupta, P. Blessinger, & M. Makhanya (Eds.), *Improving classroom engagement and international development pro-*

grams: International perspectives on humanising higher education (pp. 75–91). Emerald Publishing Limited.

Ailwood, J. (2022). Communities of care: A collective writing project on philosophies, politics and pedagogies of care and education in the early years. *Policy Futures in Education.* https://doi.org/10.1177/14782103211064440.

Alcoff, L. M. (1996). The problem of speaking for others. Who can speak? In J. Roof & R. Wiegman (Eds.), *Authority and Critical Identity.* Champaign, IL: University of Illinois Press.

Alcoff, L. M. (2010). Epistemic identities. *Episteme, 7*(2), 128–137. https://doi.org/10.3366/E1742360010000869.

Bakhtin, M. (1981). *The dialogic imagination: Four essays.* Austin, TX: University of Texas Press.

Barker, C., & Jane, E. (2016). *Cultural studies: theory and practice.* Los Angeles, CA: Sage.

Barnett, R., & Bengtsen, S. (2017). Universities and epistemology: From a dissolution of knowledge to the emergence of a new thinking. *Education Sciences, 7*(1), 1–12. https://doi.org/10.3390/educsci7010038.

Berg, M., & Seeber B. K. (2016). *The slow professor: challenging the culture of speed in the academy.* Toronto: University of Toronto Press.

Biesta, G., Heugh, K., Cervinkova, H., Rasiński, L., Osborne, S., Forde, D., Wrench, A., Carter, J., Säfström, C. A., Soong, H., O'Keeffe, S., Paige, K., Rigney, L.-I., O'Toole, L., Hattam, R., Peters, M. A., & Tesar, M. (2021). Philosophy of Education in a New Key: Publicness, Social Justice, and Education; A South-North Conversation. *Educational Philosophy and Theory.* https://doi.org/10.1080/00131857.2021.1929172.

Boldrin, M., & Levine, D. K. (2008). Against intellectual monopoly. http://www.dklevine.com/general/intellectual/againstnew.htm. Accessed 12 May 2022.

Burr, V. (2015). *Social constructionism.* 3rd Ed. Abingdon: Routledge.

Burroughs, M. D., & Tollefson, D. (2016). Learning to listen: Epistemic injustice and the child. *Episteme, 13*(3), 359–377. https://doi.org/10.1017/epi.2015.64.

Callon, M. (2002). Writing and (re) writing devices. In J. Law & A. Mol (Eds.), *Complexities: Social studies of knowledge practices* (pp. 191–217). Durham, NC: Duke University Press.

Carey, P. (2013). Student as co-producer in a marketised higher education system: A case study of students' experience of participation in curriculum design. *Innovations in Education and Teaching International, 50*(3), 250–260. https://doi.org/10.1080/14703297.2013.796714.

Couples, C., & Luke, T.W. (1998). Academic Infotecture: Course Design for Cyberschool. *Social Science Computer Review, 16*(2), 136–143.

Crème, P. (2003). Why can't we allow students to be more creative? *Teaching in Higher Education, 8*(2), 273–277. https://doi.org/10.1080/1356251032000052492.

Deleuze, G. (1988). *Foucault.* Trans. S. Hand. Minneapolis, MN: University of Minnesota Press.

Deleuze, G., & Guattari, F. (1987). *A thousand plateaus: Capitalism and schizophrenia.* Trans. B. Massumi. Minneapolis, MN: University of Minnesota Press.

DeSalvo, L. (2014). *The art of slow writing: Reflections on time, craft, and creativity.* New York: St Martins Griffin.

Elbow, P. (1998). *Writing without teachers.* 2nd Ed. Oxford: Oxford University Press.

Elbow, P. (1999). Using the collage for collaborative writing. *Composition Studies, 27*(1), 7–14.

Ford, B. (2020). Neoliberalism and four spheres of authority in American education: Business, class, stratification, and intimations of marketisation. *Policy Futures in Education, 18*(2), 200–239. https://doi.org/10.1177/1478210320903911.

Foucault, M. (1998). The thought of the outside. In J. D. Faubion (Ed.), *Essential works of Foucault 1954–1984, volume 2: Aesthetics, method and epistemology* (pp. 147–169). New York: New Press.

Freire, P. (1970). *Pedagogy of the oppressed.* Freiburg: Herder & Herder.

Freire, P. (1997). *Teachers as cultural workers: Letters to those who dare teach.* Boulder, CO: Westview Press.

Fricker, M. (2007). *Epistemic Injustice: Power and the Ethics of Knowing.* Oxford: Oxford University Press.

Gale, K., & Bowstead, H. (2013). Deleuze and collaborative writing as a method of inquiry. *Journal of Learning Development in Higher Education, 6*, 1–15. https://doi.org/10.47408/jldhe.v0i6.222.

Geoghegan, W., & Pontikakis, D. (2008). From ivory tower to factory floor? How universities are changing to meet the needs of industry. *Science and Public Policy, 35*(7), 462–474. https://doi.org/10.3152/030234208X329095.

Gibbons, A. N., & Craw, J. (2018). The importance of knowledge in early childhood education: On knowledge: Towards understandings of the place(s), space(s) and role(s) of knowledge in and for education. New Zealand: The Education Hub. https://theeducationhub.org.nz/. Accessed 1 June 2022.

Giroux, H. A., & Searls Giroux, S. (2006). *Take back higher education.* Cham: Palgrave Macmillan.

Guattari, F. (2015). Transdisciplinarity must become transversality. *Theory, Culture, & Society, 32*(5–6), 131–137. https://doi.org/10.1177/2F0263276415597045.

Guttorm, H., Hohti, R., & Paakkari, A. (2015). 'Do the next thing': An interview with Elizabeth Adams St. Pierre on post-qualitative methodology. *Reconceptualizing Educational Research Methodology, 6*(1). https://doi.org/10.7577/rerm.1421.

Hall, R. (2021). *The hopeless university: Intellectual work at the end of the end of history.* Mayflybooks/Ephemera.

Hayes, S. (2021). *Postdigital Positionality: developing powerful inclusive narratives for learning, teaching, research and policy in Higher Education.* Leiden: Brill.

Hayes, S., & Jandrić, P. (Eds.). (2017). Special Issue: Learning Technologies and Time in the Age of Global Neoliberal Capitalism. *Knowledge Cultures, 5*(2). https://www.addletonacademic-publishers.com/contents-kc#catid1069. Accessed 1 June 2022.

Hayles, N. K. (1990). Postmodern parataxis: Embodied texts, weightless information. *American Literary History, 2*(3), 394–421. https://doi.org/10.1093/alh/2.3.394.

Haynes, B. (Ed.). (2020). *Trust and schooling.* New York: Routledge.

hooks, b. (1992). *Black Looks: Race and Representation.* Brooklyn, NY: South End Press.

hooks, b. (1994). *Teaching to transgress: education as the practice of freedom.* London: Routledge.

Jackson, L., Peters, M. A., Benade, L., Devine, N., Arndt, S., Forster, D., Gibbons, A., Grierson, E., Jandrić, P., Lazaroiu, G., Locke, K., Mihaila, R., Stewart, G., Tesar, M., Roberts, & Ozoliņs, J. (2018). Is peer review in academic publishing still working?. *Open Review of Educational Research, 5*(1), 95–112.https://doi.org/10.1080/23265507.2018.1479139.

Jaldemark, J. (2021). Formal and informal paths of lifelong learning: Hybrid distance educational settings for the digital era. In M. Cleveland-Innes & D. R. Garrison (Eds.), *An introduction to distance education: Understanding teaching and learning in a new era.* 2nd Ed. (pp. 25–42). Abingdon: Routledge.

Jandrić, P. (2018). Postdigital Openness. *Open Review of Educational Research, 5*(1), 179–181. https://doi.org/10.1080/23265507.2018.1547943.

Jandrić, P., Devine, N., Jackson, L., Peters, M. A., Lăzăroiu, G., Mihăilă, R., Locke, K., Heraud, R., Gibbons, A., Grierson, E., Forster, D., White, J., Stewart, G., Tesar, M., Arndt, S., Brighouse, S., & Benade, L. (2017). Collective writing: An inquiry into praxis. *Knowledge Cultures, 5*(1), 85–109. https://doi.org/10.22381/KC5120177.

Jandrić, P., Fuentes Martinez, A., Reitz, C., Jackson, L., Grauslund, D., Hayes, D., Lukoko, H. O., Hogan, M., Mozelius, P., Arantes, J. A., Levinson, P., Ozoliņš, J., Kirylo, J. D., Carr, P. R., Hood, N., Tesar, M., Sturm, S., Abegglen, S., Burns, T., Sinfield, S., Stewart, G. T., Suoranta, J., Jaldemark, J., Gustafsson, U., Monzó, L. D., Batarelo Kokić, I., Kihwele, J. E., Wright, J., Kishore, P., Stewart, P. A., Bridges, S. M., Lodahl, M., Bryant, P., Kaur, K., Hollings, S., Brown, J. B., Steketee, A., Prinsloo, P., Hazzan, M. K., Jopling, M., Mañero, J., Gibbons, A., Pfohl, S., Humble, N., Davidsen, J., Ford, D. R., Sharma, N., Stockbridge, K., Pyyhtinen, O., Escaño, C., Achieng-Evensen, C., Rose, J., Irwin, J., Shukla, R., SooHoo, S., Truelove, I., Buchanan, R., Urvashi, S., White, E. J., Novak, R., Ryberg, T., Arndt, S., Redder, B., Mukherjee, M., Komolafe, B. F., Mallya, M., Devine, N., Sattarzadeh, S. D., & Hayes, S. (2022). Teaching in the Age of Covid-19—The New Normal. *Postdigital Science and Education, 4*(1), 877–1015. https://doi.org/10.1007/s42438-022-00332-1.

Jandrić, P., Hayes, D., Levinson, P., Lisberg Christensen, L., Lukoko, H. O., Kihwele, J. E., Brown, J. B., Reitz, C., Mozelius, P., Nejad, H. G., Fuentes Martinez, A., Arantes, J. A., Jackson, L., Gustafsson, U., Abegglen, S., Burns, T., Sinfield, S., Hogan, M., Kishore, P., Carr, P. R., Batarelo Kokić, I., Prinsloo, P., Grauslund, D., Steketee, A., Achieng-Evensen, C., Komolafe, B. F., Suoranta, J., Hood, N., Tesar, M., Rose, J., Humble, N., Kirylo, J. D., Mañero, J., Monzó, L. D., Lodahl, M., Jaldemark, J., Bridges, S. M., Sharma, N., Davidsen, J., Ozoliņš, J., Bryant, P., Escaño, C., Irwin, J., Kaur, K., Pfohl, S., Stockbridge, K., Ryberg, T., Pyyhtinen, O., SooHoo, S., Hazzan, M. K., Wright, J., Hollings, S., Arndt, S., Gibbons, A., Urvashi, S., Forster, D. J., Truelove, I., Mayo, P., Rikowski, G., Stewart, P. A., Jopling, M., Stewart, G. T., Buchanan, R., Devine, N., Shukla, R., Novak, R., Mallya, M., Biličić, E., Sturm, S., Sattarzadeh, S. D., Philip, A. P., Redder, B., White, E. J., Ford, D. R., Allen, Q., Mukherjee, M., & Hayes, S. (2021). Teaching in the Age of Covid-19 – 1 Year Later. *Postdigital Science and Education, 3*(3), 1073–1223. https://doi.org/10.1007/s42438-021-00243-7.

Jandrić, P., Hayes, D., Truelove, I., Levinson, P., Mayo, P., Ryberg, T., Monzó, L.D., Allen, Q., Stewart, P.A., Carr, P.R., Jackson, L., Bridges, S., Escaño, C., Grauslund, D., Mañero, J., Lukoko, H.O., Bryant, P., Fuentes Martinez, A., Gibbons, A., Sturm, S., Rose, J., Chuma, M.M., Biličić, E., Pfohl, S., Gustafsson, U., Arantes, J.A., Ford, D.R., Kihwele, J.E., Mozelius, P., Suoranta, J., Jurjević, L., Jurčević, M., Steketee, A., Irwin, J., White, E.J., Davidsen, J., Jaldemark, J., Abegglen, S., Burns, T., Sinfield, S., Kirylo, J.D., Batarelo Kokić, I., Stewart, G.T., Rikowski, G., Lisberg Christensen, L., Arndt, S., Pyyhtinen, O., Reitz, C., Lodahl, M., Humble, N., Buchanan, R., Forster, D.J., Kishore, P., Ozoliņš, J., Sharma, N., Urvashi, S., Nejad, H.G., Hood, N., Tesar, M., Wang, Y., Wright, J., Brown, J.B., Prinsloo, P., Kaur, K., Mukherjee, M., Novak, R., Shukla, R., Hollings, S., Konnerup, U., Mallya, M., Olorundare, A., Achieng-Evensen, C., Philip, A.P., Hazzan, M.K., Stockbridge, K., Komolafe, B.F., Bolanle, O.F., Hogan, M., Redder, B., Sattarzadeh, S.D., Jopling, M., SooHoo, S., Devine, N., & Hayes, S. (2020). Teaching in The Age of Covid-19. *Postdigital Science and Education, 2*(3), 1069–1230.https://doi.org/10.1007/s42438-020-00169-6.

Jandrić, P., Ryberg, T., Knox, J., Lacković, N., Hayes, S., Suoranta, J., Smith, M., Steketee, A., Peters, M. A., McLaren, P., Ford, D. R., Asher, G., McGregor, C., Stewart, G., Williamson, B., & Gibbons, A. (2019). Postdigital Dialogue. *Postdigital Science and Education, 1*(1), 163–189. https://doi.org/10.1007/s42438-018-0011-x.

Khan, H. (1979). The Expert and Trained Incapacity. The Hudson Institute. https://www.hudson.org/research/2219-the-expert-and-educated-incapacity#:~:text=The%20original%20phrase%2C%20E2%80%9Ctrained%20incapacity,had%20not%20had%20this%20training. Accessed 1 June 2022.

Koro-Ljungberg, M., Cirell, A. M., Gong, B., & Tesar, M. (2017a). The importance of small form: 'Minor' data and 'BIG' neoliberalism. In N. Denzin & M. D. Giardina (Eds.), *Qualitative Inquiry in Neoliberal Times* (pp. 59–73). New York: Routledge.

Koro-Ljungberg, M., Löytönen, T., & Tesar, M. (Eds.). (2017b). *Disrupting data in qualitative inquiry: Entanglements with the post-critical and post-anthropocentric.* New York: Peter Lang.

Koro-Ljungberg, M., Tesar, M., Carlson, D. L., Montana, A., & Gong, B. (2019). Aporetic and productive undecidedness of ('data' in) neoliberalism. *Qualitative Inquiry, 25*(8), 725–733. https://doi.org/10.1177/1077800418809533.

Lorde, A. (1984). *Sister Outsider: Essays and Speeches.* Trumansburg, NY: Crossing Press.

Luke, T.W. (1999). The Discipline as Disciplinary Normalisation: Networks of Research. *New Political Science, 21*(3), 345–363.

MacKenzie, A. (2022). Down to earth transdisciplinarity. Response to 'The Struggling Towards a Transdisciplinary Metaphysics' (Gibbs 2021). *Postdigital Science and Education.* https://doi.org/10.1007/s42438-022-00298-0.

MacKenzie, A., Bacalja, A., Annamali, D., Panaretou, A., Girme, P., Cutajar, M., Abegglen, S., Evens, M., Neuhaus, F., Wilson, K., Psarikidou, K., Koole, M., Hrastinski, S., Sturm, S., Adachi, C., Schnaider, K., Bozkurt, A., Rapanta, C., Themelis, C., Thestrup, K., Gislev, T., Örtegren, A., Costello, C., Dishon, G., Hoechsmann, M., Bucio, J., Vadillo, G., Sánchez-Mendiola, M., Goetz, G., Gusso, H. L., Aldous Arantes, J., Kishore, P., Lodahl, M., Suoranta,

J., Markauskaite, L., Mörtsell, S., O'Reilly, T., Reed, J., Bhatt, I., Brown, C., MacCallum, K., Ackermann, C., Alexander, C., Leah Payne, A., Bennett, R., Stone, C., Collier, A., Lohnes Watulak, S., Jandrić, P., Peters, M., & Gourlay, L. (2021). Dissolving the Dichotomies Between Online and Campus-Based Teaching: a Collective Response to *The Manifesto for Teaching Online* (Bayne et al. 2020) (2021). *Postdigital Science and Education, 4*(2), 271–329. https://doi.org/10.1007/s42438-021-00259-z.

Martin, B., Stewart, G., Watson, B. K., Silva, O. K., Teisina, J., Matapo, J., & Mika, C. (2020). Situating decolonisation: An Indigenous dilemma. *Educational Philosophy and Theory, 52*(3), 312–321. https://doi.org/10.1080/00131857.2019.1652164.

Medina, J. (2012). *The Epistemology of Ignorance: Gender and Racial Oppression, Epistemic Injustice, and Resistant Imaginations.* Oxford: Oxford University Press.

Mika, C., Stewart, G., Watson, K., Silva, K., Martin, B., Matapo, J., & Galuvao, A. (2018). What is indigenous research in philosophy of education? And what is PESA, from an indigenous perspective? *Educational Philosophy and Theory, 50*(8), 733–739. https://doi.org/10.108 0/00131857.2017.1317042.

Molinari, J. (2022). *What makes writing academic: Rethinking theory for practice.* London: Bloomsbury.

Murray, D. (1972). Teach writing as a process not a product. *The Leaflet, 71*(3), 11–14.

Neary, M. (2020). *Student as Producer: How Do Revolutionary Teachers Teach?* Winchester and Washington: Zero Books.

Networked Learning Editorial Collective (2021). Networked Learning: Inviting Redefinition *Postdigital Science and Education, 3*(2), 312–325. https://doi.org/10.1007/s42438-020-00167-8.

Networked Learning Editorial Collective, Gourlay, L., Rodríguez-Illera, J. L., Barberà, E., Bali, M., Gachago, D., Pallitt, N., Jones, C., Bayne, S., Hansen, S. B., Hrastinski, S., Jaldemark, J., Themelis, C., Pischetola, M., Dirckinck-Holmfeld, L., Matthews, A., Gulson, K. N., Lee, K., Bligh, B., Thibaut, P., Vermeulen, M., Nijland, F., Vrieling-Teunter, E., Scott, H., Thestrup, K., Gislev, T., Koole, M., Cutajar, M., Tickner, S., Rothmüller, N., Bozkurt, A., Fawns, T., Ross, J., Schnaider, K., Carvalho, L., Green, J. K., Hadžijusufović, M., Hayes, S., Czerniewicz, L., & Knox, J. (2021). Networked Learning in 2021: A Community Definition. *Postdigital Science and Education, 3*(2), 326–369. https://doi.org/10.1007/s42438-021-00222-y.

Nussbaum, M. (2010). *Not for profit: Why democracy needs the humanities.* Princeton, NJ: Princeton University Press.

Peters, M. A. (2014). Openness and the intellectual commons. *Open Review of Educational Research, 1*(1), 1–7.https://doi.org/10.1080/23265507.2014.984975.

Peters, M. A. (2021). Knowledge socialism: The rise of peer production – collegiality, collaboration, and collective intelligence. *Educational Philosophy and Theory, 53*(1), 1–9. https://doi.org/10.1080/00131857.2019.1654375.

Peters, M. A., & Jandrić, P. (2018). *The Digital University: A Dialogue and Manifesto.* New York: Peter Lang.

Peters, M. A., & Roberts, P. (2011). *The virtues of openness: Education, science, and scholarship in the digital age.* Boulder, CO: Paradigm Publishers.

Peters, M. A., Besley, T., Jandrić, P., & Zhu, X. (2020a). *Knowledge socialism: The rise of peer production: Collegiality, collaboration, and collective intelligence.* Singapore: Springer.

Peters, M. A., Besley, T., Tesar, M., Jackson, L., Jandrić, P., Arndt, S., & Sturm, S. (2021a). *The Methodology and Philosophy of Collective Writing: An Educational Philosophy and Theory Reader Volume X.* Abingdon and New York: Routledge.

Peters, M. A., Jandrić, P., & Hayes, S. (2021b). Biodigital Philosophy, Technological Convergence, and New Knowledge Ecologies. *Postdigital Science and Education, 3*(2), 370–388. https://doi.org/10.1007/s42438-020-00211-7.

Peters, M. A., Jandrić, P., & McLaren, P. (2020b). Viral modernity? epidemics, infodemics, and the 'bioinformational' paradigm. *Educational Philosophy and Theory.* https://doi.org/10.108 0/00131857.2020.1744226.

Peters, M. A., Jandrić, P., Fuller, S., Means, A. J., Rider, S., Lăzăroiu, G., Hayes, S., Misiaszek, G. W., Tesar, M., McLaren, P., & Barnett, R. (2021d). Public intellectuals in the age of viral modernity: An EPAT collective writing project. *Educational Philosophy and Theory*. https://doi.org/10.1080/00131857.2021.2010543.

Peters, M. A., Jandrić, P., Irwin, R., Locke, K., Devine, N., Heraud, R., Gibbons, A., Besley, T., White, J., Forster, D., Jackson, L., Grierson, E., Mika, C., Stewart, G., Tesar, M., Brighouse, S., Arndt, S., Lazariou, G., Mihalia, R., Bernade, L., Legg, C., Ozolins, J., Roberts, P. (2016). Toward a Philosophy of Academic Publishing. *Educational Philosophy and Theory, 48*(14), 1401–1425. https://doi.org/10.1080/00131857.2016.1240987.

Peters, M. A., McLaren, P., & Jandrić, P. (2020c). A Viral Theory of Post-Truth. *Educational Philosophy and Theory*. https://doi.org/10.1080/00131857.2020.1750090.

Peters, M. A., Oladele, O. M., Green, B., Samilo, A., Lv, H., Amina, L., Wang, Y., Chunxiao, M., Chunga, J. O., Rulin, X., Ianina, T., Hollings, S., Yousef, M. F. B., Jandrić, P., Sturm, S., Li, J., Xue, E., Jackson, L., & Tesar, M. (2020d). Education in and for the Belt and Road Initiative: The pedagogy of collective writing. *Educational Philosophy & Theory, 52*(10), 1040–1063. https://doi.org/10.1080/00131857.2020.1718828.

Peters, M. A., Tesar, M., Jackson, L., Besley, T., Jandrić, P., Arndt, S., & Sturm, S. (2021c). Exploring the philosophy and practice of collective writing. *Educational Philosophy and Theory*. https://doi.org/10.1080/00131857.2020.1854731.

Peters, M. A., White, E. J., Grierson, E., Stewart, G., Devine, N., Craw, J., Gibbons, A., Jandrić, P., Peters, M. A., Novak, R., White, E. J., Heraud R., & Locke, K. (2018). Ten theses on the shift from (static) text to (moving) image. *Open Review of Educational Research, 5*(1), 56–94. https://doi.org/10.1080/23265507.2018.1470768.

Pfohl, S., Ayes, B., Turner, A., Amoo-Adare, E., Zecchin, M., Borowski, M., Ito, K., Efeoglou, E., Moore, R., Wittig, M. D., Young, C., tujak, l., Thorne, A., Fletcher, B., Stevenson, D. E., Mañero, J., Maeso-Broncano, A., Mesías-Lema, J. M., Escaño, C., Hurley, Z., Spear, K., Brynjolson, N., Sanders, J. T., Lewis, T. E., & Blas, N. (2021). Simple, Dark, and Deep: Photographic Theorisations of As-Yet Schools. *Postdigital Science and Education, 3*(3), 793–830. https://doi.org/10.1007/s42438-021-00233-9.

Proctor, R. (2008). Agnotology: A Missing Term to Describe the Cultural Production of Ignorance (and Its Study). In R. Proctor & L. L. Schiebinger (Eds.), *Agnotology: The making and unmaking of ignorance* (pp. 1–33). Stanford, CA: Stanford University Press.

Roberts, P. (2022). *Performativity, politics and education: From policy to philosophy*. Leiden: Brill.

Robinson, W. I. (2020). Global capitalism post-pandemic. *Race & Class, 62*(2), 3–13. https://doi.org/10.1177/2F0306396820951999.

St. Pierre, E. A. (2018). Writing post qualitative inquiry. *Qualitative Inquiry, 24*(9), 603–608. https://doi.org/10.1177/2F1077800417734567.

Stewart, G. T., Hogarth, M., Sturm, S., & Martin, B. (2022). Colonisation of all forms. *Educational Philosophy and Theory*. https://doi.org/10.1080/00131857.2022.2040482.

Stewart, G. T., MacDonald, L., Matapo, J., Fa'avae, D. T. M., Watson, B. K., Akiu, R. K., Martin, B., Mika, C., & Sturm, S. (2021). Surviving academic Whiteness: Perspectives from the Pacific. *Educational Philosophy and Theory*. https://doi.org/10.1080/00131857.2021.2010542.

Stewart, G., Mika, C. T. H., Cooper, G., Bidois, V., & Hoskins, T. K. (2014). Introducing the Indigenous Philosophy Group (IPG). *Educational Philosophy and Theory, 47*(9), 851–855. https://doi.org/10.1080/00131857.2014.991540.

Tesar, M., Hytten, K., Hoskins, T. K., Rosiek, J., Jackson, A. Y., Hand, M., Roberts, P., Opiniano, G. A., Matapo, J., St. Pierre, E. A., Azada-Palacios, R., Kuby, C. R., Jones, A., Mazzei, L. A., Maruyama, Y., O'Donnell, A., Dixon-Román, E., Chengbing, W., Huang, Z., Chen, L., Peters, M. A., & Jackson, L. (2021). Philosophy of Education in a New Key: The Future of Philosophy of Education. *Educational Philosophy and Theory*. https://doi.org/10.1080/00131857.2021.1946792.

Torres-Olave, B., & Lee, J. J. (2019). Shifting positionalities across international locations: embodied knowledge, time-geography, and the polyvalence of privilege. *Higher Education Quarterly, 74*(2), 136–148. https://doi.org/10.1111/hequ.12216.

Winn, J. (2015). The co-operative university: Labour, property and pedagogy. *Power and Education, 7*(1), 39–55. https://doi.org/10.1177/2F1757743814567386.

Wyatt, J., Gale, K., Gannon, S., & Davies, B. (2011). *Deleuze and collaborative writing: An immanent plane of composition*. New York: Peter Lang.

Afterword: So, What *Is* Postdigital Research?

Neil Selwyn

While I consider myself to be a relative outsider, the steady stream of writing being produced under the 'postdigital science and education' banner is always worth paying attention to. At the very least, this is work that provides interesting and insightful takes on the fast-changing nature of education and technoscience. This present collection is no exception, and I am sure that readers will have already found a few new lines of thinking and inquiry to have emerged over the past fourteen chapters.

Of course, while most postdigital authors are keen to celebrate the open-ended nature of the concept, this remains a difficult prospect for many casual readers to fully buy into. In some instances, this reticence seems to stem from a too-literal interpretation of the phrase 'postdigital'. For example, when taken at face value, the term 'postdigital' might easily be presumed to denote a progression *beyond* the capabilities of current digital technology (the computers, Internet, and smartphones of the past 40 years or so) and somehow into a new era of super-advanced 'more-than-digital' technologies. This misreading can prompt people to disregard postdigital as something akin to the problematic hyping of 'general artificial intelligence', the singularity and other techno-fascistic imaginaries.

Conversely, the idea of postdigital can also cause alarm for those whose work is concerned with the social inequalities, harms, and injustices that have long been perpetuated through the ongoing digitisation of society. Many social scientists consider it incredibly important to continue to draw attention to 'the digital' as a matter of specific concern. Entertaining the notion of 'postdigital' might therefore be construed to infer that the digital is no longer a matter of societal or political importance – in a similar manner to contestable ideas of 'post-racial society' and so on. Indeed, there have long been concerned efforts from those with vested interests in

N. Selwyn
Monash University, Clayton, VIC, Australia
e-mail: neil.selwyn@monash.edu

© The Author(s), under exclusive license to Springer Nature Switzerland AG 2023
P. Jandrić et al. (eds.), *Postdigital Research*, Postdigital Science and Education,
https://doi.org/10.1007/978-3-031-31299-1

the digital economy to promote the idea that everyone is now online, that 'we are all digital now', and that matters of digital inequality and disadvantage are just a passing phase. As such, the postdigital turn might be seen as a dangerous distraction from efforts to tackle issues of digital inequality and data justice.

As this book demonstrates, these are clearly not the intentions of scholars working under the postdigital banner. Nevertheless, it remains important to develop more clarity around what this area of scholarship is actually trying to achieve. In this sense, one of the benefits to be drawn from this book is further elaboration of the postdigital sensibility. Here, we find useful discussions expanding upon the deeply entwined and enmeshed nature of the digital and analogue, the messiness of current digital ways-of-being, and the blurring of any boundaries that were once imposed around 'new' technologies. So, for me, this book is useful in providing further refinement around postdigital ambitions to move away from the 'digital dualisms' that grew up around the emergence of computers and the internet into late twentieth century/early twenty-first century society (Jurgensen 2011).

In this sense, these chapters certainly prompt reflection on the 'so what?' of postdigital scholarship. I finished this book thinking that there is perhaps value in embracing the notion of 'postdigital' as a corrective – i.e., a means of intellectually adjusting to a near-future when many of the concepts we have become accustomed to using around 'digital' matters will fast fall out of favour. In a similar manner to people in the mid-twentieth century eventually moving on from talking about the 'electrical age', we might anticipate any talk of the 'digital age' to soon appear quaint and anachronistic in the mid-twenty-first century. Of course, not everyone in the world will have direct access to digital technology (or to electricity for that matter), yet digital technologies might soon become such an embedded element of everyday life that they will not merit a second thought.

By the same token, it perhaps makes sense to anticipate the term 'postdigital' to only be of temporary use (in the same way that we don't talk of 'post-electrical'). As such, the emphasis currently being placed on postdigital matters might be welcomed as a necessary provocation for us to all begin moving on from the familiar mindset of digital-as-novelty to impending times of digital-as-commonplace.

Yet, this is not just a book about the postdigital sensibility. In addition, a second benefit that can be drawn from this book is specific elaboration of what it means to apply postdigital thinking to the practice of 'research'. Here, while things remain a little less clear, the book certainly raises a number of discussion points that I am sure will continue to be discussed within the Postdigital Science and Education community over the next few years. Of course, some readers might be disappointed that no one cogent sense of 'postdigital research' emerges from this book, or that it does not conclude with a rousing methodological manifesto. Yet, I get the sense that this book was never conceived as a conventional set of research-related chapters that converge around one set of approved approaches or traditions.

That said, a strong sense emerges from these chapters that postdigital research and inquiry is not simply a complete 'free-for-all' where any methodological or empirical orientation will fit. By its nature, postdigital thinking is never going to be satisfied with conventional methodological distinctions between qualitative/quantitative, primary/secondary, discovery/applied, and other such methodological binaries. As such, this volume does develop a sense of educational scholars who are interested in moving beyond such research dualisms and engaging with recent developments in a few of the more interesting enclaves of social research thinking (many of which share a 'post' suffix).

For example, this collection of chapters contains recurring nods to the traditions of historical materialism, Feminist posthumanism, sociomaterialism, and other similar lines of thought. One obvious set of cognate interests that recurs throughout the book clearly lies in actor-network theory. As such, it seems that there are strong grounds for the postdigital science and education community to further engage with ontological developments in the 'after ANT' and 'post-ANT' turns that have developed over the past 20 years or so (Law 1999; Gad and Jensen 2010). Some of these chapters also show clear affinities with the post-qualitative turn originating out of post-structuralist and post humanist thinking – not least the 'refusal of method' associated with the conventional humanist social science research methodologies of the twentieth century (St. Pierre 2021). Again, this would seem to be a fitting line of thought to guide future efforts in sketching out postdigital research.

Indeed, the more one delves into these chapters, then the more interesting avenues for further thinking come to the fore. For example, the idea of postdigital scholars finding space for what might be conventionally considered to be 'bad research' - especially the idea of engaging in the creation of non-knowledge and impossible solutions - chimes with moves in sociology during the 2010s toward 'live methods' and 'idiotic method' (Back and Puwar 2012; Michael 2012). Similarly, the origins of postdigital thinking in the arts also draws links to research-related developments in the fields of digital humanities and digital arts – not least a shared interest in compositional approaches, the creation of fictions, and other inventive and creative methodologies.

In short, this book throws up plenty of established research approaches from outside of educational scholarship that are compatible with the postdigital sensibility. As such, it is not up to those scholars working in the area of postdigital science and education to invent a distinct form of 'postdigital research'. Instead, it will be worth continuing these conversations and further exploring what (post)methodological ideas and innovations might fit best with the postdigital sensibility, and then applying them in as many educational contexts as possible. Even for those readers who do not see themselves as fully signed up to the postdigital project, these are certainly worthwhile discussion to keep track of!

References

Back, L., & Puwar, N. (2012). A manifesto for live methods: provocations and capacities. *The sociological review, 60*, 6–17. https://doi.org/10.1111/j.1467-954X.2012.02114.x.

Gad, C., & Jensen, C. (2010). On the consequences of post-ANT. *Science, Technology, & Human Values, 35*(1), 55–80. https://doi.org/10.1177/0162243908329567.

Jurgenson, N. (2011). Digital Dualism and the fallacy of web objectivity. Cyborgology, 13 September. https://thesocietypages.org/cyborgology/2011/09/13/digital-dualism-and-the-fallacy-of-web-objectivity/. Accessed 6 March 2023.

Law, J. (1999). After ANT: complexity, naming and topology. *The Sociological Review, 47*(S1), 1–14. https://doi.org/10.1111/j.1467-954X.1999.tb03479.x.

Michael, M. (2012). De-signing the object of sociology: toward an 'idiotic' methodology. *The Sociological Review, 60*(S1), 166–183. https://doi.org/10.1111/j.1467-954X.2012.02122.x.

St. Pierre, E. (2021). Why post qualitative inquiry? *Qualitative Inquiry, 27*(2), 163–166. https://doi.org/10.1177/1077800420931142.

Index